The Halbrook - Freeman Debate

On
Marriage, Divorce, & Remarriage

Ron Halbrook
West Columbia, Texas

Jack Freeman
Las Vegas, Nevada

February 26 - March 2, 1990
Junior High School Auditorium
West Columbia, Texas

First Edition

Published By
Guardian of Truth Foundation
Bowling Green, Kentucky

1995

© **Guardian of Truth Foundation 1995.** All rights reserved. No part of this book may be reproduced in any form without written permission from the publisher. Printed in the United States of America.

The charts used by Ron Halbrook in this debate are the joint property of Ron Halbrook and David A. Padfield.
©1990 David A. Padfield, All Rights Reserved

ISBN 1-58427-061-6

Guardian of Truth Foundation
P.O. Box 9670
Bowling Green, Kentucky 42102

Table Of Contents

Publisher's Preface iii
Introduction by Halbrook's Moderator viii
Introduction by Freeman's Moderator xi

First Proposition: The Scriptures teach that two people joined by God in marriage are bound for life, the only exception being that an innocent partner may put away a mate guilty of fornication and remarry.

Monday Night

Halbrook's First Affirmative 1
Freeman's First Negative 18
Halbrook's Second Affirmative 36
Freeman's Second Negative 53
Halbrook's Third Affirmative 68
Freeman's Third Negative 74

Tuesday Night

Halbrook's First Affirmative 80
Freeman's First Negative 96
Halbrook's Second Affirmative 109
Freeman's Second Negative 125
Halbrook's Third Affirmative 140
Freeman's Third Negative 148

Second Proposition: The Scriptures teach that a person who is divorced by his mate for committing fornication is free to marry another.

Thursday Night

Freeman's First Affirmative	154
Halbrook's First Negative	168
Freeman's Second Affirmative	187
Halbrook's Second Negative	200
Freeman's Third Affirmative	218
Halbrook's Third Negative	224

Friday Night

Freeman's First Affirmative	233
Halbrook's First Negative	246
Freeman's Second Affirmative	264
Halbrook's Second Negative	279
Freeman's Third Affirmative	296
Halbrook's Third Negative	300

Addendum No. 1:	Authorship Acknowledged by Freeman	309
Addendum No. 2:	Halbrook's Response to Freeman	310
Chart Index		312

PUBLISHER'S PREFACE

In the fall of 1988, Jack Freeman with the other elders of the North Las Vegas church of Christ in North Las Vegas, Nevada terminated their support of Wayne Goforth at the church on 25th and Hawaii in Alamogordo, New Mexico because of his stand for the truth on marriage, divorce, and remarriage. At the urging of the elders at the church in West Columbia, Texas, which continued to support brother Goforth, a report was published in the *Guardian of Truth* magazine asking brethren to replace the money he lost from North Las Vegas. This report commended him for not bowing his knee "to the Baal of false doctrine" (Ron Halbrook, "Opportunities to Sound Out the Word," *Guardian of Truth*, Feb. 16, 1989, pp. 108-109). As it turned out, Truman Smith, who was then at Alexandria, Louisiana, suffered the same fate for not bowing his knee to Baal: the North Las Vegas church terminated his support.

After seeing the report in the Guardian of Truth, Jack Freeman wrote a letter to Ron Halbrook challenging him to debate. When brother Halbrook had to delay answering because of his involvement in three gospel meetings in a row, brother Freeman took out an ad in the newspaper in West Columbia designed to suggest that brother Halbrook was ignoring and dodging the challenge to debate. The ad said,

> PERSONAL NOTICE
> On 2-27-89 Ron Halbrook received a challenge to debate the divorce and remarriage question. Will he accept the challenge? 1-702-642-3687 *(Brazoria County News,* March 23, 1989, p. 20)

After his meetings, brother Halbrook sent signed propositions for brother Freeman to sign (the same propositions appearing in this book). He signed the second one but refused to sign the first one in April 1989. He still had not signed in May, in June, in July, in August, in September, and in October.

In October of 1989 brother Halbrook sent a report to the *Guardian of Truth* detailing brother Freeman's refusal to finalize the debate arrangements, and in fairness to brother Freeman, provided him an advance copy. Brother Freeman then called the editor, Mike Willis, and wanted to respond to the article. Mike persuaded him to sign the unsigned proposition so the debate could occur, rather than debating why it would not occur. Brother Freeman professed to fear that brother Halbrook would not discuss the case of a believer deserted by an unbeliever. To pacify brother Freeman, brother Willis worded an announcement of the debate showing it would include the question of a believer deserted by an unbeliever, an issue brother Halbrook had already agreed to cover in a letter to brother Freeman many months before. Brother Halbrook's article was therefore shelved, and plans for the debate were announced. When it was later rumored by brother Freeman's camp that brother Willis had to pressure brother Halbrook to debate, brother Willis responded that such an account "is wholly fictitious and false" (Willis, "Halbrook-Freeman Debate," information sheet distributed at the second debate). It was brother Freeman who had to be persuaded.

Two debates were held with identical propositions and procedures. The propositions read as follows. "The Scriptures teach that two people joined by God in marriage are bound for life, the only exception being that an innocent partner may put away a mate guilty of fornication and remarry" (affirmed by Halbrook, denied by Freeman). "The Scriptures teach that a person who is divorced by his mate for committing fornication is free to marry another" (affirmed by Freeman, denied by Halbrook).

The first debate was conducted at the North Las Vegas Church of Christ. Attendance ran about 120 to 140 each night, which was good considering the geographical isolation of Las Vegas. The elders of the church of Christ in West Columbia, Texas arranged for the second debate to be held in the Junior High School auditorium to accommodate the large crowds expected. This expectation was confirmed by excellent attendance, which reached a high point of about 400-500. Good order prevailed during both debates, with many people utilizing Bibles and note pads. A large number of young people attended the second debate, took notes, and commented on how much they learned from the discussion.

There are many other evidences of the good accomplished by the Halbrook-Freeman debates. For instance, as events unfolded leading up to the debates, Keith Greer began to awaken to the clarity of the truth of Jesus' teaching on divorce and remarriage, and was disturbed by brother Freeman's unrelenting tirades against the truth and against brother Halbrook. He left the North Las Vegas church where he had been a strong member for five years, where he had studied under Jack Freeman, and where he himself had preached many times. In the providence of God, the Vegas Drive church in Las Vegas was looking for a preacher and brother Greer began his labors there in July of 1989. As he continued his studies, he resolved to stand for the truth on this issue. Brother

Introduction v
___

Greer sat at the table with brother Halbrook and helped in many ways during both debates. He said the debates clarified some questions and fully confirmed his faith in the truth.

As further evidence of the good accomplished by the Las Vegas debate, brother Greer brought the following letter from the Vegas Drive church with him to West Columbia, which was read during the introductory remarks at the debate there.

Church of Christ
3816 Vegas Drive
Las Vegas, Nevada 89108
648-4827
Keith M. Greer, Minister

January 28, 1990

To our brethren in Christ:
"Ye are the light of the world. A city that is set on an hill cannot be hid...Let your light so shine before men, that they may see your good works, and glorify your Father in heaven" (Matthew 5:14-16).
Dear brethren,
For much too long we have been silent concerning where we stand on the issue of Divorce and Remarriage, and we do not wish to remain so any longer.

On January 15th, 16th, 18th, and 19th, a debate was held between Ron Halbrook and Jack Freeman at the Northside church of Christ. Many of the members of the Vegas Drive church of Christ attended the debate, and following the discussions, the men held a business meeting on Sunday afternoon, January 21, 1990. It was agreed upon by all of the men that we would send a letter to be read at the debate between Ron Halbrook and Jack Freeman in West Columbia, Texas. We want all of the brethren to know where we stand on these matters.

The scriptures teach that two people joined by God in marriage are bound for life, the only exception being that an innocent partner may put away a mate that is guilty of fornication and remarry. We at Vegas Drive AFFIRM that the Bible teaches this to be true.

We also want all to understand that we stand against the "two-law" doctrine of marriage that is being taught by many of our brethren.

1 Corinthians 7:15 does not teach that a Christian has other grounds for divorce or remarriage, and we cannot agree with those who practice and teach the doctrine of "desertion."

We do not agree with the position that Jack Freeman and the Northside church of Christ in Las Vegas hold concerning divorce and remarriage, and we do not want to be associated with what they are teaching. They do not speak for us, and we do not speak for them. We want all to know that we stand firmly on God's word; nothing more and nothing less.

We hold no animosity towards the brethren at Northside. We love them, and would be only too happy to open up the Bible and study with them. We do not "count them as an enemy" but "admonish" them as a "brother" (2 Thessalonians 3:15).

The purpose of this letter is to let others know that there is a church in Las Vegas that is trying to stand upon the word of God. We want those brethren who come to our city to know that we are earnestly striving to teach and practice the truth.

May God bless you and keep you until the coming of His dear Son.

>Yours in Him,
>The men of the Vegas Drive church of Christ

The Vegas Drive church has continued to stand firm in the faith and to proclaim "all the counsel of God" to a lost and dying world (Acts 20:27).

In February of 1990, the disputants signed an agreement to publish the West Columbia debate. A team of transcribers worked on the debate, checking and double checking the manuscripts against the tapes. This has been a slow, tedious process but it assures the accuracy of the published debate. All of this work has been done on a voluntary basis. Thanks are due to Scott Finley, Randy Harshbarger, Sandra Nite, and Steve Curtis, along with David Padfield, who helped in the early stage of preparing charts for insertion in the book. Mike Hughes then worked on laying out the text and charts for the book, a task completed by Norris Long. The disputants did a final reading and correction of all the speeches.

The copyright which appears in the front of the book should not be interpreted to prohibit brethren from using the contents to prepare teaching materials for sermons and classes. The contents of Halbrook's charts were prepared by him (in consultation with Harry Osborne, Mike Willis, and others). Halbrook sent many handwritten charts to David Padfield who capably arranged the layout of those charts, while Harry Osborne and Scott Finley helped with others. Padfield designed both the contents and layout of chart 235 on "How Do You Show Repentance" (except for the "Note" added by Halbrook). To clarify the copyright notice on the charts, the contents belong to Halbrook and the layout done by Padfield belongs to him (with the exception noted on 235).

The Guardian of Truth Foundation is confident that the publication of the Halbrook-Freeman debate will accomplish much good for many years to come. All the teaching of Christ, including what he taught on marriage, divorce, and remarriage, was sealed and sanctified by the blood which he shed on the cross of Calvary. Those who depart from the doctrine of Christ make themselves "the enemies of the cross of Christ" (2 Jn. 9-11; Phil. 3:18). Love and loyalty to Christ require fidelity to his teaching. We urge everyone who reads this book to test its arguments by the Scriptures (1 Jn. 4:6). We urge no one to line up with men, papers, colleges, or foundations, but we urge everyone to stand within the lines of truth drawn by divine revelation. In short, we urge the reader to "remember the words of the Lord Jesus," which is the word of God's grace (Acts 20:35,32).

Introduction By Halbrook's Moderator

On this side of eternity, I have no better, dearer friend than Ron Halbrook. Often the more you know great men, the less is your regard for them. This is not true of brother Halbrook. Having worked closely with him for many years, the greater is my love, respect, and admiration of him. Truth, purity, "reverence and godly fear" have no greater friend than Ron, while, as this debate exemplifies, evil, error, and hypocrisy have no greater foe.

However, neither the discussion nor this introduction is designed to advance or advertise our brother's attributes. Our goal ought to be that God may be glorified in all things through our Lord Jesus Christ. With that in mind, let us cite some items for your meditation and reflection as you study this debate.

First, debates of this kind are necessary and beneficial to the cause of our Lord. As the lives of Jesus and the apostles demonstrate, the word of God survives and thrives in controversy (Acts 6:7; 9:22,29; 19:20; 2 Cor. 10:3-5; Jude 3). Indeed, the history of the past two centuries shows that the faith grew when the "sword of the Spirit" was used in an aggressive, combatant manner against denominationalism in general and "every false way" in particular. Spiritual stagnation, weakness, softness, and compromise find fertile soil in the absence of confrontation. Where there is a lack of militant controversy against evil, one often finds those who would rather "apologize" for the truth than antagonize error. Hence, we commend this debate to you to help you see the truth on this important topic.

Second, as you study this debate, examine the attitude toward divine authority that is expressed. Note the appeals, or the lack thereof, of the disputants toward Scripture. Even the devil himself may cite Scripture (Matt. 4:6), so weigh the positions that are set forth, "handling aright the word of truth" (2 Tim. 2:15). In any such discussion, both sides cannot be right. Both may be wrong, but both cannot be right. Lay aside prejudices and personalities that may obscure the truth. Concentrate on those arguments that appeal to the text of the Bible and do not be swayed by those that base their acceptance on emotions or difficult circumstances. This debate is not about "who" is right or wrong; it is about *what* is right. The word of God is right and true. It will stand when this old world is on fire. You may safely trust that position which is based on the word of truth.

Keep that in mind as you read this debate.

Third, this debate indicates, in my judgment, one of the dangers that we face in this present, perilous time. Questions regarding divorce and remarriage are symptomatic of a general compromise with error on many fronts. There are men who would broaden the border of the faith once delivered. Their design is incipient, subtle, and destructive. They house and espouse hidden agendas to weaken the truth as it is in Jesus. They seek to remain above the fray of contention and condemn those who will not. Theirs is a spiritual elitism which disdains debates such as this and says harsh things only against those who are set for the defense of the gospel. Beware of the spirit that has words of praise and acceptance for denominationalism but only skeptical questions about the church and doctrine of our Lord.

In essence, the issues of this debate are not the only ones where there is error being taught and tolerated if not altogether embraced. There is a much wider front afoot to change the nature and pattern of the New Testament church and its work and worship. The "marriage question" is only the tip of the iceberg. The softening, compromising acceptance of error on this issue will pave the way for future errors and changes in the doctrine of Christ on other topics. Consequently, this debate will assist you in becoming aware of the twists and turns that error makes in order to sustain itself. Accordingly, you will be strengthened to recognize false doctrine whenever it manifests itself.

Fourth, both men would, doubtless, contend for the ideal marriage, one man, one woman for life. However, as you read, note the position and argument which tends to promote this ideal. Observe the pleas for purity and godly living. Mark the arguments that would sanction and justify marriages contrary to God's original plan for man. In this perverse generation, where nearly any kind of immorality is tolerated, compare the calls of the disputants for holiness and cleanliness in the heart and hearth of home. That which appeals to righteous living and that which would justify ungodly living must be sifted and tested. This debate affords you the opportunity to do that as you seek to serve God in your life.

Fifth, this discussion was conducted, to the credit of both disputants, without overt rancor or wrangling. However, it did not take place in an ethical vacuum. Controversy tests the character. One's inner, personal honor, honesty, integrity, humility, and forthrightness are exhibited in the crucible of controversy. This debate was no exception. False doctrine intensifies the temptation to hedge and dodge, to refuse candor and to hide behind the skirt of subterfuge and equivocation, as one seeks to escape the consequences of error. Some men, hemmed in and pinned down by the withering fire of truth, cannot resist the temptations alluded to above. You may profit from this debate, not only in the issues discussed, but also in the observance of the behavior and conduct of character when it is under pressure.

It was a pleasure and privilege to work with Ron Halbrook in this debate. No one has to look for a place to hide when he assists Ron in a study of the truth! Thank you, my friend and brother, for a job well done.

Larry Ray Hafley
February 18, 1992

Introduction By Freeman's Moderator

There are those who believe debating to be wrong or sinful. Generally they use Romans 1:29 as proof of their position. But, the word "debate" as it appears in the King James Version does not prove the point. Debate in the above passage means "contention, strife, and wrangling." The word debate is rendered *strife* in the New King James, and 1901 American Standard Version. It is proven to be honorable by Jesus using this method of exposing error. Disputants may conduct themselves in an unbecoming way, which is wrong, but this in no way proves debating to be wrong.

Brethren Jack Freeman and Ron Halbrook engaged in debates January 15, 16, 18, 19, in North Las Vegas, Nevada and February 26, 27, March 1, 2, in West Columbia, Texas, 1990. It was my pleasure to moderate for Jack Freeman and brother Larry Ray Hafley moderated for Ron Halbrook. The first four nights were in North Las Vegas, in the building where Jack preaches, the last four nights in West Columbia where Ron preaches.

The attendance was good throughout the discussion. However, the gatherings were larger in West Columbia due to the number of brethren within driving distance of that area. It would have been good if all brethren could have attended. Perhaps those who could not attend will be able to read the debate.

I am doubtful that the marriage, divorce, and remarriage issue will ever be settled to the satisfaction of all. It would be good if brethren would study this important question with a sincere desire to know the truth. There is no question in my mind as to the Bible teaching being sufficient on this subject. There is difficulty in defining some words that are used in the teaching on this subject. This in part is due to human frailty and situations, not because it is impossible to understand. There are so many emotional problems involved that create in the mind of some people a cloud which makes it difficult to arrive at a right or scriptural conclusion. Not that this excuses anyone, but it is a simple fact.

The propositions discussed concerned the right of both parties in a divorce for fornication having the right to remarry. It is my observation that tradition has clouded the issue at hand till the subject of remarriage has become increasingly difficult to understand. It is my sincere desire and prayer that reading this book may be helpful in better understanding the subject of marriage, divorce, and remarriage.

Seeing that each one of us will have to give an account to God for our lives (2 Cor. 5:10), let us take our Bible in hand as we read this book, weighing the arguments made, reading the Scripture used to see if it proves the thought set forth. Remember, the Bible is the only accepted authority on this or any other religious subject.

These brethren who conducted this debate were in general a good example as to how brethren should treat one another in such discussions. During the debate neither moderator had to call anyone down. The audience in both parts of this confrontation were orderly and quiet. This is to be commended on their part.

I have known brother Freeman for many years, and believe him to be honest and capable of expressing what he believes the Scriptures teach on any subject. I want to commend both Jack and Ron for their willingness to publicly defend what they teach. I am aware that many brethren do not believe that we should debate each other. But God authorized disagreements among brethren in the early church to be put into the inspired record, for every one to see. These can be found in the books of Acts, Corinthians, Galatians, and others. The disagreements contained in the Bible will remain there to be read by all people who read the Bible even into eternity. Therefore I do not believe it to be wrong to discuss our difference before the world.

All of us know that where there is disagreement on any subject one of the disputants must be wrong. Both could be wrong, but both cannot be right. So, as suggested above, take your Bible and carefully investigate the arguments made in this book on the subject of marriage, divorce, and remarriage. Keep in mind that you will have to stand before God and be judged individually for what you believe and practice (Rom. 14:12; Rev. 20:12,13). As is seen we shall all be judged by the Scripture (John 12:48). Read carefully, think soberly and make up your own mind what is right or wrong according to Bible teaching.

Homer W. Walker, Sr.
February, 1992

First Evening
Halbrook's First Affirmative

[Proposition: The Scriptures teach that two people joined by God in marriage are bound for life, the only exception being that an innocent partner may put away a mate guilty of fornication and remarry.]

Brother Freeman, brethren moderators, ladies and gentlemen, we welcome you to this study of God's Word. I want you to know that I have no malice toward brother Freeman. He has a soul as I do and we will both stand before the same God to be judged by the same truth. May God help us to show our love for each other by seeking the truth in this debate.

If you will notice my affirmative proposition: *"The Scriptures teach,"* sixty-six books of the Bible. Jesus said, "Have ye not read," Old Testament, and then, "I say unto you," and there you have New Testament revelation.

"Two people joined by God in marriage are bound for life." As the Lord quoted from Genesis, we must leave father and mother and cleave to our mate, become one flesh, and, "What God hath joined together, let not man put asunder." *"The only exception being that an innocent partner may put away a mate guilty of fornication and remarry."* So the Lord said, "Whosoever shall put away his wife, except it be for fornication, and shall marry another, committeth adultery."

Halbrook Affirms

Passage	Proposition
Have ye not read - I say unto you (Matt. 19:9)	The Scriptures teach that
Leave, cleave, 1 flesh What God joined, let not man put asunder (Matt. 19:5-6)	Two people joined by God in marriage are bound for life
Whosoever shall put away his wife, except for fornication, & shall marry another, committeth adultery (Matt. 19:9)	The only exception being that an innocent partner may put away a mate guilty of fornication and remarry

Affirm: Ron Halbrook
Deny: Jack Freeman

And so I am affirming tonight the proposition of this passage. Brother Freeman is denying the proposition of this passage.

Now, let me read to you the questions that I have given to him that he will discuss:

1. Is it necessary to have positive divine authority for all that we preach and practice? Are we obligated to put our finger on the verse that authorizes

what we preach and practice?

2. Does Matthew 19:9 teach that, after God joins two people in marriage, an innocent partner may put away a mate guilty of fornication and marry another?

3. Is there any marriage between one male and one female which people can enter under civil law, but which they must end in order to be right with God?

4. Which passages speak of marrying another? (A) Romans 7:2-3, (B) Matthew 19:9, (C) 1 Corinthians 7:15.

My friends, he argued in Las Vegas that 1 Corinthians 7:15 speaks of it along with these others. But I predict that this debate will end and he will never ever once find "marry another" in that passage. You watch throughout the debate and see if he does.

5. Since you say 1 Corinthians 7:10-11 does not give any reason for divorce in your "Marriage" series (no. 5) [sermons taped at North Las Vegas church of Christ], what must the Christian do if there is a divorce and remarriage violating this passage? (A) Divorce the second mate and return to the first mate or remain unmarried? (B) Pray for forgiveness and remain in the second marriage. (C) "I refuse to answer on the grounds that it may incriminate me."

Well, we will look forward to his answers and comments.

Now, notice on my charts 6, 7, and 8 where we are dealing with the authority of the Word of God. Jesus said, *"All authority hath been given unto me in heaven and in earth." "All truth"* was revealed by the Spirit, sent down from heaven. We are to *"speak the same thing,"* the very words of the Spirit, *"that which is written"* (1 Cor. 1). Galatians 1 teaches that we are to teach and proclaim no other message than this one. 2 John 9, that we must *"abide in the doctrine of Christ";* if we depart from it we

---

Authority Of Christ
(Matthew 28:18)

Expressed In The Bible:

* All Truth (John 16:13)

* Speak Same Thing - Words of Holy Spirit - That Which Is Written (1 Cor. 1:10; 2:13; 4:6)

* No Other Message (Gal. 1:8-9)

* Abide In Doctrine Of Christ (2 John 9)

* Contend For The Faith (Jude 3)

6

"have not God." And Jude 3, we must *"earnestly contend for the faith."*

We notice on my chart number 7 that the authority of Christ can be expressed in *general* terms. Mark 16:15 says, "Go into all the world." We can walk, run, ride; we have authority. Sometimes God is *specific.* In Acts 20:7, *"the first day of the week,"* one day out of seven days, specific authority. And then it is expressed in three ways: direct statement, approved example, or necessary implication.

Then, notice that there was a debate in Jerusalem in Acts 15 — see chart 8. What is commanded to be bound upon the Gentiles, the gospel alone or also the law of Moses? Peter argued that God gave the same gift to the Gentiles that He gave to the Jews, and this *necessarily implies* God's acceptance of the Gentiles. And then we find Paul argued that God *approved his example* of preaching to the Gentiles.

Authority Of Christ: How Expressed

Two Kinds:

General - "Go" in Mark 16:15

Specific - "Day" in Acts 20:7

In Three Ways:

Direct Statement

Approved Example

Necessary Implication

James quoted *direct statements* where God said that in the day that the Jew is saved by the gospel, the Gentile will be saved by the same gospel. So, there was authority for them preaching the gospel. But verse 24 says that some went out teaching that the law of Moses can be bound, *"to whom we gave no such commandment."* No implication, no example, no direct statement, means the Bible is silent. *Where the Bible is silent, we cannot act.*

Now then, we want to notice next chart 13.

What Is Commanded?

The Gospel	Law Of Moses
Acts 15:7-11 God gave the same gift to the Gentiles [Imply God accepts them - Jews must, too]	No Implication - Silent! (Vs. 24)
Vs. 12 God **Approved Example** of preaching to Gentiles	No Example - Silent! (Vs. 24)
Vv. 16-18 God Made **Direct Statement**	No Statement - Silent! (Vs. 24)

On the matter of God being specific, out of the class of all possible woods, you remember in Genesis 6 that God specified *gopher wood* for building the ark. That excluded all other woods. The tribe of *Levi* for the priesthood excluded all other tribes. And then, the action in water is *immersion,* and that excludes all other actions. The music we offer in worship is *singing*. God specified that (Eph. 5:19). It excludes all other music.

My friends, here is the *simplicity* of our study tonight. Out of the class of all possible divorced people, the Lord *specified* that the innocent party can put away the one guilty of fornication and marry another (Matt.

When God Is Specific

CLASS	SPECIFIC	EXCLUDE
Woods	Gopher Wood (Gen. 6:14)	All Other Woods
Tribes	Levi (Heb. 7:14)	All Other Tribes
Action - Water	Immerse (Acts 2:38; 8:38)	All Other Actions
Music	Sing (Eph. 5:19)	All Other Music
Divorced People	Innocent Put Away Guilty & Remarry (Matt. 19:9)	All Other Divorced Persons

13

19:9). That excludes all other divorced persons from the right of marrying another. God is *specific*.

And then notice, *the unity that we find in divine truth*, chart 37. (I want to remember to give the numbers — that was chart 13 on "God is Specific," and then 37 on "Unity"). In John 17, the Lord prayed for unity, *"Sanctify them through thy truth, thy word is truth."* And then he prayed that we all might be one on the basis of that truth. And did you know that we can be one in the matter of *immersion?* If we read Acts 8:38, "they went down…into the water," came "up out of the water," we can all understand that. Divine truth unites us. But someone wants to sprinkle a little baby and he thinks he can find some kind of an inference for it in Acts 16:15. There is no clear passage for that, no direct statement, no approved example, and no *necessary* implication.

Unity In Truth
(John 17:17-21)

Divine Truth Unites All Agree:	Human Theory Divides Men Differ:
1. Immerse (Acts 8:38)	1. Sprinkle Baby (Acts 16:15?)
2. Lord's Supper 1st Day (Acts 20:7)	2. Any Day (1 Cor. 11:26?)
3. Sing (Eph. 5:19)	3. Play (Rev. 5:8?)
4. Preach (1 Tim. 3:15)	4. Meal, Party, Gym (Jude 12?)
5. Hope - Heaven (1 Pet. 1:4)	5. 1,000 Years On Earth (Rev. 20:4?)
6. Innocent Put Away Fornicator & Remarry (Matt. 19:9)	6. Others Remarry (1 Cor. 7?)

37

Human theories divide us! And that is why we are divided in religion today. *The Lord's Supper on the first day* — divine truth will unite us. But, taking it any day — oh, someone can *claim* a passage, an inference out of a passage, a *human* inference out of a passage — but, my friend, these human theories are dividing the religious world.

We have authority to *sing* and we can be united on it. But when we play the instrument we have division. We have authority for *the church to preach the gospel*. But when we have the meals and the parties in the name of the church, then we have division.

We have *the hope of heaven* specified. None of us disagrees. We are united on it. But the thousand year reign on earth brings the division.

Now, my friends, *we can agree — and my opponent will agree — the innocent can put away the guilty fornicator and marry another*. He will agree to that. We can all agree to that. *Divine truth unites us*. But when he makes the argument that others can marry again, then, my friend, comes the division. And what is dividing us? The human theory is dividing us. He may *claim* to find an inference out of a passage somewhere, but he will not find any passage that says someone can put away his mate, be divorced, and marry another, *except as it is taught in Matthew 19:9*.

Then, notice that unity has in fact been realized on the basis of restoring New Testament Christianity, asking for the "old paths," and taking the Bible pattern of faith and practice. See chart 23. In the book *Quest For A Christian America* by Ed Harrell, he showed the result of the restoration plea in the 1800's. "No release" was given to a husband or wife "unless the other party has been guilty of fornication." The claim of "desertion" as "a just cause for divorce and remarriage" was rejected by these pioneer preachers who were going back to "what saith the Scripture." And church discipline was practiced, and that means they withdrew from those who married contrary to Bible teaching. My friend, *we can be united!* Brethren have been united in the past, but it is the teaching of the human theory that brings the division.

Restoration Plea
1. "Ask for the old paths"
2. "What saith the scripture?"
3. Christ only as the head of the church
4. Bible only as guide
5. N. T. Pattern of faith & practice

Result On Marriage
1. "No release" given to a husband or wife "unless the other party has been guilty of fornication."
2. Claim of "desertion" as "a just cause for divorce and remarriage" rejected.
3. Church discipline practiced [See Ed Harrell, *Quest For A Christian America*, pp. 197-198].

23

I believe *my opponent can understand these principles*. We can see that from his article in the *Gospel Guardian* of April 1960, on chart 15. Things "not authorized...are...sinful," he said. If you have "no passage of Scripture," you cannot act. Well, my friend, there is no clear passage that will authorize the put-away fornicator or the deserted believer to marry another. You just remember that and write that down. It will stand. Such marriages are sinful and I proved it out of the mouth of brother Freeman.

And then my chart 16. Now, he talked about God's "perfect plan" in another *Gospel Guardian* article. We cannot change God's perfect "plan of salvation" and "worship"; we cannot change it "for daily living." But, my friend, God's plan for daily living includes marriage, divorce, and remarriage. And, indeed, we cannot change it, and I simply appeal to my opponent for that.

And then, notice now chart 41. As we think about surveying what the Bible teaches on marriage, divorce, and remarriage, Jesus explained Genesis 2:24, in that God requires one man for one woman, "a man" and "his wife." It excludes all immorality because it says "a man" and "his wife" and they are to be *"one* flesh." No fornication, adultery, polygamy, and such like. This implies that immorality desecrates such a union as that, and so becomes the ground for the innocent to put away the guilty.

This excludes the put-away fornicator from marrying another. Obedience is

---

Not Authorized = Sinful

1. Things "not authorized within the doctrine of Christ are not only non-essential but sinful as well."

2. An author defended sponsoring church but had "no passage of Scripture to show that such a plan is authorized by the Lord" (Jack Freeman, <u>Gospel Guardian,</u> 28 April 1960, pp. 8-9).

3. No clear passage authorizes put-away fornicator or deserted believer to marry another.

4. Conclusion: such marriages are sinful!

15

God's Perfect Plan

1. We must not change God's perfect "plan of salvation... plan of worship ... plan for the life of the individual ... plan of the work for the church."

2. "When the individual engages in dishonest activity; when his thoughts, words, or actions are evil; he has departed from the perfect plan for daily living" (Jack Freeman, <u>Gospel Guardian,</u> 24 Oct. 1957, pp. 8-9).

3. God's perfect plan for daily living includes marriage, divorce, & remarriage.

16

blessed and sin brings hardship, not privileges. And the fornicator does not win the privilege of marrying another by his sin. And it implies the bond is only in this life, "one *flesh.*" These relations have to do with the fleshly body.

Then we notice my chart 43. *God's ideal was given in the beginning in Genesis 2,* as our Lord taught, but men quickly fell into sin — bigamy, giving their wives to others, and having children through their handmaids, and all such as that. The Gentiles went so far until God cast them off.

> **Genesis 2:24 Law**
> **Explained By Jesus In Matthew 19:3-9**
>
> 1. **Requires** One Man For One Woman - "A Man," "His Wife"
> 2. **Excludes** All Immorality - "A Man," "His Wife," "<u>One</u> Flesh" - No Fornication, Adultery, Polygamy, Concubines, Homosexuals, Bestiality
> 3. **Implies** Immorality Desecrates The Union - Ground For The Innocent To Put Away The Guilty - "A Man," "His Wife," "Cleave," "One Flesh"
> 4. **Excludes** The Put Away Fornicator From Marrying Another
>   * Obedience Is Blessed (Deut. 10:13)
>   * Sin Brings Hardship, Not Privileges (Prov. 13:15)
> 5. **Implies** Bond Only In This Life - "One <u>Flesh</u>" - Life And Relations In The Fleshly Body

But you will remember that God in compassion toward a lost world made the promise of a Savior to come, and later added the law of Moses because of transgression. In Exodus 20 he taught they were not to commit adultery, and the death penalty was attached to that law. Do you see God in that law *emphasizing even that original ideal?*

But the Jews had to be regulated in their stubbornness of heart. And

> | God's Ideal | Promise Salvation ➡ | Law Of Moses | Ex. 20:14, 17 Lev. 20:10 ➡ | Gospel Of |
> | --- | --- | --- | --- | --- |
> | Gen. 2:24 | 12:1-3 | Gal. 3:19 | Deut. 22:22 | Christ |
>
> **From The Beginning Until Now - Matt. 19:8b**
>
> | | | |
> | --- | --- | --- |
> | | 4:19 Bigamy | |
> | | 12:10-20 Wife Offered | **Jews Regulated** |
> | 6:2 | 16:1-3 Maid | |
> | 11:1-9 | 25:1-6 Concubines | Deut. 24:1-4 |
> | | 26:1-11 Wife Offered | Mal. 2:14-16 |
> | | 30:4, 9 Maid | |
>
> **Gentiles Cast God Off**
> Rom. 1:18-32; Eph. 2:12; Acts 17:30

we notice this in *Deuteronomy 24* now. That is my chart 44. God restrained, but did not initiate, the practice of divorce in Deuteronomy 24. God restrained, but did not initiate, such practices. He made a temporary concession to their stubbornness as Jesus himself explained.

But, what we find in the passage is that He allowed them to put away their wives only for shameful indecency. And so He decreased the reasons by which they were doing that. He guaranteed her freedom to marry another. He prohibited the first man ever having her back after she remarried.

Now, on my chart 48 we see *God's ideal in the New Testament*. The plan had come to fruition, and Christ came and reinforced God's original ideal. In Matthew 5, he ended the Mosaic concession. In Matthew 19, what God joins man is not to break asunder. In Romans 7, marriage is used as an illustration. We will study that some. In 1 Corinthians 7, we have questions in the view of a crisis at hand. And there are various other New Testament passages. *From the beginning until now,* this is God's ideal.

I want you to see how simple this matter is as we notice my chart 54, "How Do We Know?" The simplicity of truth is expressed in the song we teach to the children, "Yes, Jesus loves me, *the Bible tells me so.*" How do you *know* you can remarry? Because in Romans 7:2-3, he said that if your mate dies you can marry another. *"Married to another,"* it said. That is how we know. In Matthew 19:9, if you put your mate away for fornication, you can "marry another." That is how we know. Where does the Bible say, "Marry another," *to the put-away fornicator and those unscripturally divorced?* It is not in the Bible! And to affirm such a practice, my friend, is to launch out into the area of divine silence where there is darkness of revelation and no certainty of truth at all.

What Deut. 24:1-4 Accomplished

Restrain, Not Initiate, Their Practices:
▶ Men sent wives away at will
▶ Women had no recourse or protection
▶ Treated as property - pawns of man's unbridled passion

Temporary Concession To Stubbornness In Order To:
▶ Curb their reckless practices
▶ Regulate their stubbornness
▶ Soften abuses suffered by women

Vs. 1 Decrease Reasons - Shameful, Indecent
Vv. 1-2 Guarantee Freedom To Remarry
Vv. 3-4 Prohibit 1st Man Ever Having Her Back After She Remarried

44

| God's Ideal Gen. 2:24 | Promise Salvation 12:1-3 | → | Law Of Moses Gal. 3:19 | → | Gospel Of Christ Reinforce God's Original Ideal |

From The Beginning Until Now - Matt. 19:8b

Matt. 5:31-32 - End Mosaic Concession

Matt. 19:3-12 - God Joins, Man Not To Break

Rom. 7:1-4 - Marriage As An Illustration

1 Cor. 7 - Questions & Crisis At Hand

Eph. 5:22-33 - Conduct Of Husband & Wife

48

> ### How We Know
>
> **Simplicity Of Truth:** "Yes, Jesus loves me, the Bible tells me so" (Rom. 4:3; Eph. 3:4).
>
> **Know We Can Remarry:**
> 1. If mate dies (Rom. 7:2-3)
> 2. If put away mate for fornication (Matt. 19:9)
>
> **Where Does The Bible Authorize These To Remarry:**
> 1. The put-away fornicator?
> 2. Those unscripturally divorced?
>
> 54

Now notice Matthew 5:32 [chart 60]. "But I say unto you, That whosoever shall put away his wife, saving for the cause of fornication, causeth her to commit adultery: and whosoever shall marry her that is divorced committeth adultery," my Lord said.

Now notice on my chart 62 [next page] that we have *the rule* and *the exception*. "Whosoever shall put away his wife, saving for the cause of fornication, causeth her to commit adultery: and whosoever shall marry her that is divorced committeth adultery." Now, watch it as you put the exception into effect. "Whosoever shall put away his wife for fornication" *is not responsible for her subsequent adultery*. But it still stands that "whosoever shall marry her that is divorced committeth adultery." Notice up here the emphasis on the *cause* of a sin, but in the case of the exception, you are *not guilty of causing* that sin when it occurs.

> ### Matthew 5:32
>
> "But I say unto you, That whosoever shall put away his wife, saving for the cause of fornication, causeth her to commit adultery: and whosoever shall marry her that is divorced committeth adultery."
>
> 60

And then, my chart 63 [next page]. *The exception does not exempt the fornicator*. Matthew 5:32 and 19:9 are compound, complex sentences. Each one contains two independent clauses joined by the conjunction "and." The exception stated in the first independent clause has no force in the second independent clause. Therefore, the force of the exception in the first independent clause does *not* yield the meaning in the second clause, "Whosoever shall marry her that is divorced for fornication doth not commit adultery." There is no way in all the world in terms of the rules of grammar that you can make that exception travel from the first independent clause to the second independent clause. And I challenge my opponent to make the attempt, if he thinks it can be done.

And then, next we notice my chart 67. Notice the difference between *the law of Moses* and *the law of Christ*. Under the law of Moses when you were guilty of fornication, you were put away indeed, you were put away by death. And so, certainly you *could marry no other*. Under the law of Christ, the fornicator is to be put away *by divorce* — and *has no authority to marry another*.

> **Rule & Exception**
> **Matt. 5:32**
>
> 1. "Whosoever shall put away his wife, saving for the cause of fornication, causeth her to commit adultery: and whosoever shall marry her that is divorced committeth adultery."
>
> 2. Whosoever shall put away his wife **for fornication** is not responsible for her subsequent adultery: and whosoever shall marry her that is divorced committeth adultery.
>
> 62

Then you had divorce for a cause short of fornication, but *now* no divorce for any cause short of fornication. So the cause changed, didn't it?

But then notice, under Deuteronomy 24, the mate who was divorced is not guilty of fornication if she married another. Alright, there has been no fornication committed and she married another — it is still not adultery under the concession that He made to their hardness of heart. But in the same situation in Matthew 5:32 and Matthew 19:9, if you are divorced and there is no fornication and you marry another, then, my friend, *you are committing adultery*. That is what Jesus said. So, the cause changed and the *effect* changed, brother Freeman. *Cause* and *effect*.

> **The Exception Does Not Exempt The Fornicator**
>
> Matt. 5:32 & 19:9 are compound, complex sentences. Each one contains two independent clauses, joined by the conjunction "and."
>
> The exception stated in the first independent clause has no force in the second independent clause.
>
> THEREFORE, the force of the exception in the first independent clause does NOT yield the meaning in the second, "Whosoever shall marry her that is divorced FOR FORNICATION doth not commit adultery."
>
> 63

Now, a man who married her under Deuteronomy was *not in adultery*, i.e.

First Evening: Halbrook's First Affirmative

MOSES	CHRIST
1. Fornication - Put Away By Death (Marry No Other)	1. Fornication - Put Away By Divorce (Marry No Other)
2. Divorce - Cause Short Of Fornication	2. No Divorce For Any Cause Short of Fornication
3. Mate Divorced - No Fornication - Marry Another w/o Adultery ↓	3. Same Situation - BUT Marry Another = Adultery ↓
4. Man Who Marries Her Not In Adultery ↓	4. Man Who Marries Her In Adultery ↓
5. First Man Can't Have Her	5. First Man Can Have Her

67

married that one put away not for fornication. But the man who marries her *is in adultery* in Matthew 5. And under that first law, the first man could not have her back after she married again. But under this law there is no such prohibition at all. Now, my friend, you see the distinction in these two laws.

Alright, next we want to notice my charts 72 and 73. Matthew 19:9, "And I say unto you, Whosoever shall put away his wife, except it be for fornication, and shall marry another, committeth adultery. And whoso marrieth her which is put away doth commit adultery."

And, my friend, notice my chart 73 now. We have *the rule* and *the exception* again. "Whosoever shall put away his wife, except it be for fornication, and shall marry another, committeth adultery: and whoso marrieth her which is put

Matthew 19:9

"And I say unto you, Whosoever shall put away his wife, except it be for fornication, and shall marry another, committeth adultery: and whoso marrieth her which is put away doth commit adultery."

72

away doth commit adultery." And you want to notice those two independent clauses joined by the coordinating conjunction *"and" — separate independent clauses*. Now then, notice the exception: "Whosoever shall put away his wife for fornication and shall marry another, doth not commit adultery: and whoever marries her which is put away doth commit adultery." That second clause stands unchanged by that expression that was in the first clause alone. There is no way in the world, brother Freeman, that you can respect the rules of grammar and make that exception travel to the second clause. It cannot be done.

Alright, notice then my chart 74. My Lord said, *"Except* it be for fornication." Except means *if and only if.* Matthew 18:3, "Except ye become as a little child you cannot enter the kingdom." So, *if and only if* you become as a child you can enter the kingdom. Nicodemus in John 3:2, *"If and only if* God is with our Lord, he could do the miracles." But he expressed that with an *except* — "except God be with him." "Except ye are born of water and of the Spirit ye cannot enter the kingdom," means *if and only if* ye are born of the water and the Spirit you enter the kingdom.

> **Rule & Exception**
> **Matt. 19:9**
>
> 1. "Whosoever shall put away his wife, except it be for fornication, and shall marry another, committeth adultery: and whoso marrieth her which is put away doth commit adultery."
>
> 2. Whosoever shall put away his wife **for fornication** and shall marry another, doth not commit adultery: and whoso marrieth her which is put away doth commit adultery.
>
> 73

> **Except = If & Only If!**
>
> * Matt. 18:3 Become as little child → Enter kingdom
> * John 3:2 God with Him → Do miracles
> * John 3:5 Born of water & Spirit → Enter kingdom
> * Matt. 19:9 Put away wife for fornication & marry another → Not adultery
>
> 74

Now, in Matthew 19:9, it has exactly the same effect and force. Think about it. If you put your wife away for fornication and marry another, it is not adultery. But it did not just say that [i.e., in those very words]. It said *"except,"* that *if and only if* term. So, it is *if and only if,* brother Freeman, *if and only if* you put your wife away for fornication, you can marry another and it would not be adultery. That is what the Bible teaches in plain terms.

Now, notice here on my chart 81, that all cases of divorce and remarriage are *adulterous.* They are *adulterous relationships* and *adulterous marriages,* brother Freeman. Notice, "whosoever" is comprehensive. If you divorce your mate and marry another, it is *adultery.* If you marry the one divorced without cause, it is *adultery.* If the put-away fornicator takes a new mate, it is *adultery.* All cases of divorce and remarriage are adulterous unions and relationships. But there was one *"except."* Whoever divorces his mate for fornication and marries another, that is *not adultery.* Now, that is how simple it is to understand that passage.

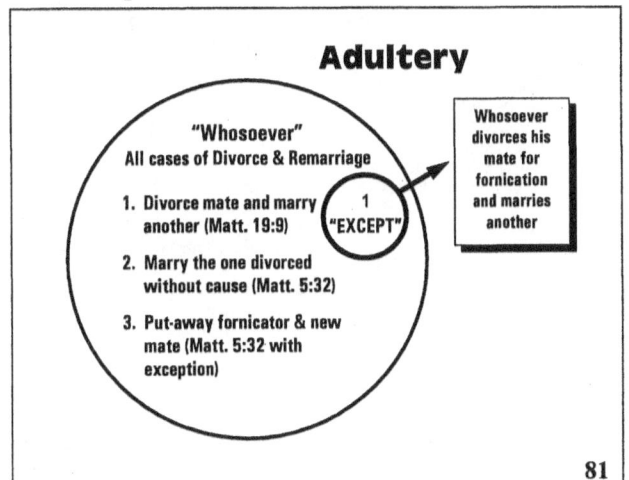

Now then, we want to notice my charts 100 and 100-A. And I want you to notice that we have shown here that *all cases of marriage, divorce, and remarriage are subject to God's law.* Starting in Genesis 2, God ordained it, defined it, regulated it. And just because a person was single, it did not mean he could just marry according to his own desire. There were laws, rules, regulations, and here you have fifteen of them from these passages and eight more again on the chart 100-A [next page]. The conclusion is that *no one is free to marry in violation of God's law.*

Now, let me focus in on that with this next chart, 101 [next page]. *Divorced people remain under the constraint of law.* In Deuteronomy 24, you could divorce your wife, but you could not have her back after she married another. The divorcee could marry another, but then she could never return to the first mate. In Leviticus 21, the divorcee is free from marriage but cannot marry a priest. Why not? She is free, she is "single," as brother Freeman likes to put it. I will tell you why not: because *God rules over all cases of marriage, divorce, and remarriage — all cases.*

Now then, notice Matthew 5 and 19. The pure can divorce the impure, the immoral, and marry another. But the new mate cannot be one put away for fornication or for some other cause. Divorced people remain *under the constraint of law*, brother Freeman.

And then, he did not authorize a put-away person to marry another, whether put away for fornication or some other cause. In 1 Corinthians 7:10-11, if two Christians are divorced, they must remain unmarried or reconcile. In 1 Corinthians 7:12-15, the believer cannot give up Christ to keep the unbeliever. But there is no authority for either to *"marry another."* That is the expression he will never find in that passage. Now, my friend, unscriptural divorce releases neither party from marriage obligations. And the scriptural divorce releases both parties from the marriage, but *not from the constraint of marriage law*. So, you keep that in mind.

Now, you may be wondering, "How can brother Freeman offset these clear and simple passages?" I want you to notice these three points. If you want to make a note, I want you to notice these three points. If you want to make a note on your pad, here are the three routes he can go. He will try to take Matthew 5 and 19 and *transfer the exception* from the first independent clause to the second. He has got to do that. He may make several arguments, but it will come under that category. Number two, he will make various *perversions of 1 Corinthians 7*. You watch him do it. I predict he will do

---

All Cases
Of Marriage, Divorce & Remarriage
Are Subject To God's Law (Continued)

16. Lev. 21:7, 13-14 Priest marry virgin, but not whore, divorcee, or widow
17. Lev. 21:7, 13-14 Whore, divorcee & widow free to marry, but not free to marry priest
18. Matt. 5:32; 19:9; Mk. 10:11-12; Lk. 16:18 Not divorce and remarry except for fornication
19. Matt. 5:32; 19:9 One free to marry, but not to a put-away person (whether put away for fornication or other cause)
20. Matt. 5:32; 19:9 Not authorize a put-away person (whether put away for fornication or other cause) to remarry
21. 1 Cor. 7:10-11 If 2 Christians divorce, must remain unmarried or reconcile
22. 1 Cor. 7:12-15 Believer not give up Christ to keep unbeliever (no authority for either to marry another)
23. Rom. 7:2-3; 1 Cor. 7:27, 39 Man & wife bound by marriage law for life

Conclusion: No one is "free to marry" in violation of God's law!

100-A

Divorced People Remain Under Constraint Of Law

1. Deut. 24:1-4 Divorce wife but can't have her back after her 2nd marriage
2. Deut. 24:1-4 Divorcee marry another but then can't ever return to 1st mate
3. Lev. 21:7, 13-14 Divorcee free from marriage but can't marry a priest
4. Matt. 5:32; 19:9 Pure divorce impure and marry another (new mate can't be one put away for fornication or other cause)
5. Matt. 5:32; 19:9 Not authorize a put-away person (whether put away for fornication or other cause) to marry another
6. 1 Cor. 7:10-11 If 2 Christians divorce, must remain unmarried or reconcile
7. 1 Cor. 7:12-15 Believer not give up Christ to keep unbeliever (no authority for either to marry another)

CONCLUSION:
1. Unscriptural divorce releases neither party from marriage!
2. Scriptural divorce releases both parties from marriage, but not from the constraint of the law!

101

it. He will go to 1 Corinthians 7 and try to find "marry another," and he will not ever find it. But you watch him go down that route. Number three, he will make *a false plea on mercy and forgiveness*. Mercy and forgiveness. Those are the three routes he will go.

Now then, chart 325. You want to watch for these false claims that are made when my opponent feels weak. I have cited to you the *passages* as final authority — he will want to claim that I cite *none*, if he gets to feeling weak. And when I refer to *sources of study*, if he feels real weak he will claim that I have been using them *in place of* the Bible. You watch and see how weak he feels. If I show you *the doctrine of Christ*, which I did, he will claim it is *the doctrine of demons*. And if he does that, you will know how weak he feels, and he is grasping for straws. I *teach* God's mercy and yet he will claim I am *denying* God's mercy. Watch and see how weak he feels tonight.

> **False Claims Made When Opponent Feels Weak**
> 1. I cite passages as final authority - he <u>claims</u> I cite none.
> 2. I refer to sources of study - he <u>claims</u> I use them in place of the Bible.
> 3. I show doctrine of Christ - he <u>claims</u> it is the doctrine of demons.
> 4. I find his doctrine in the Catholic Catechism - he <u>claims</u> I agree with Catechism.
> 5. I teach God's mercy (Mk. 6:17-18; 1 Cor. 5; 6:9-11) - he <u>claims</u> I deny mercy.
>
> 325

And then again, you will hear him use another approach. And that is that "brother Halbrook is a liar" — if he follows the course that he did before in the Las Vegas debate. Now, you know, if I am a liar and a horse thief, *if I am a liar and a horse thief,* you still need to listen for *the passage* that proves his case. You want to remember that, my friend. If he proves me a liar and a horse thief, and still does not have book, chapter, and verse for someone to *marry another,* other than the innocent party that put away the guilty, they can hang me for being a horse thief, *but he will still be on unscriptural ground,* won't he?

So after all that, he might say now as he said before that *he never had such lies told on him* and that *one of the biggest lies* I have told on him was concerning charts 15 and 16, *where I showed what he wrote and what he taught in the Gospel Guardian*. He made a categorical statement that he did *not* write these articles and that I *lied* on him when I said that he wrote these. He said, furthermore, there are *two* Jack Freeman's and that he knows it because he has met the other one. He said it must have been the *other one* at San Pablo, California. That is the address on these articles — San Pablo, California — 1957 and 1960. So, my friends, I apologized, and I would apologize again if it is called to my attention that I misrepresented something.

But, do you know, I talked to the editor of the *Gospel Guardian*, brother Freeman, and he says *this Jack Freeman is you*, sir. He knows you, and held meetings with you, and *this Jack Freeman is you*, sir. Yes, it is! And then I got word from the San Pablo church, that, yes, there were *two occasions of a Jack Freeman preaching there*.

> **Not Authorized = Sinful**
>
> 1. Things "not authorized within the doctrine of Christ are not only non-essential but sinful as well."
> 2. An author defended sponsoring church but had "no passage of Scripture to show that such a plan is authorized by the Lord" (Jack Freeman, Gospel Guardian, 28 April 1960, pp. 8-9).
> 3. No clear passage authorizes put-away fornicator or deserted believer to marry another.
> 4. Conclusion: such marriages are sinful!
>
> 15

But, brother Freeman, *both* of them were *you!* That is what they are saying at the San Pablo church. Yes sir, *you did write these articles*. Yes, you did! And then, I have word from the *other* Jack Freeman. Do you know that when these articles were written he was still a little school boy? Yes, he was still a little school boy. He did not write these articles, brother Freeman.

It reminds me of the Watergate fiasco. Some began to say, "Oh, they did not remember if they did this or that." And I

> **God's Perfect Plan**
>
> 1. We must not change God's perfect "plan of salvation... plan of worship ... plan for the life of the individual ... plan of the work for the church."
>
> 2. "When the individual engages in dishonest activity; when his thoughts, words, or actions are evil; he has departed from the perfect plan for daily living" (Jack Freeman, Gospel Guardian, 24 Oct. 1957, pp. 8-9).
>
> 3. God's perfect plan for daily living includes marriage, divorce, & remarriage.
>
> 16

believe if I were you, I would get up and say, "I do not remember if I did it." But, my friend, they were reminded by *the facts*. And I am reminding brother Freeman of *the facts* tonight, so that it will not do to say his case is proved because Ron Halbrook lied about these articles. What will you say about *the Las Vegas fiasco?* It is beginning to look like the Watergate fiasco.

First Evening: Halbrook's First Affirmative 17

See my chart 54 now. You remember, my friend, the simplicity of divine truth. "Yes, Jesus loves me, *the Bible tells me so.*" You know that you can *marry another* if your mate dies because Romans 7 said it in plain language. If you put your mate away for fornication, you know you can *marry another* because the Bible puts it in plain language. Now, you listen to my opponent as he comes, and can he produce the passage where the put-away fornicator can marry another or those unscripturally divorced *marry another?* You watch for that. Thank you.

How We Know

Simplicity of Truth: "Yes, Jesus loves me, the Bible tells me so" (Rom. 4:3; Eph. 3:4)

Know We Can Remarry:
1. If mate dies (Rom. 7:2-3)
2. If put away mate for fornication (Matt. 19:9)

Where Does The Bible Authorize These to Remarry:
1. The put-away fornicator?
2. Those unscripturally divorced?

54

First Evening
Freeman's First Negative

It is good to be back in the great state of Texas. I began my preaching career in this state a little over forty years ago. I was reminded of this just before we left home as my wife and I celebrated our forty-fourth wedding anniversary, Saturday.

I do not like to refer to things like this, as brother Halbrook did not bring it up, but his moderator did. I would like to make a brief statement in regard to how this debate took place, at the moment. *First of all, the letter that he read from the Vegas Drive Church of Christ.* I am glad it was read and we know where some stand now. This is one good thing that came out of the debate. I would like to make this observation: not all the members there agree with that statement. No one — not one person signed the letter. As a result of the position taken by those brethren, I just mention two cases. One couple (married eighteen years) had been told they can live together, but can have no sex. Married with children for eighteen years, you can live together, but have no sex. Another couple who had been married for ten years were told you can live together with no sex. In other words, you are not married in God's sight, your children are illegitimate.

As for the origin of the debate, an article in the *Guardian of Truth* in which in essence *myself and other elders at North Las Vegas in Nevada were charged with bowing our knees to the doctrine of Baal,* in regard to that, I did challenge brother Halbrook. But a month or more went by and I had no answer. I did call down here and I found out they had a weekly paper and asked if they would put an ad in it. They said they would. It only cost me four dollars. Yes, I put it in. I did not even suggest that my opponent, brother Halbrook, was a coward. It simply asked the question. First, it stated that he was challenged to debate on a certain date. A very brief ad, as you saw it on the chart. The second statement was really a question, *"Will he debate?"* It does not infer anything. We had no way of knowing whether he was a coward or not, whether he would debate or not. He could have said, "I will not, I prefer to get someone else." In fact, in the first one I wrote to him in which I challenged him, I said if you will not, perhaps you can put me in touch with someone who will. And let me add this: I had already decided if they would sell me the ad, the space in the paper, if I did not hear, *every month I would enlarge the ad until it went to a full page.*

I will have you know this, regardless of how busy brother Halbrook is, all preachers doing their work are busy — myself included — regardless of how busy he had been, the day after that ad appeared in the paper, the phones began to ring off of the walls in North Las Vegas.

As for a delay in the debate, there was no delay. My opponent wrote the agreement, the statement to be read by moderators, and I signed it. It was he who chose the dates. He chose the dates for North Las Vegas. He chose the dates for the debate here. And we are here tonight because brother Ron Halbrook chose these dates. I did not. I wanted it earlier. He said, "This is the earliest I can get to it." Fine. These are the dates. The debate was not delayed. It took place in North Las Vegas on the date that he selected. It is taking place here on the dates that he has selected also.

My reference to his first speech. Let us see his charts numbers 6, 7, and 8. I am going to refer to his like he did mine — just flip them on the screen and off. *These have to do with authority.* These are brother Halbrook's charts numbers 6, 7, and 8 — I would appreciate it if you have them ready. These charts have to do with authority and I agree with these charts. There is no disagreement and that is why I did not refer to some of these charts in North Las Vegas. There was agreement in many of these charts — 6, 7, and 8 one after another.

In regard to what he has to say about authority, I agree. Let us turn to his chart number 13 [next page] now. When you get to that, this is entitled, "When God Is Specific."

Authority Of Christ

(Matthew 28:18)

Expressed In The Bible:

* All Truth (John 16:13)

* Speak Same Thing - Words of Holy Spirit - That Which Is Written (1 Cor. 1:10; 2:13; 4:6)

* No Other Message (Gal. 1:8-9)

* Abide In Doctrine Of Christ (2 John 9)

* Contend For The Faith (Jude 3)

6

Authority Of Christ: How Expressed

Two Kinds:

General - "Go" in Mark 16:15

Specific - "Day" in Acts 20:7

In Three Ways:

Direct Statement

Approved Example

Necessary Implication

7

What Is Commanded?

The Gospel	Law Of Moses
Acts 15:7-11 God gave the same gift to the Gentiles [**Imply** God accepts them - Jews must, too]	No Implication - Silent! (Vs. 24)
Vs. 12 God **Approved Example** of preaching to Gentiles	No Example - Silent! (Vs. 24)
Vv. 16-18 God Made **Direct Statement**	No Statement - Silent! (Vs. 24)

8

When God Is Specific

CLASS	SPECIFIC	EXCLUDE
Woods	Gopher Wood (Gen. 6:14)	All Other Woods
Tribes	Levi (Heb. 7:14)	All Other Tribes
Action - Water	Immerse (Acts 2:38; 8:38)	All Other Actions
Music	Sing (Eph. 5:19)	All Other Music
Divorced People	Innocent Put Away Guilty & Remarry (Matt. 19:9)	All Other Divorced Persons

13

I want you to notice the last point down here. *Matthew 19 does not deal with a divorce for fornication.* I am going to make that clear to all, and I am going to deal with a series of charts in which everything he has presented on Matthew 19 will be answered. And what I have to show from Matthew 19 will show that his whole plan, and every chart that he used, is false and his whole position will not stand.

Let us look at his chart number 37. On this chart I want to note point six. Chart 37 has to do with unity. That chart, point number six, the put-away fornicator, the innocent puts away a fornicator and remarries. *There is nothing about this in Matthew 19:9.* You will see it when I get to these charts. Now, I am going to answer most of these in the charts that I have already.

Unity In Truth
(John 17:17-21)

Divine Truth Unites All Agree:	Human Theory Divides Men Differ:
1. Immerse (Acts 8:38)	1. Sprinkle Baby (Acts16:15?)
2. Lord's Supper 1st Day (Acts 20:7)	2. Any Day (1 Cor. 11:26?)
3. Sing (Eph. 5:19)	3. Play (Rev. 5:8?)
4. Preach (1 Tim. 3:15)	4. Meal, Party, Gym (Jude 12?)
5. Hope - Heaven (1 Pet. 1:4)	5. 1,000 Years On Earth (Rev. 20:4?)
6. Innocent Put Away Fornicator & Remarry (Matt. 19:9)	6. Others Remarry (1 Cor. 7?)

37

Let's see his chart number 23. You will note this is absolutely human opinion. No Scripture was used and none was referred to. On chart number 23, no Scripture is used, it says "restoration plea." He quotes a single person, one man, Ed Harrell. But then, he took something that was written but he does not give any Scripture, this

Restoration Plea
1. "Ask for the old paths"
2. "What saith the scripture?"
3. Christ only as the head of the church
4. Bible only as guide
5. N. T. Pattern of faith & practice

Result On Marriage
1. "No release" given to a husband or wife "unless the other party has been guilty of fornication."
2. Claim of "desertion" as "a just cause for divorce and remarriage" rejected.
3. Church discipline practiced [See Ed Harrell, *Quest For A Christian America*, pp. 197-198].

23

is some man's opinion. Evidently, it is brother Halbrook's opinion along with other men. No book, chapter, and verse. I am not obligated or entitled to give an opinion.

Next his chart number 15. *He says that which is not authorized is sinful, that is right.* And he says that no clear passage authorized the put-away fornicator or deserted believer to marry another. I gave him in North Las Vegas the passage — he would not accept it, he would not even refer to it. *I read from 1 Corinthians 6:9-11 where some of those added to the church by the Lord there* (before they believed and were saved, before they believed and were baptized and were saved according to Acts 18:8) *had been fornicators, adulterers.* They were not to enter the church in such a manner, as sinners. They were washed, sanctified, justified, 1 Corinthians 6:11. Prior to that they had been — "such were some of you" — fornicators, adulterers. Now they were told what to do — 1 Corinthians 7:2 and 1 Corinthians 7:27-28. "To avoid fornication, let every man have his own wife, let every woman have her own husband." And he spoke about those who had been fornicators and those who had been adulterers. He did not refer to that, 1 Corinthians 6, at all.

> **Not Authorized = Sinful**
>
> 1. Things "not authorized within the doctrine of Christ are not only non-essential but sinful as well."
> 2. An author defended sponsoring church but had "no passage of Scripture to show that such a plan is authorized by the Lord" (Jack Freeman, <u>Gospel Guardian</u>, 28 April 1960, pp. 8-9).
> 3. No clear passage authorizes put-away fornicator or deserted believer to marry another.
> 4. Conclusion: such marriages are sinful!
>
> 15

Let's turn to his next chart, chart number 16, which went hand in hand with this, on "God's Perfect Plan." No one is trying to change God's perfect plan, I agree that God's plan is perfect. But, you will see if you will listen honestly (and I will bet it is difficult if you have already made up your mind to hold one position), if you will listen, listen honestly, you will see that I am not trying to change God's perfect plan at all.

> **God's Perfect Plan**
>
> 1. We must not change God's perfect "plan of salvation... plan of worship ... plan for the life of the individual ... plan of the work for the church."
> 2. "When the individual engages in dishonest activity; when his thoughts, words, or actions are evil; he has departed from the perfect plan for daily living" (Jack Freeman, <u>Gospel Guardian</u>, 24 Oct. 1957, pp. 8-9).
> 3. God's perfect plan for daily living includes marriage, divorce, & remarriage.
>
> 16

Next chart please, his number 41. I want to call your attention here to point number four where he refers to Proverbs 13:15. Proverbs 13:15 says nothing about privilege at all — it does not say anything about it. It does not say anything about it. That is his opinion about it. If it says something about it, let him get up and read where Proverbs 13:15 deals with privileges. It does not deal with privileges; that is what he has to say about it.

His chart number 43. In chart number 43, *we agree here with the beginning of this chart, "from the beginning until now," Matthew 19:8.* We agree that bigamy was wrong, is today. We agree with some of these other things. But we cannot agree with all of his *conclusions* that he has reached. I do not disagree with any Scripture.

Let's see his chart number 44 [next page], exactly what it is. Here he says what Deuteronomy 24:1-4 accomplished. And I want you to see again his opinion has been inserted. God made a temporary concession to stubbornness. *Where does the Bible say so?* That is his opinion. God made a concession, and he said in earlier speeches in order to protect the women He made a temporary concession. Well, that is his opinion. But here is something that he has not thought of — perhaps you have. In Deuteronomy 24:1-4 it is clearly stated that the woman can be put away for *any cause*, not just for the causes he listed. Incidentally, there is a later verse where if the second man

---

Genesis 2:24 Law
Explained By Jesus In Matthew 19:3-9

1. **Requires** One Man For One Woman - "A Man," "His Wife"
2. **Excludes** All Immorality - "A Man," "His Wife," "One Flesh" — No Fornication, Adultery, Polygamy, Concubines, Homosexuals, Bestiality
3. **Implies** Immorality Desecrates The Union - Ground For The Innocent To Put Away The Guilty - "A Man," "His Wife," "Cleave," "One Flesh"
4. **Excludes** The Put Away Fornicator From Marrying Another
   * Obedience Is Blessed (Deut. 10:13)
   * Sin Brings Hardship, Not Privileges (Prov. 13:15)
5. **Implies** Bond Only In This Life - "One Flesh" — Life And Relations In The Fleshly Body

41

| God's Ideal Gen. 2:24 | Promise Salvation → 12:1-3 | Law Of Moses Gal. 3:19 | Ex. 20:14, 17 Lev. 20:10 → Deut. 22:22 | Gospel Of Christ |

From The Beginning Until Now - Matt. 19:8b

| 6:2 11:1-9 | 4:19 Bigamy
12:10-20 Wife Offered
16:1-3 Maid
25:1-6 Concubines
26:1-11 Wife Offered
30:4, 9 Maid | **Jews Regulated**
Deut. 24:1-4
Mal. 2:14-16 |

Gentiles Cast God Off
Rom. 1:18-32; Eph. 2:12; Acts 17:30

43

What Deut. 24:1-4 Accomplished

Restrain, Not Initiate, Their Practices:
▶ Men sent wives away at will
▶ Women had no recourse or protection
▶ Treated as property - pawns of man's unbridled passion

Temporary Concession To Stubbornness In Order To:
▶ Curb their reckless practices
▶ Regulate their stubbornness
▶ Soften abuses suffered by women

Vs. 1 Decrease Reasons - Shameful, Indecent
Vv. 1-2 Guarantee Freedom To Remarry
Vv. 3-4 Prohibit 1st Man Ever Having Her Back After
     She Remarried

44

| God's Ideal Gen. 2:24 | Promise Salvation 12:1-3 | ➡ | Law Of Moses Gal. 3:19 | ➡ | Gospel Of Christ Reinforce God's Original Ideal |

From The Beginning Until Now - Matt. 19:8b

Matt. 5:31-32 - End Mosaic Concession

Matt. 19:3-12 - God Joins, Man Not To Break

Rom. 7:1-4 - Marriage As An Illustration

1 Cor. 7 - Questions & Crisis At Hand

Eph. 5:22-33 - Conduct Of Husband & Wife

48

marries her, he could put her away for hatred, and it does not say why he should hate her. You could hate a man or a woman for any reason. It may not be a reason, a just reason. But the second could put her away for hatred. Of course, the first could not then take her back. But for various reasons that woman could be put away, but she could remarry. Now, my opponent, brother Halbrook, agrees with me that the man who put her away could remarry. But let him read there in Deuteronomy 24:1-4, where does that say the man who put her away could remarry? He says he can. That passage does not say so.

Go now to the next chart. That is his number 48. We are dealing with this first. This he calls "God's Ideal." Again, *"from the beginning until now."* The end of the Mosaic concession, again he calls it a Mosaic concession. We need to understand there that the concession was made — it was not made by Moses — it was made by God. God joined; man is not to break. *At the same time where Jesus said thou shalt not put asunder, he gave man the permission to put asunder. So putting asunder is not within itself a sin.* Man is not to break. Jesus turned right around and gave him permission to break, to put it asunder. My opponent says he can put it asunder, scripturally with God's permission, if his mate is guilty of fornication.

Marriage is an illustration. It is true in Romans 7:1-4. 1 Corinthians 7 does deal with a crisis at hand, but it also deals with various cases of marriage and we will deal with that in other charts. Ephesians 5:22-33, the conduct of husband and wife. I agree that it deals with that and so do other passages.

Let's see his chart number 54. This chart, "How Do We Know?" And so, again, the last question, *"Where does the Bible authorize these to marry: the put-away fornicator, and those not scripturally divorced?"* Well, the put-away fornicator is authorized to remarry in 1 Corinthians 7:2 and 1 Corinthians 7:27-28. "Art thou loosed from a wife?" Now, in direct answer to a direct question. Incidentally, he did not answer my questions tonight in the first speech, and so I will answer his in the

How We Know

Simplicity Of Truth: "Yes, Jesus loves me, the Bible tells me so" (Rom. 4:3; Eph. 3:4)

Know We Can Remarry:
1. If mate dies (Rom. 7:2-3)
2. If put away mate for fornication (Matt. 19:9)

Where Does The Bible Authorize These To Remarry:
1. The put-away fornicator?
2. Those unscripturally divorced?

54

second speech. And he can answer mine in the second speech. That will be fair, I believe, won't it? Alright, we are dealing anyway with the put-away fornicator, then I am going to show in a moment that *Matthew 19:9 does not deal at all with the put-away fornicator*. But in 1 Corinthians 6 he is dealt with; in 1 Corinthians 7 he is dealt with. There is a passage which authorizes it, the put-away fornicator to marry. Incidentally, if he married, he is going to marry *another*. You cannot have marriage without *another* being involved.

His chart on Matthew 5:32, number 60 [see page 9]. This is just the scripture out there and we agree with it.

Let's turn to his chart number 62 on "Rule And Exception." I want you to notice something here. Matthew 5:32, "Whosoever shall put away his wife, saving for the cause of fornication, causeth her to commit adultery: and whosoever shall marry her that is divorced committeth adultery." "Whosoever shall put away his wife *for fornication* is not responsible for her subsequent adultery: and whosoever shall marry her that is divorced committeth adultery." This, perhaps as I would say, "Well, Jesus, debate yourself." This is the teaching of Matthew 19:9 even though it is not stated exactly like it. Here, rather than saying "except" for the cause of fornication, it says "saving" for the cause of fornication. I am going to deal with that as already stated in a series of charts. Most of what he said I am already prepared to deal with in a series of charts dealing with Matthew 19:9.

Rule & Exception
Matt. 5:32

1. "Whosoever shall put away his wife, saving for the cause of fornication, causeth her to commit adultery: and whosoever shall marry her that is divorced committeth adultery."

2. Whosoever shall put away his wife **for fornication** is not responsible for her subsequent adultery: and whosoever shall marry her that is divorced committeth adultery.

62

His chart number 63 says the exception clause did not exempt the fornicator. Again, *I am going to show that Matthew 19:9 does not deal with the fornicator at all*. And so, the exception clause in that verse is not dealing with the fornicator. That is not the subject that matters.

Next, his chart 67, he has a chart in regard to Moses and Christ. Once again, back there this cause was changed. There were several causes for divorce, Deuteronomy 24; one cause according to Matthew chapter 19. Incidentally,

> **The Exception Does Not Exempt The Fornicator**
>
> Matt. 5:32 & 19:9 are compound, complex sentences. Each one contains two independent clauses, joined by the conjunction "and."
>
> The exception stated in the first independent clause has no force in the second independent clause.
>
> THEREFORE, the force of the exception in the first independent clause does NOT yield the meaning in the second, "Whosoever shall marry her that is divorced FOR FORNICATION doth not commit adultery."
>
> 63

when Jesus taught *one cause for divorce and one cause for remarriage in Matthew 19*, there was not a contradiction in what Paul taught in Romans 7:2-3 when he taught there was *a second cause for remarriage* and that is the death of your partner. Jesus never mentioned that case at all. But it is true, and it is not a contradiction of Matthew 19:9.

Let's look at the next chart, his number 72 and 73 [next page] together. This is just a quotation from Matthew 19:9. Chart number 73 follows it, on "Rule and Exception." And again, he is simply showing how *he* would use the exception in another case. This is how *he* would choose to use it. It is not necessarily how *others* would choose to use it.

Now let's come to his chart number 74. And I want you to notice something here, *"If and Only If."* You notice that little — two little marks

MOSES	CHRIST
1. Fornication - Put Away By Death (Marry No Other)	1. Fornication - Put Away By Divorce (Marry No Other)
2. Divorce - Cause Short Of Fornication	2. No Divorce For Any Cause Short of Fornication
3. Mate Divorced - No Fornication - Marry Another w/o Adultery	3. Same Situation - BUT Marry Another = Adultery
4. Man Who Marries Her Not In Adultery	4. Man Who Marries Her In Adultery
5. First Man Can't Have Her	5. First Man Can Have Her

67

[for the *equals* sign] between "Except" and "If and Only If"? Now brethren, if you do not learn anything else in this debate, you learn this. If *"except"* means *"if and only if,"* I could use "if and only if" in place of the word except. That is true, isn't it? Okay, let's read: *Except ye be converted*, notice this, *if and only if ye become, be converted, as little children, you cannot enter the kingdom of heaven.* Notice, if you are converted you cannot enter that kingdom, Jesus said. That completely reverses the meaning. Now if this, *if and only if,* is a legitimate

Matthew 19:9

"And I say unto you, Whosoever shall put away his wife, except it be for fornication, and shall marry another, committeth adultery: and whoso marrieth her which is put away doth commit adultery."

72

Rule & Exception
Matt. 19:9

1. "Whosoever shall put away his wife, except it be for fornication, and shall marry another, committeth adultery: and whoso marrieth her which is put away doth commit adultery."

2. Whosoever shall put away his wife **for fornication** and shall marry another, doth not commit adultery: and whoso marrieth her which is put away doth commit adultery.

73

First Evening: Freeman's First Negative

> ### Except = If & Only If!
>
> * Matt. 18:3 Become as little child → Enter kingdom
>
> * John 3:2 God with Him → Do miracles
>
> * John 3:5 Born of water & Spirit → Enter kingdom
>
> * Matt. 19:9 Put away wife for fornication & marry another → Not adultery
>
> 74

synonym for this, *except*, you can use it every place the word "except" is found — including here, including here, including here, and including here [pointing to passages listed on chart]. And then we would read this: a man that puts his wife away, *if and only if, for fornication* and marries another commits fornication. My opponent does not believe that. No, he does not believe that. He believes if you put her away for fornication, you can marry and not commit adultery. But if we use his reasoning here (and this is his idea, it is not mine — this is his chart), he says *"except"* means, is equal to, *"if and only if."*

And so, what Jesus is saying there (just forget about the word except and use this [if and only if] in place of the word except), if a man put away his wife, *if and only if for fornication,* now that makes it a divorce for fornication, doesn't it? Now we are getting into divorce for fornication. Well, what happens if I get a divorce for fornication? If I marry another, Jesus said I commit adultery. You can have that if you want to. You see what trouble we get into when we pick up our word and try to insert it into what this means? *If and only if* — I hope you come back to that one throughout this debate — *if and only if.* If you do become as a little child, you cannot enter into the kingdom of heaven. If you are born again, or, if God would be with him. What now? If and only if God be with him he could not do these miracles. That is what it comes out to. If God is with him, if and only if God is with him, then he cannot do these miracles. If and only if a man is born of the water and the Spirit he cannot enter the kingdom. Well, how is he going to get in? Not by being born of the water and the Spirit if "if and only if" is true.

Now, let's show some of my charts dealing with Matthew 19. We will get back to some of his charts as time permits. We want to begin with chart number 424. Some of this material has already been covered. On the exception clause of Matthew 19, Halbrook says, and he made the statement tonight, you cannot apply this exception to the second independent clause. Why? He used it to modify the first independent clause. And the two independent clauses are separated by the conjunction "and."

Let's see my next chart here, which is number 747. In turning to this [in Las Vegas] I showed from Revelation 2:22-23 three independent clauses separated by the conjunction "and." And then Halbrook replied — let's see that same chart we just turned from [chart 424]. First he said it does not apply in Matthew 19:9 because you have two independent clauses joined together by the conjunction "and," and then he said he can apply it if the independent clauses all deal with the same case as in Revelation 2:22-23. Now, why don't you ask yourself a question. I want you to ask the question, *"When was brother Halbrook telling the truth?"* When he said the exception clause cannot modify the second independent clause in Matthew 19:9 because the two different clauses are separated by the conjunction "and"? And he just said it tonight in his first speech. Or, was he telling the truth here when he said the exception clause can modify more than one independent clause when the independent clauses have to do with the same case? We are going to show that in Matthew 19:9 both independent clauses have to do with the very same case. But when was he telling the truth? Here he says it can apply, he did not say anything about different cases here. He simply says he cannot apply it because

---

THE EXCEPTION CLAUSE OF MATT. 19:9

HALBROOK SAYS: "CANNOT APPLY THE SECOND INDEPENDENT CLAUSE"
WHY? IT IS USED TO MODIFY THE FIRST INDEPENDENT CLAUSE AND THE TWO INDEPENDENT CLAUSES ARE SEPARATED BY THE CONJUNCTION "AND".

NOW HALBROOK ADMITS THAT THE EXCEPTION CLAUSE OF REV. 2:22-23 MODIFIES THREE INDEPENDENT CLAUSES SEPARATED BY THE CONJUNCTION "AND".
WHY? THE THREE INDEPENDENT CLAUSES OF REV. 2:22-23 HAVE TO DO WITH THE SAME CASE.

424

EXCEPTION CLAUSES:

DO EXCEPTION CLAUSES MODIFY SENTENCES WITH INDEPENDENT CLAUSES?

*HALBROOK'S ASSERTION: NO! THE EXCEPTION CLAUSE CANNOT MODIFY THE ENTIRE SENTENCE IN MATT. 19:9, BECAUSE THE SENTENCE HAS TWO INDEPENDENT CLAUSES.

*THE BIBLE: REV 2:22-23 ← APPEARS ONLY ONCE
"...EXCEPT THEY REPENT..."

INDEPENDENT CLAUSE #1 - "BEHOLD I WILL CAST HER INTO BED"
--- AND ---
INDEPENDENT CLAUSE #2 - "THEM THAT COMMIT ADULTERY WITH HER INTO GREAT TRIBULATION"
--- AND ---
INDEPENDENT CLAUSE #3 - "I WILL KILL HER CHILDREN"

747

you have two independent clauses joined together by the conjunction "and."

When I showed the other charts up in North Las Vegas he backed off of that and he gave this explanation. The exception clause can apply. It would not make any difference how many different clauses are separated by the conjunction "and" as long as they all deal with the very same case.

Let's deal now with chart number 428. *How do we know? How do we know what is discussed in Matthew 19:9?* If and only if. Let's go to the first independent clause. Divorce *except* it be for fornication. Is he dealing with a divorce for fornication? Not according to my opponent. *If and only if* — if the divorce is, if indeed, *for fornication,* what would be the spiritual state of the man who marries when he has put away his wife? It would be adultery. You have got a scriptural divorce. He is the innocent one. He put away the guilty wife who committed fornication but he got the divorce for fornication. According to my opponent's interpretation of this — *if and only if,* in place of *except* — if and only if it be for fornication, then what is his spiritual state when he remarries? Why, he commits adultery. The wife was not put away for fornication, however, this is what he is dealing with there. And brother Halbrook agrees with that. Now, what this really means and says — if we think about it — *if the divorce is for any reason other than fornication, the man who puts her away commits adultery.* You could see how that could legitimately be used, but you cannot use "if and only if." It completely turns the thing around, makes it mean the very opposite.

Let's see my next chart please, chart 49. Part of the discussion in Matthew 19:9, the second independent clause. What is the spiritual state of one who marries a wife who is put away, except it be for fornication, if and only if for fornication? Adultery? Why? In those cases, if it is for any reason other than fornication, they are still married to one another. The put-away wife is still the wife, in God's sight, of the man who put her away. But if he puts her away for fornication, she is not his wife; he is not her husband. Both are *single.* My

---

WHAT IS DISCUSSED IN MATT. 19:9?

FIRST INDEPENDENT CLAUSE:

DIVORCE "EXCEPT IT BE FOR FORNICATION" -- NOT DIVORCE FOR FORNICATION.

THE SPIRITUAL STATE OF THE MAN WHO REMARRIES WHEN HE HAS PUT AWAY HIS WIFE

"EXCEPT IT BE FOR FORNICATION" -ADULTERY- WHY?
STILL MARRIED (IN GOD'S SIGHT)

428

opponent admitted that. They are not tied to one another. Oh, he says, *bound by law*. But I will show you by one of his own witnesses, that is not the meaning at all. Both independant clauses deal with the very same case. Putting away except it be for fornication, for any reason other than fornication, thus *"except for fornication" modifies both independent clauses*. By my opponent's own argument, they deal with the very same case, the very same case.

> **WHAT IS ADULTERY?**
> THAYER: page 417
>
> "TO HAVE UNLAWFUL INTERCOURSE WITH ANOTHER'S WIFE, TO COMMIT ADULTERY" MATT. 5:32, MATT. 19:9
>
> MAN DIVORCES FOR CAUSE OF FORNICATION HAS NO WIFE. IF HE MARRIES A WOMAN WHO HAS NO HUSBAND, HE CANNOT COMMIT ADULTERY WITH HER. (HIS OWN WIFE) ANY MAN WHO HAS NO WIFE MAY SCRIPTURALLY HAVE A WIFE.
>
> 49

My next chart please, number 430. Halbrook uses *the exception clause*. Now he does not mind taking it out of Matthew 19, responding to it tonight, and putting it over in Mark 10 and other places. He takes it out of Matthew 19:9, puts it in Mark 10:11-12 where nothing is said about any reason, scriptural reason, for divorce and remarriage. Nothing is said about any scriptural reason for divorce and remarriage in Luke 16:18. Just think about this, brethren. Does Matthew 19:9 have Jesus contradicting what he taught here and here — no reason for divorce and remarriage here, no reason for divorce and remarriage here, no reason for divorce and remarriage here (at least not referred to in those passages) — but did Jesus contradict those when he gave the statement of his teaching of Matthew 19:9? Of course not. This is a part of the law, this is a part of the law, this is a part of the law, this is a part of the law [indicating the various passages on the

> **HALBROOK'S USE OF - EXCEPTION CLAUSE IN MATT. 19:9**
>
> HE TAKES IT OUT OF MATT. 19:9 & PUTS IT IN MK. 10:11-12
> HE TAKES IT OUT OF MATT. 19:9 & PUTS IT IN LUKE 16:18
> HE TAKES IT OUT OF MATT. 19:9 & PUTS IT IN ROM. 7:2-3
> HE TAKES IT OUT OF MATT. 19:9 & PUTS IT IN 1 COR. 7:2
> HE TAKES IT OUT OF MATT. 19:9 & PUTS IT IN 1 COR. 7:10-11
> HE TAKES IT OUT OF MATT. 19:9 & PUTS IT IN 1 COR. 7:12-16
>
> HE TAKES THE EXCEPTION CLAUSE OUT OF THE VERSE, OUT OF THE BOOK AND APPLIES IT TO DIFFERENT CASES IN DIFFERENT BOOKS -- BUT SAYS IT CANNOT APPLY TO THE SECOND CLAUSE IN MATT. 19:9!
>
> 430

chart]. You put all these passages together and you have the entire law. Of course, God does not contradict himself. But he takes his exception clause, he calls it, out of Matthew 19 and puts it in Mark 10; out of Matthew 19 and puts it in Luke 16; out of Matthew 19 and puts it in Romans 7; out of Matthew 19 and puts it in 1 Corinthians 7:2; out of Matthew 19 and puts it in 1 Corinthians 7:10-11; out of Matthew 19 and puts it in 1 Corinthians 7:12-16. But he says you cannot let it apply to a second phrase in the same verse. You can take it out of the book, out of the verse, throw it all over the Bible, but, brother Freeman, don't you dare let it apply to a same case in the same verse, the second clause of the very same verse.

Let's deal with my chart number 1. *How do we know?* What is false doctrine and what is the truth? How do we know? God anticipated false doctrine. And Paul says that "the Spirit speaketh expressly, that in the latter times some shall depart from the faith," (1 Tim. 4 beginning with verse 1). They will "give heed to seducing spirits, and doctrines of devils," and, he says, those who give heed to seducing spirits and doctrines of devils will forbid to marry. Think about this: you have the faith in contrast with the doctrines of devils. The faith does not forbid marriage from this passage; doctrines of devils does, does forbid marriage. Who demands celibacy? Who is forbidding to marry? A simple question, do you want the doctrine of devils or the faith? The faith, the gospel does not forbid marriage. Incidentally, you will hear a lot of things about me, but I am here for one reason: I believe that every unmarried person, every person *single* in the sight of God has a right to a spouse, *has a right to marry,* that is all I believe. I am not affirming adultery, I do not believe it; I am against it. I am not in favor of homosexuality or anything like that regardless of what my opponent is saying. I am affirming that unmarried people have God's permission to marry. If you have no wife, you have a right to a wife.

Let's leave that and go on to chart number 2. You know, Jesus taught while

---

HOW DO WE KNOW?
GOD ANTICIPATED FALSE DOCTRINE

1 TIM. 4:1-3
*"...*__SOME SHALL DEPART FROM THE FAITH__
GIVING HEED TO SEDUCING SPIRITS
AND __DOCTRINES OF DEVILS, FORBIDDING TO__
__MARRY__*..."*

WHO IS DEMANDING CELIBACY?
WHO IS FORBIDDING TO MARRY?

__DO YOU WANT THE DOCTRINES OF DEVILS__
OR
__THE FAITH ???__

1

on earth as we already mentioned these passages. Here he taught no cause for divorce, no cause for remarriage, these go together. And Paul said that is what Jesus taught there in 1 Corinthians 7:10-11. So, no scriptural way to put asunder.

But here in Matthew 19 he gave one cause for divorce, one cause for remarriage. And how do we know that? Not because it says divorce for cause of fornication. This you know by inference. This is how he says — he admits that is one way of knowing — that is he knows it. One cause for remarriage, Matthew 5:32, one other passage teaches the same. One scriptural way to put asunder husband and wife.

**JESUS TAUGHT
(WHILE ON EARTH)**

<u>NO SCRIPTURAL WAY TO PUT ASUNDER HUSBAND AND WIFE</u>

<u>NO CAUSE</u> FOR DIVORCE ——— MK. 10:11-12, LK. 16:18
<u>NO CAUSE</u> FOR REMARRIAGE —— 1 COR. 7:10-11

<u>ONE SCRIPTURAL WAY TO PUT ASUNDER HUSBAND AND WIFE</u>

<u>ONE CAUSE</u> FOR DIVORCE ——— MATT. 19:9
<u>ONE CAUSE</u> FOR REMARRIAGE —— MATT. 5:32

2

Let's take a look at my next chart, number 3. Now, there are other New Testament teachings on the same subject and they do not contradict the other passages. In fact, Jesus said, "I have other things to say, you are not ready to bear them, the Holy Spirit will guide you into all truth." Here is a second cause for remarriage: *death* (Rom. 7:2-3). 1 Corinthians 7:39 does not contradict any other passage. A scriptural way to put asunder. If I die, I have not sinned. I have a scriptural right to die. There is cause for remarriage given in 1 Corinthians 7; we will not have time to get that in this speech; I will get to it tonight. The believer divorced from the unbeliever is not under bondage. Paul said this is what I say, the Lord did not deal

---

**OTHER NEW TESTAMENT TEACHING
ON THE SAME SUBJECT.**

(JNO. 14:26, JNO. 16:12-13)

<u>SECOND CAUSE FOR REMARRIAGE (DEATH)</u>
ROM. 7:2-3, 1 COR. 7:39
A SCRIPTURAL WAY TO PUT ASUNDER
HUSBAND AND WIFE.

IS IT SCRIPTURAL TO DIE?

<u>THIRD CAUSE FOR REMARRIAGE</u> 1 COR. 7:12-15
BELIEVER DIVORCED BY UNBELIEVER.
TO THE REST SPEAK I, NOT THE LORD.

3

First Evening: Freeman's First Negative 35

with this. My opponent, in North Las Vegas, said, "The Lord did not deal *directly* with the case stated in 1 Corinthians 7:12-15." He said it. The Lord did not deal directly with it.

Well, let's look at my next chart, as much as we can get in tonight. Chart number 4. Again, let's consider what is said here. It has to do with passages again which deal with God's law pertaining to marriage and divorce. All of these: Matthew 5, Matthew 19, Mark 10, Luke 16, Romans 7, 1 Corinthians 7. Here we have, "What part of the law applies to a Christian married to an alien? 1 Corinthians 7:12-15." That is the case my opponent has admitted Jesus did not *directly* deal with. But Paul dealt with it and was guided by the Holy Spirit to deal with it. Jesus did not say anything about this case. But my opponent will look over to this as a different case, he says, than that in Matthew 19. But he will slide Matthew 19 and the exception clause over here. This is the same case. Jesus did not deal with that at all. "To the rest speak I, not the Lord, if any brother hath a wife that believeth not...the woman which hath an husband that believeth not." Jesus did not talk about such cases as that. Thank you very much.

HOW DO WE KNOW?
BOND BETWEEN HUSBANDS & WIVES

* **WHAT BOND IS DISCUSSED IN ROM. 7:2-3?**
  "**WOMAN** BOUND BY THE LAW TO HER **HUSBAND**"

* **WHAT BOND IS DISCUSSED IN 1 COR. 7:39?**
  "**WIFE** IS BOUND BY LAW AS LONG AS HER **HUSBAND** LIVETH"

* **WHAT BOND IS DISCUSSED IN 1 COR. 7:27?**
  "**BOUND UNTO A WIFE**" "**LOOSED FROM A WIFE**"

* **WHAT BOND IS DISCUSSED IN 1 COR. 7:12-15?**
  "IF ANY **BROTHER** HATH A **WIFE**"
  "THE **WOMAN** WHICH HATH A **HUSBAND**"

4

First Evening
Halbrook's Second Affirmative

Brother Freeman, brethren moderators, ladies and gentlemen, I am glad to stand before you as we continue in our affirmation tonight. We have affirmed the principle of this passage and the proposition is simply taken from the passage. "The Scriptures teach that two people joined by God in marriage are bound for life, the only exception being that an innocent partner may put away a mate guilty of fornication and remarry." *I am affirming the principle and the proposition of this passage* and he is *denying* the principle and proposition of this passage.

Let me observe that he had some comments about the *Vegas Drive church,* of which he is *not* a member. *We have a member here* (Keith Greer, preacher for the Vegas Dr. church, had been sent to the debate by that church). The men decided how that letter would be put together and how it would be signed and composed. And so you (brother Freeman) are not a member there; you do not know the firsthand facts about that.

Now, as to *the newspaper ad.* He, apparently somewhat embarrassed, said that he did not necessarily put that in there to imply that I would not debate. So, I guess you put it in there to imply I *would* debate. Is that it?

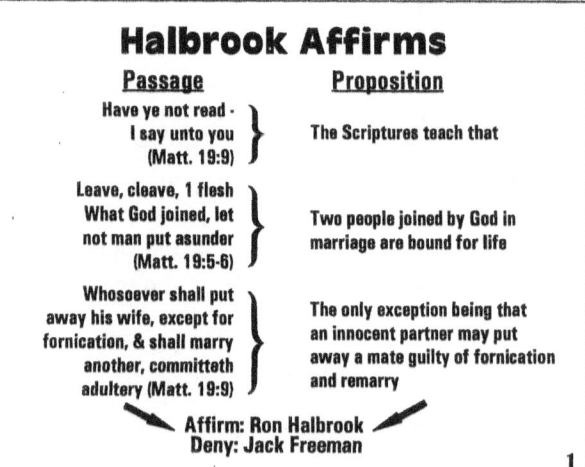

And then you said you were going to *enlarge* it. And each time you enlarged it, was that to imply that I *would* debate or that I *would not?* Now, each enlargement would be designed to reflect what the first one was designed to reflect. You were trying to imply and suggest that we are unwilling to meet this test and to debate you. And I am about as afraid of debating you, brother Freeman, as a woman that has never been married might be afraid of getting a date and being kissed! I am *glad* to take my turn!

As to there being a delay in the debate, he would not sign the first proposition

First Evening: Halbrook's Second Affirmative

> **BRAZORIA COUNTY (TX) NEWS**
> **23 MAR. 1989 p.20**
>
> FREEMAN AD IN OUR COUNTY WIDE NEWSPAPER SUGGESTS HALBROOK WON'T DEBATE
>
> **PERSONAL NOTICE**
> On 2-27-89 Ron Halbrook received a challenge to debate the divorce and remarriage question. Will he accept the challenge 1-702-642-3687.
>
> 3

month after month after month. That is the simple truth about it.

Now furthermore, I want you to notice that *he did not answer the questions which I read into the record*. And he understands that, because we discussed it at Las Vegas. I told him the first night there that *I would read my questions into the record* and that would call upon him to answer, then *he would read his into the record*, and then I would answer. But I am not going to take up my speech reading *your* questions, brother Freeman. That is silly and ludicrous. All he is doing is dodging. Now, he dodged out there in Las Vegas. It took him five speeches to answer the question number five that we have got on this list.

But I want you to notice again just *why* he would like to dodge and duck these questions. *"Is it necessary to have positive authority for all that we preach and practice?"* He knows the answer is *yes*. But if he tells you yes, then he is in the embarrassed position that he does *not have positive divine authority for the guilty put-away fornicator to marry another*. And his speech is the best evidence for it you could ever have. Do you see why he does not want to answer it? He will not answer it; he will not call for these. He will go on ducking and dodging. I read it into the record. I have met my part of the obligation, and now he will not meet his. You will just have to decide as an audience what kind of debating that is, and *why* a man would conduct himself that way.

And, *"Does Matthew 19:9 teach that after God joins people together in marriage, an innocent partner can put away a mate guilty of fornication and marry another?"* You [brother Freeman] know good and well *it does*. *I* know good and well it does. *This audience* knows good and well it does. And that is *the ground of unity*. That is how simple God's plan and God's pattern is. No wonder you do not want to answer the questions.

"Is there any marriage between one male and one female which people can enter under civil law but which they must end in order to be right with God?" Unscriptural marriages must be brought to *an end*, like in Mark 6:17-18. And he

does not want to have to get tangled up in that again like he did in the first debate. And so he will just "observe the passover" on this. And he does not want to talk about questions. No wonder. I would not either.

And then, he does not want to talk about question number four *["Which passages speak of marrying another? (A) Romans 7:2-3, (B) Matthew 19:9, (C) 1 Corinthians 7:15.]*, because in Las Vegas — I will just let the secret out of the bag — he answered this by saying that *all of these passages speak of marrying another* [pointing to Rom. 7:2-3, Matt. 19:9, and 1 Cor. 7:15 on the question chart]. Do you still believe that tonight? Do you want to nod your head or blink your eye? Do you still believe that tonight? Oh, he is like a statue or something there. My friend, which one of these passages says *marry another?* Just open your Bible if you want to know what this debate is about. When you read *Romans 7:2-3*, your mate dies, and it says you can *marry "another."* It says it in *Matthew 19:9, "marry another."* It does *not* say it in *this* passage [pointing to 1 Cor. 7:15]. But he said in Las Vegas that it is in *all* of those passages. Will you say it again? Will you tell this audience again? I predict he will not call for this and he will not answer this even when the week is out.

Now, *since you say 1 Corinthians 7:10-11 "does not give any reason for divorce,"* that such a divorce is wrong, *what must a Christian do if he divorces like that and gets involved in a remarriage.* And he does not want to answer that. He has already seen my follow-up charts — if he says "A" *["Divorce the second mate and return to the first mate, or remain unmarried."]*, I will follow him; if he says "B" *["Pray for forgiveness and remain in the second marriage."]*, I will follow him; if he says "C" *["I refuse to answer on the grounds that it may incriminate me."]*, I will follow him. He has been down this road, and he does not want to go back again. I will tell you why he does not want to go back again, because this passage does *not authorize the divorce* and it does *not authorize a remarriage,* and when a person does that *he has got to get out of that marriage to be right.* He does not want to have to face that. There is no authority for such a remarriage just like there is *no authority for the put-away fornicator to remarry.* That is the pickle he is in, and he does not want to talk about it.

Well, we will just simply request in an humble way that you come and fulfill your obligation on the questions. I am ready to answer yours if you will only read them into the record.

Well then, let's notice our charts 6, 7, and 8 on authority. And my friend, he said that he would agree that Christ had all authority and that we must speak the very words of the Holy Spirit. Brother Freeman, *we are looking for the words of the Holy Spirit that the put-away fornicator can marry again.* Do you really agree with this or not? And if you do, give us that passage, sir.

And then we notice again my chart 7. Two kinds of authority. Give us the *direct statement for the fornicator to marry another*. Or the *approved example*. Or the *necessary implication*. Will you? Won't you? I plead for you to do it. You say you accept the authority of Christ, that you agree with these charts, and so that is why he flips through them: snap, snap, snap. He does not want to have to stop and talk about the fact that he has *no authority for the put-away fornicator to marry another*. See?

> **Authority Of Christ**
> (Matthew 28:18)
>
> **Expressed In The Bible:**
>
> * All Truth (John 16:13)
> * Speak Same Thing - Words of Holy Spirit - That Which Is Written (1 Cor. 1:10; 2:13; 4:6)
> * No Other Message (Gal. 1:8-9)
> * Abide In Doctrine Of Christ (2 John 9)
> * Contend For The Faith (Jude 3)
>
> 6

And then again we notice on my chart 8. Where there is no implication and you have divine silence, then *we are not permitted to teach or practice or act*. But he is teaching that the put-away fornicator can marry another. And the Bible is silent about it. He is in the same condition as the Judaizing teachers — teaching something for which there is *no positive divine authority*.

Then, on my chart 13. He said he would answer later. That is a fine how-do-you-do. I never did get to *"later."* Did any of the rest of you? Now, that would be like debating a man on instrumental music, and you show him there is a class of things, *woods* — God specifies *gopher, excludes all others*. And you show him the parallel to the instrument: class of *music* — God specified *singing, excludes all others*. And he

> **Authority Of Christ: How Expressed**
>
> | Two Kinds: | In Three Ways: |
> |---|---|
> | General - "Go" in Mark 16:15 | Direct Statement |
> | Specific - "Day" in Acts 20:7 | Approved Example |
> | | Necessary Implication |
>
> 7

says, "*I will talk about it later.*" I guess he will. He does not want to have to face the fact that the gopher wood excludes all other woods.

And brother Freeman does not want to face the fact that *out of the class of all divorced people* [pointing to "Innocent Put Away Guilty and Remarry (Matt. 19:9)" on chart 13] —

What Is Commanded?

The Gospel	Law Of Moses
Acts 15:7-11 God gave the same gift to the Gentiles [**Imply** God accepts them - Jews must, too]	No Implication - Silent! (Vs. 24)
Vs. 12 God **Approved Example** of preaching to Gentiles	No Example - Silent! (Vs. 24)
Vv. 16-18 God Made **Direct Statement**	No Statement - Silent! (Vs. 24)

8

the Bible said it so plainly a little child can understand it. There are little children here ten and twelve — I have a daughter that age, and she can understand this.

When God Is Specific

CLASS	SPECIFIC	EXCLUDE
Woods	Gopher Wood *(Gen. 6:14)*	All Other Woods
Tribes	Levi *(Heb. 7:14)*	All Other Tribes
Action - Water	Immerse *(Acts 2:38; 8:38)*	All Other Actions
Music	Sing *(Eph. 5:19)*	All Other Music
Divorced People	Innocent Put Away Guilty & Remarry *(Matt. 19:9)*	All Other Divorced Persons

13

We have read the verses and studied them, and she asked in puzzlement why people cannot understand that. A child can understand it: *The innocent can put away the guilty and marry another.* No, he does not want to talk about it except *later*. My friend, that *excludes all other divorced persons from marrying another!*

And then, we notice [on chart 37] the "Unity in the Truth." *Divine truth unites.* He believes the innocent can put away the fornicator and marry again. I believe that. And, my friend, *there is the ground for us to shake hands in unity* — if we will stand with that, and stay with that. The same way that we do with immersion, the Lord's Supper every first day, singing, and preaching, and the hope of heaven. Let us then join our hands: *The innocent can put away the fornicator and marry another.* God's word *unites* people religiously. We are in a divided religious world because of *human theories,* and *that* is the problem

First Evening: Halbrook's Second Affirmative   41

> **Unity In Truth**
> (John 17:17-21)
>
> | Divine Truth Unites All Agree: | Human Theory Divides Men Differ: |
> |---|---|
> | 1. Immerse (Acts 8:38) | 1. Sprinkle Baby (Acts 16:15?) |
> | 2. Lord's Supper 1st Day (Acts 20:7) | 2. Any Day (1 Cor. 11:26?) |
> | 3. Sing (Eph. 5:19) | 3. Play (Rev. 5:8?) |
> | 4. Preach (1 Tim. 3:15) | 4. Meal, Party, Gym (Jude 12?) |
> | 5. Hope - Heaven (1 Pet. 1:4) | 5. 1,000 Years On Earth (Rev. 20:4?) |
> | 6. Innocent Put Away Fornicator & Remarry (Matt. 19:9) | 6. Others Remarry (1 Cor. 7?) |
>
> 37

tonight! Where are we parting company? When he affirms that *others* can remarry. Just as we part with those who claim a thousand year reign on earth, and we part with those who want the meals and the parties sponsored by the church, and so on. My friend, *there is unity in truth.*

And then, look at my chart 23. He said, well, this was just somebody's opinion and he did not have to comment on it. Brother Freeman, I am simply showing you *the result* when we demand, *"What saith the Scripture?"* like I am asking you, *"What saith the Scripture?,"* and we insist on the Bible only as our guide. The result is this [pointing to bottom half of chart 23], on the marriage and divorce subject, as brethren put it into practice. That is my argument. Brethren put it into practice that no release was given to a husband or wife, unless the other party had been guilty of fornication.

> **Restoration Plea**
> 1. "Ask for the old paths"
> 2. "What saith the scripture?"
> 3. Christ only as the head of the church
> 4. Bible only as guide
> 5. N. T. Pattern of faith & practice
>
> **Result On Marriage**
> 1. "No release" given to a husband or wife "unless the other party has been guilty of fornication."
> 2. Claim of "desertion" as "a just cause for divorce and remarriage" rejected.
> 3. Church discipline practiced [See Ed Harrell, *Quest For A Christian America*, pp. 197-198].
>
> 23

Brother Ed Harrell has read more of the restoration literature probably than any man alive, and he is simply showing you the conclusion they came to. Whether he agrees with these conclusions or not, he is saying that is the fact of the record of history, and I am simply saying to you, *God's word unites people!* And then he says, "That is just somebody's opinion. I do not have to comment on that." Are we here to strive to get together on the Book or not? We can do it if we will simply take the principles they took.

And then again, we notice my charts 15 and 16. *Whatever is not authorized is sinful.* And there is no clear passage authorizing the put-away fornicator or the deserted believer to marry another. The conclusion is that such marriages are *sinful*. He *did not* produce the passage, nor *can* he produce the passage, nor *will* he produce the passage. Such marriages are sinful, and the principle that condemns them as such has been taught even by brother Jack Freeman.

Now, I was the worst liar he had ever met, and told more lies on him than he had ever heard of. And so, I apologized in Las Vegas because I *thought* I had made an error on this. But I have talked to the editor of the *Gospel Guardian*. And what did my opponent say about that, after calling me publicly a liar and I apologized on my own? The next night in Las Vegas he said I did *not* apologize, so I ate another bite of humble pie, and I did it gladly and graciously. I am not complaining. I ought to do it. *If I make a mistake,* I ought to apologize. And so, I apologized *again* the second time. And brother Freeman, I have now talked to the editor of the *Gospel Guardian:* He says it was *you.* Was it you or was it not? Do you want to nod your head or shake your head? Or, he does not remember, I guess, like these politicians who get on the hot-seat and they cannot remember what they did and what they said.

You wrote this article, and there is no shame in that. Brethren, I was trying

---

Not Authorized = Sinful

1. Things "not authorized within the doctrine of Christ are not only non-essential but sinful as well."

2. An author defended sponsoring church but had "no passage of Scripture to show that such a plan is authorized by the Lord" (Jack Freeman, <u>Gospel Guardian</u>, 28 April 1960, pp. 8-9).

3. No clear passage authorizes put-away fornicator or deserted believer to marry another.

4. Conclusion: such marriages are sinful!

15

God's Perfect Plan

1. We must not change God's perfect "plan of salvation... plan of worship ... plan for the life of the individual ... plan of the work for the church."

2. "When the individual engages in dishonest activity; when his thoughts, words, or actions are evil; he has departed from the perfect plan for daily living" (Jack Freeman, <u>Gospel Guardian</u>, 24 Oct. 1957, pp. 8-9).

3. God's perfect plan for daily living includes marriage, divorce, & remarriage.

16

to introduce that in Las Vegas to show *we have a common starting place*. Whatever is not authorized, and when you cannot give a passage of Scripture, then it is *sinful*, it is *excluded. There is no Scripture tonight for the put-away fornicator or the deserted believer to marry another*. No one in the world knows it better than brother Freeman, because he struggled and tried so desperately to find it, and it is not there, and he still cannot. Do you see why "no comment" about what the *Gospel Guardian* editor said and all of that? And what the brethren said at San Pablo? No, he does not want to face the facts on it. Did you write it or not? Could you just tell us? Well, he does not want to.

Well, we notice further, we talked about chart 41, Genesis 2. The only thing he could find to say about that is that Proverbs 13:15 does not say anything about privileges. *Amen* and *amen*, and that is my point! Now, you watch it, friend. Jesus explained Genesis 2:24 in such a way that will exclude the put-away fornicator from marrying another. For, you see, obedience is always blessed (Deut. 10:13). The law is for our good, but sin brings hardship and *not privileges* (Prov. 13:15). You are right. It says nothing about privileges — that is my point. And when the fornicator gets the *privilege* out of fornicating to go marry another, then you contradict the principle of this passage. Now, you think about that. The way of the transgressor is what? *Hard*. So, what that means is, *if you commit fornication, go marry another?* Is that what it means? It cannot mean that. And my Lord shows it cannot mean that.

Genesis 2:24 Law
Explained By Jesus In Matthew 19:3-9

1. **Requires** One Man For One Woman - "A Man," "His Wife"
2. **Excludes** All Immorality - "A Man," "His Wife," "<u>One</u> Flesh" = No Fornication, Adultery, Polygamy, Concubines, Homosexuals, Bestiality
3. **Implies** Immorality Desecrates The Union - Ground For The Innocent To Put Away The Guilty - "A Man," "His Wife," "Cleave," "One Flesh"
4. **Excludes** The Put Away Fornicator From Marrying Another
   * Obedience Is Blessed (Deut. 10:13)
   * Sin Brings Hardship, Not Privileges (Prov. 13:15)
5. **Implies** Bond Only In This Life - "One <u>Flesh</u>" = Life And Relations In The Fleshly Body

---

And then on my chart 43 [next page]. We talked about God's ideal in the Old Testament, and how men have departed from that. The way they have departed from it is by not maintaining what the Book taught. Just as you are not maintaining it. And you are opening a door to things that are reprehensible even to you, just as the history of man shows that it will happen.

And then, next my chart 44, on *Deuteronomy 24*. Why, he said there was another cause given in verse 2, that if a man just hated his wife he could put her away. Well now, let's look at chart 67-A [next page]. Was hatred another cause? The truth is that brother Freeman is too liberal for Moses or Christ. The law of Moses said they could put her away for *shameful, indecent, filthy conduct* — that was *the hateful thing*, that is *the hateful thing*. That is just a parallel statement is all that is.

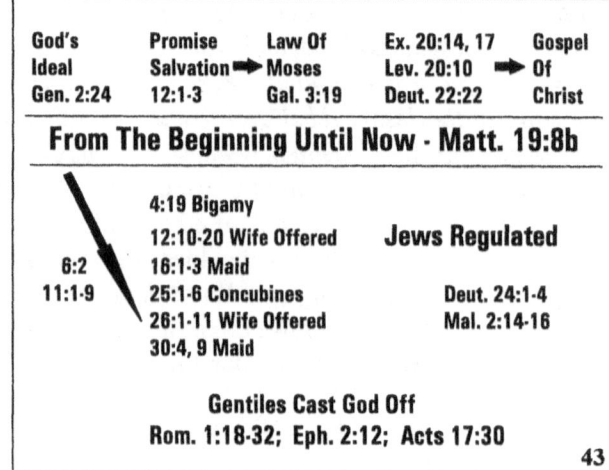

But brother Freeman said in his "Marriage" series (part no. 1), "God was allowing divorce if she burnt the toast or the biscuits…. He did under the law of Moses, under the law that He gave through Moses." Friend, you let that sink in. Here sits the man who believes God actually allowed divorcing of a woman if she merely burned a piece of bread. He is too liberal even for Moses, let alone my Lord and Savior. Oh, he would say [in reference to his explanation of Deut. 24], "Now that law has been changed." But that is his explanation of it, and he is explaining it *just like the sinful Pharisees did*.

Notice the next one, chart 67-B. Now, *the law of Christ versus liberalism today* (Matt. 5:32 and 19:9). The innocent mate can put away the fornicator and marry another. But the liberal position is, the fornicator can marry another and the deserted believer marry another. And so you are too liberal for Moses and too liberal for Christ!

And then we notice my chart 54. *How do we know? Because the Bible tells*

Opponent Too <u>Liberal</u> For Moses Or Christ

<u>Law Of Moses</u>	<u>Vs.</u>	<u>Liberalism</u>
Deut. 24:1 - Put her away for shameful, indecent, filthy conduct		"God was allowing... divorce if she burned the toast or the biscuits... He did under the Law that He gave thru Moses." (Freeman, Marriage Series, 1988, #1)

67 - A

Law Of Christ Vs. Liberalism

Matthew 5:32; 19:9
Innocent mate put away fornicator and marry another

Fornicator <u>can</u> marry another

Deserted Believer marry another

67 - B

me so. And there are little children here tonight that can take that down and think about it and understand it just as clear as crystal. "Yes, Jesus loves me," we sing it, what a beautiful song. And one of the great truths that it teaches us, *"the Bible tells me so,"* is that when the Bible tells you so, you can *know* that it is right and true. So, Romans 7:2-3, if your mate dies, you can marry another. And then, if you put away your mate for fornication, you can marry another. The Bible says so. He did *not find* the put-away fornicator may marry another — or the unscripturally divorced may marry another — and he will not have found it when this debate is ended. Simple truths, simple truths.

> **How We Know**
>
> **Simplicity Of Truth:** "Yes, Jesus loves me, the Bible tells me so" (Rom. 4:3; Eph. 3:4)
>
> **Know We Can Remarry:**
> 1. If mate dies (Rom. 7:2-3)
> 2. If put away mate for fornication (Matt. 19:9)
>
> **Where Does The Bible Authorize These To Remarry:**
> 1. The put-away fornicator?
> 2. Those unscripturally divorced?
>
> 54

Then we notice, let's look at my chart 62 about the exception. The simplicity of *the rule* and *the exception.* "Whosoever shall put away his wife, saving for the cause of fornication, causeth her to commit adultery: Whosoever shall marry her that is divorced committeth adultery." Now, my friend, you take this home and study it; you circle that word *"causeth"* in your Bible so that you can see the thing that this passage revolves around. It is whether you have *caused* sin. The sin happened, but the question is, did you *cause* it? When she married another, she committed adultery, but did you *cause* it? Yes, you did if you put her away in that circumstance.

Well then, my friend, the exception has the

> **Rule & Exception**
> **Matt. 5:32**
>
> 1. "Whosoever shall put away his wife, saving for the cause of fornication, causeth her to commit adultery: and whosoever shall marry her that is divorced committeth adultery."
>
> 2. Whosoever shall put away his wife **for fornication** is not responsible for her subsequent adultery: and whosoever shall marry her that is divorced committeth adultery.
>
> 62

same force. It centers on the *cause* of sin. Whoever puts away his wife for fornication is not the cause, and is not responsible for her subsequent sin in adultery. "But whoever marries her that is divorced committeth adultery," *that stands!*

And then, chart 63, *the exception does not exempt the fornicator.* You have compound, complex sentences in these passages. Each one contains two independent clauses joined by the conjunction "and." The exception stated in the first clause has no force in the second. The force of the exception in the first clause does *not* yield the meaning in the second clause, "Whoever marries her that is divorced *for fornication* doth not commit adultery." And that is the only hope, that is the only straw in all the world he has got to produce his case from the Bible that the guilty, put-away fornicator could marry another. And that straw is gone with the wind. Grammatically, it is an absolute impossibility. The passage does not exist that he is looking for.

And then, Moses and Christ, my chart 67. Brother Freeman talked about this chart a little bit. It kind of amuses me the way he can talk about something and not answer the points that are on it. The fornicator was put away by death and could not marry another. Do you see that? And so *under the law of Christ,* God does not attach the death penalty, but *the fornicator is put-away by divorce and certainly cannot marry another.*

The Exception Does Not Exempt The Fornicator

Matt. 5:32 & 19:9 are compound, complex sentences. Each one contains two independent clauses, joined by the conjunction "and."

The exception stated in the first independent clause has no force in the second independent clause.

THEREFORE, the force of the exception in the first independent clause does NOT yield the meaning in the second, "Whosoever shall marry her that is divorced FOR FORNICATION doth not commit adultery."

63

MOSES	CHRIST
1. Fornication - Put Away By Death (Marry No Other)	1. Fornication - Put Away By Divorce (Marry No Other)
2. Divorce - Cause Short Of Fornication ↓	2. No Divorce For Any Cause Short of Fornication ↓
3. Mate Divorced - No Fornication - Marry Another w/o Adultery ↓	3. Same Situation - BUT Marry Another = Adultery ↓
4. Man Who Marries Her Not In Adultery ↓	4. Man Who Marries Her In Adultery ↓
5. First Man Can't Have Her	5. First Man Can Have Her

67

There is no authority for it. Divorce for a cause short of fornication was allowed under Moses, but no divorce for any cause short of fornication under Christ. The *cause* changed, and the *effect* changed. The mate who is divorced where there is no fornication marries another; it is not adultery under Moses. But in that situation, it *is* adultery under Christ. The cause and the effect both changed. No, he did not want to talk about this — just show it and then move on. The man that marries her was not in adultery over there (under Moses), but now, you watch it, the man who marries her is in adultery over here (under Christ).

And then, we notice again my chart 72 [text, Matt. 19:9]. How simple is the wording of the Lord, "Whosoever shall put away his wife, except it be for fornication, and shall marry another, committeth adultery: And whoso marrieth her which is put away doth commit adultery." She might be put away *without cause* — you marry her, you commit adultery. She might be put away *for fornication* — you marry her, you commit adultery. That is simple to understand, simple to understand.

And then notice my chart 73. He did not answer this, *the rule* with *the exception*. The force of the exception is, "Whoever puts away his wife for fornication and marries another, doth not commit adultery: but whoever marries her which is put away does commit adultery." And he did not answer it. It cannot be answered.

And then, chart 74. *Except, if and only if.* Let's just take a moment, my friend, and read the passage. I never heard such a garbled speech in

> ## Rule & Exception
> ## Matt. 19:9
>
> 1. "Whosoever shall put away his wife, except it be for fornication, and shall marry another, committeth adultery: and whoso marrieth her which is put away doth commit adultery."
>
> 2. Whosoever shall put away his wife **for fornication** and shall marry another, doth not commit adultery: and whoso marrieth her which is put away doth commit adultery.

all my life. I doubt if there is anybody here who can understand what he said. I could not, but maybe my intelligence is not up to par. Matthew 18:3, "Except ye be converted, and become as little children, ye shall not enter into the kingdom of heaven." He wants me to assign the meaning "if and only if," but leave the *"not"* in it. Who in the world cannot understand that? You just think about it, my friend. The force of the exception is, *"If and only if* you are converted, become as little children, you *can* enter." That is giving the exception its force. "Whoever

> **Except = If & Only If!**
>
> * Matt. 18:3 Become as little child → Enter kingdom
>
> * John 3:2 God with Him → Do miracles
>
> * John 3:5 Born of water & Spirit → Enter kingdom
>
> * Matt. 19:9 Put away wife for fornication & marry another → Not adultery
>
> 74

puts away his wife and marries another, except it be for fornication," you see, "commits adultery." Well, if you put her away *for fornication* and marry another, the force of the exception is you do *not* commit adultery.

Look at John 3:5, John 3:2. This is just too simple to miss. John 3:2, "No man can do these miracles that thou doest *except* God be with him." That means *if and only if God is with him* he *can* do the miracles. That is the point about the *except*. There is a "not" condition there, but then the exception means, *in the case of the exception, the not is removed.* That is the simple meaning of the grammar. And if he cannot understand that, I do not know what to do to help him. What does *except* mean?

Now then, I want to notice his chart 747, which is on Revelation 2:22. Alright, in Revelation 2:22 he proposes to find where an exception in one independent clause has been moved to another clause. Look at how he has that. He has as the first independent clause, "I will cast her into bed," and I want you to look at his next independent clause, "them that commit adultery with her into great tribulation." Send him back to the first grade. I do not mean that unkindly. But is that an *independent clause?* My lands! That is *not* an independent clause. And

> **EXCEPTION CLAUSES:**
>
> DO EXCEPTION CLAUSES MODIFY SENTENCES WITH INDEPENDENT CLAUSES?
>
> *HALBROOK'S ASSERTION: NO! THE EXCEPTION CLAUSE CANNOT MODIFY THE ENTIRE SENTENCE IN MATT. 19:9, BECAUSE THE SENTENCE HAS TWO INDEPENDENT CLAUSES.
>
> *THE BIBLE: REV 2:22-23   APPEARS ONLY ONCE
>   "...EXCEPT THEY REPENT..."
>
> INDEPENDENT CLAUSE #1 - "BEHOLD I WILL CAST HER INTO BED"
>   --- AND ---
> INDEPENDENT CLAUSE #2 - "THEM THAT COMMIT ADULTERY WITH HER INTO GREAT TRIBULATION"
>   --- AND ---
> INDEPENDENT CLAUSE #3 - "I WILL KILL HER CHILDREN"
>
> 747

number three, independent clause number three, "I will kill her children." He said, now "except they repent" is in the first clause, but not in the others, and therefore it will carry over. And, that is suppose to be his carry-over from Matthew 19 [i.e., this is the basis for his argument that the exception in the first independent clause of Matt. 19 carries over to the second].

Now, I made the point in Las Vegas that both clauses in Matthew 19 do not deal with the same person. In the first case, you have the innocent man putting away his wife, for instance, that is one case. But the next case is somebody marries her. That is another case.

Now look at his chart 113. Now, in Revelation 2:22 does "except" in one independent clause modify other independent clauses? When he claims three independent clauses, he errs, not knowing his grammar. Secondly, my opponent claims the exception for Jezebel and her children. And when I first read that, I followed him. I made the mistake of following him and thinking it was all talking about the same ones. I went back and read the context when I got home. He errs not knowing the Scriptures and I erred right behind him. It was the blind leading the blind. The passage says, *"She repented not,"* and that is why it says, "I will cast her...and I will kill her children." There was not any exception *for Jezebel and her children.*

> **Revelation 2:22 "Except" In One Independent Clause Modify Other Independent Clauses?**
> 1. Opponent claims three independent clauses - Errs, not knowing grammar.
> 2. Opponent claims "exception" for Jezebel and her children - Errs, not knowing scripture: "She repented not ... I will cast her ... I will kill her children" (Vv. 21-23).
> 3. Brethren who compromise with immorality will perish, "Except they repent" (Vs. 22).
> 4. "Except" in one independent clause does NOT modify other independent clauses - Matt. 5:32; 19:9; Rev. 2:22.
> 5. EXCEPT = IF AND ONLY IF!
>
> 113

Go back and read your passage, brother Freeman.

And I will tell you what it said: *Brethren who compromise with immorality will perish, "except they repent."* There was the exception. And *except* my brother will repent of the doctrine he is teaching, he finds himself in this same position. Will he repent? We beg him to do it. "Except" in one independent clause does not modify other independent clauses. And, my friend, notice the "except" — *if and only if.* This is my passage all the way. *If and only if* these compromising brethren repent, they escape the condemnation that Jezebel faces. If and only if — just like Matthew 19:9.

Alright, and then I want us to notice now Freeman's chart 428. Alright, how do you know what is discussed in Matthew 19:9? He is trying to get this thing about the first independent clause with the exception, and he is all confused about what does "if and only if" mean.

Now, you notice my chart 70 on this, the simplicity of this thing. Alright, notice that Jesus said, "For this cause shall a man leave father and mother, and cleave to his wife: and they twain shall be one flesh. Wherefore they are no more twain, but one flesh. What...God hath joined together, let not man put asunder." Now, there you have a plain statement that what God joins, men cannot break.

WHAT IS DISCUSSED IN MATT. 19:9?

FIRST INDEPENDENT CLAUSE:

DIVORCE "EXCEPT IT BE FOR FORNICATION" -- NOT DIVORCE FOR FORNICATION.

THE SPIRITUAL STATE OF THE MAN WHO REMARRIES WHEN HE HAS PUT AWAY HIS WIFE

"EXCEPT IT BE FOR FORNICATION" -ADULTERY- WHY?
STILL MARRIED (IN GOD'S SIGHT)

428

Now again, the passage Matthew 19:9 with it. Alright, now watch, this is the same context. What God joins, men cannot put asunder; but whoever puts away his wife, except it be for fornication, and marries another committeth adultery. Whoever marries her which is put away, doth commit adultery. Now, you notice the *simplicity* of that exception. He is so confused that he acts like it cannot be understood. My friend, it is simple to see that in the case of the exception, that if you put your wife away

---

Matthew 19:3-6

"The Pharisees also came unto him, tempting him, and saying unto him, Is it lawful for a man to put away his wife for every cause? And he answered and said unto them, Have ye not read, that he which made them at the beginning made them male and female, And said, For this cause shall a man leave father and mother, and shall cleave to his wife: and they twain shall be one flesh? Wherefore they are no more twain, but one flesh. What therefore God hath joined together, let not man put asunder."

70

---

and marry another, it is not adultery. I believe he can see that. I do not believe it is that hard to understand.

Now, my friend, I have an eighteen year old son who will marry in the next few years. And I want him taught the restraints and the constraints of God's Word. Is there anyone else here who is raising an eighteen year old or a teenager? And do you want them taught a doctrine that if they marry and commit fornication, they will have the privilege out of that to marry another? And *if they commit fornication, the privilege that grows out of that is to marry another?* Or do you want them taught that there is *the one and only the one exception,* and they are to keep themselves faithful to Almighty God? You think of the force of this.

Now, my chart 333. My friend, I want you to notice what has happened in the passing of time by teaching this doctrine. As the *International Standard Bible Encyclopedia* points out, when courts allow remarriage to the "guilty and innocent alike," "We invite the very evils we seek to remedy. We make it the interest of the dissatisfied party to create" the grounds that "free" him to marry another. And my friend, this will result in opening the door to all kinds of sin, even sins that brother Freeman would not want and he would repudiate.

> **Remarriage Of Guilty Party Invites Sin!**
>
> I.S.B.E. article (II:865-866) warns that when courts allow remarriage to "guilty and innocent alike," "We invite the very evils we seek to remedy. We make it the interest of a dissatisfied party to create" the grounds that "free" him to marry another.
>
> The Law of Christ opens no such door to invite sin!
>
> 333

Next, chart 108. I want you to notice that it is *God versus Satan*. God said, "Whosoever marrieth her which is put away doth commit adultery." My opponent says, "Whoever marries her which is put away doth *not* commit adultery." God versus Satan's doctrine.

> **God -vs- Satan**
>
> 1. If you eat, "surely die" (Gen. 2:17)
> 2. Believe & "Baptized shall be saved" (Mk. 16:16)
> 3. "Whoso marrieth her which is put away doth commit adultery" (Matt. 5:32; 19:9)
>
> 1. If you eat, "NOT surely die" (Gen. 3:4)
> 2. Believe and NOT baptized shall be saved
> 3. Whoso marrieth her which is put away doth NOT commit adultery
>
> 108

First Evening
Freeman's Second Negative

Brethren and friends, moderators, brother Halbrook, I would like to in a moment review some things that have been said, but I would like to correct one thing. I said that at Vegas Drive two couples have been told to refrain from sex, but they could live together. Keith Greer told me after the speech that in the case of one of those couples, the woman had decided that she would accept that man as her husband, scriptural husband. I am thrilled to hear that. Yes, debates do good.

Brother Halbrook, I did not take time to read the agreement tonight, but I do not remember reading in the agreement anything having to do with just when questions would be answered. So, I do not know that that is written in the agreement. And I did not recall exactly how we conducted that in North Las Vegas. So, I guess we just—but I did not expect you to use your time. I was going to use mine reading your questions, but since you did not read mine, why, we can do as you please about it, anything that you suggest. We could use the last ten minutes for the questions. I will be happy to answer yours now. While we have to answer them, I will be happy to read them regardless of how much time it takes. And you can make any comments you care to. I will read mine to you:

1. Is 1 Corinthians 7:12-16 a part of God's marriage law?

2. The Christian is not required to stay married to the unbeliever against the unbeliever's wishes. True or False.

3. To be "loosed" is the opposite of being bound; hence, it means not under obligation regarding duty enjoined in marriage. True or False.

4. The innocent person (free of fornication) who has been put away without God's or his or her approval and against whom adultery has been committed may remarry (scripturally). True or False.

5. The innocent believer (free from fornication) who has been put away by the unbeliever without God's or his or her approval and against whom adultery has been committed may scripturally remarry. True or False.

His questions to me: 1. *"Is it necessary to have positive divine authority for all that we preach and practice? That is, are we obligated to put our finger on the verse that authorizes what we preach and practice?"* I answer it yes. We must see it authorized either by command, by example, or by necessary implication. I am not afraid to answer it. That is what I have taught for years.

2. *"Does Matthew 19:9 teach that after God joins two people in marriage,*

an innocent partner may put away a mate guilty of fornication and marry another?" Yes, it does. An innocent partner, not only according to Matthew 19, but wherever the Scriptures deal with it, has always had the right to put away the one who is guilty of fornication.

3. *"Is there any marriage between one male and one female which people can enter under civil law but which they must end in order to be right in the sight of God?"* Yes; Herod had another man's wife. And he was not allowed to have her according to the Scripture. I am not defending a man having another man's wife, but he has a right to his own. That is what I am defending. Herod had a right to his own wife.

4. *"Which passages speak of marrying 'another'?"* [The passages offered were Rom. 7:2-3, Matt. 19:9, and 1 Cor. 7:15.] Well, he predicted how I would answer because that is the same question he asked in North Las Vegas. *Which passages speak of marrying "another"?* I might ask him which passage speaks of the fornicator being guilty of sin when he remarries. None. He only gets it by inference. And the word "another" is kind of a catch word. You cannot marry without another being involved. You cannot have a marriage when you have one person. If you marry, you marry another. And so, inference. And I will try to get this in tonight; if not, I will get it in tomorrow night. I have a good many charts for 1 Corinthians 7 showing exactly what is taught there.

5. *"Since you say 1 Corinthians 7:10-11 'does not give any reason for divorce'* (he refers to a series of sermons I preached in the fall of 1988), *what must the Christian do if there is a divorce and remarriage violating this passage? (A) Divorce the second mate and return to the first mate, or remain unmarried? (B) Pray for forgiveness and remain in the second marriage? (C) 'I refuse to answer on the grounds that it may incriminate me?'"* And brethren, I want you to be honest, and just listen to these. I have asked him very straightforward and simple questions, not a catch question in the whole bunch. You will see that is true in five questions I give him each night — not a catch question. Every question he asked me is meant to be a trick question, a catch question. Yet, I do my best to answer and so I am adding point "D" and this is my answer. You know, I do not have to choose his answers; I have the right to answer as the Bible does. The divorce is only a legal document, they are still married to one another. Well, when the remarriage, the legal marriage, takes place, they are still married to one another. But now, by marrying, the one has committed adultery, and so the other has grounds for divorce and remarriage in God's sight and that according to your own passage, Matthew 19:9.

Now, let's get on and answer what he has to say. And incidentally, he talked about the fact that I would not answer his charts. He did not call for the majority of mine, left the majority of them out in his speech. You know that he did.

Let's look at charts 6, 7, and 8 having to do with authority. And we agree that you must have book, chapter, and verse. You have got to have command, or approved example, or necessary implication. After this, we are going to be using 13 and 37 and 23, 41 and 67-A. Alright, authority of Christ. And we agreed on this. And number 7, he says we just flash it up there. Well, I do not have to do any more than that because I did not even have to call for it to be put up, because you have already seen them and I agree with this. And number 8. I agree with this teaching on authority. I have used the same charts myself teaching on authority. And so, there is no point in going over things that we agree on. That is not what the debate is about. If we agreed, then we would not be here debating one another.

And let me insert this: I think you can see that brother Halbrook and I have no hatred for one another. But you need to understand this: he believes I am a false teacher and will be responsible for people going to hell. I believe he is a false teacher and those who believe him on this question will certainly end up at the very same place. We need to be honest enough to admit it. Even though we are brethren, we differ. And this is *not a matter of opinion*, this is a matter of

---

Authority Of Christ
(Matthew 28:18)

Expressed In The Bible:

* All Truth (John 16:13)
* Speak Same Thing - Words of Holy Spirit - That Which Is Written (1 Cor. 1:10; 2:13; 4:6)
* No Other Message (Gal. 1:8-9)
* Abide In Doctrine Of Christ (2 John 9)
* Contend For The Faith (Jude 3)

6

Authority Of Christ: How Expressed

Two Kinds:	In Three Ways:
General - "Go" in Mark 16:15	Direct Statement
Specific - "Day" in Acts 20:7	Approved Example
	Necessary Implication

7

what the Bible teaches.

Now, you say, now we must have this authority. We must have *command,* we must have an *approved example,* or we must have a *necessary implication.* Alright, this is what I want. I want a command, I want approved example, or necessary inference *where any inspired man in the New Testament ever told anyone you will have to leave your spouse to get to heaven.* Now, if any of you have ever read that, you catch me on the way out tonight, and just give me that passage. Where did any inspired writer, after Jesus gave his lesson, after the Apostles began to preach, where did any inspired writer say you will have to leave that woman, your mate, to get to heaven?

2. We are talking about authority. This is his subject. *Where did any of the inspired writers, Apostles or others, ever tell a man he would have to leave or remain unmarried to get to heaven?* Now, there are two very important questions. That is what this debate is all about. Do you know the book, chapter, verse? If you do, you give it to me; I will appreciate it very much. I want the truth on this subject. I admit to human imperfections. I am going to deal with that a little more when we get to his charts 15 and 16 in a moment.

His chart number 13. I did answer and on many other charts also with my charts dealing with Matthew 19. All of these charts that have to do with Matthew 19, I dealt with, and they are each deal-

What Is Commanded?

The Gospel	Law Of Moses
Acts 15:7-11 God gave the same gift to the Gentiles [**Imply** God accepts them - Jews must, too]	No Implication - Silent! (Vs. 24)
Vs. 12 God **Approved Example** of preaching to Gentiles	No Example - Silent! (Vs. 24)
Vv. 16-18 God Made **Direct Statement**	No Statement - Silent! (Vs. 24)

8

When God Is Specific

CLASS	SPECIFIC	EXCLUDE
Woods	Gopher Wood *(Gen. 6:14)*	All Other Woods
Tribes	Levi *(Heb. 7:14)*	All Other Tribes
Action - Water	Immerse *(Acts 2:38; 8:38)*	All Other Actions
Music	Sing *(Eph. 5:19)*	All Other Music
Divorced People	Innocent Put Away Guilty & Remarry *(Matt. 19:9)*	All Other Divorced Persons

13

ing with this. It was the whole point of this chart to get down to Matthew 19:9, where the chart says, "Innocent put away the guilty party and remarried." Well, I agree the innocent party can put away the guilty party and remarry. We were talking about guilt and the fact that he says he was guilty of fornication. Yes, they can put them away. But I answered everything in which we disagreed on Matthew 19 with six charts from Matthew chapter 19.

> **Unity In Truth**
> (John 17:17-21)
>
> | Divine Truth Unites All Agree: | Human Theory Divides Men Differ: |
> |---|---|
> | 1. Immerse (Acts 8:38) | 1. Sprinkle Baby (Acts16:15?) |
> | 2. Lord's Supper 1st Day (Acts 20:7) | 2. Any Day (1 Cor. 11:26?) |
> | 3. Sing (Eph. 5:19) | 3. Play (Rev. 5:8?) |
> | 4. Preach (1 Tim. 3:15) | 4. Meal, Party, Gym (Jude 12?) |
> | 5. Hope - Heaven (1 Pet. 1:4) | 5. 1,000 Years On Earth (Rev. 20:4?) |
> | 6. Innocent Put Away Fornicator & Remarry (Matt. 19:9) | 6. Others Remarry (1 Cor. 7?) |
>
> 37

His chart number 37. I answered this also with my charts dealing with Matthew 19.

Let's notice his chart number 23. Notice what the brethren did. You know, the brethren did not release the guilty party. If you are going to go by what the brethren did, no. "'No release' given to husband or wife 'unless the other party has been guilty of fornication.'" "'No release' given," — now who says that? "Claim of 'desertion' as 'a just cause for divorce and remarriage' rejected." Who said it was

> **Restoration Plea**
> 1. "Ask for the old paths"
> 2. "What saith the scripture?"
> 3. Christ only as the head of the church
> 4. Bible only as guide
> 5. N. T. Pattern of faith & practice
>
> **Result On Marriage**
> 1. "No release" given to a husband or wife "unless the other party has been guilty of fornication."
> 2. Claim of "desertion" as "a just cause for divorce and remarriage" rejected.
> 3. Church discipline practiced [See Ed Harrell, *Quest For A Christian America,* pp. 197-198].
>
> 23

rejected? My opponent said that Ed Harrell did not necessarily say that or agree with it. He wrote it, but he did not necessarily agree with it. It is the conclusion that he reached, from what had been done in past years. That is beside the point; that has nothing to do with this debate.

Let's turn now to his chart 41. I am referring to his charts, he did not refer to mine, and I am going to refer to his. Genesis 2:24, the marriage law, explained by Jesus in Matthew 19:3-9. The things that it excludes — implies bound only in this life. That is true, I agree with that. *"Excludes the put-away fornicator from marrying another"* — I do not agree with that. Now, he says I have never given a passage and will not in all this debate. Every night for four nights in North Las Vegas I gave it. You heard me mention it tonight. Did you hear him talk about 1 Corinthians 6:9-11? Acts 18:8? 1 Corinthians 7:2? Did you hear it? He did not refer to it. He wants book, chapter, and verse. He says we have got to have it; I gave it to him. He will not even read it. He will not even mention it. I gave him book, chapter, and verse. Will he give me book, chapter, and verse where it says, where it was ever taught, that a man must put away his wife to get to heaven, must remain single to get to heaven? I give him passages, he will not have them — will not even refer to them. He will get up here and tell you I did not give it, I will not find it. In eight nights of debating I have given it to him already. This is the fifth night, and for the fifth time he has completely ignored it.

Genesis 2:24 Law
Explained By Jesus In Matthew 19:3-9

1. **Requires** One Man For One Woman - "A Man," "His Wife"
2. **Excludes** All Immorality - "A Man," "His Wife," "One Flesh" - No Fornication, Adultery, Polygamy, Concubines, Homosexuals, Bestiality
3. **Implies** Immorality Desecrates The Union - Ground For The Innocent To Put Away The Guilty - "A Man," "His Wife," "Cleave," "One Flesh"
4. **Excludes** The Put Away Fornicator From Marrying Another
   * Obedience Is Blessed (Deut. 10:13)
   * Sin Brings Hardship, Not Privileges (Prov. 13:15)
5. **Implies** Bond Only In This Life - "One Flesh" - Life And Relations In The Fleshly Body

41

His chart number 67-A. In chart number 67-A, "opponent is too liberal for Moses or Christ." Well, that is his opinion. That is his opinion. Moses' law, again, I want to ask him — *and he agrees the man who puts the woman away has the right to remarry* — I ask him to tell us how he knows that. He says, where is the passage that

---

Opponent Too Liberal For Moses Or Christ

Law Of Moses	Vs.	Liberalism
Deut. 24:1 - Put her away for shameful, indecent, filthy conduct		"God was allowing... divorce if she burned the toast or the biscuits... He did under the Law that He gave thru Moses." (Freeman, Marriage Series, 1988, #1)

67-A

says thus and so? Well, where is the passage that says (and those verses are in that context) the man that puts away his wife can remarry? It says plainly the wife can. Now, he comes on down to the latter where the second husband has her. That is what I talked about, not the *first husband* — he puts her away for shameful, indecent conduct. That is not what the passage says exactly, but I agree that is so. And that could cover a multitude of things. He admits it is not fornication. Alright, that would cover a multitude of things. And then you get down to the second husband who marries her can put her away, and only it says it is for hatred, if he hates her. It does not say *why* he hates her. My opponent comes back and says, well, this is why he hates her. How does he know? Moses did not say so. God did not say so. But my opponent would have you to think that he knows. Well, I would like to know how he knows.

Let's come back to chart number 74. Chart number 74, this *"if and only if."* I hope you noticed how he dealt with it. *"If and only if."* You know, now he has got to change the second phrase to make the Scripture teach the truth — or what he believes is the truth. *Except* ye be converted and become as little children. *If and only if* ye become as little children, you *cannot* enter the kingdom. Oh, he says, you have got to take the "not" out of it. *Why?* Because you have changed the meaning of *except*. You have completely reversed the Lord's meaning. Otherwise, you could leave the rest of it alone. No one gave you permission to change the rest of this anyway. Now, if you wanted to use a synonym, if it really is a synonym, it can be used without taking the "not" out of the last phrase. You try it on any passage of the Bible. If you find a word that is a synonym for a word used in the Bible, you could use it without changing any other word in the passage. It will not reverse the meaning; if it is a synonym, it leaves the meaning just like it is. Think about it. You have grade school children, he thinks a lot of them, so do I. I love you and want you to go to heaven. You just think about this: if you can use a word as a synonym in place of a word that is used, you use a synonym which

---

Except = If & Only If!

* Matt. 18:3 Become as little child → Enter kingdom

* John 3:2 God with Him → Do miracles

* John 3:5 Born of water & Spirit → Enter kingdom

* Matt. 19:9 Put away wife for fornication & marry another → Not adultery

74

means exactly the same thing, a word or phrase — you do not have to change the rest of the sentence. That synonym will not change the meaning. You do not have to take a "not" out of the sentence.

That is what he had to do in all of these. He had to do it here, change it, because — you just listen to this, now this is a sad mistake he made — if I become as a little child, I *cannot* enter the kingdom. If God was with Jesus, then Jesus could do *no* miracles. If a man is born of the water and of the Spirit, he *cannot* enter the kingdom. If I put away my wife for fornication, I *cannot* remarry without committing adultery. That is exactly what happens when you toy with the word of God. Why not leave it like it is? Now, if this is a legitimate synonym, alright, use it, but do not try to change the rest of it. You know, if this is a legitimate synonym, you are not changing the meaning here by using it. So, you do not have to change this [pointing to right side of chart 74]. But if it is not a legitimate synonym, you put it in here [left side], then you have no right to change this [pointing to the right side of chart 74]. And so he has made all those passages teach exactly the opposite. What did he say? Why, that is the funniest thing I have ever heard, that is the funniest thing I have ever heard.

My chart number 747. Now, he admitted here that he had made a mistake in Las Vegas. We all do. This was where I referred to the clauses in Revelation 2. And he said there in Las Vegas he did not catch it. But there he did say that they were referring to the same case, and now he changes his mind about it. Well, you have a right to change your mind. He says that these were not actually clauses. He picks on one of these and says, well, all of the wording is not listed here. All of the wording there is not listed here. This is what God was going to do, and three things that God said He was going to do, *except they repent*. God was going to do three different things to these people, but every one had to do, as you admitted, with the very same case. Now, even if this is not a complete clause, one that is not, then you have admitted the other two are and they are joined together by

EXCEPTION CLAUSES:

DO EXCEPTION CLAUSES MODIFY SENTENCES WITH INDEPENDENT CLAUSES?

***HALBROOK'S ASSERTION**: NO! THE EXCEPTION CLAUSE CANNOT MODIFY THE ENTIRE SENTENCE IN MATT. 19:9, BECAUSE THE SENTENCE HAS TWO INDEPENDENT CLAUSES.

***THE BIBLE: REV 2:22-23** — APPEARS ONLY ONCE
"...EXCEPT THEY REPENT..."

INDEPENDENT CLAUSE #1 - "BEHOLD I WILL CAST HER INTO BED"
--- AND ---
INDEPENDENT CLAUSE #2 - "THEM THAT COMMIT ADULTERY WITH HER INTO GREAT TRIBULATION"
--- AND ---
INDEPENDENT CLAUSE #3 - "I WILL KILL HER CHILDREN"

747

"and," and they deal with this — you said the same case. I have already shown that Matthew 19:9 deals with the very same case, both phrases.

> **All Cases**
> **Of Marriage, Divorce & Remarriage**
> **Are Subject To God's Law**
> 1. Gen. 2:24 Ordain, define, regulate
> 2. Deut. 7:3 Jew not marry Gentile
> 3. Deut. 23:1-8 Not marry a man with mutilated sex organs
> 4. Deut. 23:1-8 Not marry one of illegitimate birth
> 5. Deut. 23:1-8 Not marry Ammonite or Moabite
> 6. Deut. 23:1-8 Not marry 1st or 2nd gen. Edomite or Egyptian
> 7. Deut. 24:1 Divorce for indecency
> 8. Deut. 24:2 Divorcee allowed to remarry
> 9. Deut. 24:3 After remarry, not return to 1st mate
> 10. Deut. 22:13-19 Falsely accused wife, no divorce
> 11. Deut. 22:28-29 Rape victim, must marry, no divorce
> 12. Num. 36:8-9 Heiress marry within her tribe
> 13. Lev. 18:7-17 Not marry 15 relatives - Jews found no "ethical cause" but "positive law, the cause of which cannot be divined by human reason" (McClintock & Strong, Cyclopedia of Bibl., Theol., & Eccl. Lit., V:782-783)
> 14. Lev. 18:8 Not marry wife's sister in her lifetime
> 15. Deut. 25:5 Widow without children marry man's brother
>
> 100

Let's deal with his charts 100 and 100-A, on "All Cases of Marriage, Divorce, and Remarriage, are Subject to God's Law." Well, we did not have any quarrel with what the Scripture says. Sometimes we have to take issue with men's interpretation, what they say the Scripture says or what they say the Scripture means. Incidentally, we both agree that the Scriptures can teach something without saying it directly. We both agree with that.

I want to see his charts 15 and 16 since I did not get to them in my first speech. I tried to refer to all of your charts, I missed one. Why, we will give it attention now. Here, I do not see any reason to debate about this. But I can tell you frankly: I preached in San Pablo. I edited a paper called *The Eye Opener* there for the six years that

> **All Cases**
> **Of Marriage, Divorce & Remarriage**
> **Are Subject To God's Law (Continued)**
> 16. Lev. 21:7, 13-14 Priest marry virgin, but not whore, divorcee, or widow
> 17. Lev. 21:7, 13-14 Whore, divorcee & widow free to marry, but not free to marry priest
> 18. Matt. 5:32; 19:9; Mk. 10:11-12; Lk. 16:18 Not divorce and remarry except for fornication
> 19. Matt. 5:32; 19:9 One free to marry, but not to a put-away person (whether put away for fornication or other cause)
> 20. Matt. 5:32; 19:9 Not authorize a put-away person (whether put away for fornication or other cause) to remarry
> 21. 1 Cor. 7:10-11 If 2 Christians divorce, must remain unmarried or reconcile
> 22. 1 Cor. 7:12-15 Believer not give up Christ to keep unbeliever (no authority for either to marry another)
> 23. Rom. 7:2-3; 1 Cor. 7:27, 39 Man & wife bound by marriage law for life
>
> **Conclusion: No one is "free to marry" in violation of God's law!**
>
> 100 - A

I preached there. I did not, so far as I know, even receive the *Gospel Guardian*, as it was called then. I do not recall who the editor was. I certainly do not recall any editor of any paper being in a meeting while I was there. But, I am getting old, maybe my memory is bad. But notice here, this [referring to bottom part of chart], who said this? Who said this? I did not. If this is me, or whoever wrote this [top of chart], did not write this [bottom of chart]. Notice, one, two, three, four. One and two were written by someone called Jack Freeman. If it was me, he says, "Well, it is good writing, I agreed with it." Well, I do too. But the same man did not write this [referring to bottom of chart]. Brother Halbrook wrote this. Brother Halbrook wrote this, didn't you? Yeah, brother Halbrook wrote this right here.

Now, I have talked to the elders in San Pablo, or those who were elders when I was there. I have talked to all of the members that I can recall.

> **Not Authorized = Sinful**
>
> 1. Things "not authorized within the doctrine of Christ are not only non-essential but sinful as well."
> 2. An author defended sponsoring church but had "no passage of Scripture to show that such a plan is authorized by the Lord" (Jack Freeman, <u>Gospel Guardian</u>, 28 April 1960, pp. 8-9).
> 3. No clear passage authorizes put-away fornicator or deserted believer to marry another.
> 4. Conclusion: such marriages are sinful!
>
> 15

Most of them are gone now, that I knew when I was there. I have talked to preachers who were in that area when I was there. And none of them recall me writing for the *Gospel Guardian* or any other paper while I was there and that is all that I can tell you about it. The articles could have been taken from *The Eye Opener* that I published, I do not know. If I did, well, I did. But no one can remember it. And my wife cannot remember it. She has got a lot better memory than I have.

> **God's Perfect Plan**
>
> 1. We must not change God's perfect "plan of salvation... plan of worship ... plan for the life of the individual ... plan of the work for the church."
> 2. "When the individual engages in dishonest activity; when his thoughts, words, or actions are evil; he has departed from the perfect plan for daily living" (Jack Freeman, <u>Gospel Guardian</u>, 24 Oct. 1957, pp. 8-9).
> 3. God's perfect plan for daily living includes marriage, divorce, & remarriage.
>
> 16

Now, if that proves anything, you have already said you agree with the teaching. But be careful when you add something. If I am going to use a chart of yours and add something, I will make it clear it is my conclusion and it is not yours.

Let's go now to 4. It is my chart 4, I believe. Start right there on 4, and then 5 and 6, right on down the line. Well, there was another one I intended to use, just wait a minute, if I can think of it. I had a chart laid out there, Glen, that had to do with testimony, introduced some testimony from McClintock and Strong. Alright, 748. Yes, I want to use that. 748, 749, and 750. I want to use these first. Now, "Halbrook says that his uninspired witness shows what Jack Freeman teaches causes people to sin." I am going to read what Halbrook's own witness, McClintock and Strong, tells about evils brought in the world by forbidding to marry. His own witness, this is his witness, I am not introducing his witness to prove anything, but this is his witness he used to teach that Jack Freeman has brought a lot of sin into the world by what he teaches. Now, here is one quotation, "With what impunity fornication rages among them it is unnecessary to remark. Embolden by their polluted celibacy they have become hardened to every crime. In the first place it was on no account lawful for men to prohibit that which the Lord left free."

Next chart, 749. We are quoting from the same book. "Secondly, that God has expressly provided in His word, that liberty should not be infringed. It is too clear to require much proof." Well, you say, I do not agree with him there. Well, what you are saying is, I introduced a witness who was a liar. He lied over something about celibacy but told the truth when he agreed with me. This is your witness. This is what he said about what you would teach, forbidding to marry. You say it is not the doctrine of devils. Here is what your witness has

---

WITNESS

* HALBROOK SAYS THAT HIS UNINSPIRED WITNESS SHOWS THAT WHAT JACK FREEMAN TEACHES CAUSES PEOPLE TO SIN.

* HALBROOK'S OWN WITNESS TELLS ABOUT THE EVILS BROUGHT INTO THE WORLD BY FORBIDDING TO MARRY:

"WITH WHAT IMPUNITY FORNICATION RAGES AMONG THEM IT IS UNNECESSARY TO REMARK; EMBOLDENED BY THEIR POLLUTED CELIBACY, THEY HAVE BECOME HARDENED TO EVERY CRIME."

"IN THE FIRST PLACE, IT WAS ON NO ACCOUNT LAWFUL FOR MEN TO PROHIBIT THAT WHICH THE LORD LEFT FREE."

748

WITNESS
(Cont)

"SECONDLY, THAT GOD HAS EXPRESSLY PROVIDED IN HIS WORD THAT LIBERTY SHOULD NOT BE INFRINGED, IS TOO CLEAR TO REQUIRE MUCH PROOF."

"WHEN AN INSTITUTION HAS BEEN TRIED A DOZEN CENTURIES IN ALL PARTS OF THE WORLD, AND HAS UNIFORMLY BEEN FOUND PRODUCTIVE OF THE SAME EVIL EFFECTS, THERE CANNOT BE A DOUBT WHAT SENTENCE OUGHT TO BE PASSED ON IT. CUT IT DOWN."

"THE APOSTLE PAUL DENOMINATES THAT A DOCTRINE OF DEVILS FORBIDS MARRIAGE."

749

to say about it, "When an institution," he is talking about celibacy, "has been tried a dozen centuries in all parts of the world and has uniformly been found productive of the same evil effects, there cannot be a doubt what sentence ought to be passed on it. Cut it down." Still quoting from the same book, "The Apostle Paul denominates that a doctrine of devils forbids marriage." That is your witness, brother Halbrook. Examine him further if you want to.

Now, let's come to my chart number 4 and go on where he left off in the last speech. How do we know? What bond is discussed in these passages? Do we need a Greek lexicon? Do we need a dictionary? Do we need any help outside the Bible? Incidentally, I do not oppose the use of other books. I just oppose trying to prove what you believe by it. How do we know what is discussed in Romans 7:2-3? Because he talks about a woman that is bound to the law to her husband, not bound to the

HOW DO WE KNOW?
BOND BETWEEN HUSBANDS & WIVES

* WHAT BOND IS DISCUSSED IN ROM. 7:2-3?
 "<u>WOMAN</u> BOUND BY THE LAW TO HER <u>HUSBAND</u>"

* WHAT BOND IS DISCUSSED IN 1 COR. 7:39?
 "<u>WIFE</u> IS BOUND BY LAW AS LONG AS HER <u>HUSBAND</u> LIVETH"

* WHAT BOND IS DISCUSSED IN 1 COR. 7:27?
 "<u>BOUND UNTO A WIFE</u>" "<u>LOOSED FROM A WIFE</u>"

* WHAT BOND IS DISCUSSED IN 1 COR. 7:12-15?
 "IF ANY <u>BROTHER</u> HATH A <u>WIFE</u>"
 "THE <u>WOMAN</u> WHICH HATH A <u>HUSBAND</u>"

4

law, but bound *by* the law to her husband. That is 1 Corinthians 7:39. He is talking about the very same case. He is talking about a wife that is bound by the law as long as her husband liveth. A wife and a husband, woman and husband. What is he talking about in 1 Corinthians 7:27, "Art thou bound unto a wife?" "Art thou loosed from a wife?" He is talking about the husband and wife relationship. What bond is he talking about in 1 Corinthians 7:12-15? I asked my opponent in North Las Vegas. What does the word "bondage" mean? He said "slavery." He did not tell me where he got that answer. He said "slavery." Paul says, "If any brother hath a wife." "The woman which hath a husband." The wife that believeth not, the woman that hath a husband that believeth not. What is discussed there? What bond? Why, it is the bond between husbands and wives.

Let's go to the next chart, number 5. You do not have to be college graduates to understand that. Again, the children can understand that. How do we know? How do we know that the bond, that he is talking about the bond between husbands and wives. All these passages discuss the same bond, that between a husband and a wife. If not under bondage, you are loosed, and those loosed from

> **HOW DO WE KNOW?**
> **BOND BETWEEN HUSBANDS & WIVES**
> (Cont)
> <u>ALL THESE PASSAGES DISCUSS THE SAME BOND</u>:
> THAT BETWEEN A HUSBAND AND A WIFE.
> IF NOT UNDER BONDAGE, YOU ARE LOOSED AND
> THOSE <u>LOOSED FROM A WIFE</u> ARE TOLD:
>
> **"BUT IF THOU MARRY, THOU HAST NOT SINNED."**
> **1 COR. 7:27-28**
>
> GOD SAYS THEY DO NOT SIN - <u>MY OPPONENT SAYS</u>
> <u>THEY DO SIN.</u>
>
> <u>WHOM SHALL WE BELIEVE?</u>
>
> 5

a wife are told, 1 Corinthians 7:27-28, "But if thou marry thou hast not sinned." My opponent says this man sins if he marries. Oh, if he is the one who was guilty of fornication and his wife put him away, *if he marries he sins*. God says he does not! Now I ask you, do you have any trouble deciding who you are going to believe? It is God or brother Halbrook. You cannot accept both. It is one or the other. "If thou marry thou has not sinned." God says he does not sin, my opponent says they do sin. Whom shall we believe?

My next chart please, number 6. A believer married to an unbeliever, it is dealing with it now. In some of these cases or marriages, the believer is pleased to dwell with the unbeliever. In that case, Paul says, "Let him not put her away." In talking to the woman, "Let her not leave him." That means among other things that that marriage is pleasing in the sight of God. It is a legitimate marriage. It is scriptural marriage. They are not just living together. They are not in what he just calls an *adulterous relationship*.

> **BELIEVER MARRIED TO AN UNBELIEVER**
>
> **1 COR. 7:12-16**
>
> 1. IN SOME OF THESE CASES (MARRIAGES)
>   A. THE UNBELIEVER IS PLEASED TO DWELL WITH THE BELIEVER
>   1) "LET HIM NOT PUT HER AWAY"
>   2) "LET HER NOT LEAVE HIM"
>
> *NECESSARILY INFERRED: A BROTHER OR SISTER
> <u>IS UNDER BONDAGE IN SUCH CASES</u> (MARRIAGES)
>
> 6

It is a marriage in the sight of God, necessarily inferred. The Bible teaches by necessary implication, usual word for inference. A brother or sister is under bondage in such cases or marriages. If the unbeliever is pleased to dwell with him or her, then they are not to put him away, they are not to leave.

Let's see the next chart please, number 7. Well, we see the next case is the same context here. How do we know about the believer married to an unbeliever? Well, let's look at the context. In some of these cases or marriages the unbeliever departs—divorces the unbeliever, or the believer. Unbeliever divorces the believer. What did God say? "Let him depart. A brother or sister is not under bondage in such cases." Not under bondage, not under constraint of law or necessity in some matter.

> **HOW DO WE KNOW?**
> **BELIEVER MARRIED TO AN UNBELIEVER**
>
> (Cont)
>
> 2. IN SOME OF THESE CASES (MARRIAGES)
>   A. THE UNBELIEVER DEPARTS (DIVORCES THE BELIEVER)
>   1) LET HIM DEPART
>   2) A BROTHER OR SISTER IS <u>NOT UNDER BONDAGE</u> IN SUCH CASES
>
> *<u>NOT UNDER BONDAGE</u> = NOT UNDER THE CONSTRAINT OF LAW OR NECESSITY IN SOME MATTER.
> NOT BOUND BY THE LAW TO A SPOUSE.
>
> 7

I want to show I am not opposed to using those books; I want to use brother Halbrook's witness. He used a witness over in New Mexico when questioned after a speech there, in reply to what brother Hailey had preached [reference to video tape of opposite views taught by Homer Hailey and Ron Halbrook on divorce and remarriage on March 22 and 31, 1988 at Belen, NM]. He was questioned by a woman and some others and one wanted to know, "Brother Halbrook, what does the word 'bondage' mean in 1 Corinthians 7?" And he said according to Henry Thayer it means slavery. That was his witness. According to Henry Thayer it means slavery. That is absolutely not so. You come right on down that same page, and Henry Thayer will say that is the literal meaning of the word, it literally means slavery. But then he says the metaphorical or figurative meaning of the word in 1 Corinthians 7:15 is "bondage, under constraint of law or necessity in some matter." It does not say a word about slavery. And there is a negative there. And so "not under bondage" means not under constraint of law.

And what has been his whole argument? Why, they are under constraint of law, that is why they cannot remarry. They are under constraint of law. This is not what the Bible says. It says "not under bondage," therefore, not under constraint of law. Bring all the witnesses you want to, but be ready to accept what they say. Alright, "not under bondage," it means "not under constraint of law or necessity in some matter." Not bound by the law to a spouse, not bound by the law to a spouse.

Look at chart number 9 if we have time for it. Not under bondage in such cases. And these are simply a summing up of quotations. These are not history books or encyclopedias, but several different translations of the Bible. And they all contain the expression, "in such cases." Now, if this does not mean in the case where the unbeliever departs they were not bound "in such cases," — or that phrase should not be there — it has absolutely no meaning at all. In such cases, in these cases the believer is not under bondage. In other cases where the unbeliever is pleased to dwell with him, he is under bondage, in those cases. Is that the time?

---

1 COR. 7:15
(Cont)

"NOT UNDER BONDAGE IN SUCH CASES"

NEW KING JAMES VERSION - 47 TRANSLATORS:
"...IS NOT BOUND IN SUCH CASES..."

*POINT: IF, IN THIS CONTEXT, "NOT UNDER BONDAGE" MEANT THE BELIEVER IS NOT AND NEVER WAS BOUND, THE WORDS "IN SUCH CASES" MEAN NOTHING.

*FACT: THE FOREGOING TRANSLATORS AGREE THAT THE WORDS "IN SUCH CASES" BELONG IN THE TEXT.

Rebuttals:
First Evening
Halbrook's Third Affirmative

Brother Freeman, gentlemen moderators, brothers and sisters in Christ, I am thankful to conclude the affirmation tonight and I want to notice the questions that we dealt with.

I gave him the question, *"Is it necessary to have positive authority for all that we preach and practice?"* He says *yes,* but he *produces none* for the guilty, put-away fornicator to marry another.

"Does Matthew 19:9 teach that after God joins two people in marriage, an innocent partner may put away a mate guilty of fornication and marry another?" He said *yes.* So, there is *the unity ground!* Remember that? The ground of unity.

And then, *"Is there any marriage which people can enter under civil law but which they must end in order to be right with God?"* And he said *yes,* Herod. Well, I guess then when John preached to Herod, he had to do *"a marital check"* before he could baptize him. Brother Freeman says you cannot do that. Tell us more about it.

And then, *"Which passages speak of marrying 'another'?"* He still answers like he did in Las Vegas. I want you to notice chart 150-X, please, on that. He still says that all of those passages speak of marrying another. You can read it in Romans 7, read it in Matthew 19:9. Now, you look at the text [1 Cor. 7:15], my friend. We are slaves to Christ, not to men. "But and if the unbelieving depart, let him depart, a brother or sister is not under bondage" (literally, "has not been enslaved," look at

---

**Slaves To Christ, Not To Men
1 Corinthians 7:15, 23**

But if the unbelieving depart, let him depart. A brother or a sister is not under bondage (lit.: *has not been enslaved)* in such cases; but God has called us to peace.

Ye are bought with a price; be not ye the servants (lit.: *slaves)* of men.

150-X

---

your interlinear) "in such cases, but God has called us to peace." And, my friend, you look at the text of that, and if you can find *"marry another"* in there, I will give you the keys to my car tonight, right now! Can you find *"marry another"* in there? If you can see it, you can see something I cannot see.

But when you look at *Matthew 19:9*, let's look at Matthew 19:9, chart 72. Let's see if we can see "marry another." He says it is in *all* of them. Let's see if it is or not. Some of you have your Bible and you can turn right there and read it. Let's see, is it there? *"Marry another,"* yes sir, it is there. And he says, "Oh, it is in 1 Corinthians 7:15." He has got to say that in order to get his doctrine. It reminds me of these people defending instrumental music — they can find an instrument in passages where there is not one within a hundred miles of it.

> **Matthew 19:9**
>
> "And I say unto you, Whosoever shall put away his wife, except it be for fornication, and shall marry another, committeth adultery: and whoso marrieth her which is put away doth commit adultery."
>
> 72

And then on *1 Corinthians 7:10-11*, I asked him, *"What would a Christian do if there is a divorce and a remarriage violating this?"* And then he wants to get into saying, "Well, that makes it into a case of adultery and the other person can put them away." But that does not give you authority for that guilty one to marry another; you still do not have your *"marry another,"* brother Freeman.

Now then, he gave me these questions. *"Is 1 Corinthians 7:12-16 a part of God's marriage law?"* Yes.

"A Christian is not required to stay married to an unbeliever against the unbeliever's wishes." Now, that is true, he would be *unmarried,* as in verse 11.

Then, *"To be loosed is the opposite of being bound."* True. The person in 1 Corinthians 7:27b is loosed, *having never been bound.*

And then, four and five. He has the same question, simply that he made it a person or a believer. I will answer this together. *"The innocent person, or believer, who has been put away without God's approval and against whom adultery has been committed may remarry scripturally."* It is true. The right to remarry does not depend on who gets to the courthouse first. I have with me here tonight the Texas Family Code, 1990 edition. And, brother Freeman, a person could be guilty of fornication, and go in and sue for insupportability, which means no-fault divorce. You can come in and counter sue for adultery and they will not give it to you; they will give it to the other person. Talk to a lawyer about that. My friends, this matter of divorce and remarriage does not depend on who can get to the courthouse first. When there is fornication involved, you have grounds. When there is no fornication involved, you do not have grounds, brother Freeman. Now, that is the truth about it.

Let's look at 59-X. I want you to notice that there is no authority in that passage or any passage to *marry another*. Now, my friend, you look at this case of Herod and Herodias. And here is a case where Herodias had been married to Philip and she marries Herod. "For he had married her, for John said to Herod, It is not lawful for thee to have thy brother's wife." Now, brother Freeman, that means that *they have got to get out of that unscriptural marriage!* And it also means that *God's law over-rules man's law!*

> **Mark 6:17-18**
>
> "For Herod himself had sent forth and laid hold upon John, and bound him in prison for Herodias' sake, his brother Philip's wife: for he had married her. For John had said unto Herod, It is not lawful for thee to have thy brother's wife."
>
> 59 - X

Did you know in this case, listen to me closely, historians will tell you that Herodias walked off and left Philip and then married Herod. Now, according to what you said awhile ago, all Philip had to do was put her away for fornication now, and let her stay in this second marriage. That is the answer you gave awhile ago. How ludicrous. John said, "It is not lawful for thee to have thy brother's wife." I want the audience to see this. He had the situation awhile ago where a woman did like Herodias did. Now, since she is in adultery, why Philip can just say, "I put you away," and she can now *stay* in that state. John did *not* say anything like that! Apparently, you are preaching a *different doctrine* than those who were inspired.

Now then, I want to notice he said he did not remember how we did the questions. And he did not remember who wrote from San Pablo that had the name Jack Freeman and had articles published in the *Gospel Guardian*. Here are the articles, one after another. Here is one, here is another, here is another, here is another [holding up articles in the *Gospel Guardian* dated July 25 and Oct. 24, 1957, and Mar. 3 and Apr. 28, 1960]. Now, he does not remember any of them.

First Evening: Halbrook's Third Affirmative

Yes sir, I will make you copies of them, I surely will. All of them say, *San Pablo, by Jack Freeman. San Pablo, California* — every one of them do. Now, if you could figure out if he has admitted yet whether he wrote those or not, again you are a lot smarter than I am. He just does not remember things. I apologized when you pointed out I had made a mistake.

Now, I want us to notice that on the authority charts he said where we really differ is that brother Halbrook is leading people to hell by teaching Matthew 19:9. Look at chart 72 [text, Matt. 19:9]. Is this why I am going to go to hell? Here is what I am teaching. Here is the text, my friend. And he said, "We differ, I think he is a false teacher, he thinks I am." And so here is how I am sending people to hell: *"Whosoever shall put away his wife, except it be for fornication, and shall marry another, committeth adultery; and whoso marrieth her which is put away doth commit adultery."* And so, now, for teaching that, I will go to hell. There is your doctrine.

And he wanted to know, "Where does it say you have to leave your mate to go to heaven?" *Mark 6:17-18 said it.* You admitted it said it in the case of Herod. Yes, you did, do not shake your head "no" [which Freeman was doing]. You said they *could not stay* in that marriage. Now, the tapes will show that.

Alright, and then I want us to notice number 13. And he said I had not called for all his charts. It is not my obligation to call for all his charts; he is supposed to be calling for mine. I am in the *affirmative* tonight, and in debating, the affirmative is *followed* by the negative.

When God Is Specific

CLASS	SPECIFIC	EXCLUDE
Woods	Gopher Wood (Gen. 6:14)	All Other Woods
Tribes	Levi (Heb. 7:14)	All Other Tribes
Action - Water	Immerse (Acts 2:38; 8:38)	All Other Actions
Music	Sing (Eph. 5:19)	All Other Music
Divorced People	Innocent Put Away Guilty & Remarry (Matt. 19:9)	All Other Divorced Persons

13

Now, his comment here was that he agrees down here about divorced people, that the innocent mate could put away the guilty one and remarry. Okay now, brother Freeman, stay with me. He agrees to that. Now then, I am debating a man on instrumental music, and he agrees that it specified *singing*. The effect is that all other music is excluded and he cannot have the instrument. Now, you agree that the innocent who puts away the guilty can remarry. The effect is that all other divorced persons are *excluded*. See it?

See it, friend? *He agrees that out of the class of divorced people, God specified this.* When God specified gopher wood, it excluded all others. When God specified this, and he agrees God specified it, all others are *excluded*. Thank you, brother Freeman. Thank you.

Alright, and then he talked about when at Belen, New Mexico, I gave *Thayer,* and gave first the basic definition; and if you look at the rest of the tape, I explained 1 Corinthians 7:15 in detail. Many of you have seen that tape and know that to be the case. I do not know what he hopes to gain by references like that.

Then he referred to McClintock and Strong, his charts 747 and 749; you do not have to put them up on the screen, I agree with them. These historians pointed out those who teach celibacy, the doctrine of celibacy, forbidding men to ever be married, create great evils.

Notice my chart 316. Now, my friend, do we forbid to marry? No indeed! *Everyone has a right to marry and a responsibility to obey God's marriage law.* But now, watch it: God's law forbids divorce without cause of fornication and marriage to another again, and again, and again, and again. God's law forbids that. But, will *you* forbid it? And if you forbid it, would it be *celibacy?* God's law forbids a man to commit adultery. Listen friend: Be divorced, marry another, commit adultery; be divorced, marry another, again and again and again and again. That is what we are forbidding, brother Freeman. No sir, we do not forbid men the privilege to marry, but with the right to marry comes what? Responsibility to obey God's marriage law!

Do We Forbid "To Marry"?

1. **NO! Everyone has a right to marry and a responsibility to obey God's marriage law (Gen. 2:24; Matt. 19:9; 1 Cor. 7:2).**

2. **God's law forbids divorce without cause of fornication and marriage to another again and again and again (Matt. 19:9).**

3. **God's law forbids a man to commit adultery, be divorced, marry another and do it all over again and again and again (Matt. 19:9).**

316

Now, my friend, notice chart 108. The issue between us is simply this: In the beginning God said, "If you eat, you will surely die." Satan said, "If you eat, you will not surely die." "Believe and *baptized*—shall be saved." "Believe and *not baptized*—shall be saved." Now, the Lord said, "Whoso marrieth her which is put away *doth commit adultery.*" And Satan is teaching, "Whoso marrieth her which is put away *doth not commit adultery.*" See the difference? If you eat, you die, God said. Whoever marries her which is put away commits adultery, God said. But Satan said, if you eat you shall *not* surely die; and whoever marries her which is put away doth *not* commit adultery. And so that is the issue between us.

And if we want our children to have happy, secure marriages, we are going to have to teach them the limits and the constraints and the restraints of God's divine law for the salvation of their souls and for the good of their homes. Thank you.

God -vs- Satan

1. If you eat, "surely die" (Gen. 2:17)
2. Believe & "Baptized shall be saved" (Mk. 16:16)
3. "Whoso marrieth her which is put away doth commit adultery" (Matt. 5:32; 19:9)

1. If you eat, "NOT surely die" (Gen. 3:4)
2. Believe and NOT baptized shall be saved
3. Whoso marrieth her which is put away doth NOT commit adultery

108

Rebuttals:
First Evening
Freeman's Third Negative

I would like to see his chart number 150-X [page 68]. In the last ten minute speech I want to deal with as much of this as I can. Slaves to Christ, not to men, 1 Corinthians 7:15, 23. It is true in the latter verse, Paul does talk about physical slavery. That is not true in 1 Corinthians 7:15. His own witness says it is not. We will show that in just a moment. "If the unbelieving depart, let him depart, a brother or sister is not under bondage" — literally, has not been enslaved — "in such cases."

Let's look at my chart now, charts 11 and 12. This is his witness, his witness. He said in Belen, New Mexico, this Greek word found in 1 Corinthians 7:15, *bondage,* literally means "to make a slave of, reduce." That is what Thayer says, "reduce to bondage." Literally, it means to make a slave of, reduce to bond-

THAYER
PG. 158

DOULOO - prop.(LITERALLY) - TO MAKE SLAVE OF, REDUCE TO BONDAGE. <u>ACTS 7:6</u>
METAPH. (FIGURATIVELY) - TO BE UNDER BONDAGE HELD BY CONSTRAINT OF LAW OR NECESSITY IN SOME MATTER. <u>1 COR. 7:15</u>

WHAT IS THE MATTER UNDER CONSIDERATION IN 1 COR. 7:15? THE DEPARTURE (DIVORCE) FROM THE BELIEVER BY THE UNBELIEVING SPOUSE...
<u>THE MARRIAGE BOND</u>.
THUS, WHEN THE UNBELIEVING SPOUSE DIVORCES THE BELIEVER, THE BELIEVER <u>IS NOT</u> HELD BY CONSTRAINT OF LAW OR OF NECESSITY IN SOME MATTER.

11

age. It gives the expression where the Israelites were slaves to Egypt, as in Acts 7:6. Then he says it has a metaphorical or figurative meaning, "to be under bondage, held by constraint of law or necessity in some matter," and Mr. Thayer puts 1 Corinthians 7:15 right there. I did not. I did not put it there. Now, if you are going to use one of these — incidentally, do not try to consult these to prove anything, I am not using it for that. If it cannot be proved with the Bible, it cannot be proved. But you introduced a witness, this is his witness that he introduced over there. And when they asked him what that word "bondage" means, he said it means slavery. I asked in North Las Vegas, what does it mean, he said, slavery. It means that. What does Mr. Thayer say it means in 1 Corinthians 7:15? It means "to be under bondage, held by constraint of law or necessity in some matter." But "not under bondage," we are dealing with a negative, and so you are not under bondage. You are not held by constraint of law or necessity in some matter. And

> **THAYER**
> (Cont)
>
> PG. 158
>
> *THE BELIEVER, IN SUCH CASES, NO LONGER HAS A WIFE/HUSBAND AND IS THEREFORE FREE TO MARRY... 1 COR. 7:27-28
>
> *LITERAL SLAVERY IS DISCUSSED BY THAYER UNDER THE GREEK WORD "DOULOS" AND MR. THAYER TELLS US THAT THIS WORD USED IN 1 COR. 7:21 (SERVANT) AND THIS WORD ALSO HAS A FIGURATIVE MEANING 1 COR. 7:22 "SERVANT OF CHRIST".
>
> 12

he said all the time this fornicator does not have a husband, does not have a wife, they cannot marry because they are still bound by the law, under constraint of law. His own witness says, "not under constraint of law or necessity in some matter."

So what is the matter under consideration? It is not slavery. The matter under consideration is the unbeliever divorcing the believer. That is when God says no longer under bondage. That is what I said the Bible teaches in that passage, that the believer has a right to marry. I did not say it says it. You have said a lot of things that this verse says it or teaches it. I agree sometimes a verse teaches things that it never says in so many words.

Let's have chart number 59-X [text of Mk. 6:17-18]. What about Herod? I asked him the question, notice he did not answer it. My question was, "Was not Herod allowed by God to have his own wife?" He did not touch it. I did not say that John the Baptist or God or anyone else allowed Herod to have his brother's wife. John said, "It is not lawful for thee to have her." John did not say, "It is not lawful for thee to have a wife." Now, let's get the record straight. I asked you, now you have no more opportunity to answer tonight but answer it sometime during the debate, *was it lawful for Herod to have a wife?* Was it or not?

Let's go to another chart. I want to refer again to these articles in San Pablo. I do not know what it has to do with this debate. Those articles had nothing to do with the subject of marriage, divorce, or remarriage. I can only tell you, everyone I know who was in that area at the time, and whoever has known me, has never known me to write an article for the *Gospel Guardian* or any other paper, except the one I edited myself for six years. If I did, why he agrees it is fine writing, he agrees with what was written. So what are we haggling about? He said what was written was the truth. And it had nothing to do with divorce and remarriage. It had to do with institutionalism which was dividing the church in those days, as the marriage and divorce question is now.

He says you get over there in Mark 6:17-18, "Why, Freeman will not touch it." I did, I said Herod had a right to his own wife; he had no right to his brother's wife.

Alright, let's have this chart now, but first, I want to refer to something else he said over here on chart 13 where he used the word "sing." And then he said divorced people — you said something about the word "sing." If there was a verse in there that gave us the authority to "play," it would not contradict "sing." It would just be another revelation from God, and so we could sing *and* play. But there is none, is there? But in Matthew 19:9, there is *one cause* for divorce given, and remarriage, in Romans 7:2-3, *another* cause for remarriage, not divorce, another cause

When God Is Specific

CLASS	SPECIFIC	EXCLUDE
Woods	Gopher Wood (Gen. 6:14)	All Other Woods
Tribes	Levi (Heb. 7:14)	All Other Tribes
Action - Water	Immerse (Acts 2:38; 8:38)	All Other Actions
Music	Sing (Eph. 5:19)	All Other Music
Divorced People	Innocent Put Away Guilty & Remarry (Matt. 19:9)	All Other Divorced Persons

13

for remarriage is given — death. That does not contradict. You know, if I say it, it contradicts another verse; if he says it, fine. If he gets it out of some secular book, it is fine. But if I find a passage that he thinks disagrees with his, then it has got to be a contradiction. No, God did not contradict himself. You put all the passages together, and you add everything that God said on this subject.

Well, you have seen it clearly. We saw it in North Las Vegas four nights; you will see it here for four nights. Everything he says hinges around and hangs upon Matthew 19:9. I have already shown that here is a case in 1 Corinthians 7:12-15 that Jesus did not deal with. He said Jesus did not deal with it. But God dealt with it through Paul. It had to do with divorced people, had to do with divorced people. *So here is the divorced person that can remarry that Jesus did not personally say anything about.* But he taught it through the Apostle Paul nonetheless. You know, this is the gospel of Christ.

Now, let's go on with these charts that I have selected. Chart number 15, "God versus Halbrook." You know, since we have stepped aside from the gospel, we have got to come up with a new plan of salvation. I ask you to read it. If you can find it, you read it to me. God says, "Repent and be baptized every one of you in the name of Jesus Christ for the remission of sins" (Acts 2:38). Brother Halbrook says that there are some aliens that must *repent, put away their spouse,* be baptized, and remain single the rest of your life. Book, chapter and verse? Acts 2:38 is the one I believe. Book, chapter, and verse — he cannot give it. He asks me: book, chapter, and verse? I give it. Book, chapter and verse —

GOD VS. HALBROOK

GOD TO:	HALBROOK TO:
ALL ALIENS "REPENT, AND BE BAPTIZED EVERY ONE OF YOU IN THE NAME OF JESUS CHRIST FOR THE REMISSION OF SINS..." SCRIPTURE: ACTS 2:38	**SOME ALIENS** "REPENT, PUT AWAY YOUR SPOUSE, BE BAPTIZED AND REMAIN SINGLE THE REST OF YOUR LIFE". SCRIPTURE: _____
SINFUL MEMBERS OF THE CHURCH "REPENT AND PRAY..." ACTS 8:22 CONFESS OUR SINS" 1 JNO. 1:9	**SOME SINFUL MEMBERS OF THE CHURCH** "REPENT, PUT AWAY YOUR SPOUSE, REMAIN UNMARRIED THE REST OF YOUR LIFE". SCRIPTURE: _____
"GOD IS FAITHFUL AND JUST TO FORGIVE US OUR SINS, AND TO CLEANSE US FROM ALL UNRIGHTEOUSNESS" 1 JNO. 1:9	"REPENT, REMAINED UNMARRIED THE REST OF YOUR LIFE". SCRIPTURE: _____

15

and I want you to give it to me if you have it. Where did any of the Apostles ever tell this: "You have to get rid of that wife and remain single to be saved?"

Sinful member of the church, what must they do? Acts 8:22, repent and pray. 1 John 1:9, confess our sins. Also, 1 John 1:9, God is faithful to forgive us. But brother Halbrook says that some sinful members of the church, not all, but *some* must put away their spouse and remain unmarried the rest of their life. Scripture? He says that others must remain unmarried the rest of their life. Scripture? You will find that woefully lacking throughout this debate. Oh, I know how tough it is to change your mind. Someone said to me, "That is all I have ever heard, that is the way I was raised." That has nothing to do with it. Can you give book, chapter and verse? You know, if you are out here teaching an alien, you will give book, chapter, and verse, "Repent and be baptized"; "believe and be baptized"; "arise and be baptized"; "repent and be converted." You give him book, chapter, and verse. But then, you begin to teach him Halbrook's doctrine on marriage, divorce, and remarriage. And he says, "I want book, chapter, and verse, Mister." I want book, chapter, and verse. Can you find it? No, you will not find it.

Let's go on to my next chart, chart number 16. Mark 16, Matthew 28, Colossians 1:6, 23. Jesus sent the Apostles to preach the gospel to all the world; Paul affirmed in these verses that had been done. Heard by every creature under heaven. Not one person was told to leave a husband or wife. Not one person was told to remain single for life. People were saved, they were added to the church, they had the hope of eternal life. *Who needs Halbrook's doctrine?* And that is the doctrine that it is. Also the doctrine of devils, 1 Timothy 4:1-3. Now, look at this, you cannot miss this, it is too simple. You cannot miss it: Not one person was told to leave husband or wife, not one person was told to remain single for life. People were saved, added to the church, and had the hope of eternal life. Now, go back and try to bring Herod into this. Herod lived back there under a different law. But if he lived after the gospel came, he has to put his wife away. And he did not have his own wife to leave, he had another man's wife. We are talking about a man that has a wife, not about the wife of someone else. People were saved and added to the church and had the hope of eternal life without Halbrook's doctrine.

Let's see the next chart please, chart 21. We find a contrast between God and Halbrook. God says in 1 Corinthians 7 it is not good for man to be alone. Halbrook says it does not matter what God says, some are going to have to be alone. See the difference between those two statements? "It is not good for man to be alone." Halbrook says some will have to be alone. God says, 1 Corinthians 7, "It is better to marry than to burn." My opponent says some will have to burn anyway. God says, Hebrews 13:4, "Marriage is honorable." Halbrook says some cannot do that which is honorable. They are going to have to do penance the rest of their life; God will never forgive them. God says, 1 Corinthians 7:2, to avoid fornication, marry. My opponent says some cannot use this means of avoiding fornication. God says, 1 Corinthians 7:28-29, "If loosed, you do not sin when you marry." My opponent says, some who are loosed do sin when they marry. Now, who is right? Both cannot be, you have God or brother Halbrook.

Let's have the next chart, please, chart number 1. God anticipated false doctrine, 1 Timothy 4:1-3. "Some shall depart from the faith." When they depart from the faith, what will they teach? Among other things, they will forbid us to marry. Which of us is forbidding marriage now? He says, "Freeman forbids

---

MK. 16:15 - MATT. 28:19-20 - COL. 1:6, 23

GOSPEL PREACHED TO EVERY CREATURE - ALL NATIONS

*NOT ONE PERSON WAS TOLD TO LEAVE HUSBAND OR WIFE.

*NOT ONE PERSON WAS TOLD TO REMAIN SINGLE FOR LIFE.

*BUT PEOPLE WERE SAVED - ADDED TO THE CHURCH AND HAD HOPE OF ETERNAL LIFE.

WHO NEEDS HALBROOK'S DOCTRINE?

16

A CONTRAST:

GOD	HALBROOK
IT IS NOT GOOD FOR MAN TO BE ALONE	SOME WILL HAVE TO BE ALONE
IT IS BETTER TO MARRY THAN TO BURN	SOME WILL HAVE TO BURN
MARRIAGE IS HONORABLE	SOME CANNOT DO THAT WHICH IS HONORABLE
TO AVOID FORNICATION, MARRY	SOME CANNOT USE THIS MEANS TO AVOID FORNICATION
IF LOOSED, YOU DO NOT SIN WHEN YOU MARRY	SOME WHO ARE LOOSED DO SIN WHEN THEY REMARRY

WHO IS RIGHT?

21

> **HOW DO WE KNOW?**
> **GOD ANTICIPATED FALSE DOCTRINE**
>
> 1 TIM. 4:1-3
> "...**SOME SHALL DEPART FROM THE FAITH**
> **GIVING HEED TO SEDUCING SPIRITS**
> **AND DOCTRINES OF DEVILS, FORBIDDING TO**
> **MARRY**..."
>
> WHO IS DEMANDING CELIBACY?
> WHO IS FORBIDDING TO MARRY?
>
> **DO YOU WANT THE DOCTRINES OF DEVILS**
> OR
> **THE FAITH ???**

Herod to marry." Oh, no I did not, John did not either. He had the right to marry. But he did not have the right to take another man's wife. That is not what I am contending for. But, if you are unmarried in the sight of God, you have the right to your own wife. Do not go out and try to get another man's wife. Find someone who is not the wife of another. Get your own wife. Do not ask me to help you out, I am not a good match-maker either. But you have the right to have a wife.

Second Evening
Halbrook's First Affirmative

[Proposition: The Scriptures teach that two people joined by God in marriage are bound for life, the only exception being that an innocent partner may put away a mate guilty of fornication and remarry.]

Brother Freeman, brethren moderators, ladies and gentlemen, I am thankful for the opportunity to stand before you in the affirmative tonight.

"The Scriptures teach," sixty-six books of the Bible, Old and New Testaments. Jesus said, "Have ye not read," Old Testament Scripture, "and I say unto you," New Testament revelation. *"Two people bound by God in marriage are bound for life."* They must "leave," and "cleave," and become "one flesh." What God joined, "let not man put asunder." *"The only exception being that an innocent partner may put away a mate guilty of fornication and remarry."* Jesus said, "Whosoever shall put away his wife, except it be for fornication, and shall marry another, committeth adultery."

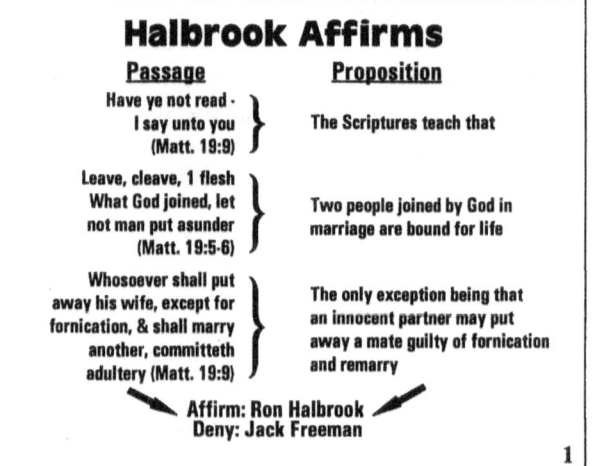

So we affirm tonight the principle and proposition of this passage. And my opponent, of course, is denying it.

We want to notice these questions:

1. Which passages speak of marrying another, i.e. a subsequent mate? (A) Romans 7:2-3, (B) Matthew 19:9, (C) 1 Corinthians 7:15.

2. When did the call to peace occur in 1 Corinthians 7:15? (A) When the believer obeyed the gospel, (B) When the unbeliever departed.

3. In the case of Mark 6:17-18, would the marriage of Herod and Herodias be lawful if Philip would say he put her away? (A) Yes, (B) No.

4. On January 16, 1990, you said that a Christian who violates 1 Corinthians

Second Evening: Halbrook's First Affirmative 81

7:10-11 by divorcing his mate and marrying another *cannot continue* in the marriage. But on January 18, 1990 you said he *can continue* in the marriage. What will you say now? (A) Can continue, (B) Cannot continue.

On chart number 146, I want to document what I just said. "If a Christian violates 1 Corinthians 7:10-11 by divorcing his mate and marrying another, when he repents, what must he do?" That was my chart number 141, and then brother Freeman answered, *"He has no right to wife number two."* No right to her, cannot be married to her. Alright, then we asked him later, "If an erring Christian in a second marriage following a divorce not for fornication desires to be acceptable to God," — *"he,"* brother Freeman answered, *"may continue in the marriage."* So, up here, he said "no right" to the marriage — cannot live in the marriage — cannot abide in the marriage — cannot maintain the relationship. But down here, "May continue in the marriage" — maintain the relationship. Now, *which* is it? What will he say tonight?

1 Cor. 7:10-11
Contradictions of Error

1. If a Christian violates 1 Cor. 7:10-11 by divorcing his mate and marrying another, when he repents, what must he do? (My chart #141)

    FREEMAN: "He has no right to wife #2" (16 Jan. 1990)

2. If an erring Christian in a second marriage following a divorce not for fornication desires to be acceptable to God, he:

    FREEMAN: "May continue in the marriage" (18 Jan. 1990, answer to my question 4)

146

5. When Paul told slaves not to be "the servants of men," did he mean they were free from their slave relationships? (A) Yes, (B) No.

And so we look forward to his dealing with those questions tonight.

Now then, we want to notice my chart 13. We studied the principle of Bible authority. And we saw that when there is a

When God Is Specific

CLASS	SPECIFIC	EXCLUDE
Woods	Gopher Wood (Gen. 6:14)	All Other Woods
Tribes	Levi (Heb. 7:14)	All Other Tribes
Action - Water	Immerse (Acts 2:38; 8:38)	All Other Actions
Music	Sing (Eph. 5:19)	All Other Music
Divorced People	Innocent Put Away Guilty & Remarry (Matt. 19:9)	All Other Divorced Persons

13

class of things, and God *specifies one* out of that class, it *excludes all others*. When God said, "Build an ark of gopher wood," that excluded all other woods. When God said that we are to sing, out of the class of music, then all other music is excluded.

Out of the class of divorced people, Jesus specified the innocent can put away the guilty and marry another. My opponent called for this chart and he agreed with that point — had no dispute with that point. Then, my friend, even though he does not want to admit it, he has admitted it: *All other divorced persons are excluded*. The only possible escape is if he can find another clear passage that affirms *someone else* — a guilty party — can marry another. He cannot find *the deserted party* can marry another (1 Cor. 7:15). He will try to do that. He will make a feeble attempt at it. And you will see this debate will close without him ever finding "marry another" in 1 Corinthians 7:15. He will not find it for the guilty party — he cannot find it anywhere. But he agrees the innocent can put away the guilty party and marry another. Now, brother Freeman, all other divorced persons are *excluded*. That is the principle of Bible authority.

And notice my chart number 54. "How Do We Know?" "Yes, Jesus loves me, the Bible tells me so." *We know we can marry another if our mate dies, Romans 7:2-3*. Now give us my chart 59-B, which is Romans 7. I want to show you how we know. Now notice this, "If, while her husband liveth, she be married to another man, she shall be called an adulteress: but if her husband be dead, she is free from that law; so that she is no adulteress, though she be" — *though she be what?* — "though she be married" — *married to whom?* — "married to another man." That is what he cannot find in 1 Corinthians 7:15. But you can find it in Romans 7:2-3. I can find it, he can find it, children can find it, all can find it. That is how we know!

Now, how do we know again? Alright, if your mate is guilty — *if you put away your mate for fornication, Matthew 19:9*. Are we certain, are we sure about it? Let's look at my next chart on that. Here is the text, my chart 72 [text, Matt.

How We Know

Simplicity Of Truth: "Yes, Jesus loves me, the Bible tells me so" (Rom. 4:3; Eph. 3:4)

Know We Can Remarry:
1. If mate dies (Rom. 7:2-3)
2. If put away mate for fornication (Matt. 19:9)

Where Does The Bible Authorize These To Remarry:
1. The put-away fornicator?
2. Those unscripturally divorced?

54

19:9]. "I say unto you, Whosoever shall put away his wife, except it be for fornication, and shall"—*and shall, and shall what?*—"marry"—*marry whom?*—"marry another, committeth adultery: and whoso marrieth her which is put away doth commit adultery." If you put her away for fornication, you marry another without committing adultery. We all can see it, we all know it, children can see it, brother Freeman can see it, *because the text says "marry another."* That is how we know, friend. Isn't that simple? The power of the word of God. That is how we know *immersion.* That is how we know *singing.* See it? That is how we know *the Lord's Supper on the first day of the week.* How do we know? The Bible tells me so.

> **Romans 7:2-3**
>
> "For the woman which hath an husband is bound by the law to her husband so long as he liveth; but if the husband be dead, she is loosed from the law of her husband. So then if, while her husband liveth, she be married to another man, she shall be called an adulteress: but if her husband be dead, she is free from that law; so that she is no adulteress, though she be married to another man."
>
> 59 - B

Where does the Bible authorize the put-away fornicator to marry another? Let him put the text on the chart and flash it up here and show you just as I have shown you what the word of God says. I beg you to do it, brother Freeman. I plead for you to do it, brother Freeman. *And those unscripturally divorced — where are they authorized to marry another?* The more I listen to him, the more I realize he has a way to explain how *every* unscripturally divorced person can ultimately *stay* in the marriage. Say "hocus-pocus," say you "repent," and do not get out of it. Or somebody says [to a former mate now in a new marriage], "I put you *away*" [the idea being that such action releases the former mate to stay in the new marriage]. He will move the checkers around on the board until *every last one of them can stay in that marriage.* Now, I charge that is your position, and if it is not, you deny it. But the more I listen to you, the more I realize that *is* your position.

Now then, we notice my chart 74. Remember, "except it be for fornication" — *if and only if.* Just like Matthew 18:3, except ye become as a little child, you cannot enter the kingdom. Now, "except" in that case works with the word "not." And the *effect* is, if you become as a little child, *if and only if* you become as a little child, you can enter the kingdom. He tried to make it say you cannot enter the kingdom. My friend, the *force* of "except" is "if and only if." That is the force of it.

John 3:2, "No man can do these miracles…, except God be with him." Alright, that means if God is with him, *if and only if* God is with him, he can do the miracles. John 3:5, "born of water and the Spirit." Now, it said, "except" you are born of water and the Spirit, you cannot enter the kingdom. You see that word *"except"* working with the

> **Except = If & Only If!**
>
> * Matt. 18:3 Become as little child → Enter kingdom
> * John 3:2 God with Him → Do miracles
> * John 3:5 Born of water & Spirit → Enter kingdom
> * Matt. 19:9 Put away wife for fornication & marry another → Not adultery
>
> 74

"not"? Now then, if you are born of the water and of the Spirit, *the "not" goes away,* doesn't it, brother Freeman? And you enter the kingdom.

And he tried to talk about it and explain it, and the more he talked, the more he got covered up and stuck in the tar baby! I never heard such a bowl of mush in my life. And I know the audience felt that way. I am not saying that to be unkind or ugly in any sense. But people could not understand for their life what you were talking about.

The Bible is simple, my friend. You can understand it and put your finger on the passage. *If you put away your mate for fornication and marry another, you do not commit adultery.* Now, that is the force of the passage, and if I cannot help him to see it, maybe my eighteen year old son can help him to see it. Look at my chart 74-A. My son suggested this one last night. "Except it be for fornication." Like "except it miss the hoop." Now watch it: "Whoever shoots a basketball, except it misses the hoop, scores two points." The *force* of the exception is: *If and only if* your shot

misses the hoop, you do *not* get two points. *"If and only if you put your wife away for fornication,* and marry another, you do *not* commit adultery." He may not be able to understand it, but every young child here tonight can understand that. That is the force of the exception.

If the children cannot teach him, we will turn him over to the women. One of the women gave me this one, "Except you make an 'A' on the test, you cannot go to the party." That means, *"If and only if you make an 'A' on the test, you can go to the party."* Everybody here understands that but brother Freeman.

My Lord made it plain and simple. Go back to my chart number 72 [text, Matt. 19:9] again and see the text. You can understand it, I can understand it, brother Freeman may not ever understand it, but we *must* understand it if we save our soul. "Whosoever shall put away his wife, except it be for fornication, and shall marry another, committeth adultery." The *effect* of that is, *"If you put your mate away for fornication,* and marry another, you do *not* commit adultery." We can understand that, brother Freeman, whether you can or not. And then you have the second independent clause, "Whosoever marrieth her which is put away doth commit adultery." And my friend, that will stand when the world is on fire. That is the truth about it. The Lord gave it in language that is so plain even a child and a woman can understand it. No, I am not making fun of the women. *I am wondering why brother Freeman cannot understand it.* That is the point.

Now then, notice my chart 15. We have pointed out this principle of truth. I am thankful to God that brother Jack Freeman has taught it in the past. *Things not authorized in the doctrine of Christ are sinful. If you have no passage of Scripture, you have no right to act.* Now then, my friend, if you have no clear passage to authorize the put-away fornicator or deserted believer to marry another, then it is *sinful* to act in that realm or teach in that realm, and such marriages are *sinful.* I introduced that chart in Las Vegas to show we have common ground, a common principle, and we must work to understand it and properly apply it. And his response was that

---

Not Authorized = Sinful

1. Things "not authorized within the doctrine of Christ are not only non-essential but sinful as well."
2. An author defended sponsoring church but had "no passage of Scripture to show that such a plan is authorized by the Lord" (Jack Freeman, <u>Gospel Guardian</u>, 28 April 1960, pp. 8-9).
3. No clear passage authorizes put-away fornicator or deserted believer to marry another.
4. Conclusion: such marriages are sinful!

15

he had never had such awful *lies* told on him in all of his life. He emphatically said I had lied on him. And he has not withdrawn that charge or corrected that false accusation yet. Now, if I lied, *he still does not have the clear passage that authorizes the put-away fornicator to marry another* — still does not have it.

But, my friend, we have the facts from the editor of the *Gospel Guardian*, facts from the San Pablo church where he lived when he wrote it, facts from the other Jack Freeman. And notice my chart 16-A. I want you to see, brother Freeman, here are articles that you had in the *Gospel Guardian* during those years. There they are. And I am going to offer you copies of them tonight in the hope that it might not only *refresh your memory* but that it might even *prick your conscience*. I am going to offer those to you when you come up here tonight. I want you to see them and see your name, and I want you to see "Jack Freeman, San Pablo, California" on

Gospel Guardian Articles by Jack Freeman
"WITHOUT FACILITIES, TRAINING, AND ADEQUATE FINANCIAL MEANS" Jack Freeman, San Pablo, California 25 July 1957 *Gospel Guardian*
"ARE YE NOW MADE PERFECT BY THE FLESH?" Jack Freeman, San Pablo, California 24 Oct. 1957 *Gospel Guardian*
"NOT CONFORMED -- BUT TRANSFORMED" Jack Freeman, San Pablo, California 3 Mar. 1960 *Gospel Guardian*
"NECESSARY THINGS" Jack Freeman, San Pablo, California 28 Apr. 1960 *Gospel Guardian*

16-A

there. Yes sir, that is what it says. And it is high time that you just acknowledged this, repented of it, confessed it, and put it behind us, and cleared the record of our debates of the ugly, uncalled-for charge that I am a liar. *Help us to focus on the principles and the passages that we need to be studying*.

He tried to make a little "out" that, well, he might have had it in some paper and they *[Gospel Guardian]* picked it up. Well, if they did, then who *wrote* it? You wrote it! That is the only point I was making. And when brother Tant [editor of *Gospel Guardian*] did that, he ordinarily put where he got it when he borrowed it. There is an example of that out of the same years that your article appeared. But he does not give a credit line [in connection with the Freeman articles]. But, so what if the credit line is there or not there, the issue is — *did you write it? Yes, you wrote it*.

The principle is true, the principle is right [the principle of Bible authority taught in Freeman's articles]. Why in the world is it necessary to call me a liar to deal with it? *Now according to his doctrine*, I am wondering, *if he truly repents, will he inform the brethren at Las Vegas?* Will you, brother Freeman, will you go back home where you called me a liar in front of all those people and tell them that you are sorry that you said that? Will you look at me right now and nod that you will? I ask you, I plead that you will do it. I apologized in front of those people *twice* because you asked for it. Will you apologize to them even *once?* No indication.

Now, my friend, *does repentance include works meet for repentance?* Listen to me tonight. You say, "Why did Ron bring this up again?" Listen to me. *According to his doctrine, people in all sorts of unscriptural marriages can somehow work it out to say they "repent," but stay in those marriages.* A doctrine of repentance which does not require works meet for repentance in cases of unscriptural marriage would not require such works in case of false accusations either, brother Freeman.

I turn your attention to 1 Corinthians 7, hoping that he will clear that up and clear the record of the charge of lying so that we can go forward. We are going to study from 1 Corinthians 7. He will make every possible attempt to find the put-away fornicator marrying another in 1 Corinthians 7. You are the audience; you be the judge whether he finds it or not.

I notice my chart 122. Now, brethren in Corinth asked about several cases, but *the put-away fornicator is not in the chapter*. They did not ask about it. Notice in 1 Corinthian 7:1, you can open your Bible and follow because we will stay in this chapter. And you will notice Paul says, *"Now concerning the things whereof ye wrote unto me."* They wrote to him about several things and that is the principle that guides you in studying the rest of the chapter. And *there is not one single question in the chapter about the put-away fornicator*.

You have "the unmarried" in verse 8, referring to those never married. It does not refer to previously married people who are unscripturally divorced and the put-away fornicator. And I know that to be the case, brother Freeman, because Paul adds one case of the previously married. When he wanted to indicate the previously married, he did

---

Put-Away Fornicator Not In 1 Cor. 7

1. Brethren asked about several cases, but not that one (vs. 1).
2. "Unmarried" in vs. 8 refers to those never married.
   a. Not refer to previously married (unscriptural divorce; put-away fornicator).
   b. Adds one case of previously married: "widows."
3. "Unmarried" in vs. 11 unscripturally divorced & not free to marry another - same in vs. 15.
4. "Loosed" or free man in vs. 27 is counterpart to virgin in vs. 28 (i.e. never married).
5. "Unmarried woman" in vs. 34 is "virgin."

122

it, and he said *"widows."* And if he wanted to indicate the *previously married, put-away fornicator,* he would have said that. "The unmarried" there are those *never married.*

In verse 11, *the "unmarried"* (unscripturally divorced in that case) are not free to marry another, just like verse 15. You have *the "loosed" or the free man* in verse 27, the counterpart to the "virgin" in verse 28. We will look at that. She was never married. You have *"the unmarried woman"* in verse 34, "a virgin." So every time you have an unmarried person, the context makes it clear what Paul is talking about, and never ever is it the put-away fornicator.

Now chart 122-A. Does 1 Corinthians 7 authorize the put-away fornicator to marry another? The text says (you have got your Bible open, now look at the text), "Let every man have his own wife." It is not this, brother Freeman, "Every man who wrecks his marriage, and throws away his own wife." You see, I believe every man can have his *own wife.* [Freeman looked up and grinned at this point.] The issue is when a man throws away his own wife, brother Freeman. Grinning won't answer it. The issue is throwing away your own wife by fornication or unscriptural divorce. "Go get *another* wife." He is going to try to make you think that is what that verse says; you watch him.

Does 1 Cor. 7 Authorize
The Put-Away Fornicator To Marry Another?

Text Says This:	Not This:
Vs. 2 "Every man have his own wife"	Every man who wrecks his marriage & throws away his own wife by fornication or unscriptural divorce, gets another wife!
Vs. 9 "Unmarried...widows... better to marry than to burn"	Unscripturally divorced & put-away fornicator... better to commit adultery than fornication!
Vv. 27-28 A man "loosed from a wife" (free, never married) and "a virgin" (free, never married) may marry.	A man unscripturally divorced or a divorced fornicator may marry a woman in the same condition!

122 - A

Now notice verse 9. Paul said to *the widows,* "It is better to marry than to burn." It does not say, "Unscripturally divorced and put-away fornicator, it is better for you to commit adultery than fornication. Get in this unscriptural marriage — no positive divine authority for it — but you better go ahead and marry anyhow." "It is better to marry than to burn." Freeman is taking it out of the context.

Verses 27-28, *a man "loosed from a wife" (free, never married),* and *"a virgin" (free, never married),* they may marry. But Freeman will try to convince you *a man unscripturally divorced or a divorced fornicator may marry a woman in the same condition* (also unscripturally divorced or else a divorced fornicator). And they [those teaching Freeman's doctrine] can move the checkers around until they can get it right for him to stay in it. Now, he is going to try to prove that in 1 Corinthians 7:27 and he cannot do it.

Now notice, going back to chart 121 now. You have a *universal provision, conditional enjoyment* in verse 2. *"Every man have his own wife."* What does it mean? It is a provision for all within the terms and conditions set by God. These marriages are authorized: (1) *those never married,* we all agree; (2) *the mate is dead,* we all agree; (3) *innocent mate can put away the fornicator and marry another,* we all agree. Why can we all agree? The Bible tells me so.

These marriages are unauthorized and division comes when men will try to defend such: a put-away person (whether for fornication or other cause) would marry another. And my friend, "Every man have his own wife," you remember that. It is not, "Every man throw away his own wife and go marry another." It is not there, brother Freeman. And we are going to help the audience understand that. "Jesus tasted death for every man": universal provision, conditional enjoyment. The provision is for all, yes, but within the terms and conditions set by God. Those terms: hear, believe, repent, confess, and be baptized. Unauthorized offer of salvation: faith only, pray through, Holy Ghost baptism, and so on. So, you remember *universal provision, conditional enjoyment.*

See my chart 125. Now, brother Freeman explains 1 Corinthians 7:2 when he says, "It is lawful for every man to have his own wife, that is, in accord with the gospel." Well, what does he mean? *Any* and *every* marriage is in accord with the gospel? Just like when Herod married Herodias, is that the kind of thing included in this? Or does he mean — I hope he means, I think he means — that every marriage which is in accord with the gospel is acceptable to God. And if that is what he means, then verse 2 is a *universal provision* with a *conditional application,* and we can agree and understand that. Limited, not unlimited, only those in accord with the gospel. Tell us if that is what you meant, and we hope

---

1 Corinthians 7:2
Universal Provision BUT Conditional Enjoyment

1. "Every man have his own wife" - Provision for all within the terms & conditions set by God!
   a. Authorized Marriages: Never married; Mate dead; Innocent mate put away fornicator.
   b. Unauthorized Marriages: A put-away person (whether for fornication or other cause) marry another.

2. Jesus tasted "death for every man" (Heb. 2:9) - Provision for all within the terms & conditions set by God!
   a. Authorized Salvation: Hear, believe, repent, confess, be baptized.
   b. Unauthorized Salvation: Faith only; Pray through; Holy Ghost baptism; Sprinkle infants; Etc.

121

that it is more common ground there.

Next, my chart 126. Now notice 1 Corinthians 7:2, "Nevertheless, to avoid fornication, let every man have his own wife, and let every woman have her own husband." Here is the consequence of brother Freeman's position. Now, don't do like you did at Las Vegas and say

> **Freeman Explains 1 Cor. 7:2**
>
> "It is lawful for every man to have his own wife, that is, in accord with the gospel. It's not talking about civil law, it's talking about God's law. It is lawful, permissible by God." (Marriage Sermons, Fall 1988, #6)
>
> **What Does He Mean?**
>
> 1. Any & every marriage is "in accord with the gospel" -OR-
> 2. That every marriage which is "in accord with the gospel" is acceptable to God.
>
> If the latter, then vs. 2 is a universal provision with a conditional application or enjoyment!
>
> 125

that I said you embrace the consequence. I did not say it then and I am not saying it now. But this is the consequence whether you can see where it leads or not: "Let every man have as many wives as he wants and every woman have several husbands." Or, "Let each man have someone else's wife and every woman have someone else's husband, and we will move the checkers around and it will all come out." He does not mean for it to end up there, but you watch and see if it does not end up there. And

> **1 Corinthians 7:2**
>
> "Nevertheless, to avoid fornication, let every man have his own wife, and let every woman have her own husband."
>
> **Consequence Of Freeman Position**
>
> "Let each man have as many wives as he wants, and let every woman have several husbands."
>
> or
>
> "Let each man have someone else's wife, and let every woman have someone else's husband."
>
> *Who Will You Believe?*
>
> 126

you will have to make the choice on what you believe tonight.

And then we notice my chart 129. Let's apply 1 Corinthians 7:2 to Mark 6:17-18. "Every man have his own wife,...every woman have her own husband." Now that would be Philip has Herodias. But it is *not this* — Herodias has Herod. God's law would not join them. It is not lawful for him to have her. *Could we take "every man have his own wife" and try to get Herod and Herodias in that?* And if we could not, then you remember 1 Corinthians 7:2 is not universal in its *application*. It is universal in the *provision*, but there are *limitations* as to

Second Evening: Halbrook's First Affirmative

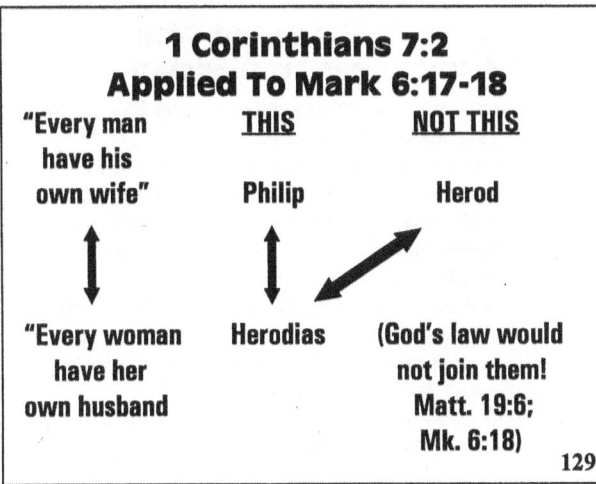

the application of it.

Alright, let's notice then my chart 130. My opponent makes it absolute. He disregards the context, other passages, and other factors. What about these passages that say every spirit who confesses Jesus is "of God," or who believes in Jesus is "born of God"? "Every one that loveth is born of God." Hitler loved Eva Braun. Was he born of God? Is that thing unlimited or not? Let him tell us, and if he says *limited*, then you will remember 1 Corinthians 7:2 is limited like that too.

Now my chart 135. Notice verse 9. We are dropping down to verse 9, and it does not have or give a universal application either. Now verse 9, *"But if they cannot contain, let them marry: for it is better to marry than to burn."* Now, watch the context, look at verse 8, it is *those never married, or widows*. It is *not discussing other cases*.

1 Cor. 7:2 "Every Man"

Opponent makes it absolute - disregards context, other passages & other factors.

How about this:

1. "Every spirit that confesseth that Jesus Christ is come in the flesh is of God" (1 John 4:2).
2. "Whosoever shall confess that Jesus is the Son of God, God dwelleth in Him" (1 John 4:15).
3. "Whosoever believeth that Jesus is the Christ is born of God" (1 John 5:1).
4. "Every one that loveth is born of God, and knoweth God" (1 John 4:7).

And he can agree with me it is not discussing other cases to this extent, for he commented on verses 10 and 11, "It would be unlawful for her to marry someone else at that time." Do you see that? "Unlawful to marry someone else." Suppose she wanted to appeal to verse 9. Brother Freeman would block her and say, *"No, it is unlawful for you to marry."* So that is not included, is it? Well, friend, neither is *the wife divorced for serving Christ* authorized to marry another. She is not included in that. That is not the context. *The wife divorced for fornication* is not authorized to marry another. *The wife divorced for other causes* is not authorized to marry another.

We notice then my chart 136. Notice my opponent's position on 1 Corinthians 7:1-2 and verse 9 results in this *consequence*—results in this *consequence*. You can tell whether you embrace it or not, but I am not saying you embrace it. I am telling you this is *the consequence* if this thing is *unlimited:* *"Any man burning with passion always has a right to take a wife."* If that is true, then all these can marry another: the put-away fornicator, and the man whose wife is in an asylum, or his wife is an invalid. Then he is burning with passion, so let him marry another. You see, *"marry another"* is *not* the context here.

> **1 Cor. 7:9 Does Not Give A Universal Application**
> 1. Context: Those never married or widowed (vs. 8)
> 2. Simply not discussing other cases:
>   a. Freeman on divorced wife of vv. 10-11, "It would be unlawful for her to marry someone else at that time. The law is that she is to remain unmarried. It would not be permitted for her to marry." (Marriage Sermons, Fall 1988, #6)
>   b. Wife divorced for serving Christ not authorized to marry another (vs. 15)
>   c. Wife divorced for fornication not authorized to marry another (Matt. 5:32; 19:9)
>   d. Wife divorced for other causes not authorized to marry another (Matt. 5:32; 19:9)
>
> 135

> **Opponents Position On 1 Cor. 7:1-2, 9:**
> **Any Man Burning With Passion Always Has A Right To Take A Wife**
>
> If true, then all of these can marry another:
>
> 1. Put-away fornicator
> 2. Person put away for other cause
> 3. Person who put away mate for other cause
> 4. Man - Wife held indefinitely in foreign country
> 5. Man - Wife serving life sentence
> 6. Man - Wife in asylum (Insane, T.B., Leprosy)
> 7. Man - Wife has AIDS
> 8. Man - Wife an invalid (Disease, accident, etc.)
>
> 136

Alright, now, we notice my chart 138. Jumbling these passages together uses a text out of context. You know, he said something about a Judas in the audience out in Las Vegas — I would not want to be in the position of a Judas like this. Somebody tries to read the Bible and reads, "Judas went out and hanged himself." The next verse they read, "Go thou and do likewise." And the next verse, "What thou doest, do quickly." That is the way you are jumbling up 1 Corinthians 7, brother Freeman.

Now then, we notice my chart 139. He is trying to make an argument from 1 Corinthians 6:9-11 on those washed, sanctified, and justified from adultery

> **OPPONENT HANGS HIMSELF**
> *Uses Text Out of Context*
>
> 1. Judas "Went And Hanged Himself" (Matt. 27:5)
> 2. "Go Thou And Do Likewise" (Luke 10:37)
> 3. "What Thou Doest, Do Quickly" (John 13:27)
>
> 138

and fornication, that you have fornicators and adulterers there that could include divorced fornicators. And this is his bridge from that to 1 Corinthians 7:2, "Let every man have his own wife," applied this way: *"Let the divorced fornicator marry another."* Now, there is your argument, there is your bridge, but it is falling down. My friend, here are your divorced fornicators in chapter 6, so what about in 9:22? "I am made all things to all men." "I marry, fornicate and divorce that I may save divorced fornicators." Is that it? It is addressed to them. Tell us about it.

Now, notice 1 Corinthians 7:10-11 next. Here is the text. "And unto the married I command, yet not I, but the Lord, Let not the wife depart from her husband: But and if she depart, let her remain unmarried, or be reconciled to her husband: and let not the husband put away his wife." That is what the Bible says. Now notice chart 140. This passage versus brother Freeman on all unmarried can marry. He said if he is unmarried, then he has God's permission to marry *again,* but the scripture says, "But and if she depart, let her remain unmarried, or be reconciled to her husband." Now, let him explain it to us.

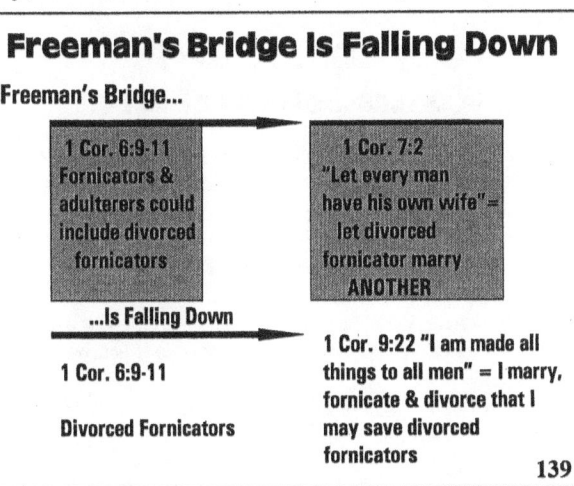

And then chart 146. Now, notice the contradiction that he is in. If a Christian violates 1 Corinthians 7:10-11 by divorcing his mate and marrying another, when he *repents,* what must he do? *"He has no right to wife number two,"*

Freeman said. And I say, amen and amen, and I hear all of these brethren saying amen with me. Now, if an erring Christian in a second marriage (following a divorce not for fornication) desires to be acceptable to God, that is the very thing you have up there. Then he answered, *"May continue in the marriage."* Continue in it or *get out of it?*

> **1 Cor. 7:10-11 -VS- Freeman On All Unmarried Can Marry**
>
> **Freeman says:**
>
> "If he is unmarried, then he has God's permission to marry again." (Freeman, June 1988 tape)
>
> -VS-
>
> **Scripture says:**
>
> "But and if she depart, let her remain unmarried, or be reconciled to her husband."
>
> **Who Will You Believe?**
>
> 140

Which is it, brother Freeman? We want you to tell us. Which is it?

Now then, I want us to notice my chart 54. We are going to resume in our next speech taking up 1 Corinthians 7:15. It is his duty to call for these charts and answer these passages and these principles tonight. We will see if he does it. And we are going to study verses 15 and 27 in my next speech. I want you to notice chart 54. How do we know? The simplicity of divine truth. The Bible tells me so. If your mate dies, if you put away your mate for fornication — the Bible tells me so. *Where does it say the put-away fornicator can marry another?* It is not there.

> **1 Cor. 7:10-11 Contradictions of Error**
>
> 1. If a Christian violates 1 Cor. 7:10-11 by divorcing his mate and marrying another, when he repents, what must he do? (My chart #141)
>
>   FREEMAN: "He has no right to wife #2" (16 Jan. 1990)
>
> 2. If an erring Christian in a second marriage following a divorce not for fornication desires to be acceptable to God, he:
>
>   FREEMAN: "May continue in the marriage" (18 Jan. 1990, answer to my question 4)
>
> 146

And then chart 122-A. Remember that we read in Romans 7, *marry another,* if your mate dies. We read it in Matthew 19, *marry another,* if you put one away for fornication. Now you remember tonight, *1 Corinthians 7 did not authorize the put-away fornicator to marry another.* You remember when he talks about verse 2, it does not say every man who wrecks his marriage and throws away *his own* wife by fornication can get *another* wife. It will not be there. "Unmarried"

> **How We Know**
>
> Simplicity Of Truth: "Yes, Jesus loves me, the Bible tells me so" (Rom. 4:3; Eph. 3:4)
>
> **Know We Can Remarry:**
> 1. If mate dies (Rom. 7:2-3)
> 2. If put away mate for fornication (Matt. 19:9)
>
> **Where Does The Bible Authorize These To Remarry:**
> 1. The put-away fornicator?
> 2. Those unscripturally divorced?
>
> 54

and "widows" — "it is better to marry than to burn." It does not say the put-away fornicator had better get into an adulterous relationship rather than commit fornication.

The man and the woman in verses 27-28 were *never married*. It is not saying that the divorced fornicator could marry a woman that is a divorced fornicator — that is not the context, brother Freeman.

Thank you for your good listening.

> **Does 1 Cor. 7 Authorize**
> The Put-Away Fornicator To Marry Another?
>
> | Text Says This: | Not This: |
> |---|---|
> | Vs. 2 "Every man have his own wife" | Every man who wrecks his marriage & throws away his own wife by fornication or unscriptural divorce, gets another wife! |
> | Vs. 9 "Unmarried...widows... better to marry than to burn" | Unscripturally divorced & put-away fornicator... better to commit adultery than fornication! |
> | Vv. 27-28 A man "loosed from a wife" (free, never married) and "a virgin" (free, never married) may marry. | A man unscripturally divorced or a divorced fornicator may marry a woman in the same condition! |
>
> 122 - A

Second Evening
Freeman's First Negative

Brethren, moderators, brother Halbrook, it is my pleasure again to stand in defense of the gospel of Christ. I realize that what I am setting forth is new to many of you, perhaps to most. What brother Halbrook set forth in Nevada was without doubt new to a lot of people there. Because we have never heard it, does not mean it is so. Because it is new to us, does not mean it is new to God.

Brother Hafley made a point in his speech before the debate began tonight that it was not Ron's duty to reply to the arguments made by the negative. We both agreed, Ron and I, and signed an agreement which was published in the *Guardian of Truth* that we would include in our first proposition a discussion of 1 Corinthians 7:12-16, and it is being included. I did so last night and brother Halbrook has done so tonight. And it was my right to include it. Even though it is a general proposition and I am in the negative, I have the right to include it just as much as he has the right to include it. When he signed it, he gave me the right to include it. When I signed it, I gave him the right to include it.

I want to see brother Halbrook's chart on the proposition. If you will look at the proposition carefully, I want you to notice, "Whosoever shall put away his wife, except it be for fornication, and shall marry another, committeth adultery," Matthew 19:9. Look on the right hand side: "the only exception being that an innocent partner may put away a mate guilty of fornication and remarry." Look back at Matthew 19:9. Do you see the word "only" there? Do you see anything about "only" there? I do not.

I want to call your attention to something else. I would like for you to turn in your New Testaments and read Matthew 5:42. "Give to him that asketh thee, and from him that would borrow of thee turn not thou away." This is a commandment given by Jesus. "Give to him that asketh thee, and

Halbrook Affirms

Passage	Proposition
Have ye not read - I say unto you (Matt. 19:9)	The Scriptures teach that
Leave, cleave, 1 flesh What God joined, let not man put asunder (Matt. 19:5-6)	Two people joined by God in marriage are bound for life
Whosoever shall put away his wife, except for fornication, & shall marry another, committeth adultery (Matt. 19:9)	The only exception being that an innocent partner may put away a mate guilty of fornication and remarry

Affirm: Ron Halbrook
Deny: Jack Freeman

Second Evening: Freeman's First Negative

from him that would borrow of thee turn not thou away." Now we have another commandment, just as forceful even though written by the Apostle Paul. He was guided by the Holy Spirit. 2 Thessalonians 3:10, "If any would not work, neither should he eat." They seem like opposites but they are not. One does not contradict the other. One says, "If he asks, give." The other says, "If he would not work, neither should he eat." There is no contradiction between these. When you read Matthew 19:9, there only becomes a contradiction between that and 1 Corinthians 7:15 when you insert a word that is not there, *and that is the word "only."*

I would like at this time to read the questions that I have presented to brother Halbrook:

1. If a man divorces his wife for any cause other than adultery, and then commits adultery, can she scripturally remarry?

2. When a husband obtains a civil divorce from his wife for any cause other than adultery, are the two still married in God's sight?

3. In Matthew 5:32 and Matthew 19:9, adultery means to have unlawful intercourse with someone else's wife. True or false?

4. If a wife refuses sex with her husband, can she scripturally divorce him when he commits adultery?

5. Does God demand that the innocent human being, one not guilty of adultery, suffer because of the sins of the guilty party, one who obtains a divorce for the cause of adultery?

Now, the questions that he presented to me and my answers:

1. *"Which passages speak of marrying 'another' (a subsequent mate)?* (A) Romans 7:2-3, (B) Matthew 19:9, (C) 1 Corinthians 7:15."

All of them, as I answered last night. 1 Corinthians 7:15 gives a person a right to marry by saying he is not under bondage, which means he is not under constraint of law. And I pointed out to his own authority, the one that he used in New Mexico to answer Homer Hailey. He quoted from Henry Thayer. And Henry Thayer says the word "bondage" there does not mean "slavery," it means "not under constraint of law." What law is he talking about? The law that bound husband and wife together. "Not under constraint of law or necessity in some matter." And the matter under consideration is marriage. While you might not find the exact words there, my opponent has inferred several things from other passages that he cannot read directly there; the teaching is there.

2. *"When did the call to peace occur in 1 Corinthians 7:15?"*

Well, does he mean peace with God? It occurred *when he obeyed the gospel.* If he means peace with his marriage partner, that peace occurred *when the marriage took place.* He is also called to peace with God and remained in peace with God even though the marriage breaks up, when the husband and wife depart. So there man is to be at peace with God at all times, at peace with his mate when he is married. At peace with all men, Paul said, "as much as lieth within you."

3. *"In the case of Mark 6:17-18, would the marriage of Herod and Herodias be lawful if Philip would say he put her away?"*

I have never seen what Herod and Herodias have to do with our debate. And I have pointed out from time to time, and my opponent agrees with me, that Herod and Herodias were not married in the first place. Now here is the difficulty we have in understanding the debate: We use the word "marriage," we use the term "divorce," sometime we talk about the "courthouse marriage," the "courthouse divorce." Brother Halbrook agrees with me that Herod and Herodias were not married in God's sight even though the Bible says he married her. Legally, civilly, yes, but *not in the sight of God*. And I think all of you who hold brother Halbrook's position will agree with that. In the sight of God these two were not married. That is why Herod could not have her, it was his brother's wife. It was against the law to have his brother's wife. But the law did not say he could not have *his own wife*. Now that is the point that I have tried to get before this audience and before my opponent. The law did not say he could not have his own wife.

4. *"On January 16, 1990, you said a Christian who violates 1 Corinthians 7:10-11 by divorcing his mate and marrying another* CANNOT CONTINUE *in the marriage. On January 18, 1990 you said he* CAN CONTINUE *in the marriage. What will you say now?"*

I say this: At the point of divorce he is *still married to the first wife*. I think we agree there. In the sight of God — still married to the first wife. Even though it may have the word "depart" there, it means "divorce." But he is still married in the sight of God. *When he remarries he commits adultery.* This gives the mate the right to divorce him on grounds of adultery. Now, you think that is difficult to understand? Brother Halbrook agrees with me on 1 Corinthians 7:12-16, that when the unbeliever departs from the believer, they are still married even though they have obtained a divorce. But if that unbeliever becomes guilty of adultery, that gives the believer the right to obtain a scriptural divorce. The unbeliever obtained a civil divorce. That does not prohibit the Christian from getting a scriptural divorce.

5. *"When Paul told slaves not to be the servants of men (1 Corinthians 7:23), did he mean they were free from their slave relationship?"*

Second Evening: Freeman's First Negative 99

Well, he points out in verse 21 that servants of men can be made free. But our proposition does not have to do with slavery. There were those who were born slaves who had purchased their freedom; others, their master had turned them loose. That is not the point of our discussion. Our discussion has to do with marriage, divorce, and remarriage.

I would like to see his chart number 13. This is where he deals with all other divorced persons. And he says, "God is specific." And God is specific here in Matthew 19:9. That does not mean He cannot be just as specific in another verse that does not contradict Matthew 19:9, even when it allows someone else to remarry. *Jesus did not put the word "only" in Matthew 19:9 — my opponent does.* Think about that. Who put the word "only" in Matthew 19:9? My opponent did. He even wrote it in his proposition, *"only."* We saw his proposition again just a moment ago. Matthew 19:9 has to do with one particular group of people. But there are other people talked about in other passages, such as 1 Corinthians 7:12-15.

When God Is Specific

CLASS	SPECIFIC	EXCLUDE
Woods	Gopher Wood (Gen. 6:14)	All Other Woods
Tribes	Levi (Heb. 7:14)	All Other Tribes
Action - Water	Immerse (Acts 2:38; 8:38)	All Other Actions
Music	Sing (Eph. 5:19)	All Other Music
Divorced People	Innocent Put Away Guilty & Remarry (Matt. 19:9)	All Other Divorced Persons

13

Chart number 74. He comes to the *"if and only if"* again. And I admire his son for drawing the illustration that we will notice in a moment. But it still does not help him any. You know, to get by with *Matthew 18:3* and use "if and only if," and to get by with *John 3:5*, he has to take a "not" out of each verse. But to use it in *Matthew 19:9*, he has

Except = If & Only If!

* Matt. 18:3 Become as little child → Enter kingdom
* John 3:2 God with Him → Do miracles
* John 3:5 Born of water & Spirit → Enter kingdom
* Matt. 19:9 Put away wife for fornication & marry another → Not adultery

74

to put a "not" in the verse. He takes it out of two or three and puts it into the other one. You have to put a "not" in one and take it out of the others. Why? Now that is not so if "if and only if" are synonyms for the word "except." And so, "if and only if you become as a little child you *cannot* enter the kingdom." That is what the passage says if "if and only if" means the same as "except." If "if and only if" means the same as "except" in John 3:2, it is saying, "If God was with you, you could *not* do the miracles that you are doing." In John 3:5, "You have to be born of water and of the Spirit to enter the kingdom," would mean exactly the opposite; "if and only if you are born of water and of the Spirit you *cannot* enter the kingdom." And, "if and only if a man puts away his wife for fornication, and marries another, he is guilty of *adultery."* The one who divorces on grounds of fornication is guilty of adultery. My opponent does not believe it; I do not believe it. I do not think anyone in this audience believes it. Well, when you begin to play around with the Scriptures you get yourself in trouble, and so you have got to take words out and put words in — you cannot leave it like it is.

Let's see the chart 74-A. Now let us talk about the shot through the hoop. Now let us just think about this a moment. Let us say, *"Except* the shot goes through the hoop, you do not get two points. *If and only if* your shot goes through the hoop, you *do not* get two points." Exactly the opposite of what you would be saying. We know that the basketball player wants the shot to go through the hoop so he would get two points. But if you put "if and only if" there — "if and only if it goes through the hoop you do not get two points."

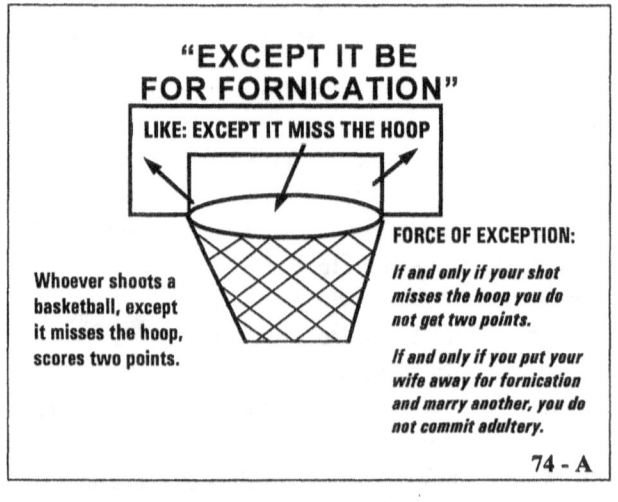

Let us go to chart number 122. When he deals with these charts, most of them are dealing with *the put-away fornicator,* and that is what we are going to be dealing with Thursday and Friday nights. That is all we will be dealing with as long as I am speaking. But most of his speeches thus far in this debate have had to do with the put-away fornicator. That is our subject for Thursday and Friday night. I am glad to see that he did get to 1 Corinthians 7 some tonight.

> **Put-Away Fornicator Not In 1 Cor. 7**
>
> 1. Brethren asked about several cases, but not that one (vs. 1).
> 2. "Unmarried" in vs. 8 refers to those never married.
>   a. Not refer to previously married (unscriptural divorce; put-away fornicator).
>   b. Adds one case of previously married: "widows."
> 3. "Unmarried" in vs. 11 unscripturally divorced & not free to marry another - same in vs. 15.
> 4. "Loosed" or free man in vs. 27 is counterpart to virgin in vs. 28 (i.e. never married).
> 5. "Unmarried woman" in vs. 34 is "virgin."
>
> 122

The articles from the *Gospel Guardian*, as I have pointed out, he agreed with them. They were not false teaching. He made some assumptions from them. Do as you please with them. God will judge us all for it. I explained those articles the best I could last night. And they have nothing to do with the subject of marriage, divorce, and remarriage. It had to do with the institutional question by which the church was being divided at that time, according to the articles that I have looked at.

Let us look at chart number 122. Okay, let us look at chart number 122 *again*. I want to notice a point here. I want you to notice number three. "'Unmarried' in verse 11 unscripturally divorced and not free to marry another — the same as in verse 15." But, if you begin in verse 10 Paul is dealing with the same thing that Jesus taught. And beginning in verse 12 he is dealing with something else that Jesus did not teach. And my opponent has admitted that Jesus did not deal with the case of the believer married to an unbeliever, but Jesus did deal with the case discussed in 1 Corinthians 7:10-11. Read Mark 10:11-12 and Luke 16:18. You will see Jesus is dealing with the very same thing. He does not deal with the case where the believer is married to an unbeliever. And so this has nothing to do with it.

Let us look at number 122-A in a moment, but go back there. You think about this chart 122, point three, these people are still married. And he says that they are still married in God's sight even if the one gets a divorce on unscriptural grounds. They are still married in the sight of God. But even if it is adultery, he brings in Matthew 19 as it applies. Well and good.

Chart 122-A [next page]. Now when you think about this, Ron believes every man can have his own wife, he believes every woman can have her own husband. Now, I ask him, does the put-away fornicator have a wife? He said, "No, he has no wife." That is the person, I am affirming, who has the right to a wife. Where he has never married, or has no wife because his wife died, or because his wife put him away because of the sin of fornication, *when he has no wife, he has a God-given right for a wife.* God has never given any of us the right to have our brother's wife, another man's wife. But He has given each man, each woman, the right to have a wife, or the woman the right to have a husband. That is the right that God has given us.

Does 1 Cor. 7 Authorize The Put-Away Fornicator To Marry Another?	
Text Says This:	**Not This:**
Vs. 2 "Every man have his own wife"	Every man who wrecks his marriage & throws away his own wife by fornication or unscriptural divorce, gets another wife!
Vs. 9 "Unmarried...widows... better to marry than to burn"	Unscripturally divorced & put-away fornicator... better to commit adultery than fornication!
Vv. 27-28 A man "loosed from a wife" (free, never married) and "a virgin" (free, never married) may marry.	A man unscripturally divorced or a divorced fornicator may marry a woman in the same condition!

122 - A

And brother Halbrook with one side of his mouth says, "Yes, I believe that man has a right to have a wife, but not all men, you see, not all men have the right to have their wife." *He admits that every man actually can have his own wife.* Then he turns around and says, "No, here are some that cannot — here are some that cannot have their own wives." And among other things he says, "There is the put-away fornicator." Why not? Because brother Halbrook says so. But does that fornicator have a wife? "No," he says. He is unmarried. "Yes," he says, "he is unmarried." Why can't he have a wife? Because brother Halbrook says so. God does not say so. God said to that man, "To avoid fornication, let every man have his own wife." And to that wife who has no husband, "To avoid fornication, let every woman have her own husband," 1 Corinthians 7:2.

And he admitted that 1 Corinthians 6:9-11 discusses fornicators and adulterers. And 1 Corinthians 7 is still speaking to the same people. These are the same people that back in Acts 18:8 were washed, sanctified, and justified when they were baptized, *putting the passages together*. And those people who had been fornicators and adulterers, they were not added to the church like that, they were cleansed from all sin. They were added to the church as saved people. Now they were not fornicators and adulterers, but they had been. And to these who had been fornicators, Paul said, "Let every man have his own wife;" he is speaking to the same people. He has not switched horses; he is writing to the same church; he is talking to the same people.

So Halbrook takes away Herod's right to have *his own* wife. I do not mind anyone saying that Herod had no right to his brother's wife. That is what John the Baptist said to him: "You have no right to her; it is not lawful for you to have her." But I cannot admire my opponent when he tries to take away Herod's right to have a wife. God did not say, "You cannot have a wife." John the Baptist did not say to Herod, "You cannot have *your own* wife." He said, "You cannot have your brother's wife," or words to that effect, "It is not lawful for you to have your brother's wife." That is a long way from saying, "It's not lawful for you to have *your own* wife."

Chart number 139. Now, he did call for 1 Corinthians 6:9-11. He referred to that. Fornicators and adulterers could include divorced persons. I guess he admits that. 1 Corinthians 7:2, writing to these very same people, "Let every man have his own wife." *That equals up to a divorced fornicator marrying*. And whether he is a divorced fornicator or not, if he marries at some point, it necessarily involves another, someone else. "Well," he says, "Freeman's bridge is falling down." It was not my bridge, I did not build it. Over in 1 Corinthians 6:9-11, if you have the divorced fornicators, then over here *you said,* "Paul is made a fornicator." That does not follow. "I am made all things to all men." It does not follow that Paul became a sinner. That has nothing to do with our subject. If there is any bridge God built it. And you do not need a bridge to cross over when you have the word of God, "Let every man have his own wife." Now, you bring that put-away fornicator to God, and he says to God, "I want to know how I can avoid fornication," and God says, "To avoid fornication, you get your own wife." My opponent says, "You cannot have her, you cannot have her." Now, who is right?

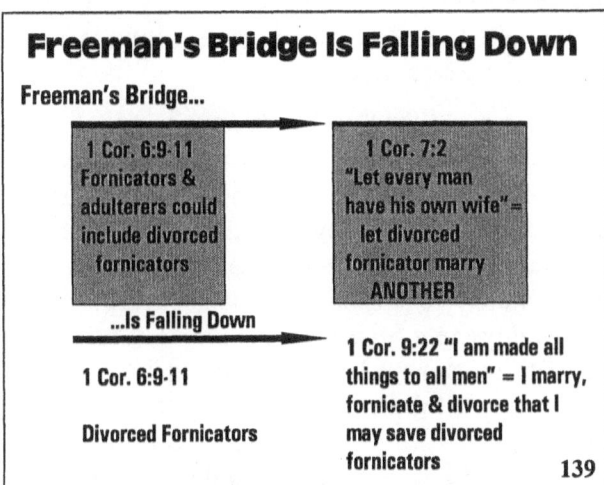

Let us turn now to chart number 140. His chart number 140. "1 Corinthians 7:10-11 versus Freeman on all unmarried can marry." Freeman says, "If he is unmarried then he has God's permission to marry again." *Yes, if he is unmarried.* "But and if she depart, let her remain unmarried, or be reconciled to her husband." Well, think about this again, here the breakdown is, and I think brother Halbrook is aware of it. When He says, "Let her remain unmarried," God recognizes that she is still married to the man from whom she departed. She is still married to him. In God's sight the marriage still stands; and so *she is to remain unmarried.* That is, do not go marry someone else because you are still married to this one. And if he disagrees with that let him say so. But if, on the other hand, her husband commits *adultery,* she has *scriptural grounds for divorce.* Now, if you say, "Adultery has to come first and divorce second," there it is. They are still married. But if he commits adultery, becomes unfaithful, she has the right to obtain a divorce in God's sight. Now, they become unmarried in God's sight and both are *single* in God's sight. And *God said to single people, unmarried people,* "Let every man have his own wife, and let every woman have her own husband."

Now, I realize that it is difficult to follow this because we do not always remember (I do not, Ron does not) to say we are talking about a *civil* marriage. Courthouse records do not mean anything. You cannot go down to the courthouse to prove how many people in this audience are married. But God knows how many of us are married. And God knows how many of us do not have husbands and wives. God is aware of that.

I want to see my chart number 1. Of course, brother Halbrook did not like this chart. I did not expect him to. "How do we know?" Well, God anticipated false doctrine. How do you know which is false doctrine tonight?

---

1 Cor. 7:10-11 -VS- Freeman On All Unmarried Can Marry

Freeman says:

"If he is unmarried, then he has God's permission to marry again." (Freeman, June 1988 tape)

-VS-

Scripture says:

"But and if she depart, let her remain unmarried, or be reconciled to her husband."

Who Will You Believe?

140

HOW DO WE KNOW?
GOD ANTICIPATED FALSE DOCTRINE

1 TIM. 4:1-3
"...SOME SHALL DEPART FROM THE FAITH GIVING HEED TO SEDUCING SPIRITS AND DOCTRINES OF DEVILS, FORBIDDING TO MARRY..."

WHO IS DEMANDING CELIBACY?
WHO IS FORBIDDING TO MARRY?

DO YOU WANT THE DOCTRINES OF DEVILS
OR
THE FAITH ???

1

Second Evening: Freeman's First Negative

"Now the Spirit speaketh expressly, that in the latter times some shall depart from the faith, giving heed to seducing spirits, and doctrines of devils; Speaking lies in hypocrisy; having their conscience seared with a hot iron; Forbidding to marry, and commanding to abstain from meats." Well, you have "the faith" which does not forbid marriage according to this passage. You have the doctrine of devils which does forbid marriage according to this passage. *God never forbade marriage.* Now, he forbade adultery, people living together when they were not married. But he did not forbid marriage. "Marriage is honourable in all," Hebrews 13:4. God found no fault with marriage. Now, he might find fault with what some men call marriage. But when God recognizes that a marriage does exist, God does not find fault with that as a marriage; it does exist. He might find fault with how a husband and wife treat one another, but the marriage itself is considered by God to be honorable. Why? It is a marriage in His sight.

Chart number 2. Jesus taught while he was on earth, Mark 10:11-12, Luke 16:18, and also 1 Corinthians 7:10-11. None of these give any cause for divorce or any cause for remarriage. Just read them. No cause for divorce and no cause for remarriage found. And *if the Bible stopped there,* if that was the law on marriage, today there would be absolutely no cause, *not one,* none, no cause for divorce and no cause for remarriage. But, Jesus continued to teach: Matthew 19:9, Matthew 5:32, one cause for divorce and one cause for remarriage — fornication or adultery — one scriptural way to put asunder a husband or wife. Now there is no contradiction, no contradiction there at all, you just have more of the law added. All of these passages are part of the marriage law.

**JESUS TAUGHT
(WHILE ON EARTH)**

NO SCRIPTURAL WAY TO PUT ASUNDER HUSBAND AND WIFE

NO CAUSE FOR DIVORCE — — — MK. 10:11-12, LK. 16:18
NO CAUSE FOR REMARRIAGE — — 1 COR. 7:10-11

ONE SCRIPTURAL WAY TO PUT ASUNDER HUSBAND AND WIFE

ONE CAUSE FOR DIVORCE — — — MATT. 19:9
ONE CAUSE FOR REMARRIAGE — — MATT. 5:32

2

Let us have my next chart, number 3. Other New Testament teaching on the same subject. Jesus said in John 14:26, "The Holy Spirit will remind you of all things that I have taught you." "I have other things to say unto you now, you are not yet able to bear them" (John 16:12). "But when He, the Spirit of Truth is come He will guide you into all truth" (John 16:13). And so Paul gives a second cause for remarriage, Romans 7:2-3 and 1 Corinthians 7:39. I did not say a second cause for *divorce*, but a second cause for *remarriage*, the death of a spouse. Jesus never said one word about it. But that is not a contradiction of Matthew 19 or Mark 10:11-12, Luke 16:18; it is not a contradiction. It is just as much a revelation from God as any of these other passages — *a second cause for remarriage*, and my opponent admits this is a second cause. And it is not a contradiction, he admits that. *It is scriptural for a man to die*, not to commit suicide, but a man to die of old age, sickness, disease. We all will some day. We need to keep that in mind.

> **OTHER NEW TESTAMENT TEACHING ON THE SAME SUBJECT.**
>
> (JNO. 14:26, JNO. 16:12-13)
>
> **SECOND CAUSE FOR REMARRIAGE (DEATH)**
> ROM. 7:2-3, 1 COR. 7:39
> A SCRIPTURAL WAY TO PUT ASUNDER HUSBAND AND WIFE.
>
> IS IT SCRIPTURAL TO DIE?
>
> **THIRD CAUSE FOR REMARRIAGE** 1 COR. 7:12-15
> BELIEVER DIVORCED BY UNBELIEVER.
> TO THE REST SPEAK I, NOT THE LORD.
>
> 3

Well, in 1 Corinthians 7:12-15, God gives a *third cause* for remarriage. What is it? When the believer is divorced by the unbeliever. "To the rest, speak I, not the Lord." How do we know? God said, "But if the unbelieving depart, let him depart. A brother or a sister is not under bondage in such cases."

> **HOW DO WE KNOW?**
> GOD'S LAW PERTAINING TO DIVORCE & REMARRIAGE
>
> | | WHAT PART OF THE LAW APPLIES TO: |
> |---|---|
> | MATT. 5:32 | A CHRISTIAN MARRIED TO AN ALIEN? 1 COR. 7:12-15 |
> | MATT. 19:9 | "TO THE REST SPEAK I, NOT THE LORD" |
> | MK. 10:11-12 LUKE 16:18 | "IF ANY BROTHER HATH A WIFE THAT BELIEVETH NOT..." |
> | ROM. 7:2-3 1 COR. 7 | "THE WOMAN WHICH HATH AN HUSBAND THAT BELIEVETH NOT" |
>
> 3-A

Chart number 3-A. Alright, how do we know? Well, we see God's law now, putting all of the passages together pertaining to divorce and remarriage: Matthew 5:32, Matthew 19:9, Mark 10:11-12, Luke 16:18, Romans 7:2-3, and the law stated in 1 Corinthians 7. What part of that law applies to this case, where a Christian is married to an alien or one who is not a Christian? 1 Corinthians 7:12-15, "If any brother hath a wife that believeth not" (or the woman which has a husband that believeth not), this law, that part stated in 1 Corinthians 7:12-15, applies to that situation; other passages do not.

See my chart number 4. How do we know what the bond between husbands and wives is or which passage discusses it? Romans 7:2-3, a woman is "bound by law to her husband." That is what he is talking about: the bond between husband and wife. 1 Corinthians 7:39, a parallel passage. The same: the bond between husband and wife. 1 Corinthians 7:27, what bond is discussed? If you are bound to a wife or loosed from a wife, he is talking about the marriage bond. *Well, what bond is discussed in 1 Corinthians 7:12-15?* "If any brother hath a wife" (or a woman which hath an husband), you do not have to have a Greek lexicon or dictionary to understand what these passages are talking about. Not one of them is talking about slavery. Every one of them is talking about the marriage bond, the relationship between a husband and wife.

HOW DO WE KNOW?
BOND BETWEEN HUSBANDS & WIVES

* WHAT BOND IS DISCUSSED IN ROM. 7:2-3?
  "WOMAN BOUND BY THE LAW TO HER HUSBAND"

* WHAT BOND IS DISCUSSED IN 1 COR. 7:39?
  "WIFE IS BOUND BY LAW AS LONG AS HER HUSBAND LIVETH"

* WHAT BOND IS DISCUSSED IN 1 COR. 7:27?
  "BOUND UNTO A WIFE" "LOOSED FROM A WIFE"

* WHAT BOND IS DISCUSSED IN 1 COR. 7:12-15?
  "IF ANY BROTHER HATH A WIFE"
  "THE WOMAN WHICH HATH A HUSBAND"

4

And when the unbeliever departs, God said, "Let him depart. A brother or sister is not under bondage in such cases." Not under constraint of law — not bound by that law to that mate; *that marriage no longer exists in the sight of God.* You know, we are not as far apart on this as you might think. Brother Halbrook admits that *if a mate dies* the believer can remarry. And further, *if the departing mate commits adul-*

BELIEVER MARRIED TO AN UNBELIEVER

1 COR. 7:12-16

1. IN SOME OF THESE CASES (MARRIAGES)
   A. THE UNBELIEVER IS PLEASED TO DWELL WITH THE BELIEVER
      1) "LET HIM NOT PUT HER AWAY"
      2) "LET HER NOT LEAVE HIM"

*NECESSARILY INFERRED: A BROTHER OR SISTER IS UNDER BONDAGE IN SUCH CASES (MARRIAGES)

6

tery, then the believer can obtain a scriptural divorce and remarry. The only point of our difference, as far as I can see, is that I believe further that *at the point of departure, the marriage is gone in the sight of God*. It is not the courthouse that approves it. He agrees with that. That is what I am saying — we are only one point away from agreement on that so far as I know.

Let us take a moment to look at my chart number 6 [previous page] if we have time. Well, we have the believer married to an unbeliever. In some cases, some of these marriages, the believer is pleased to dwell with her. What is the instruction? "Let him not put her away." Let her not leave him; it is necessarily inferred a brother or sister is under bondage in these cases.

Second Evening
Halbrook's Second Affirmative

Brother Freeman, brethren moderators, ladies and gentlemen, I direct your attention to the proposition: "The Scriptures teach that two people joined by God in marriage are bound for life, the only exception being that an innocent partner may put away a mate guilty of fornication and remarry."

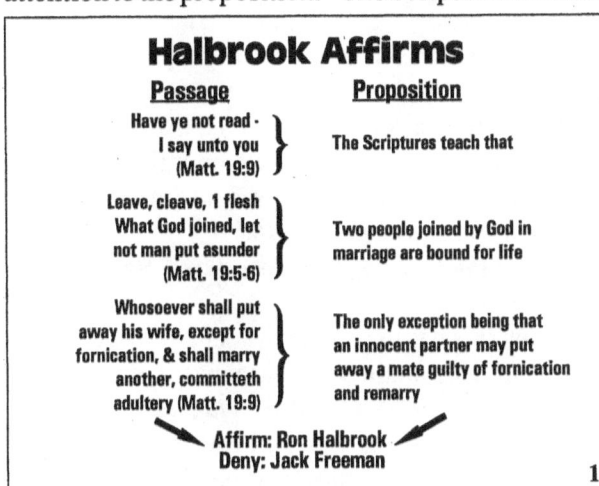

Now, he said that he agreed with the passage but he objected to my putting the word *"only"* in there. He said the word "only" is not over here. Sure it is — that is the force of "except," brother Freeman. "Except" — *if and only if* — there is the "only." Yes, it is in there. Everybody else can see it whether you can see it or not.

Now, he said that what I preached in Las Vegas is *"new."* I want to show you what I preached in Las Vegas on my chart 72 [text, Matt. 19:9]. *This is new, brother Freeman? This is new in Las Vegas? "Whosoever shall put away his wife, except it be for fornication, and shall marry another, committeth adultery: and whoso marrieth her which is put away doth commit adultery."* Yes, it is new compared to what you are teaching. This is new indeed! And I can realize they had not known it — had not known the truth about it.

"Well," he says, "as to the exception, if you take Matthew 5:42, 'Bless those who ask,' and 2 Thessalonians 3:10, 'Do not feed the lazy,' why these two do not conflict." No, they do not, but they have the force of another *"except."* "Bless those who ask, except the lazy." And I wonder if he will know what "except" means in that. But my friend, it still says, *"Except it be for fornication,"* and you will remember that tonight. And you understand that tonight.

Now then, I want to notice the questions I asked him:

1. *Which passages speak of marrying "another"?*

And he said, "All of them — all of them." But he said, "Now, it is inferred in 1 Corinthians 7:15." I did not ask you which passages inferred something. This question was *"speak of — speak of,"* and I put *"another"* in quotation marks because that is what the text says. The text of Romans 7 says *"another."* The text of Matthew 19 speaks of *marrying "another."* The text of 1 Corinthians 7:15 does *not* say "marry another." And it is no more inferred than in Acts 16:15, sprinkling little babies is inferred. No, it is not even inferred. But he said, "All of them speak of it." That was his answer.

2. *When did the call to peace occur in 1 Corinthians 7:15?*

Oh, he said, "Well, it depends on which peace, and when they married that was peace." But I said the peace in 1 Corinthians 7:15. Now, that is the thing you did not answer, you just dodged it. Come back and tell us. And I will show you why he would rather not answer that this time — he answered it the right way in Las Vegas. It is *when the believer obeyed the gospel,* and he did not want to have to say that tonight. I will show you why in a minute.

3. *In the case of Mark 6, would the marriage of Herod and Herodias be lawful if Philip would say he put her away?*

Well, he said he cannot see what this has to do with the debate. Let us show him. Chart 59-X [text, Mk. 6:17-18]. He cannot see what it has to do with the debate. Here is what it has to do: *it was an unscriptural marriage.* Herodias left Philip and married Herod. Now then, "he had married her," the Bible says; and this is not just *a courthouse record* by the way — the Bible says he married her; *the Bible* says it. *The Bible* says he married her, brother Freeman. "John had said unto Herod, It is not lawful for thee to have thy brother's wife." *Unscriptural marriages.*

But now we want you to tell us the effect if Philip would say, "Well, I put her away." He just does not know what that has to do with the debate — and he forgot to answer it, in addition. The thing is, you will move the checkers around and let her *become* the lawful wife. Oh, you say "not lawful" right now, but she would *become* the lawful wife if Philip would say, "Well, I do not want her anymore." How do you *make it lawful?* That is what I asked you to answer. I know your answer. Your answer is, "It can be made lawful if Philip just says he does not want her." But he does not know what it has to do with anything.

Now then, I asked him about his two conflicting answers. A person who violates 1 Corinthians 7:10-11 *cannot continue* in the marriage, and then, on the other side of it he said the person *can continue* in the marriage [pointing to chart, question four: *On January 16, 1990 you said that a Christian who violates 1 Corinthians 7:10-11 by divorcing his mate and marrying another CANNOT CONTINUE in the marriage. But on January 18, 1990 you said he CAN*

CONTINUE in the marriage. What will you say now?]

He said at the point of the divorce the man was still married to the first mate. Well, when did they *become* lawful mates? Because you said, "Well, they can continue in the marriage." "Well," he said, "they committed *adultery* by it and so then they could continue in it, and that is what made it alright to continue."

Now, do you see what Mark 6 has to do with it? That is the same point I was asking you about in Mark 6. According to you, all Philip would have to do is say, "Well, I am through with her," and now it has *become* a scriptural marriage. That is what it has to do with this debate. Brother Freeman, you come back and answer these questions. You did not answer them. You danced around them and did not answer them.

5. *"When Paul told slaves not to be servants of men, did he mean they were free from their slave relationship?"*

Well, the answer to that is, properly, "No, they were not." And he answered it right in Las Vegas, but not tonight. No, he said in verse 21, servants can be *made* free. Look at chart 150-X. Look at the text. Look at the text. Now, my friend, "If the unbelieving depart, let him depart. A brother or a sister is not under bondage in such cases" — literally, "has not been enslaved" — "but God has called us to peace."

And lest I forget it, by the way, this fits exactly with Thayer; Freeman made a play that I was some way trying to pervert Thayer. Do you know if you take off "en," you have the word *"slave."* Thayer said that is the primary meaning. And so the law that they are not under constraint to is *the law of this husband making demands that over-rule the law of Christ,* brother Freeman. That is what this passage teaches. No, I did not pervert Thayer.

Alright now notice, "Not under bondage in such cases, but God hath called us to peace." Then, notice in verse 23, "Ye are bought with a price; be not ye the servants" — literally, *slaves,* it is the same word, that same word for *enslave* — "of men." Now see, I asked him, "When Paul said, 'Be not servants of men,' did

---

**Slaves To Christ, Not To Men
1 Corinthians 7:15, 23**

But if the unbelieving depart, let him depart. A brother or a sister is not under bondage (lit.: *has not been enslaved)* in such cases; but God has called us to peace.

Ye are bought with a price; be not ye the servants (lit.: *slaves*) of men.

150 X

he mean they were free from the slave relation?" Well, he said, "They could *get free* in verse 21." And she can *get* free too, if there is death, brother Freeman. If there is death she can get free, but *there is no freedom given in verse 23 from the slave relation* and *no freedom given from the marriage relation in verse 15.* There is the point. And he can see the point. Running off does not free *him* and does not free *her.* Unscriptural divorce does not free either one of them [i.e., husband or wife].

Now then, the questions he gave me:

1. *"If a husband divorces his wife for any cause other than adultery, and then commits adultery, can she scripturally remarry?"*

I have said over and over again, and he understands it about as well as he understands "except," the only way *anyone* — capital letters, ANYONE — can remarry is *if they put their mate away for fornication.* Now, you can juggle the circumstances a thousand ways, but there is no scriptural right *except it be for fornication.* (We will put chart 72 [text, Matt. 19:9] up there again, put it up there again in a moment.) You try to make a scenario dealing with *when do you have that innocent party.* I know what you are driving at in that question. But I want you to know that is no help to you, brother Freeman, at all. You have got to find a passage and then a scenario *for the guilty, put-away fornicator to marry another.* Don't you forget what this debate is about.

Now, my friend, it will have to meet this test or it is unscriptural. *"Whosoever shall put away his wife, except it be for fornication, and shall marry another, committeth adultery: and whoso marrieth her which is put away doth commit adultery."* If you marry one unscripturally put away, you commit adultery. If you marry the put-away fornicator, you commit adultery. But if you put your wife away for fornication, you do *not* commit adultery.

You can juggle it a thousand different ways, brother Freeman, but *you have got to have an innocent party that did not commit adultery. And your proposition is, "The guilty party that did commit adultery can marry another"* — that is what this debate is about. Chasing rabbits, the very idea, about when do you have the *innocent* party! We are not differing over the *innocent* party, *we agree the innocent party can marry another.* We want to know about the *guilty* party — ask me about the *guilty* party — that is what this debate is about. If you want to sign a proposition on another discussion we can do that, but this debate is, *"Can the guilty party marry another?"*

2. *"When a husband obtains a civil divorce for any cause other than adultery are the two still married in God's sight?"*

The scriptural bond of marriage is still there in spite of man's rebellion

Second Evening: Halbrook's Second Affirmative

against it. And, let me tell you that somebody juggling it around like Philip saying, "I do not want her anymore," deciding, "I do not want her anymore," *will not change that unscriptural marriage into a scriptural marriage,* either. And you watch and see if he says any more about Mark 6. I bet he is done with it, he is washed out on it. I have exposed him on it. He does believe that could *become* a scriptural marriage, don't you, brother Freeman? Would you shake your head and deny that you believe it could *become* a scriptural marriage that way? Shake your head. Now, he will not shake it and you can see the conclusion — you can see the conclusion.

3. *"In Matthew 5:32 and Matthew 19:9 adultery means to have unlawful sexual intercourse with someone's wife."* And he wants me to say true or false.

Well, it could include that, but not that alone. It could be a single person, a married man *with* a single person. And furthermore, see my chart 85, adultery is unlawful sexual intercourse by one who is under the constraint of law. Here is your Bible definition, adultery defined *by use*. The Lord used the term of unlawful sexual intercourse involving someone under constraint of God's marriage law. A married man having sex with another man's wife. Or, a man puts away his wife without cause, and marries another. And, friend, it is adultery and nobody juggling it around later can make it anything else than adultery. It is adultery. The woman put away without cause marries another — that is adultery.

Adultery Defined By Use:
Unlawful Sexual Intercourse Involving Someone Under Constraint Of God's Marriage Law

1. Married man with another man's wife (Jn. 8:4)

2. Man puts away wife w/o cause and marries another (Matt. 19:9; Mk. 10:11-12; Lk. 16:18)

3. Woman put away w/o cause marries another (Matt. 5:32; 19:9)

4. Put-away fornicator marries another (Matt. 5:32 & 19:9 read with exception)

85

The put-away fornicator marries another. That is a different case of adultery than these other cases, I realize that, but my Lord and Savior said it is adultery. Whether you ever understand why it is or not, *it is adultery if the Lord says it is.* The Lord says it is. Whoever puts his mate away for fornication is not guilty of causing the subsequent adultery. The Lord called it adultery, brother Freeman.

4. *"If a wife refuses sex with her husband can she scripturally divorce when he commits adultery?"*

Why, certainly not! She violates 1 Corinthians 7:4-5. Jesus taught you cannot reap the benefit of sin (Matt. 5:32).

And then he had a question that is so garbled and confused I do not know what to make of it: 5. *"Does God demand that the innocent human being (one not guilty of adultery) suffer because of the sins of the guilty party (one who obtains a divorce for a cause other than adultery)?"*

The *innocent* and the *guilty.* You say that this is a *guilty party* but there is *no adultery.* I do not really know what he means. I know the innocent suffer, not because God desires or demands it, but because of Satan and because of sin, I know that.

And I want to take up again in our study of 1 Corinthians 7 — just taking you through it. I want to notice now, 1 Corinthians 7:15, on my chart 150-X. And we know that here, by inspiration, Paul said that we are slaves to Christ, not to men. And therefore, "If the unbelieving depart, let him depart. A brother or sister is not under bondage," not enslaved to men in matters of this kind, "but God hath called us to peace.... Ye are bought with a price; be not ye the servants (slaves) of men."

> **Slaves To Christ, Not To Men**
> **1 Corinthians 7:15, 23**
>
> But if the unbelieving depart, let him depart. A brother or a sister is not under bondage (lit.: *has not been enslaved)* in such cases; but God has called us to peace.
>
> Ye are bought with a price; be not ye the servants (lit.: *slaves*) of men.
>
> 150 X

Not enslaved to men, even though in a slave relation. *Not enslaved to a husband, even though in a marriage relation,* brother Freeman, that is what it teaches. How simple it is.

And then notice my chart 150. There are difficulties in this chapter. I am not trying to pretend there are not. If he believes Paul did not write any difficult passages, I will let him debate the Apostle Peter on it. Peter said he did. Maybe you know more about it than Peter knew about it. Now, you interpret the difficult chapter in a way to contradict the clear and simple teaching of Jesus in Matthew 5 and Matthew 19, "Whoso marrieth her which is put away doth commit adultery." And, he is trying to get the meaning out of 1 Corinthians 7:15, "Whoso marrieth her which is put away doth *NOT* commit adultery." Now, you call for chart one-five-0, that is it — 150. And you just come up here and admit that you are creating this contradiction. Here is your position. Jesus said, *"Whoever*

Interpret Difficult Passage - Contradict Clear & Simple One	
Matthew 5:32; 19:9 Clear and Simple	**1 Corinthians 7:15** Interpretation of Difficult Text
"Whoso marrieth her which is put away doth commit adultery"	Whoso marrieth her which is put away doth NOT commit adultery

150

marrieth her which is put away doth commit adultery," and you say, *"They do not commit adultery."* So you can just debate the Lord on it!

Now then, we notice chart 151. Now, he had his discussion about "bondage." Well, let us study about bondage. "A brother or sister is not under bondage" — *has not been bound and is not now* — that is the force of it. *Simultaneous* with that, "God hath called us to peace" — has been called and right now is abiding in that same peace. Now, when did it begin? Did it begin when they were deserted? Now, think about that. "Not under bondage," he wants to make that begin when they were deserted, but, see, *it is parallel to "hath called us to peace."* It is *simultaneous:* at the same time you are not under bondage to men — not slaves to men, but to Christ — that is *because* you are

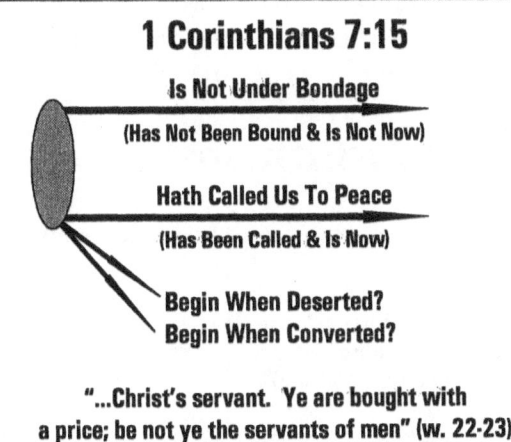

called into the peace of God. It is a simultaneous thing. And so whenever one of these began is when the other did, and they began *at conversion*.

Alright then, we notice the next one, my chart 151-A. And here you have the parallel in Psalm 1:1-2, "Blessed is the man that walketh not in the counsel of the ungodly," now simultaneous with that, "But his delight is in the law of the Lord." He does *not* mean one of these started *one time* and then the other a *later time*. Now watch it, friend: "A brother or a sister is not under bondage in such cases," but, "called to peace." These are *parallel statements*, you see. See the parallel here, "Blessed is the man that walks not." While he is walking not, what is he? Why, "delighting in the law." And while he is "not under bondage," what is he? *"Called into peace."* While he is in that peace, what is he? *"Not under bondage."* See that?

And then we notice my chart 150-X [page 114] again. Notice the text. Now here we are, I want to see the text again, *"Ye are bought with a price; be not ye the servants of men."* Not the slaves of men. Now, that is that same word — that word *douloo* here for "bondage" in verses 15 and 23. Up here the *verb* [verse 15]; down here the *noun* form [verse 23] — same word, same concept.

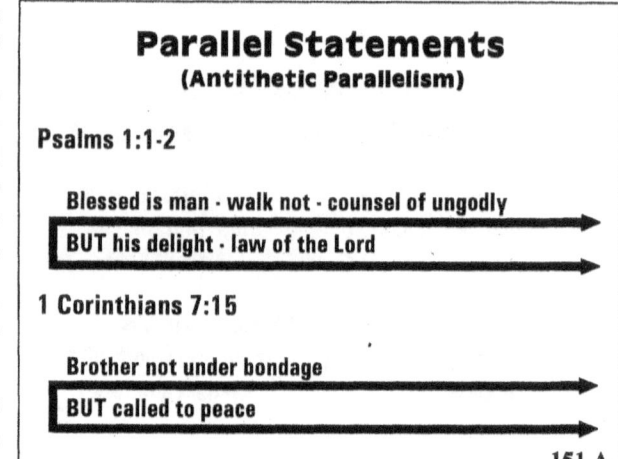

Now, watch it on my chart 152. Call for 152 and tell us about it, brother Freeman. If my opponent can understand verses 22 and 23, he can understand verse 15. Now, in his "Marriage" series he said "not servants of men" refers to "spiritual relationship." God has called us to freedom when we obey the gospel. Right. Right, brother Freeman. Now watch it: *"Not under bondage" refers to spiritual relationship.* I just know he can see that — I know he can see that. Paul said, "I am dealing with cases of this kind." *Human relationships.* "Not under bondage," all the time "God has called us to peace" — when we obey the gospel. He can understand it just like you and me.

Now see my chart 154. He brought up this matter of different groups

> **Address Separate Groups Does Not Mean Give Contradictory Information**
>
> 1. Coach Separates Old & New Players
>   a. Tell old group to run fast
>   b. Tell new group to run slow???
>   c. NO, but new group has more questions!
>
> 2. Apostles Address Separate Groups (Languages - Acts 2:1-13)
>   a. Tell one group the Kingdom is now
>   b. Tell other group the Kingdom is not now???
>   c. NO, but each group had different questions!
>
> 154

addressed in verses 10 and following, and then verses 12 and following. That does not mean you have to give *contradictory information*. The coach separates the old and the new players. Now, since you have got two groups, what? Well, he will have to have contradictory information — tell the old group, *"run fast,"* the new group, *"run slow."* Is that it? No, the new group may have more questions, but it is not necessary that they be given contradictory information. The Apostles addressed separate groups. Did they tell one group, "The kingdom is *now*," and the other group, "The kingdom is *not now*"? No, addressing several groups does not mean you have to give contradictory information.

Now, on my chart 154-A, Peter and Paul addressed separate groups. Peter, to the Jews, preached, "Be baptized to be saved." Paul, to the Gentiles, well, I suppose it is a different group, so he would have to preach, "You are saved to be baptized." No, each group may have different questions, but, my friend, they do not have to be given *contradictory information*.

Now, Paul addresses separate groups in 1 Corinthians 7:10-11, and in 12-16. I believe that. I understand that. I am not

> **Address Separate Groups Does Not Mean Give Contradictory Information**
>
> 3. Peter & Paul Address Separate Groups (Gal. 2:9)
>   a. Peter to Jews: Baptized → Saved
>   b. Paul to Gentiles: Saved → Baptized???
>   c. NO, but each group had different questions!
>
> 4. Paul Addresses Separate Groups (1 Cor. 7:10-16)
>   a. Tell believers divorced from believers, not marry another
>   b. Tell believers divorced by unbeliever, marry another???
>   c. NO, but each group had different questions in view of status, false theories, and "present distress"
>
> 154 A

trying to dodge that at all. But now watch the effect of it. And I sure hope he calls for chart 154-A, and talks about this bottom part. Sometimes he will call for a chart and he will refer to something over here and a little bit over there, and he does not get to the conclusion. You get to the conclusion on this! Paul addresses *separate groups*. He tells believers divorced from believers not to *marry another*. He says that; I say that; Paul says that. But then, according to my opponent, Paul tells believers divorced by unbelievers to *"marry another."* Do you see the *contradiction* in that? Same set of circumstances, two groups of people: "you *cannot* marry another" — "you *can* marry another." No, my friend, each group had different questions, we understand that because of their different circumstances, but we do not have to have contradictory information.

See my chart 157. And he talked about the bond. There are *two bonds* in this chapter. He keeps going through it as if there were "one bond, same bond, just the same bond" all the time. No, it is not! Now, you have "bound by God's marriage law" — tied, fastened, joined. That is from *"deo."* Now, check your *Thayer's [Greek-English Lexicon]* and *Vine's [Dictionary of New Testament Words]*. And that is used in Romans 7:2 and in 1 Corinthians 7:27 and verse 39. There is the word for God's marriage law. But, now, bondage or *enslavement to the demands of another person* is a different word, different word meaning "to make a slave of, reduce to bondage, enslave." That is from *douloo,* in 1 Corinthians 7:15. And then you have the noun form in verse 23. And when he said, "Be not servants of men," that was a figurative use too, brother Freeman. I understand all that talk about figurative use, I understand it is figurative. But he said the literal slaves are figuratively "not under bondage to men." Now, here are people married and we understand the figure in that [indicating *deo* at top of chart 157]. Marriage is not an "enslavement to men," but rather you recognize you are "enslaved" to the Lord Jesus Christ [indicating *douloo* on chart]. No, all the bonds are *not the same* in that chapter.

And it is just like Galatians 6:2 [indicating bottom of chart 157]. Each man is taught that we would "bear one another's burdens." The word for "burden" there, *"baros,"* means "a heavy or crushing load." But then "each man bear his

---

Two Bonds In 1 Cor. 7

1. BOUND by God's marriage law = tied, fastened, joined, from DEO in Romans 7:2; 1 Cor. 7:27, 39 (See Thayer, Vines, Etc.).

2. BONDAGE or enslavement to the demands of another person = to make a slave of, reduce to bondage, enslave, from DOULOO in 1 Cor. 7:15; noun form in vs. 23 (Thayer, Etc.)

LIKE:

1. BURDENS to share = a heavy or crushing load, from BAROS in Gal. 6:2.

2. BURDEN for each man alone = a normal load or cargo, from PHORTION in Gal. 6:5.

157

Second Evening: Halbrook's Second Affirmative

own burden," the Greek word is *phortion* and this is a normal load that a man can carry. Now, you have two different *"burdens"* here just like two "bounds" or two *"bonds"* up there. See that?

Then we notice now chart 150-X [see page 114]. Notice you have this same word in verses 15 and 23. "A brother or sister is not *enslaved*—not enslaved in such cases." And down here, to the slave, "Be not ye the *servants* (slaves) of men." Figurative usage in verse 15. Figurative usage in verse 23. Yes, we understand that.

Next, my chart 162. Now, the deserted believer is not to marry another. Robertson says in his *Word Pictures* the text does *not* say the believer "may marry again." And I told you this debate would end without him ever finding "marry another," "marry again," in 1 Corinthians 7:15. *Alford's Greek Testament* said it is not dealing with "remarrying after such a separation." *Expositors Greek Testament*, "freedom of remarriage" is not suggested. Gordon Fee said, "Remarriage is not an issue."

> **Deserted Believer Not To Marry Another - 1 Cor. 7:15**
> 1. Text does **not** say believer "may marry again" (Robertson, Word Pictures, IV:128)
> 2. **Not** deal with "re-marrying after such a separation" (Alford, Greek Testament, II:525)
> 3. "Freedom of remarriage" **not** suggested (Expositor's Greek Testament, p. 827)
> 4. "Remarriage is not an issue" in text (G. Fee, 1st Epistle To Corinth, pp. 302, 303)
> 5. "In such cases remarriage is not approved" (D. Lipscomb & J.W. Shepherd, 1 Cor., p. 102)
> 6. Allows separation but "not...the privilege to marry another" (H. Leo Boles, Luke, p. 317)
>
> 162

David Lipscomb, "In such cases remarriage is not approved." Allows separation but "not...the privilege to marry another," said H. Leo Boles. These brethren as well as others could see that; I believe you can.

Now notice my chart 165. *The Holy Spirit added new revelation to what Jesus said.* I believe that. Now, he had some charts (and I am covering them right now) arguing "you have got to take all the passages, it cannot be a contradiction if you take them all." Amen. But let us watch that. Jesus taught one man for one woman for life, just one exception. The Holy Spirit said it is better not to marry during "the present distress" (1 Cor. 7:1-9, 26). Now, that does not conflict with Jesus. The Holy Spirit said God accepts the marriage of the believer and the unbeliever (1 Cor. 7:12-14). No conflict. The Holy Spirit said a believer married to an unbeliever must put Christ first (1 Cor. 7:15). No conflict. Conclusion: *The Holy Spirit did not add a contradiction to what Jesus said.*

See my chart 165-A. If then, if 1 Corinthians 7:15 adds another "except" to

The Holy Spirit Added New Revelation To What Jesus Said
(John 16:12-13)

1. Jesus = One man & one woman for life; one exception (Matt. 19:9)
2. Holy Spirit = Better not to marry during "present distress" (1 Cor. 7:1-9, 26)
3. Holy Spirit = God accepts marriage of believer & unbeliever (1 Cor. 7:12-14)
4. Holy Spirit = A believer married to an unbeliever must put Christ first (1 Cor. 7:15)

Conclusion: The Holy Spirit did not "add" a contradiction to what Jesus said!

165

If - Then

IF
1 Corinthians 7:15 adds another "except" to Matt. 19:9, as per John 16:12-13,

THEN
1. Like Matt. 18:3, "Except ye be converted, and become as little children," ADD "Except ye are not converted and do not become as little children"
2. Like John 3:2, "Except God be with him," ADD "Except Beelzebub be with him"
3. Like John 3:5, "Except a man be born of water and of the Spirit," ADD "Except faith only"

My Opponent ADDS a contradiction!

165 A

Matthew 19:9, that would be like Matthew 18:3, "Except you be converted and become as little children," *add*, "Except you are not converted and do not become as little children." John 3:5, "Except a man be born of water and of the Spirit," *add*, "Except faith only." My opponent *adds* a *contradiction!*

> **1 Corinthians 7:25-28**
>
> | | |
> |---|---|
> | Now concerning virgins... | } Never Married |
> | ...for the present distress... good for a man so to be | } Never Married |
> | Art thou bound unto a wife? Seek not to be loosed | } If Married, STAY |
> | Art thou loosed from a wife? Seek not a wife. But and if thou marry, thou hast not sinned; and if a virgin marry, she hath not sinned [but best not to marry, vv. 28-38] | } If man never married, STAY
 } If woman never married, STAY |
>
> 190 X

Now we notice verse 27 on my chart 190-X. The text, and here is your setting for the passage, verse 25, "Now concerning *virgins.*" He is looking for where it says, "Now concerning *divorced fornicators.*" "Now concerning virgins" — *never married* — "for the present distress, I say, that it is good for a man so to be" — *never married.* "Art thou bound unto a wife?" — we are just reading the text — "seek not to be loosed" — if you are married, stay. "Art thou loosed from a wife? Seek not a wife. But and if thou marry, thou hast not sinned; and if a virgin marry, she hath not sinned." Now, notice you have *the man — never married —* then, *the woman — never married.* That is what you have in the context.

Chart 190. Now, "loosed" in this context. Is it *"never married"* or *"divorced,"* which? In the context, verses 25-38, is it *virgins* or *divorcees?* You read that and see. It was good to be as Paul, "so to be." Was Paul divorced? He was *loosed.* Was he *divorced?* If it meant divorced or death, if "loosed" meant divorced or death, it would read, "Seek not *another* wife, seek not *another* wife," brother Freeman.

> **1 Corinthians 7:27**
> "Loosed From A Wife"
> **Never married OR divorced?**
>
> 1. Context (vv. 25-38) - Virgins or Divorcees?
> 2. Vs. 26 - Good to be as Paul (vv. 7-8) - Divorced?
> 3. Vv. 26-27 So to be (as Paul) = Loosed - Divorced?
> 4. Vs. 27 If divorced or death, "seek not another wife" (as Matthew 19:9; Romans 7:3)?
> 5. Vv. 27-28 Unmarried male (loosed) & Unmarried Female (virgin) - Divorce?
> 6. Those never married! Virgins (25), as Paul (26), loosed (27), virgin (28), have no mate (29), unmarried man (32), virgin as unmarried woman (34), virgin (36-37)
>
> 190

That is the way it is in Matthew 19, that is the way it is in Romans 7. If it is that same thing here, it would read, "Seek not *another.*" And in verses 27 and 28, the *unmarried male* is *loosed,* the *unmarried female,* what is she, a *divorcee?* That will not work.

Now notice 191-A. See this, if this is divorced people? Every unmarried man is loosed from a wife, his female *counterpart* is a virgin—that is what you have in the passage. If the *loosed man* is divorced, then a *virgin* is a *divorcee* — that is what it would yield.

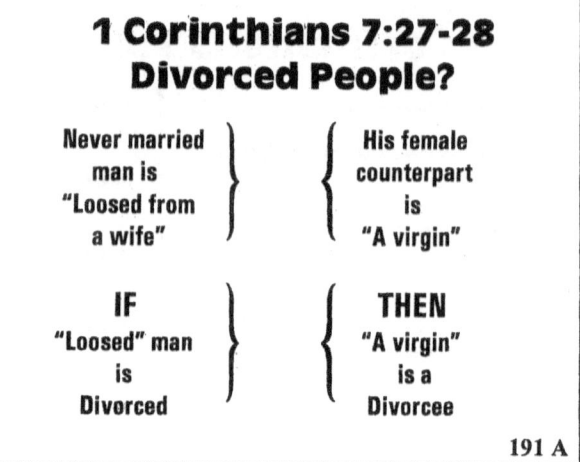

1 Corinthians 7:27-28 Divorced People?

Never married man is "Loosed from a wife" } { His female counterpart is "A virgin"

IF "Loosed" man is Divorced } { THEN "A virgin" is a Divorcee

191 A

Now look at my chart 193. These commentators point out that the word "loosed" there "does not imply previous marriage," *Alford's Greek New Testament. Meyer,* "Does not imply art thou *separated* from, but art thou *free* from." *Barnes,* "Does not imply...the person had been married" and "divorced." *Fisher,* "Perfect tense...permanent state of freedom from marriage ties" — "*permanent state.*" Now, that is what they say on it.

And now let us go down to my chart 196.

1 Corinthians 7:27 - Commentaries
Loosed (LELUSAI)

1. "Does not imply previous marriage" (Alford's Greek New Testament, II:529)
2. "Does not imply: art thou *separated* from, but art thou *free* from, unentangled with a wife, *single*" (H.A.W. Meyer, Epistle To The Corinthians, pg. 171)
3. "Does not imply ... the person had been married" and "divorced" (Barnes, First Corinthians, pg. 126)
4. "Perfect tense ... permanent state of freedom from marriage ties" (F. Fisher, 1-2 Corinthians, pg. 117)
5. 20/22 Not say divorced - "Bachelor" often; 2 include divorce; 0 say divorce only.

193

"Loose" has the same latitude in Greek and English. It can be *the simple state of freedom.* You have these Greek writers that use this very word. "Unbinding her hair." Another one said a woman was "with unbound hair." Now notice this: *If your hair is tied up, don't unbind it.* That would be parallel to: *If you are bound, don't seek to be loosed.* Now, is your hair unbound? Don't tie it up. *"Are you*

Second Evening: Halbrook's Second Affirmative 123

> **Loose: Same Latitude In Greek & English**
> **Can Be Simple State Of Freedom**
>
> 1. Bion (200 B.C.): "unbinding her hair" (Liddell & Scott, 1068) Hermas (A.D. 140): "with unbound hair" (Arndt. & Ging., 484)
>
> 2. Is your hair tied up? Don't unbind it. Is your hair unbound? Don't tie it up.
>
> 3. "Free from a state of confinement, restraint, or obligation" (Webster)
>
> **Many dogs run LOOSE, FREE - Context tells if they were ever tied up!**
>
> 196

loosed? Seek not to be married." Now see, my friend, "Is your hair *unbound?*" does not imply that it previously was bound; it just means *"free from a state of confinement."* We say, "Many dogs run loose around here, many dogs run free." Does that mean that they have been first of all tied up somewhere? No. No, my friend.

Then notice my chart 197. Here is how the Greek writers used that term. For instance, here is a Greek writer, writing a Greek commentary, that deals with this verse, and he said the meaning of that word is "not...those who have been joined together and then dissolved (the relationship)," but it is "those who have not cohabited, not entered a marital union, but being loosed/free of this bond." This is a Greek writer, writing on a Greek word, and he knows that language. Now, that is the meaning

> **Loose (LUO) Greek Writers**
>
> 1. Xenophon (400 B.C.) used "to be loosed/free from others" as equivalent to "to be independent, autonomous" (Translation from H.A.W. Meyer, Epistle To The Corinthians, pg. 171)
>
> 2. Photius (A.D. 800 - Greek Commentary - 1 Cor. 7:27): "Not ...those who have been joined together and then dissolved (the relationship)" but "Those who have not cohabitated,(i.e.) entered into a marital union, but being loosed/free of this bond" (Translation from Alford's Greek Testament, II:529)
>
> 197

of it and that is the truth about it.

Now, I want you to notice my charts 175 and 176. Notice, my friend, that the doctrine that my opponent is teaching according to the historians has brought "wide effects." Using 1 Corinthians 7:15 this way is "an entrance-wedge" for remarriage in any case of "malicious desertion." And it has resulted in "increased looseness," "shocking facility of divorce...flowed from this source." That is what the historians say. And we have our young children we are trying to raise and trying to protect, and we are trying to keep the purity of the church.

And the doctrine that he is teaching will open the door, it is an "entrance-wedge" to what? "Increased looseness" on divorce and remarriage. My friend, let us respect what the Lord said — one cause and only one cause to put our mate away, and marry another. If you love your children, teach them that. Thank you.

Misuse Of 1 Cor. 7:15

"An entrance-wedge" to "increased looseness" on divorce and remarriage. Survey history of movement from "one cause of separation with remarriage" to looser practices ("Divorce," McClintock & Strong, <u>Cyclopedia of Bibl., Theol., & Eccl. Lit.</u>, II:839-844)

1. "'Not in bondage' to keep company with unbeliever at all events" but no "remarriage."
2. Later claim it gives "Liberty to contract a new" marriage - "Had wide effects."
3. "Entrance-wedge" for remarriage in any case of "malicious desertion."
4. RESULT: Much "Increased looseness" & "Shocking facility of divorce ... flowed from this source."

175

I.S.B.E. Article Warns

If use 1 Cor. 7:15 as right to remarry, "The flood gates are open" (II:865-866)

Steps of Progression:

"If your husband deserts you, you may have another. If he is cruel, you may have another. If he fails to support you, you may have another. If he is drunken, you may have another. If he is incompatible or makes you unhappy, you may have another" - and yet others beyond these.

Results: Careless Marriages, Divorce For Any Cause, Multiplied Miseries!

176

Second Evening
Freeman's Second Negative

Brother Halbrook. In this last speech this evening, last twenty-five minute speech, I would like to refer briefly to the questions I asked brother Halbrook. He has charged me at times with not answering his questions. I wonder if you saw his answers to these.

1. *If a husband divorces his wife for any cause other than adultery, and then commits adultery, can she scripturally remarry?*

He did not answer it. He did not say she can or she cannot. That is all I asked, a very simple question. He has in every night of this debate presented me with trick questions; I have presented him just simple questions which he did not answer. Now, I know he ran a drape, went all around the mulberry bush, but he did not answer the question. He did not say she can; he did not say she cannot. I will tell you why: In the debate in North Las Vegas he said, *"We cannot play the waiting game — we cannot play the waiting game."* And even in 1 Corinthians 7:12-15, he said, the believer divorced by the nonbeliever can remarry, even though he is unscripturally divorced, *when the unbeliever commits adultery,* and the believer can obtain the divorce in God's sight. The marriage would be broken in God's sight.

2. *In Matthew 5:32 and Matthew 19, adultery means to have unlawful intercourse with someone else's wife.* True or false?

He says, "not that alone." You know where I got that statement? The first January issue of *Guardian of Truth* [in 1990]. Maybe you would like to debate one of your own brethren who claims to believe what you do. That is what he says it means and he quoted Thayer — he quotes Thayer. That is what Thayer says adultery means. But you use this witness and you referred to it again tonight, but we are not through with it yet. I am going to call upon Mr. Thayer again because he is your witness.

Now, my question 5 — he says he cannot understand the question.

Maybe you should ask your eighteen year old son. I am sorry, I should not have said that. That is a poor comment — beating on the women, beating on the children. "I will get my three year old child to explain that to you." It does not take a lot of intellect, I do not think, to understand this — let me see if I can explain it. If you have difficulty with it, let me know.

5. *Does God demand that the innocent human being (one not guilty of adultery)* — that is what I mean by innocent, an innocent person not guilty of

adultery — *suffer because of the sins of the guilty party (one who obtains a divorce for a cause other than adultery)?*

The *guilty party* obtains a divorce — why is he guilty? He obtained a divorce for a cause other than adultery. Isn't he guilty of sin? 1 John 3:4 says it is a transgression of God's law. He is a sinner. So he obtains a divorce, contrary to what God says. The question was, "Must the innocent one that he put away on unscriptural grounds suffer?" He did not answer it. He said, "I do not understand it — I do not understand that question." What made it difficult? Of course, maybe I can understand it because I wrote it. Now, if you in the audience did not understand it, I would appreciate it if you would come to me after this debate tonight and I will try my best to explain it to you.

I would like to call, first of all, for my own charts number 11 and 12. Thayer, page 158, says the literal meaning of "bondage" is "to make a slave of, reduce to bondage," and he used an illustration, Acts 7:6, Israelites in bondage to the Egyptians. Now, he points out that there is also another meaning — a metaphorical or figurative meaning. Incidentally, if you are going to use these books, you soon understand that they have a literal meaning and a figurative meaning and they cannot agree; they cannot be the same. If the figurative meaning is what he means, then the literal meaning could not be. If the literal meaning is what he means, the figurative meaning cannot be. Now, all you preachers understand that, I know. I think all and plus the children understand it too. So, literally, it means "to make a slave of." Figuratively, it means "to be under bondage, held by constraint of law or necessity in some matter, 1 Corinthians 7:15." And that is what Henry Thayer says, *word for word* — it is copied right out of his book.

> **THAYER**
> **PG. 158**
>
> DOULOO - prop.(LITERALLY) - TO MAKE SLAVE OF, REDUCE TO BONDAGE. ACTS 7:6
> METAPH. (FIGURATIVELY) - TO BE UNDER BONDAGE HELD BY CONSTRAINT OF LAW OR NECESSITY IN SOME MATTER. 1 COR. 7:15
> WHAT IS THE MATTER UNDER CONSIDERATION IN 1 COR. 7:15? THE DEPARTURE (DIVORCE) FROM THE BELIEVER BY THE UNBELIEVING SPOUSE... THE MARRIAGE BOND.
> THUS, WHEN THE UNBELIEVING SPOUSE DIVORCES THE BELIEVER, THE BELIEVER IS NOT HELD BY CONSTRAINT OF LAW OR OF NECESSITY IN SOME MATTER.
>
> 11

What is the matter under consideration in 1 Corinthians 7:15? *The departure or divorce from the believer by an unbelieving spouse.* The marriage bond. Then when the unbelieving spouse divorces the believer, the believer is *not held by constraint of necessity in that matter*. Now, if you want to throw your witness away and say he has been lying about that, then you should not have introduced him in the first place.

Let us look at chart number 12. Thayer, let's follow him. The believer in such cases no longer has a wife or a husband, so they are both free to marry. What does God say to those who have no wife or husband? 1 Corinthians 7:27-28, "Seek not a wife. But and if thou marry, thou hast not sinned." Incidentally, turn to 1 Corinthians 7. Ron would like you to believe these verses beginning in verse 25, that they all have to do with *virgins*. Now, this is a problem he had in North Las Vegas. He finally admitted that someone is here besides virgins. In 1 Corinthians 7, Ron likes to read part. Paul *starts here with virgins,* that is true. But I want to ask you, clearly now, is he talking about virgins in verse 27, "Art thou bound to a wife?" It does not sound like a virgin to me. Some could answer "yes," some would answer "no." "Art thou bound to a wife?" *If you are, you are not a virgin.* "Are you bound to a husband?" He is not talking about virgins in all of these verses.

Now let us look at my chart number 57. Yes, I want to call upon brother Halbrook's witnesses — his witnesses. I do not try to prove things by men but he does. Thayer says this word in 1 Corinthians 7:27, "loosed" — "A loosing of any bond as that of marriage; hence once in the New Testament of divorce, 1 Corinthians 7:27." That is what his witness says;

> **THAYER**
> (Cont)
>
> **PG. 158**
>
> *THE BELIEVER, IN SUCH CASES, NO LONGER HAS A WIFE/HUSBAND AND IS THEREFORE FREE TO MARRY... 1 COR. 7:27-28
>
> *LITERAL SLAVERY IS DISCUSSED BY THAYER UNDER THE GREEK WORD "DOULOS" AND MR. THAYER TELLS US THAT THIS WORD USED IN 1 COR. 7:21 (SERVANT) AND THIS WORD ALSO HAS A FIGURATIVE MEANING 1 COR. 7:22 "SERVANT OF CHRIST".
>
> 12

> **THAYER**
> page 384
>
> LUSIS - "A LOOSING OF ANY BOND, AS THAT OF MARRIAGE; HENCE ONCE IN THE NEW TESTAMENT OF DIVORCE",
>
> *1 COR. 7:27 - THUS, "ART THOU LOOSED FROM A WIFE" "ART THOU DIVORCED FROM A WIFE"
>
> *1 COR. 7:28 - "BUT AND IF THOU MARRY, THOU HAST NOT SINNED..."
>
> 57

that is what his witness says — there is the page number. And if you do not believe it, brother Homer Walker has Thayer with him. You are welcome to come up here and read it tonight. He said it is used once of divorce and that is in 1 Corinthians 7:27. Thus, "Art thou loosed from a wife?" Are you *divorced* from a wife? "And if thou marry thou hast not sinned," verse 28.

Let us look at my chart number 751. Now, brother Halbrook had — I do not know when, but sometime ago — did some preaching evidently and this is a portion of his outline. And the outline was entitled *Trends Pointing to a New Apostasy*. And this is from page two of that outline, Roman numeral II, entitled "Drinking from Sectarian and Liberal Wells." You do not have to spend most of your speech trying to get us to drink from sectarian and liberal wells — quoting from uninspired men, commentaries, and such like. Well, let us see what he says here, *"The word of God reveals the will of God. We need to fill our hearts and minds with God's Word so that we can know and do His will."* I agree one hundred percent. I think we would all agree.

**TRENDS POINTING TOWARD
A NEW APOSTASY**

(NOTES BY RON HALBROOK)

II. DRINKING FROM SECTARIAN & LIBERAL WELLS

* THE WORD OF GOD REVEALS THE WILL OF GOD

* WE NEED TO FILL OUR HEARTS & MINDS WITH GOD'S WORD SO THAT WE CAN KNOW & DO HIS WILL

1 TIM. 4:13-16, 2 TIM. 1:13, 2 TIM. 3:14-17, NEH. 13:23-24

751

**TRENDS POINTING TOWARD
A NEW APOSTASY**

(NOTES BY RON HALBROOK (Cont))

IT IS NOT WRONG TO CONSULT OR READ UNINSPIRED WRITINGS

PAUL QUOTED FROM THEM - ACTS 17:28, 1 COR. 15:32, TIT. 1:12

IT IS WRONG TO BECOME SO FASCINATED WITH SECTARIAN & LIBERAL MATERIALS THAT WE SATURATE OUR MINDS WITH IT AND CANNOT DISTINGUISH TRUTH FROM ERROR.

OBSERVATION:
PAUL NEVER QUOTED FROM UNINSPIRED WRITERS TO PROVE ANYTHING TO BE RIGHT OR WRONG!

752

Well, let us see my following chart, number 752. In the second paragraph he writes, right there, I am not taking it out of the context, it follows the first one. *Trends Pointing to a New Apostasy*, under Roman numeral II. *"It is not wrong to consult or read uninspired writings."* I do not believe that it is either. *"Paul quoted from them,"* and he gives the passages. *"It is wrong to become so fascinated with sectarian and liberal materials that we saturate our minds with it and cannot distinguish truth from error."* Whose mind is saturated with it when in a twenty-five minute speech he quotes fourteen, fifteen, sixteen uninspired men? I ask you, whose mind is saturated (saturated — filled with), who has been drinking from and trying to get us all to drink from "liberal and sectarian wells"? Brother Halbrook.

Now, this is my observation — Halbrook did not make this observation, I did, surrounded with red to remind me to make this statement [pointing to OBSERVATION at bottom of chart]. I did not charge brother Halbrook with this observation. I do not think he believes it. Paul never quoted from an uninspired writer to prove anything to be right or wrong. If Ron knew a man to go off the deep end on a certain subject, and to show that, you know, he had a lot of force, he said, "Brethren, I want you to know that I don't stand alone." And he quoted brother so-and-so, brother so-and-so, brother so-and-so. This mess is what brother Halbrook has done. "I want you to know, I don't stand alone. Here is a dictionary that confirms what I believe, it agrees with me. And this Presbyterian commentary agrees; Methodist, Methodist commentator, Greek, Methodist, Baptist commentator agrees with me, on, and on, and on." Keep a list of all the uninspired writers in the world — they would not prove his point. Paul never — no other Bible writer ever quoted uninspired writers to prove anything.

What do you brethren do in Texas when you want to prove something? When I lived here — I never lived in this part of Texas, but way down in southwest Texas — people would come to me and say, "Now, Jack Freeman, you teach that baptism is for the remission of sins, I want book, chapter, and verse." Well, the Baptist commentator says so. Well, you know it does not, but even if it did, that did not prove it. I would say his little theme, "The Bible tells me so." "How do we know?" Well, the Bible tells me so.

Let us begin now with my chart number 7; go

HOW DO WE KNOW?
BELIEVER MARRIED TO AN UNBELIEVER

(Cont)

2. IN SOME OF THESE CASES (MARRIAGES)
A. THE UNBELIEVER DEPARTS (DIVORCES THE BELIEVER)
 1) LET HIM DEPART
 2) A BROTHER OR SISTER IS <u>NOT UNDER BONDAGE</u> IN SUCH CASES

*<u>NOT UNDER BONDAGE</u> = NOT UNDER THE CONSTRAINT OF LAW OR NECESSITY IN SOME MATTER.
NOT BOUND BY THE LAW TO A SPOUSE.

7

back to where we left off in the last speech. How do we know the truth in regard to a believer married to an unbeliever? He dealt with the first case. If the unbeliever is pleased to dwell with him, then dwell with him. That is God's law. In some of these marriages God knew the unbeliever would not be pleased and so he said, "If the unbeliever depart" — divorces the believer, incidentally, Thayer also says the word "depart" means divorce — "let him depart. A brother or sister is not under bondage in such cases." Remember we just read Thayer's definition of "bondage." "Not under constraint of law or necessity in some matter." It does not say, "not a slave, never was, never has been."

I want to turn back here and pick up a statement made by brother Halbrook. He says here, "Not a slave, and never has been," he says, "marriage is a spiritual relationship." He says in 1 Corinthians 7:12-16, God is talking about a spiritual relationship. Now, he says just a little later from another passage in this, 1 Corinthians 7, we as Christians are slaves of Christ. Well, that is a spiritual relationship, isn't it? Now, if what he said about a definition of 1 Corinthians 7:15 is right, we are not slaves of Christ, and never have been. The same word, he says, is used for bondage. And, see, it figures out to be the servants of men, but we all are servants, we are slaves of Christ, and that is talking about a spiritual relationship, and he says, 1 Corinthians 7, which in truth talks about, verses 12-15, *a physical relationship: marriage*. He says that is a spiritual relationship. Well, if it is, it must be a relationship to Christ. And what he is saying, "You people where a Christian is married to a non-Christian, never were servants of Christ, and you are not now." I do not think he believes that.

I do not know whether he believes it sinful for a Christian to marry a non-Christian or not. We have not discussed that in this debate, we may not. But there is something wrong here. He says they are both spiritual relationships. If you are a slave of Christ, that is a spiritual relationship; and if you are a slave of your wife, that is a spiritual relationship, except you never have been. What word "bondage" means that? "Not now, never had been. It means that in regard to our relationship to Christ also." We do not accept that I am sure. Now, Thayer does say the primary meaning means "a slavery." But if you come down, let Thayer say what he means about "bondage" in 1 Corinthians 7:15. He does not give it the primary meaning, he gives it the metaphorical meaning.

Now, let us look for his chart number 59-X [text, Mk. 6:17-18]. We want to come back to Herodias. He has a difficult time. He says, "I just cannot understand it." I want you to understand now what he is saying: I hope you are listening to this now. He said they were joined *in God's sight* — it was a marriage in God's sight. You know what the Bible says about marriage, "What God hath joined together, let not man put asunder." My opponent is saying God joined Herod and Herodias together, and then turned right around and *condemns them for being joined together*. God did not join these two together, they were not married in God's sight. I hope you believe that. They were not married in God's sight. [Freeman looks at Halbrook, who nods agreement.] Alright, he agrees with me. They were not married in God's sight. Then God did not join them together. I did not say all Herod had to do to make it right was say, "I put her away"; I did not say that. He said that is what I said—I have never said that. That would not make it right. John said, "It is not lawful for you to have her." He could not have her according to the law.

We are not talking about a man having another man's wife. I have stated over and over again that is not my position. I uphold no man in having another man's wife — no woman in having another woman's husband. I uphold the right of single people, unmarried people, to have *their own* husband or wife. Now, I hope you can all understand that; I think my opponent can—I think he can understand that. He talks about consequences, well, he can say all he wants to. There is something in our agreement that says, point number six, a man will not be charged with a consequence of his position unless he expressly avows that. I do not avow all the ones he has charged me with.

His chart number 150. *He says that I interpret a difficult passage to conflict Matthew 19:9.* [Halbrook nods, *"yes,"* to indicate that Freeman is doing this.] Yes, he shakes his head, yes. Alright, you know half of this debate is in Matthew 19:9, Thursday and Friday night. Do you know why we are having a debate over Matthew 19:9? Because brethren have had difficulty in understanding it. I believe one thing about it and he believes something else. *I believe the put-away fornicator can remarry scripturally.* He believes they cannot. Alright — 1 Corinthians 7:15, we are divided over that; no more so than over Matthew 19:9. I will venture to say that there is just as much division in the church over *Matthew 19:9* as there is over

---

Interpret Difficult Passage - Contradict Clear & Simple One

Matthew 5:32; 19:9	1 Corinthians 7:15
Clear and Simple	Interpretation of Difficult Text
"Whoso marrieth her which is put away doth commit adultery"	Whoso marrieth her which is put away doth NOT commit adultery

150

1 Corinthians 7:12-15, maybe more — maybe more. Most of the debates have been over Matthew 19:9. Why? Because it is evident that people would not be debating over it if they understood it. Someone misunderstands it, maybe we all do. But we would not be debating one another if we understood it, if each agreed this is what it teaches. That is what this debate is all about: to try to get to be honest enough to just step out and say, "Lord, all I want is what you teach. Lord, just tell me what the truth is and I will accept it."

So, this is no way to get out of what the Bible teaches — "You are taking a difficult passage." In the first place, I have pointed out time and time again it does not contradict Matthew 19:9. Read it again, Mark 10:11-12 — *no cause for divorce;* Matthew 19:9 — *one cause for divorce;* no contradiction. Jesus said both of them. But in essence he has charged Jesus with contradicting himself, then charged Paul with contradicting Jesus when Paul said you can remarry if your mate dies, Romans 7:2-3. No, Paul did not contradict any of them. And Paul did not contradict anyone in the inspired writing including Jesus when he taught that *the Christian divorced by the non-Christian was free to marry,* when he said he is no longer held by constraint of law. No longer bound to that mate by God's law.

And he — Halbrook — goes through 1 Corinthians 7. He admits there are different situations, different circumstances. That is all I want him to see. He admitted that 1 Corinthians 7:10-11 is not the same as 1 Corinthians 7:12-16. Here [verse 11] he is dealing with one case, down here in the following verse [verse 12] he is dealing with another case. He admits that. If it is, why does he always go back to Matthew 19 and apply it to every case. He said, "Now, this is a different case, Jesus did not deal with it." Well, if he did not, you will have to forget about what he said and you will have to listen to what Paul said. And Paul said, "Jesus did not deal with this." And my opponent admitted Jesus did not deal with it. Then, we will have to take what Paul says and it is just as truthful as what Jesus said because he was guided word by word by the Holy Spirit.

Let us look at his chart number 157. Again, he says that "bondage" means that we are slaves of Jesus when it talks about our relationship to Christ. And he talks about this — remember, his own witness tells us what this word "bondage" means in 1 Corinthians 7:15. He says it means, my opponent says, *"never a slave and never has been* — and it is talking about a *spiritual relationship."* Thayer says it is talking about *marriage* because it had a figurative meaning, not the literal meaning. It does not mean slavery — it does not use the word slavery at all, it means bondage. "Held under constraint of law or of necessity in some matter." In 1 Corinthians 7 we already dealt with these supposed virgins and that

Two Bonds In 1 Cor. 7

1. **BOUND** by God's marriage law = tied, fastened, joined, from DEO in Romans 7:2; 1 Cor. 7:27, 39 (See Thayer, Vines, Etc.)
2. **BONDAGE** or enslavement to the demands of another person = to make a slave of, reduce to bondage, enslave, from DOULOO in 1 Cor. 7:15; noun form in vs. 23 (Thayer, Etc.)

LIKE:

1. **BURDENS** to share = a heavy or crushing load, from BAROS in Gal. 6:2.
2. **BURDEN** for each man alone = a normal load or cargo, from PHORTION in Gal. 6:5.

they are bound to wives. Everything there is virgins but there are some of them that are bound to wives — mighty peculiar sounding virgins to me.

Okay, my chart number 8 coming up next — 1 Corinthians 7:15. Now he said, when I got onto him a little in North Las Vegas for depending on these sectarian sources, drinking from sectarian wells, liberal wells, he said, "Brother Freeman introduced this chart and there are hundreds of witnesses." These are Bible translations. "Not under bondage in such cases." Now, the reason I use this is to show that all these translations include *"in such cases."* King James, American Standard, Revised Version, New American Standard, New International Version.

Go to my next chart please, number 9. All of those, King James Version included now, the point is — "not under bondage" — then "the believer is not and never was bound" — the words "in such cases" mean nothing; you just think about it. "Not under bondage in such cases" — he says it means *"never was in bondage."* Paul says "in such cases" — that means "in other cases you were." "In the preceding case I talked about where the believer is pleased to dwell with you, you were in bondage; but now you are not — this is a different case." That is why Thayer gives a different meaning. Now, you could argue with him about whether or not he is right or with my opponent, it is his witness not mine. So I simply use this showing all these

HOW DO WE KNOW?
1 COR. 7:15

"NOT UNDER BONDAGE IN SUCH CASES"

KING JAMES VERSION - 48 TRANSLATORS:
"...IS NOT UNDER BONDAGE **IN SUCH CASES**..."

AMERICAN STANDARD VERSION - 100 TRANSLATORS:
"...IS NOT UNDER BONDAGE **IN SUCH CASES**..."

REVISED STANDARD VERSION - 9 NT TRANSLATORS:
"...**IN SUCH A CASE** THE BROTHER OR SISTER IS NOT BOUND..."

NEW AMERICAN STANDARD VER. - 50 TRANSLATORS:
"...IS NOT UNDER BONDAGE **IN SUCH CASES**..."

NEW INTERNATIONAL VERSION - 100 TRANSLATORS:
"...IS NOT BOUND **IN SUCH CASES**..."

translations which use the phrase "in such cases" which would be absolutely meaningless if "bondage" means "you are not a slave now and never were."

Let us go to my next chart please, number 17. Demanding the impossible. I want you people to think about it. You were not in North Las Vegas. I used this. *Number one:* How can you know that the one you married was never married before? How can you know that? *Number two:* How can you know that the one you marry was not divorced because of adultery? *Number three:* How can you know that the one you married divorced their previous spouse on the grounds of fornication. *Number four:* How can you know that the one you marry was not divorced for a cause other than fornication? *Number five:* How can you know that the Christian you marry was not divorced by an unbeliever? *Number six:* How can you know that the one you baptize and fellowship as a faithful Christian and for whom you perform a marriage ceremony was not previously divorced for fornication?

> **1 COR. 7:15**
> (Cont)
>
> "NOT UNDER BONDAGE IN SUCH CASES"
>
> NEW KING JAMES VERSION - 47 TRANSLATORS:
> "...IS NOT BOUND IN SUCH CASES..."
>
> *POINT: IF, IN THIS CONTEXT, "NOT UNDER BONDAGE" MEANT THE BELIEVER IS NOT AND NEVER WAS BOUND, THE WORDS "IN SUCH CASES" MEAN NOTHING.
>
> *FACT: THE FOREGOING TRANSLATORS AGREE THAT THE WORDS "IN SUCH CASES" BELONG IN THE TEXT.
>
> 9

> **DEMANDING THE IMPOSSIBLE**
> **HOW CAN YOU KNOW:**
>
> 1. THAT THE ONE YOU MARRY WAS NEVER MARRIED BEFORE?
> 2. THAT THE ONE YOU MARRY WAS NOT DIVORCED BECAUSE OF ADULTERY?
> 3. THAT THE ONE YOU MARRY DIVORCED A PREVIOUS SPOUSE ON GROUNDS OF FORNICATION?
> 4. THAT THE ONE YOU MARRY WAS NOT DIVORCED FOR A CAUSE OTHER THAN FORNICATION?
> 5. THAT THE CHRISTIAN YOU MARRY WAS NOT DIVORCED BY AN UNBELIEVER?
> 6. THAT THE ONE YOU BAPTIZE AND FELLOWSHIP AS A FAITHFUL CHRISTIAN AND FOR WHOM YOU PERFORM A MARRIAGE CEREMONY WAS NOT PREVIOUSLY DIVORCED FOR FORNICATION?
>
> 17

Go on to the next chart, my chart 18. I want to make some observations about this one. I do not know what you brethren do down here with someone who comes along to the West Columbia congregation. *Do you question every one of them about their marriage when a person comes to make the good confession and be baptized? Do you question them about their past marriages?* You would

Second Evening: Freeman's Second Negative

> **DEMANDING THE IMPOSSIBLE**
> (Cont)
>
> <u>WHAT PROOF WILL YOU DEMAND TO SHOW THAT ONE HAS BEEN GUILTY OF FORNICATION?</u>
>
> * <u>COURT RECORDS?</u>
> * <u>THE WORD OF A FRIEND?</u>
> * <u>THE WORD OF THE ONE YOU WANT TO MARRY?</u>
> * <u>PHOTOGRAPHIC EVIDENCE?</u>
> * <u>SEEING IT WITH YOUR OWN EYES?</u>
> * <u>ASK RON HALBROOK?</u>
>
> 18

be obligated to. Do you take their word if they say, "Yes, I was married but my wife committed adultery, and I divorced for that reason." Will you take his word? Do you hire detectives to investigate?

Well, let us go on. What proof would you demand to show that one has been guilty of *fornication?* Court records? You cannot depend on them. He admits, he said, in Texas why they won't even use it and in Nevada they won't either. Lawyers make their money too easy; if you have to prove fornication, they would have to go out and work. Now, they get their money for doing nothing. So you cannot go with court records. You cannot go with the word of a friend; the word of one you want to marry, one could accept their word; or, if you wanted to demand photographic evidence. Are you going to insist that I have to see it with my own eyes before I believe it? Or will you ask brother Ron Halbrook? Do you know what his answer was? "If you cannot know, you just cannot marry."

Now, I want you older people to think about that. You women who were married to service men and they were gone for a year or two overseas; I want you men to think about it. I am not suggesting that any of you was unfaithful. How can you know if they were not? How can you know that the man you married did not marry a woman and leave some children overseas? Maybe in the Philippines, Japan, or somewhere? You know this happened a lot according to our military records, but the wife never knew anything about it. He simply got married again; it was legal over there but it was not scriptural; they were not married in God's sight. So what brother Halbrook is doing is demanding the impossible. There is no way out of it. So he can only give one answer, "Do not marry." This applies to him, it applies to him just as much as it does to us.

Let us look at my next chart, chart number 15. "God versus Halbrook." When you come up with a new doctrine, you have got to come up with a new plan of salvation. Have you ever thought of that? If you come up with a new doctrine, you have got to come up with a new plan of salvation. According to God, to all aliens, "Repent, and be baptized every one of you in the name of Jesus Christ for the remission of sins," scripture, Acts 2:38. According to Halbrook, to some aliens, "Repent, put away your spouse, be baptized and remain single the rest of your life." He has not given book, chapter, and verse. He says, "Oh, we will not hear about the fornicator having the right." I have given it to him but he just will not accept it. He has not even attempted to put a Scripture here.

GOD VS. HALBROOK

GOD TO:	HALBROOK TO:
ALL ALIENS "REPENT, AND BE BAPTIZED EVERY ONE OF YOU IN THE NAME OF JESUS CHRIST FOR THE REMISSION OF SINS..." SCRIPTURE: ACTS 2:38	**SOME ALIENS** "REPENT, PUT AWAY YOUR SPOUSE, BE BAPTIZED AND REMAIN SINGLE THE REST OF YOUR LIFE". SCRIPTURE: _____
SINFUL MEMBERS OF THE CHURCH "REPENT AND PRAY..." ACTS 8:22 CONFESS OUR SINS" 1 JNO. 1:9	**SOME SINFUL MEMBERS OF THE CHURCH** "REPENT, PUT AWAY YOUR SPOUSE, REMAIN UNMARRIED THE REST OF YOUR LIFE". SCRIPTURE: _____
"GOD IS FAITHFUL AND JUST TO FORGIVE US OUR SINS, AND TO CLEANSE US FROM ALL UNRIGHTEOUSNESS" 1 JNO. 1:9	"REPENT, REMAINED UNMARRIED THE REST OF YOUR LIFE". SCRIPTURE: _____

15

Tomorrow night I will ask him a direct question: *"Can you give one verse supporting what you believe about this?"* God said to the sinful member of the church, "Repent and pray" *(Acts 8:22);* "confess your sins" *(1 John 1:9)*. 1 John 1:9, God will forgive us. But Halbrook says to some members of the church, "Repent, put away your spouse, remain unmarried the rest of your life." Scripture please — he cannot give it. And he says to others, "Repent, remain unmarried the rest of your life." Give the book, chapter, and verse please. Now just think about that. If you have book, chapter, and verse, you give it to me tonight. I will be happy to have it.

MK. 16:15 - MATT. 28:19-20 - COL. 1:6, 23

GOSPEL PREACHED TO EVERY CREATURE - ALL NATIONS

*NOT ONE PERSON WAS TOLD TO LEAVE HUSBAND OR WIFE.

*NOT ONE PERSON WAS TOLD TO REMAIN SINGLE FOR LIFE.

*BUT PEOPLE WERE SAVED - ADDED TO THE CHURCH AND HAD HOPE OF ETERNAL LIFE.

WHO NEEDS HALBROOK'S DOCTRINE?

16

Let us look at the next one, my chart number 16. Alright, the gospel had been preached to every creature. Paul said so in Colossians 1:6, 23. Now, let us follow their preaching. When did this doctrine come into effect anyway? Did it start in Acts 2 when three thousand were baptized? Did it start a little later in Acts when thousands more were baptized? Did it start over there in Corinth when fornicators and adulterers were baptized? When did it start? Well, it had to start some place. Yet, in all the preaching that was done — go through all your New Testament, not just the book of Acts, but in other books Paul refers back. Other writers said these people — their conversion, but in all their preaching and in all their writing *not one person was told to leave* husband or wife. Not one. If you believe it is, just give me book, chapter, and verse. Not one person was told to *remain single* in life, but you [Halbrook] have been in there telling them that, aren't you? Oh, yes, you are. You are telling them that.

People were saved; they were added to the church and had the hope of eternal life. *Who needs Halbrook's doctrine?* If you can be saved, if you can be in the church, you can have the hope of eternal life without it. You know why I am not out preaching this? I cannot give book, chapter, and verse for it. I cannot say to a man or a woman, "You will have to leave your husband or wife to be a Christian. I will not baptize you, not until you leave." But, [they respond,] "Oh, we don't do that. We baptize them, then withdraw from them."

Alright, let us look at the next chart, my chart number 21. A contrast. God says, "It is not good for man to be alone." Halbrook says, "Some will have to be alone." God says, "It is better to marry than to burn." Halbrook says, "Some will have to burn." Now, he tried to wiggle out of it. He teaches that some will have to be alone, he teaches that some will have to burn — that is what he teaches; he admits he teaches it. "Marriage is honorable." He admits he teaches some cannot do that which is honorable because of a mistake they made in the past. They did a dishonorable thing and that prohibits them from doing the honorable thing. To avoid fornication, God says marry. Halbrook says some cannot use God's means of avoiding fornication.

God says, "If loosed, you do not sin when you marry." Halbrook says, "Some who are loosed do sin when they marry." He can talk about loose dogs

A CONTRAST:

GOD	HALBROOK
IT IS NOT GOOD FOR MAN TO BE ALONE	SOME WILL HAVE TO BE ALONE
IT IS BETTER TO MARRY THAN TO BURN	SOME WILL HAVE TO BURN
MARRIAGE IS HONORABLE	SOME CANNOT DO THAT WHICH IS HONORABLE
TO AVOID FORNICATION, MARRY	SOME CANNOT USE THIS MEANS TO AVOID FORNICATION
IF LOOSED, YOU DO NOT SIN WHEN YOU MARRY	SOME WHO ARE LOOSED DO SIN WHEN THEY REMARRY

WHO IS RIGHT? 21

all he wants to. Loose dogs are not marrying and not committing fornication; we are talking about people. We are talking about if you are loosed in the sight of God, not married in the sight of God, God says when you marry you do not sin. Halbrook says, "Even though you are loosed in the sight of God, when you marry you do sin."

Next chart please, my chart number 59. Halbrook used this chart in North Las Vegas. He said, "You steal another man's wife, another man's watch, another man's car — repentance demands that you give it back." *That is right; no argument.* But if this is true, if it is going to prove anything: You steal a man's watch, you give it back, you can *never* have your own. You steal his car, and you will have to give it back, and you can *never* have your own car. It is not true that when you give the man's wife back, you can never have *your own* wife. If you have your own watch, you have your car, then you can have your own wife. If not, then you can never be allowed to own a watch if you ever steal one, even though you give it back. And if you steal an automobile you will never be allowed by God to have your own even though you give that car back, repent and give it back. Well, I repent and *give the man's wife back.* He says, "Oh, oh, you can have the watch, go out and buy one; you can have a car, go out and buy one, but you can never have another wife." What did that prove? It proves too

A MAN STEALS

ANOTHER'S WIFE   ANOTHER'S WATCH   ANOTHER'S CAR

REPENTANCE DEMANDS: RETURN THE WIFE, THE WATCH, THE CAR

AND NEVER HAVE:

YOUR OWN WIFE----YOUR OWN WATCH----YOUR OWN CAR
(IF THIS IS TRUE)   (SO IS THIS)   (AND THIS)

BUT

IF AFTER REPENTANCE, A MAN CAN HAVE HIS OWN WATCH AND HIS OWN CAR; HE CAN HAVE <u>HIS OWN WIFE</u>!

59

HOW DO WE KNOW?
GOD ANTICIPATED FALSE DOCTRINE

1 TIM. 4:1-3
"...<u>SOME SHALL DEPART FROM THE FAITH</u> GIVING HEED TO SEDUCING SPIRITS AND <u>DOCTRINES OF DEVILS, FORBIDDING TO MARRY</u>..."

WHO IS DEMANDING CELIBACY?
WHO IS FORBIDDING TO MARRY?

<u>DO YOU WANT THE DOCTRINES OF DEVILS</u>
OR
<u>THE FAITH ???</u>

1

much. He admits that the man can have a watch of his own; the man can have his own car. How do we know? The Bible tells us so. That is how we know.

Again, God anticipated this false doctrine, see my chart 1 on 1 Timothy 4:3, and my opponent admits that he forbids to marry — he forbids to marry. Well, what do we read? The faith does not; the faith, the gospel, does not forbid to marry. We are talking about people who are not married. We are not talking about people who are already married in the sight of God. The devil, the doctrine of devils, forbids people to marry. The faith does not. Who is demanding celibacy, the Bible? Is God demanding celibacy or is my opponent? You do not have any difficulty answering that.

Rebuttals:
Second Evening
Halbrook's Third Affirmative

Brother Freeman, gentlemen moderators, brothers and sisters in Christ. I want to say to Larry Hafley, my moderator, that I am *already relaxed*. I never felt better or had less to do in a closing speech [alluding to Hafley's remark after the intermission that everyone should be seated for the closing speeches, then we could all go home and relax].

We have shown you tonight on our chart number 1 that *the passage Matthew 19 is embodied in our proposition,* "The Scriptures teach that two people joined by God in marriage are bound for life, the only exception being that an innocent partner may put away a mate guilty of fornication and remarry."

Notice Matthew 19:9. "Whosoever shall put away his wife, except it be for fornication, and shall marry another, committeth adultery: and whoso marrieth her which is put away doth commit adultery." My friend, you remember that was *new* preaching when I brought it to Las Vegas, but it is not new to you. You understand that when we put our mate away, if it is not for fornication, that subsequent, second marriage, that marrying another, is *adultery* in the sight of God. And no amount of moving the checkers on the checker-board can ever make it anything else.

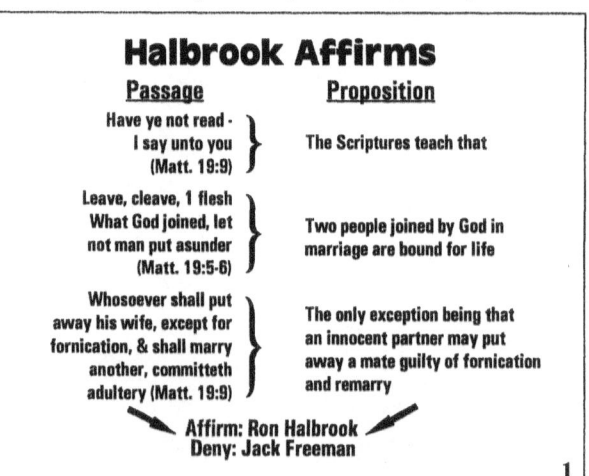

And, then, we notice again, I want our chart 74. *"Except"* — *if and only if* is the force. I did not say it was the definition of the word in the dictionary. I am showing you the force of the word. Surely, you can understand that. "Except you become as a little child, you cannot enter the kingdom." My friend, the Bible teaches that if you put your wife away for fornication and marry another, it is *not* adultery. *Except* you put your wife away — *except* — a man who puts his wife

Except = If & Only If!

* Matt. 18:3 Become as little child → Enter kingdom

* John 3:2 God with Him → Do miracles

* John 3:5 Born of water & Spirit → Enter kingdom

* Matt. 19:9 Put away wife for fornication & marry another → Not adultery

74

away, *except* it be for fornication, and marries another, commits adultery. If he puts her away for fornication, and marries another, it is *not adultery*.

See my chart 74-A. "Except it be for fornication" — except it miss the hoop. The young people here can understand this. We are not making fun of them or light of them. I was told last night the young people paid close attention; young people talked to me about the things that they had learned, brother Freeman. Whoever shoots a basketball, *except* it misses the hoop, scores two points. *If and only if* your shot misses the hoop you do *not* get two points. *If and only if* you put your wife away for fornication, and marry another, you do *not* commit adultery. We can understand it. The young people can understand it. The women, the godly women, understand it. I can understand it. And if

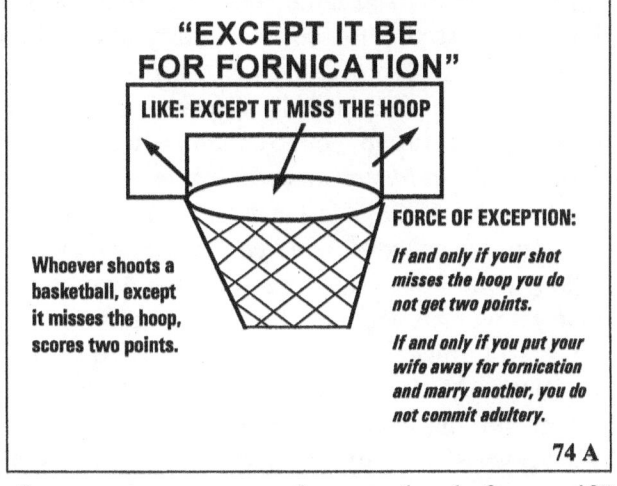

I can understand it, next to the women — you see, they are ahead of me — if I can understand it, then brother Freeman can join hands with me and understand it. Surely, we can. Surely, we can.

Alright now, go to chart 122-A. I am just trying to show you that we are following *the text*. What is my appeal tonight? Book, chapter, and verse. Book, chapter, and verse. Book, chapter and verse. How do we know? The Bible tells me so. My friend, I am interested in what the text says. "Let every man have his own wife," 1 Corinthians 7:2. *Is the guilty, put-away fornicator to marry another in this text?* Every man who wrecks his marriage and throws away his own wife by fornication or some unscriptural divorce, get *another* wife?

Now, he [Freeman] showed this chart up here and dallied around, but he never read this statement right here [pointing to top, right part of chart, "Every man who wrecks his marriage..."], be-

Does 1 Cor. 7 Authorize The Put-Away Fornicator To Marry Another?	
Text Says This:	**Not This:**
Vs. 2 "Every man have his own wife"	Every man who wrecks his marriage & throws away his own wife by fornication or unscriptural divorce, gets another wife!
Vs. 9 "Unmarried...widows... better to marry than to burn"	Unscripturally divorced & put-away fornicator... better to commit adultery than fornication!
Vv. 27-28 A man "loosed from a wife" (free, never married) and "a virgin" (free, never married) may marry.	A man unscripturally divorced or a divorced fornicator may marry a woman in the same condition!

122 A

cause that is what he is teaching and that is what he is appealing to. He knows that is *not* in the text of the scripture.

Verse nine talked about *"the unmarried* and *widows;"* Paul told us to whom it was addressed. "It is better to marry than to burn," is not addressed to the unscripturally divorced and the put-away fornicator. He did not say, "I am addressing the unscripturally divorced and the put-away fornicator. Hear ye, hear ye, it is better for you to commit adultery than fornication. Do not fall into fornication, *get into an unscriptural marriage,* instead, and *commit adultery."*

In verses 27-28, it is a man "loosed from a wife" *(free, never married)* and "a virgin" *(free, never married),* and they may marry. That is what the text is talking about. But a man unscripturally divorced or a divorced fornicator may marry a woman who is in the same condition — unscripturally divorced and divorced fornicator — that is *not* in the text anywhere.

Notice Matthew 5:32 on chart 60. "Whosoever shall put away his wife, saving for the cause of fornication, causeth her to commit adultery: and whosoever shall marry her that is divorced committeth adultery." Notice the word cause, "causeth." This passage hinges on the *cause*. Now then notice, if you put your wife away for fornication, you do not *cause* her to what? To commit the adultery. The adultery is committed, but you did not cause it.

Now, Jesus did not say, "You *cause* her to *not commit* adultery." That is brother Freeman's position, you see. It does not revolve around the *commission* of the sin, the sin is placed there. It revolves around whether you *caused* it or not. And whoever marries that woman who is put away unscripturally, or else that put-away fornicator, commits adultery in such a marriage.

> ### Matthew 5:32
>
> "But I say unto you, That whosoever shall put away his wife, saving for the cause of fornication, causeth her to commit adultery: and whosoever shall marry her that is divorced committeth adultery."
>
> 60

Alright, we want to notice chart 140-X. "Unto the married I command, yet not I, but the Lord. Let not the wife depart from her husband: But and if she depart, let her remain unmarried, or be reconciled to her husband: and let not the husband put away his wife." And I guess Paul should have put a P.S. or else let her talk to brother Freeman about moving the checkers on the board, and maybe *after that subsequent marriage* which she sinfully contracted, you can say that you do not want her, and *then she can stay in it*. A bunch of "mumbo-jumbo!" The passage is clear, plain, and simple, and if you violate this by *getting into* a marriage, the only way you can be right is to *get out* of that marriage and come back and do what the Bible says to do.

Alright, then we notice chart 59-X [text, Mk. 6:17-18]. This is the pas-

> ### 1 Corinthians 7:10-11
>
> "And unto the married I command, yet not I, but the Lord, Let not the wife depart from her husband: But and if she depart, let her remain unmarried or be reconciled to her husband: and let not the husband put away his wife."
>
> 140 X

sage that he does not know what it has to do with this debate. Well, here is what it has to do with it: Herodias *left* Philip and *went to* Herod, "for he had married her." I did not say God joined them. I said it was not a mere reference to a courthouse. This is a text of Scripture; the text of Scripture is what said he married her. *He married her in a human relationship not approved by God.* I understand that.

But now, my friend, John had said unto Herod, "It is not lawful for thee to have thy brother's wife." The difference between myself and brother Freeman is this: That *if* Philip would only say he did not want her any more, he was tired of her, *then* John could say, "It is not lawful for thee to have thy brother's wife, but of course we can work this out. We will just talk to Philip, I am sure he does not want you back anyway — now it will be lawful. Just say you repent; come on, say you repent, and then it will be lawful, it will be alright."

You know he [Freeman] would not deny that is what he believes. I could not get him to deny it. And did he deny it when he came back up here? No sir, he did not deny it. He believes that all it would take is for Philip to nod his head, "I am through with her." And now she becomes the lawful, wedded wife of Herod. There is his doctrine! Every kind of an unscriptural divorce and remarriage can be justified in this doctrine.

Chart 150-X. Slaves to Christ, not to men. "If the unbelieving depart, let him depart. A brother or sister is not under bondage (has not been enslaved) in such cases: but God has called us to peace." "Ye are bought with a price; be not ye the servants (slaves) of men." And so we understand that even though we are still in a marriage relationship, the higher bond is to the Lord. Even though we are in an economic relationship, the higher bond is to the Lord. *But that higher bond to the Lord does not free the slave from his slavery, and the higher bond to the Lord does not free you from a marriage relationship*. No, not free to *marry another*, and nowhere does it say you are.

Slaves To Christ, Not To Men
1 Corinthians 7:15, 23

But if the unbelieving depart, let him depart. A brother or a sister is not under bondage (lit.: *has not been enslaved)* in such cases; but God has called us to peace.

Ye are bought with a price; be not ye the servants (lit.: *slaves*) of men.

150 X

Chart 190-X. We noted the text in 1 Corinthians 7:25-28, "Now concerning virgins" — *never married*— "...for the present distress,...good for a man so to be" — *never married*. "Art thou bound unto a wife? seek not to be loosed" — if you are married, stay that way. But now look at his train of thought again, "Art thou loosed from a wife? seek not a wife." That is the man loosed from a wife, free from a wife — *"never cohabited"* is what the Greeks say that means. "But and if thou marry, thou hast not sinned; and if a virgin marry, she hath not sinned." So, *the man who has never married* and *the woman who has never*

1 Corinthians 7:25-28

Now concerning virgins...	} Never Married
...for the present distress... good for a man so to be	} Never Married
Art thou bound unto a wife? Seek not to be loosed	} If Married, STAY
Art thou loosed from a wife? Seek not a wife. But and if thou marry, thou hast not sinned; and if a virgin marry, she hath not sinned [but best not to marry, vv. 28-38]	} If man never married, STAY } If woman never married, STAY

190 X

married — that is what you have in that context.

Now then, he had his chart — let us look at his chart 752. Alright, now, here he is talking about that we do not prove by appeal to uninspired sources — that is right. Now, I want to just leave it [Freeman's chart number 752] there and put my chart 02 over it. Now I want you to notice, my friend, Freeman cited 355 uninspired scholars. When *he* does it, it is *right;* when *I* do it, it is *wrong*. That is how simple it is to understand that. That is just how simple that matter is.

Now, then, on the matter of there being two bonds, my chart number 157 [next page]. He said that Thayer said that in 1 Corinthians 7:15 *bondage* meant *marriage*. And I defy you from the top of your head to the bottom of your feet to find where Thayer ever said that referred to marriage, brother Freeman. It does

TRENDS POINTING TOWARD A NEW APOSTASY
(NOTES BY BOB HALBROOK) (Cont))

IT IS NOT WRONG TO CONSULT OR READ UNINSPIRED WRITINGS
PAUL QUOTED FROM THEM — ACTS 17:28, I COR. 15:32, TIT. 1:12

IT IS WRONG TO BECOME SO FASCINATED WITH SECTARIAN & LIBERAL MATERIALS THAT WE SATURATE OUR MINDS WITH IT AND CANNOT DISTINGUISH TRUTH FROM ERROR.

OBSERVATION:
PAUL NEVER QUOTED FROM UNINSPIRED WRITERS TO PROVE ANYTHING TO BE RIGHT OR WRONG.

752/02

not say that. Not only do you *pervert Christ,* you *pervert Thayer*. Never once does he say that! No sir, he does not say that. No sir, he does not say that.

Now, then, on his "Demands the Impossible" chart. Well, our time is about gone — I will pick up some of those later. I just want to notice my chart 176. My friend, here are the steps of progression as historians have pointed out. "The flood gates are open" when you take this position. "If your husband deserts you, you can have another. If he is cruel, you can have another. If he fails to support you, you may have another. If he is a drunkard, you may have another, and so

Two Bonds In 1 Cor. 7

1. **BOUND** by God's marriage law = tied, fastened, joined, from DEO in Romans 7:2; 1 Cor. 7:27, 39 (See Thayer, Vines, Etc.)

2. **BONDAGE** or enslavement to the demands of another person = to make a slave of, reduce to bondage, enslave, from DOULOO in 1 Cor. 7:15; noun form in vs. 23 (Thayer, Etc.)

LIKE:

1. **BURDENS** to share = a heavy or crushing load, from BAROS in Gal. 6:2.

2. **BURDEN** for each man alone = a normal load or cargo, from PHORTION in Gal. 6:5.

157

I.S.B.E. Article Warns

If use 1 Cor. 7:15 as right to remarry,
"The flood gates are open" (II:865-866)

Steps of Progression:

"If your husband deserts you, you may have another. If he is cruel, you may have another. If he fails to support you, you may have another. If he is drunken, you may have another. If he is incompatible or makes you unhappy, you may have another" - and yet others beyond these.

Results: Careless Marriages, Divorce For Any Cause, Multiplied Miseries!

176

on." This position leads to careless marriages, divorce for any cause, and multiplied miseries. *We protect our children by teaching them the truth.* Teach them the text, as we have shown the text time and time again.

> ## How We Know
>
> **Simplicity Of Truth:** "Yes, Jesus loves me, the Bible tells me so" (Rom. 4:3; Eph. 3:4)
>
> **Know We Can Remarry:**
> 1. If mate dies (Rom. 7:2-3)
> 2. If put away mate for fornication (Matt. 19:9)
>
> **Where Does The Bible Authorize These To Remarry:**
> 1. The put-away fornicator?
> 2. Those unscripturally divorced?
>
> 54

How do we know, chart 54, remember that? *How do we know?* Even the young people will go away, and the women go away, and even Ron will go away, and understand *how we know.* If your mate dies, you can marry another. If you put your mate away for fornication, you can marry another. He [Freeman] did *not* find the put-away fornicator could marry another — *never* found it, *cannot* find it. And those unscripturally divorced — marry another — he never found it and he cannot find it. Yes, I am raising an eighteen year old son; I am thankful for him, it is a gift from God; and I am responsible to teach him that God's marriage law is binding for life. And if we love our children and would protect them, and protect the church and the purity of truth, then let us teach them that it is *one man for one woman for life with only one exception.*

Rebuttals:
Second Evening
Freeman's Third Negative

Brethren, friends, moderators, brother Halbrook. In the final ten minutes I would again call your attention to the charts that my opponent had. I wanted to show, I want you to remember what is at the top — *"except"* — that word, and then right after that the signs were equal — two little dashes, "equals" *if and only if*. Now he is trying to get out of it, he says "That is not what I meant." Well, that is what he had up there. That equals, equals. And he saw that got him in trouble and so he had to back off of that and change that — it does not mean it is the same, a synonym. With a synonym I showed you the problem he got into.

> **Except = If & Only If!**
>
> * Matt. 18:3 Become as little child → Enter kingdom
> * John 3:2 God with Him → Do miracles
> * John 3:5 Born of water & Spirit → Enter kingdom
> * Matt. 19:9 Put away wife for fornication & marry another → Not adultery

And the appeal, he says, is for book, chapter, and verse. Did he give it for his plan of salvation? I put his plan of salvation right up there with God's, side by side. He saw God's; he did not give his, did he? Repent and put away your wife. Repent and remain single. He did not give it. You cannot give it either. If you can, I would like to hear it.

You know, his strongest argument, the only thing I could hear is *Herod and Herodias,* and then he got himself into a mess here: He says they were really married. But God did not join them together. This, brother Halbrook, if God did not join those two together, who did? Who joined them together in marriage if God did not? It had to be civil authorities. God joins together if the marriage meets his approval. You said God did not do it and yet you said they were married in God's sight. You cannot have it both ways. So, who did join them together? If God, then the marriage was pleasing. But what did John say? "It is not lawful for you to have her."

Second Evening: Freeman's Third Negative 149

Again, the reason *this has nothing to do with our debate,* I let you know again, and do not go around quoting Jack Freeman as saying, do not write me up in your paper as saying, "Jack Freeman believes that any man can go take your wife; any woman can take your husband." I do not believe that. Any unmarried person has the right to *their own* spouse. That is what I believe — you can quote me on that. Now, I did deny what you quoted me as saying about Herod. *I did not say all he had to do to make it right was to say, "I will put you away," and then keep her.* I did not say that. No, I did not say that about Herod. I said exactly what John did, it was not lawful for Herod to have her. He could have said, "I put her away, I put her away, I repent, I repent," and kept her; it was not lawful for him to have her, period. Now, that is what I said about it. I said exactly what John said about it. And I do not think that I should be criticized for saying what John said about it.

Now, he says, "Freeman called upon these hundreds of witnesses." I simply referred to Bible translations. *I am like my opponent, I do not believe it is wrong to use other books.* But I believe it is wrong to try to prove anything by any source other than the Bible.

Let us see now my chart number 15. I put on my chart as an exact quote, Thayer said — and I invite anyone to come and read it — he says I misquoted Thayer. If you believe that, you come down and read it for yourself, we will just lay it here on the desk, you can take all night if you want to. Just line up in single file, you can come down and read it. I did not misquote Thayer. A word for word. I checked it, several other people checked it before I put it on the chart. I checked it after it was put on the chart; they checked it after it was put on the chart. If that was a mistake, I want to know it. I believe I quoted it word for word exactly what he said.

GOD VS. HALBROOK

GOD TO:	HALBROOK TO:
ALL ALIENS "REPENT, AND BE BAPTIZED EVERY ONE OF YOU IN THE NAME OF JESUS CHRIST FOR THE REMISSION OF SINS..." SCRIPTURE: ACTS 2:38	**SOME ALIENS** "REPENT, PUT AWAY YOUR SPOUSE, BE BAPTIZED AND REMAIN SINGLE THE REST OF YOUR LIFE". SCRIPTURE: _____
SINFUL MEMBERS OF THE CHURCH "REPENT AND PRAY..." ACTS 8:22 CONFESS OUR SINS" 1 JNO. 1:9	**SOME SINFUL MEMBERS OF THE CHURCH** "REPENT, PUT AWAY YOUR SPOUSE, REMAIN UNMARRIED THE REST OF YOUR LIFE". SCRIPTURE: _____
"GOD IS FAITHFUL AND JUST TO FORGIVE US OUR SINS, AND TO CLEANSE US FROM ALL UNRIGHTEOUSNESS" 1 JNO. 1:9	"REPENT, REMAINED UNMARRIED THE REST OF YOUR LIFE". SCRIPTURE: _____

15

Chart number 15. God versus Halbrook. And we will leave Friday night without any Scriptures being given to repent, put away your spouse, be baptized, remain single for the rest of your life — it will not be there. He says, "That is

God's plan of salvation — that is what I preach." He will say to some sinful members of the church, repent, put away your spouse, remain single the rest of your life. Some might say when you repent you just live together, but no sex, but repent, put away your spouse, remain unmarried the rest of your life. Or to others: repent, remain unmarried the rest of your life. Book, chapter, verse, please, that is all I ask for. And he has not given it.

Let us see my chart number 16. Jesus told the Apostles to preach the gospel throughout the world; Paul said that job had been accomplished. It does not mean we do not have the same job. Others did then, and they said every creature under heaven had heard the gospel. My opponent has not denied that. So, the gospel was preached to every creature — all nations. In all their preaching, *not one person was told to leave his wife*. [Some in the audience found this statement ironic after the discussion

> **MK. 16:15 - MATT. 28:19-20 - COL. 1:6, 23**
>
> GOSPEL PREACHED TO EVERY CREATURE - ALL NATIONS
>
> *NOT ONE PERSON WAS TOLD TO LEAVE HUSBAND OR WIFE.
>
> *NOT ONE PERSON WAS TOLD TO REMAIN SINGLE FOR LIFE.
>
> *BUT PEOPLE WERE SAVED - ADDED TO THE CHURCH AND HAD HOPE OF ETERNAL LIFE.
>
> **WHO NEEDS HALBROOK'S DOCTRINE?**
>
> 16

about Herod, causing brief, subdued laughter.] Now, you want to snicker about it? I want to ask you: how much laughing will you be doing on the day of judgment when he asks you, "Where is book, chapter, and verse for what you preached on that subject? Where is it?" Do you think you can laugh your way into heaven? Where will you find that book, chapter, and verse to give to the Lord then? Where is it? *Not one person was told to leave a husband or wife.* Not one person was told to remain single for life, and yet during the time the Apostles preached, people were saved, they were added to the church; they had the hope of eternal life. And again I ask you: *Who needs Halbrook's doctrine?*

Next chart, please, number 17. "Demanding the Impossible." And you just think about what you will have to acknowledge that Halbrook and others — if you agree with it — are demanding the impossible. How can you know? And his only answer — he did not give an answer tonight, but how can you know? You have got to take his word for it. And he says the only safe way is do not marry. That would apply to all. How do you know that the one you married was never married before? How can you know that the one you have married was not

> **DEMANDING THE IMPOSSIBLE**
> **HOW CAN YOU KNOW:**
>
> 1. THAT THE ONE YOU MARRY WAS NEVER MARRIED BEFORE?
> 2. THAT THE ONE YOU MARRY WAS NOT DIVORCED BECAUSE OF ADULTERY?
> 3. THAT THE ONE YOU MARRY DIVORCED A PREVIOUS SPOUSE ON GROUNDS OF FORNICATION?
> 4. THAT THE ONE YOU MARRY WAS NOT DIVORCED FOR A CAUSE OTHER THAN FORNICATION?
> 5. THAT THE CHRISTIAN YOU MARRY WAS NOT DIVORCED BY AN UNBELIEVER?
> 6. THAT THE ONE YOU BAPTIZE AND FELLOWSHIP AS A FAITHFUL CHRISTIAN AND FOR WHOM YOU PERFORM A MARRIAGE CEREMONY WAS NOT PREVIOUSLY DIVORCED FOR FORNICATION?
>
> 17

divorced because of adultery? How can you know that the one you married divorced their previous spouse on the grounds of fornication? How can you know the one you married was not divorced for a cause other than fornication? How can you know that the Christian you married was not divorced by an unbeliever? How can you know, number six, that the one you baptized and fellowship as a faithful Christian and for whom you perform a marriage ceremony was not previously divorced for fornication?

And let us follow this with chart number 18. "Demanding the Impossible." What proof will you demand? Court records? The word of a friend? The word of one you want to marry? Photographic evidence? Seeing it with your own eyes? Or asking Ron Halbrook? And he will tell you, if he tells you the same thing he told us in North Las Vegas, the only safe course is do not marry. Then, he said what? "You have to know; you have to know according to Matthew 19." *Jesus did not say that you have to know either*.

> **DEMANDING THE IMPOSSIBLE**
> **(Cont)**
>
> WHAT PROOF WILL YOU DEMAND TO SHOW THAT ONE HAS BEEN GUILTY OF FORNICATION?
>
> * COURT RECORDS?
> * THE WORD OF A FRIEND?
> * THE WORD OF THE ONE YOU WANT TO MARRY?
> * PHOTOGRAPHIC EVIDENCE?
> * SEEING IT WITH YOUR OWN EYES?
> * ASK RON HALBROOK?
>
> 18

There may be, no doubt, many people living together with husbands and wives who had been unfaithful and they do not know anything about it. Jesus did not say you had to know. And here are some cases we talked about where you could not know.

Let us see the next chart please; go back to my chart number 1. How do we know what is false doctrine and what is not? God anticipated false doctrine; you know — isn't it wonderful we have a God that knew what would be taught and He dealt with it before it was ever taught? He took care of it before any man ever started to preach it. *"Some shall depart from the faith."* What would they do? They would "give heed to seducing spirits and doctrines of devils," and in doing that they will "forbid to marry." Who does that? Who forbids to marry? My opponent admits that he forbids to marry. Who does? The doctrines of devils, those who had departed from the faith. The faith does not forbid marriage. I am talking about marriage in God's sight. You have a right to your wife; you have a right to your husband. God did not forbid it; if you were *single, unmarried,* you had God's permission to marry. And when you have God's permission to marry, and then God's permission to divorce because a mate became guilty of fornication, and *that fornicator now has been divorced* — my opponent admits they have no spouse, they are *single.* "Oh," he says, "they are still bound by the law." To what? Not to a spouse.

> **HOW DO WE KNOW?**
> **GOD ANTICIPATED FALSE DOCTRINE**
>
> 1 TIM. 4:1-3
> "...<u>SOME SHALL DEPART FROM THE FAITH GIVING HEED TO SEDUCING SPIRITS AND DOCTRINES OF DEVILS, FORBIDDING TO MARRY</u>..."
>
> WHO IS DEMANDING CELIBACY?
> WHO IS FORBIDDING TO MARRY?
>
> <u>DO YOU WANT THE DOCTRINES OF DEVILS</u>
> OR
> <u>THE FAITH ???</u>
>
> 1

So, they have no spouse — what did God say to that person who had been a spouse or who had never had a spouse? That man who wants to avoid fornication (1 Cor. 7:2), "To avoid fornication let every man have his own wife, and let every woman have her own husband." "Oh," he [Halbrook] says, "that does not mean every." But he will take that "whosoever" in Matthew 19 and say that includes every one in the world. But this, "every man" and "every woman," that does not include every man and every woman. It includes everyone that has God's right to marry. I will say just what he did there. The one who had no wife, the one who had no husband — he admits the fornicator has no wife, has no husband. If they have none, why can't they have one?

And, again, in the day of judgment what are you going to tell the Lord and Savior? "Oh, I forbade that person to marry." Why? "Because they have been guilty of fornication." Let us bring the fornicator to the Lord himself. What did the Lord answer? The person comes to the Lord and says, "Now, Lord I would like to marry." "Well, have you ever been *married before?*" "Yes." "Are you *divorced?*" "Yes." "Why did your wife divorce you?" "Because I committed *fornication,* Lord. But Lord, I would like to avoid fornication. What can I do to avoid fornication?" What are you going to tell him? You know, one man in one of the articles in the January 1990 issue of the *Guardian of Truth* taught you could go to the hospital and be castrated. *You could become a eunuch.* He did not use the word castrated. Become a eunuch means the same thing if I read the dictionary correctly. That is one way out; that is your out. You cannot use God's way out. God said, "To avoid fornication let every man have *his own* wife, and let every woman have *her own* husband." That is what God had to say about it. And that is what Jack Freeman is saying about it. That is all I am saying about it. I am not upholding adultery and fornication, I am not upholding anything like that. I am only upholding the right of a person who is *unmarried* in the sight of God to have a wife or to have a husband. Now, is that asking too much?

If I was asking for one man to have two wives or one man to have another man's wife, why, certainly I would be wrong. But I am acknowledging, as God does, each man has a right to his own wife; each woman has a right to her own husband. Well, if I say, "Well, he had a wife, why didn't he avoid fornication then?" Well, he did not abide by God's teaching, now he wants to serve God — and he knows his sexual drives, he knows he will not be faithful to God without a wife, he wants to know whether or not he can have one. What are you going to tell him? "You can't, you will just have to burn," that is what brother Halbrook says, "You will just have to burn." God says, "It is better to marry than to burn." Halbrook says, "Well, you will have to burn anyway, regardless of what God says." God says it is better to marry. Halbrook says, "You cannot do that which is better. You will have to do then, in effect, that which is worse — whatever that is. You cannot do that which is better or best and you will have go on burning."

"To avoid fornication let every man have his own wife, and let every woman have her own husband." "It is better to marry than to burn." And if you are "loosed from a wife? seek not a wife. But and if thou marry, thou hast not sinned; and if a virgin marry," showing a distinction, "she hath not sinned." Now the *fornicator* says, "Yes, I am *loosed from a wife.*" What do you mean? "Well, she divorced me because I was a fornicator — I am loosed from a wife." Or, the other so-called innocent party, "Yes, I am loosed from a husband because he committed fornication and I divorced him." Both are loosed in God's sight, and my opponent admits that. They are not bound to one another, they are not married to one another in God's sight.

Third Evening
Freeman's First Affirmative

[Proposition: The Scriptures teach that a person who is divorced by his mate for committing fornication is free to marry another.]

Brethren, moderators, brother Halbrook, as has been indicated, it is my responsibility tonight to be in the affirmative. The proposition has been read and at this time I will define it. By *"the Scriptures"* I mean, the sixty-six books of the Bible. By *"teach,"* I mean impart information or give instruction. By the expression, "that *a person,"* I mean a husband or a wife. By the expression, *"who is divorced,"* I mean one who is put away, the marriage has been put asunder. By the expression, *"for committing fornication,"* I mean for engaging in sex with someone other than his or her spouse. By the expression, *"is free,"* I mean at liberty, has God's permission. *"To marry another,"* I mean to remarry, since he or she is now unmarried in God's sight. After all, the one guilty of fornication who has been divorced is not the one who obtained the divorce, may not even want a divorce, but when he is divorced, both brother Halbrook and I agree that he has no spouse, no wife. I am affirming that the one who has no spouse has the God-given right to marry one who has no spouse. I want to go back to a statement I made the first evening of this debate. That is all I am here for. I am defending the right of unmarried people to marry. That is all. I am defending the right of the woman who has no husband to have one, the man who has no wife to have one. That is what Paul affirmed, that is what Jesus affirmed, and that is what I affirm.

Before I go any further I want to read some questions presented me tonight by Ron and give the answers.

1. *"Cite the exact words where Thayer used any of the following terms in his comments on 'bondage' in 1 Corinthians 7:15: "marriage," "husband," "wife."* By necessary implication he refers to *marriage* and the *husband* and *wife* because that is the subject under consideration. *Thayer's* definition under the metaphorical meaning of bondage there is constraint of law, and since it is a negative term, *"not under bondage,"* not under constraint of law or necessity in some matter. And the matter under consideration is marriage.

2. *"Which verses in 1 Corinthians 7 address the put-away fornicator and tell him he can remarry: (A) Verses 1 and 2, (B) Verses 8 and 9, (C) Verses 10 and 11, (D) Verse 15, (E) Verses 27 and 28."* Verse 2, verses 8 and 9, verses 27 and

28 refer to all unmarried people, for they are unmarried because they have never married or have lost their spouse by death, have obtained a scriptural divorce, or have been *scripturally divorced*. By necessary inference verse 15 refers to the marriage bond and, as we were discussing that the first two nights of the debate, tonight we are going to be discussing *the one who is put away on grounds of fornication.*

3. *"Repentance requires severing which of the following sinful relationships: (A) homosexual marriage?"* These are not marriages. They may even, as Ron indicated, some states might authorize them, he said they would not be marriages, not in God's sight. A courthouse marriage is not necessarily a marriage in God's sight. So these would not be marriages. *"(B) Polygamous marriages?"* Again, the same answer, these are not marriages in God's sight. *"(C) Adulterous marriages?"* There is no such language in the Bible. *"(D) Incestuous marriages?"* This is not a marriage in God's sight. *"(E) Man-beast marriage?"* These are not marriages in God's sight. *"(F) A man married 100 times?"* If he has a scriptural wife at present, he is *not* required to *leave* her. And what is the difference between being married two times and being married a hundred times? Well, you might answer 98, but 100 sounds a lot worse, doesn't it? Prejudicial.

4. *"Did Paul or other Apostles ever tell anyone to remain unmarried in order to get to heaven?"* Yes, if you are talking about the one in 1 Corinthians 7:11. She was told to *remain unmarried* because she was still married. She was unmarried, legally, had divorced her husband, but still in the sight of God she was married to that man. Therefore, she was commanded to remain unmarried, do not go out and marry another man. You already have a husband. *No*, if by unmarried you mean celibate, she was never told or commanded to remain celibate. She had a husband and if she wanted to abstain from fornication, she could go back and realize she had a husband, that was his purpose.

5. *"Jack Freeman believes that the marriage of Herod and Herodias would become lawful if Philip would say he put her away."* That is false. I did not say so. He has charged me with that. I have not said it. That is not so. John the Baptist spoke the truth when he said it is not lawful for thee to have her and it was not lawful for Herod to have that woman.

Here are questions pertaining to brother Halbrook tonight and I will read them. He can answer in his speech. 1. "What is the meaning of 'adultery' as used in Matthew 19:9?"

2. "Under what conditions, if any, may the one guilty of adultery, and divorced for that reason, scripturally remarry?"

3. "If the husband is guilty of adultery, may his wife scripturally remain married to him?"

4. "Can you give one passage from the New Testament where those guided by the Holy Spirit to preach the gospel of Christ told any person that he or she must remain unmarried the rest of his or her life?"

5. "Can you give one passage from the New Testament where those guided by the Holy Spirit to preach the gospel of Christ told any person that he or she must put away his or her husband or wife in order to be saved?"

I want to remind you of the fact that in regard to the questions I presented to brother Halbrook Tuesday night, he did not answer two of them. Number one, he did not answer, he beat around the bush, but he did not answer. I want to read it again. "If a husband divorces his wife for any cause other than adultery, and then commits adultery, can she scripturally remarry?" I would still like to have an answer. Question 5. This one he did not answer because he said he could not understand it. I will read it again. "Does God demand the innocent human being," now I want to tell you why I worded this this way. I gave him a similar question in North Las Vegas, "Must the innocent suffer for the sins of the guilty?" He answered yes, Christ suffered for all the sinners. And so I worded it this way, so we are dealing with human beings. This relationship called marriage. "Does God demand that the innocent human being (one not guilty of adultery) suffer because of the sins of the guilty party (that is, the one who obtains the divorce for a cause other than adultery)?" He said I just cannot understand, I do not know what that question is.

I would like to have chart number 30. Matthew 19:9, Jesus said, "Whosoever shall put away his wife, except it be for fornication, and marrieth another, committeth adultery; whoso marrieth her which is put away doth commit adultery." We have a noun, *wife*, a pronoun, *her*. By the rules of any language, the pronoun must refer back to the noun, and the noun is *wife*, the pronoun is *her*. Incidently, brother Hal-

---

NOUN & PRONOUN IN MATT. 19:9

WHOSOEVER SHALL PUT AWAY HIS <u>WIFE</u>, EXCEPT IT BE FOR FORNICATION,
WHOSO MARRIETH <u>HER</u> WHICH IS PUT AWAY DOTH COMMIT ADULTERY.

MAN WHO PUTS AWAY HIS WIFE FOR FORNICATION HAS NO WIFE,

CAN REMARRY.

WOMAN PUT AWAY FOR FORNICATION HAS NO HUSBAND,

CAN REMARRY.

30

Third Evening: Freeman's First Affirmative   *157*

brook claimed that in his proposition he was affirming Matthew 19:9; his proposition was not a thirty-second cousin to Matthew 19:9. Matthew 19:9 discusses one who obtains a divorce for reasons other than fornication, *not for fornication,* and discusses those who marry one who has been put away on a ground other than fornication. All you have to do is read it to see that.

The man who puts away his wife for fornication has no wife. Now, here is a point upon which we both agree. He has no wife. If he has one, who is she, and where is she? Therefore, since he has no wife, I am affirming that he can remarry. *And the woman put away for fornication has no husband. Therefore, she can remarry.* If she has a husband, let brother Halbrook tell us, who is he, and where is he?

Let's see the next chart please, number 31. Again, continuing this thought on the noun and the pronoun, God says, "Art thou loosed from a wife," 1 Corinthians 7:27-28, "if thou marry thou has not sinned." I have quoted his own authority, *Thayer,* which he introduced in New Mexico. His own authority says that in 1 Corinthians 7:27 the word loosed means *divorced,* used one time in the New Testament, *divorced.* And, in regard to those loosed from a wife, Paul said, "Seek not a wife. But and if thou marry, thou hast not sinned; and if a virgin marry, she hath not sinned." My opponent says if he marries he sins, God says he does not. It ought to be easy to make up our minds who is right. A long time ago when I began to read the Bible, I decided to read it to see what God has to say. I am still doing that tonight. All I ask you to listen to is *what God has to say.* If he marries he does not sin.

NOUN & PRONOUN IN MATT. 19:9
(Cont)

GOD SAYS --- "ART THOU LOOSED FROM A WIFE.."
1 COR. 7:27-28

"...IF THOU MARRY, THOU HAST NOT SINNED".
MAN WHO PUTS AWAY HIS WIFE FOR FORNICATION HAS NO WIFE,

MY OPPONENT SAYS --- "IF HE MARRIES HE SINS"

GOD vs. HALBROOK

31

Chart number 56. Now, brother Halbrook, I am going to introduce another of your witnesses you referred to last night, Dean Alford. I am not going to go into all this diagram, but here is a diagram of Matthew 19:9. And in a moment, just looking at this briefly, there is one thing especially I want to call to your attention, that is, this exception phrase in this diagram is repeated. Brother

Halbrook says it does not belong there, but Dean Alford says that it does. Now, this is his witness he introduced last night. I am not introducing this to prove anything, I am just *impeaching* his witness. He introduced Dean Alford to prove something.

This was what Dean Alford said in regard to this. This phrase "with-

> Here is what I believe to be a correct diagram of Matthew 19:9, as it appears in the Greek text. You will note that *me epi porneia* is found a second time on dotted lines to indicate that it is understood to modify *apolelumenan*. In the paragraph following the diagram, Dean Alford is quoted in justification of this action in both Matthew 5:32 and 19:9.

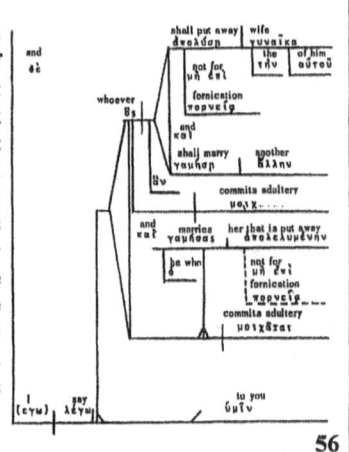

56

out the article, and thus logically confined to the case of her who has been divorced" not for fornication. "This not having been seen, expositors" — he names some — "have fallen into the mistake of supposing that the dictum applies to the marrying of the woman divorced" for fornication, "which grammatically would require" — and he gives another Greek word that is not even in Matthew 19:9. "The proper English way of rendering the word as it now stands would be, *a woman thus divorced"* — and he gives the Greek expression for that, and that means for a cause other than fornication. Now, here is your witness. That is your witness, it is not mine. I am not saying it proves anything, but you introduced it to try to prove your argument. I am introducing it and saying your own witness denies what you have to say.

And incidentally, here is a peculiar thing, an odd thing. Dean Alford, as he says, *does not agree with my position.* But he did try to be honest in explaining this passage and he gave this meaning to it. And he said the wording, the Greek word, would have to be changed if this meant "for fornication." But it is *not* "for fornication." And so, if you marry a person who is divorced, and their cause was not for fornication, you commit adultery.

Let us come to chart number 1 now. Chart number 1, we have used several times. How do we know what is false and what is not, so far as doctrine is concerned? God anticipated false doctrine. And using the Holy Spirit to guide the Apostles word by word into all truth, he caused Paul to write these words in 1 Timothy 4:1-3: "Now the Spirit speaketh expressly, that in the latter times some shall depart from the faith, giving heed to seducing spirits, and doctrines of devils; speaking lies in hypocrisy; having their conscience seared with a hot

> **HOW DO WE KNOW?**
> **GOD ANTICIPATED FALSE DOCTRINE**
>
> **1 TIM. 4:1-3**
> "...<u>SOME SHALL DEPART FROM THE FAITH</u> GIVING HEED TO SEDUCING SPIRITS AND <u>DOCTRINES OF DEVILS, FORBIDDING TO MARRY</u>..."
>
> <u>WHO IS DEMANDING CELIBACY?</u>
> <u>WHO IS FORBIDDING TO MARRY?</u>
>
> <u>DO YOU WANT THE DOCTRINES OF DEVILS</u>
> OR
> <u>THE FAITH ???</u>

iron; forbidding to marry, and commanding to abstain from meats..." etc. Now, "the faith" according to this passage does not forbid marriage. But the doctrine of devils does. What forbids marriage? Not the faith. What forbids people to marry? The doctrine of devils. *Who is demanding celibacy? Who is forbidding to marry?* Not God. Not Paul. Not the Holy Spirit. Who is forbidding to marry? Who is demanding celibacy? Well, you have to decide do you want the doctrine of devils or do you want the faith. Do you want the doctrine of Halbrook, or, do you want the faith, the gospel of Jesus Christ.

Chart number 22. I would like for brother Halbrook to use this same chart and just tell us where we reach the point of disagreement. A man and woman marry, they are married. Now, a man divorces this woman for cause other than fornication. If I understand brother Halbrook's position, I know mine, if his is the same, we agree because the divorce is for a cause other than fornication, *they are still married in God's sight*. Not in man's sight. Go down to the courthouse and get a divorce. We are not interested in the courthouse record, it does not prove anything pertaining to the Bible. They are still married in God's sight. Now, the man commits adultery.

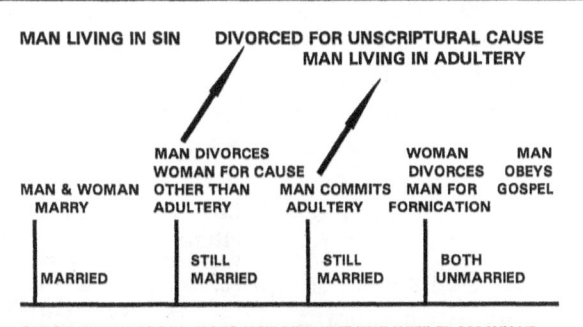

Since these are still married in God's sight, the woman then divorces her man *for fornication*. She cannot go to the courthouse and get a divorce but in the eyes of God she can. She can put him away for a scriptural cause and now *they are both unmarried.*

Now, this same man whom she put away. Incidentally, now this man whom she put away back there, when he divorced her for a cause other than fornication, he was *living in sin.* The sin, divorcing for an unscriptural cause. When he committed adultery, even if it was just once, he was *living in adultery.* Now, the woman divorces him for the sin of adultery, and they are both unmarried. Now, this man obeys the gospel. As he arises from baptism, of what sin is he guilty? In the North Las Vegas debate, brother Ron Halbrook said none. And so, he is a single man, he is not guilty of a sin, *why can't he marry?* The sin of the husband does not prohibit the wife from doing what is authorized. The innocent in this case is not punished for the sins of the guilty. The man who obtained the divorce for unscriptural grounds and then committed adultery has now been scripturally divorced by his wife, he is single. He obeys the gospel. He is not guilty of any sin. So in this case, now if you disagree at any point, just tell us. I do not know, I am trying to see just how far we agree on this chart. And, just tell us, start from the beginning and tell us when we reach the point of disagreement.

Chart number 28 please. We are talking about mercy tonight. How do we know what God's mercy is? I tell you, we should appreciate it. If you do not know anything about God's mercy, I would urge you to go to the Bible and learn what God's mercy is, what it includes. Through God's mercy our sins are remitted, (Acts 2:38, for the remission of sins). Through God's mercy our sins are blotted out, Acts 3:19. Through God's mercy our sins are washed away when we are baptized,

HOW DO WE KNOW?
MERCY

GOD THROUGH HIS MERCY:
REMITS SINS---------------------------------ACTS 2:38
BLOTS OUT SINS----------------------------ACTS 3:19
WASHES AWAY SINS----------------------ACTS 22:16
FORGIVES ALL TRESPASSES-----------COL. 2:13
DESTROYS THE BODY OF SIN-----------ROM. 6:6
REMEMBERS SINS NO MORE-------------HEB. 8:12

BUT MY OPPONENT WILL ALWAYS REMEMBER THAT ONE HAS COMMITTED FORNICATION AND WILL ALWAYS DEMAND PENANCE, EVEN WHEN GOD HAS FORGIVEN.
LET US BE THANKFUL WE DON'T DEPEND UPON "HALBROOK'S MERCY".

28

Acts 22:16. Through God's mercy our sins are forgiven, all trespasses, Colossians 2:13, all of them. Romans 6:6, through God's mercy God destroys the body of sins. And further, in Hebrews 8:12, through God's mercy He has said in this passage, "Their sins and their iniquities will I remember no more."

Now, let us bring this man who was divorced on grounds of fornication and then obeys the gospel to the Lord. And this man says to the Lord, "I want to get married." The Lord says, "Were you married?" Of course, the Lord knows. We are using a hypothetical case. The Lord says, "Were you married?" He says, "Yes." "Well, were you divorced?" *"Yes, my wife put me away because I was guilty of fornication."* "Well, what is your spiritual state now?" "Well, I repented and was baptized." The Lord says, *"You can marry."* About that time brother Halbrook stands up and says, "Now, wait a minute Lord, you are wrong. I remember back there ten years ago, this man committed fornication and his wife divorced him." The Lord says, "I do not remember that." The Lord says, "I do not remember that." Now, mark that down. You got a little black book or you keep that record in your mind, you are going to remember it all of your life. "I remember back there some time ago that person committed fornication, they can never remarry." God did not say so. God did not demand celibacy.

And we have already earlier in this debate introduced again brother Halbrook's own witnesses that pointed out the evil sins, the sins brought into the world because of the *doctrine of celibacy*. Those who forbid marriage. Now, my opponent will always remember that one has committed fornication, always demand penance, penance even after God has forgiven. Of what sin are you guilty or were you guilty when you were raised from baptism? I can look back, though I am getting up in years, I can look back to the time when I was baptized (and I have never had a doubt), as I rose from baptism I knew that God had forgiven every sin that I had committed before that. He would never hold it against me again. And yet, you are saying, some of you, "I hold it against him, I will not forget it, and as far as I am concerned, I am going to see that he is punished."

You know, one of the first arguments made to me on this subject, "That lets the fornicator off too easy." You think about it, how easy those murderers got off who crucified God's own Son. Repent and be baptized for the remission of sins, Acts 2. Wasn't that easy? Saul the persecutor, who referred to himself as the chief of sinners, was told to arise and be baptized and wash away thy sins. Oh yes, it is easy. What do you think we ought to do? Take this fornicator out here, and tie him to a post, whip him every day? No, we are going to punish him by making him remain single the rest of his life. That is not a Bible idea. That is Halbrook's idea.

Chart number 47 please. Paul was preaching to those who were aliens in Corinth, Acts 18. Verse 4, we learn that he reasoned and persuaded. What they did, Acts 18:8, they believed and were baptized. Well, what did God have to do with it? 1 Corinthians 6:22, now even though according to verse 9 and 11 *they* had been guilty of fornication and adultery, 9 and 10 later on the chart, *when they were baptized they were washed, sanctified, and justified.* Acts 2:47, they were added to the church. Now, of what had they been guilty before baptism? Verses 9 and 10, some had been guilty of fornication and adultery. Did God add fornicators to the church? No. These were baptized. God forgave their sins, remembered them no more. They were washed, sanctified, and justified.

> **PAUL PREACHING TO ALIENS**
>
> ACTS 18:4 REASONED, PERSUADED
> **WHAT THEY DID:**
> ACTS 18:8 -- BELIEVED AND WERE BAPTIZED
> **WHAT GOD DID:**
> 1 COR. 6:11 --- WASHED, SANCTIFIED, JUSTIFIED
> ACTS 2:47 ----- ADDED TO THE CHURCH
> **OF WHAT THEY HAD BEEN GUILTY OF BEFORE BAPTISM**
> 1 COR. 6:9-10 - SOME HAD BEEN GUILTY OF FORNICATION AND ADULTERY.
> **DID GOD ADD FORNICATORS TO THE CHURCH?**
> (ACTS 2:47 --- NO!)
>
> 47

Next chart please, number 48. Same thought continued. What did Paul tell these who had been fornicators and adulterers to do to avoid fornication? Still talking to the same people, writing to the same church, the same people who had been guilty of fornication and adultery. "Let every man have his own wife and let every woman have her own husband." This will avoid fornication, 1 Corinthians 7:2. *Did Paul or other Apostles ever tell any man to leave his wife in order to be saved?* Have you ever told anyone that? I know some of you that have. *Did Paul or other Apostles ever tell any woman to leave her husband in order to be saved?* Some of you have, but Paul did not. Did Paul or other Apostles ever tell anyone to remain unmarried in order to get to heaven? Oh, you say so in 1 Corinthians 7:10-11? Here was a woman who was already married in God's sight. And she was to remain unmarried legally, not go out and get another husband, because she

> **PAUL PREACHING TO ALIENS**
> (Cont)
>
> **WHAT DID PAUL TELL THOSE WHO HAD BEEN FORNICATORS AND ADULTERERS TO DO TO AVOID FORNICATION?**
>
> 1 COR. 7:2 - "LET EVERY MAN HAVE HIS OWN WIFE, AND LET EVERY WOMAN HAVE HER OWN HUSBAND."
>
> *DID PAUL OR OTHER APOSTLES EVER TELL ANY MAN TO LEAVE HIS WIFE IN ORDER TO BE SAVED?
>
> *DID PAUL OR OTHER APOSTLES EVER TELL ANY WOMAN TO LEAVE HER HUSBAND IN ORDER TO BE SAVED?
>
> *DID PAUL OR OTHER APOSTLES EVER TELL ANYONE TO REMAIN UNMARRIED IN ORDER TO GET TO HEAVEN?
>
> 48

was already married in the sight of God.

Let's come back to the closing part of these questions. *"Did Paul or other Apostles ever tell anyone to remain unmarried in order to get to heaven?"* This is question number 4. I answered it. *Yes*, if the woman in 1 Corinthians 7:10-11 was, she was told to remain unmarried because she was still married to a husband. And if you disagree with that brother Halbrook, tell us so. Did she still have a husband or not? Now, if she did not, she could be married. *No*, if by that you mean, did she have to remain unmarried the rest of her life, that is not so; her mate could have died or committed fornication. The Apostles did not demand celibacy anywhere.

Let's continue with chart number 49. *What is adultery?* Again, brother Halbrook's own witness, according to Matthew 5:32 and Matthew 19:9, in these passages, his witness says, adultery is to have unlawful intercourse with another's wife, to commit adultery. Incidentally, this was the exact quotation by one of the writers in the first issue of the *Guardian of Truth* in January 1990. Brother Halbrook says it is a broader explanation of that in Matthew 19:9, Matthew 5:32. Well, maybe these people ought to debate their own people. Why is it that when I disagree with brother Halbrook he writes me up as a false teacher? When those others who agree with him more closely than I do disagree with him, he does not write them up. Why is that?

WHAT IS ADULTERY?
THAYER: page 417

"TO HAVE UNLAWFUL INTERCOURSE WITH ANOTHER'S WIFE, TO COMMIT ADULTERY" MATT. 5:32, MATT. 19:9

MAN DIVORCES FOR CAUSE OF FORNICATION <u>HAS NO WIFE</u>. IF HE MARRIES A WOMAN WHO HAS NO HUSBAND, HE <u>CANNOT</u> COMMIT ADULTERY WITH HER. (HIS OWN WIFE) ANY MAN WHO HAS NO WIFE MAY SCRIPTURALLY HAVE A WIFE.

49

Well, a man divorced for the cause of fornication has no wife. If he married a woman who has no husband, he cannot commit adultery with her, his own wife. And any man who has no wife may scripturally have a wife. That is all I am contending for. If in the sight of God he has no wife or if in the sight of God she has no husband, she has the right to a husband, he has the right to a wife. And *Thayer* says in regard to these passages, to have unlawful intercourse with another's wife, to commit adultery.

Chart number 32, put away due to fornication. *This gives the man, a woman, the right to put away the spouse for fornication,* doesn't it? This is not a commandment and you know this by inference. It does *not* actually deal, say that, but brother Halbrook will not admit that it is necessarily inferred. Well, *must* the innocent put away the guilty? God does not say so. If not, it is not sinful to be married to a fornicator, and re-

> **PUT AWAY DUE TO FORNICATION**
>
> **Matt. 19:9**
>
> Gives MAN/WOMAN the RIGHT to put away spouse for fornication
>
> Must the innocent put away (divorce) the guilty?
> If not, it is NOT sinful to be married to a fornicator.
>
> The <u>fornicator IS</u> living in fornication.
> The <u>innocent IS NOT</u> living in fornication.
>
> To live in sin DOES NOT mean to be married to a sinner.
>
> 32

member this, brother Halbrook does not believe it is. And I do not believe it is. If your wife commits fornication, you do not have to put her away. She is a fornicator, she is living in fornication, but you are not. You can keep her. The fornicator is living in fornication, the innocent is not living in fornication.

But, *he would have you to believe that a marriage is adulterous because it is unauthorized, or if one is guilty of fornication and you marry her, then both of you are guilty of fornication.* But that cannot be the case. To live in sin does not mean to be married to a sinner. "To live in" means to be guilty of. We will illustrate that later in this debate.

> **RIGHT TO PUT AWAY**
> (Cont)
>
> * WHEN A MAN IS PUT AWAY FOR THE CAUSE OF FORNICATION, DOES HE HAVE A WIFE?
>
> * WHO IS SHE?
>
> * WHERE IS SHE?
>
> * IF HE MARRIED A WOMAN WHO HAS NO HUSBAND, DOES HE COMMIT ADULTERY WITH HER?
>
> * <u>THE MARRIAGE IS NOT ADULTEROUS.</u>
>
> 33

Chart number 33. Alright, the name of this, *when a man is put away for the cause of fornication, does he have a wife?* If so, who is she, where is she? Now, I asked this question, written question, of my opponent in North Las Vegas. He said that *he does not have any wife, but is still bound by the law.* As to what? To what? Not to his wife. *To what law is he bound?* Genesis 2:24 or Matthew 19:9, the early verses, to what law is he bound? There was that

Third Evening: Freeman's First Affirmative   165

law, God's law that bound him to his wife. Well, he has no wife, so he is not bound to a wife. If he married a woman who has no husband, does he commit adultery with her? He cannot. You cannot commit adultery with your own mate. This is not what my opponent would then call an adulterous marriage.

Chart number 451. Halbrook says only virgins are discussed in 1 Corinthians 7 beginning at verse 25. Again we have in verse 27, "Art thou bound to a wife?" That does not sound like a virgin to me. If one would answer, "Yes, I am bound to a wife," then you are not a virgin. Neither you nor your wife. "Art thou loosed from a wife? If thou marry, thou hast not sinned." That is, "Seek not a wife," then he says, "If thou marry, thou hast not sinned." "And if a virgin marry," shows he is talking to two different people — those who have been married and loosed, and the one who has never been married, the virgin. And neither one, according to God, sins if they marry. According to my opponent they do.

---

1 COR. 7:25-28

HALBROOK SAYS ONLY <u>VIRGINS</u> ARE DISCUSSED.

*V.25 - VIRGINS

*V.27 - ART THOU <u>BOUND</u> TO A WIFE?
(DIVORCED)

*V.27 - ARE THOU <u>LOOSED</u> FROM A WIFE?
IF <u>THOU</u> MARRY, <u>THOU</u> HAST NOT SINNED.

-- AND --

*V.28 - IF A VIRGIN MARRY SHE HATH NOT SINNED.

451

Chart number 57. This is again Halbrook's witness, *Thayer,* page 384. He says this word for loosed, loosed is a loosing of any bond, as that of marriage, hence, once in the New Testament of divorce, 1 Corinthians 7:27. "Art thou loosed from a wife?" He says, *Thayer* says, and I

THAYER
page 384

LUSIS - "A LOOSING OF ANY BOND, AS THAT OF MARRIAGE; HENCE <u>ONCE</u> IN THE NEW TESTAMENT OF DIVORCE",

*1 COR. 7:27 - THUS, "ART THOU <u>LOOSED</u> FROM A WIFE" "ART THOU <u>DIVORCED</u> FROM A WIFE"

*1 COR. 7:28 - "BUT AND IF THOU MARRY, <u>THOU HAST NOT SINNED</u>..."

57

---

do not think you need these Greek references to understand that, just read the English. "If thou marry thou hast not sinned."

Let me take a moment to say this. In Luke 24 Jesus said, or Luke says in regard to this account, Jesus opened their understanding, that they might understand the scriptures. And Paul wrote in Ephesians 3:3-4, I write so that when ye read ye may understand my knowledge in the mystery of Christ. They went out preaching and they understood what they were preaching. Those who heard could understand if they wanted to. We can understand today what they preached and what they wrote if we read it. That is all we have to do, is read it. Paul said, "When ye read ye may understand my knowledge in the mystery of Christ." I am not introducing *Thayer* to prove anything, I am just using these as rebuttals to show that these, his own witnesses, do not agree with what he has said.

Chart number 452. Chart number 452, we have this thought, bound by the law, Romans 7:2. Incidentally, if you use your own witness again, the word for *bound* according to your own witness does not apply to a marriage in the literal meaning [referring to Greek word *deo*]. A little three-letter word, but it does not apply to marriage, the word bondage, in 1 Corinthians 7, until you get down to the figurative meaning.

ROM. 7:2-3

"BOUND BY THE LAW TO HER HUSBAND"

BUT

"IF THE HUSBAND BE DEAD, SHE IS LOOSED FROM THE LAW"

*V.3 - "IF HER HUSBAND BE DEAD, SHE IS FREE FROM THAT LAW"

- BOUND VERSUS LOOSED.
- BOUND VERSUS FREE.

452

The literal meaning simply means bound or tied. Your authority, your witness will tell you the references to which it, the passages to which it refers, and it will tell you also the passages to which it refers when it has to do with marriage. But this passage says the husband is dead, she is loosed from the law. No longer bound by the law. If her husband be dead, she is free from that law. Bound versus loosed. Bound versus free.

Chart number 34. Alright, chart number 34, the put-away fornicator, free to marry. Either he has a wife or he does not. If he does not have a wife, he is loosed from a wife. *What is the marital state of the put-away fornicator?* Well, he has no wife, just to sum it up. If he still has a wife, the wife who put him away cannot remarry. If he still has a wife, she still has a husband. The marriage still exists in the sight of God. We both agree *that marriage does not exist* any longer. He

Third Evening: Freeman's First Affirmative

> **THE "PUT AWAY" FORNICATOR**
>
> **FREE TO MARRY**
>
> 1. HE <u>HAS A WIFE</u> (BOUND TO A WIFE)
>   OR
> 2. HE <u>DOES NOT HAVE A WIFE</u> (LOOSED FROM A WIFE)
> 3. WHAT IS THE MARITAL STATE OF THE PUT AWAY FORNICATOR?
>
>   A. DOES HE HAVE A WIFE? IF SO WHO IS SHE? WHERE IS SHE?
>   B. IF HE STILL HAS A WIFE, THE WIFE WHO PUTS HIM AWAY FOR FORNICATION CANNOT REMARRY, FOR SHE HAS A HUSBAND.
>   C. THE PUT AWAY FORNICATOR DOES NOT HAVE A WIFE.
>   1) HOW SHALL HE AVOID FORNICATION?
>   * 1 COR. 7:2 -- HAVE HIS OWN WIFE
>   2) DOES HE HAVE DIVINE PERMISSION TO REMARRY?
>   * 1 COR. 7:27-28 -- "ART THOU LOOSED FROM A WIFE..."
>   IF THOU MARRY, THOU HAST NOT SINNED."
>
> 34

does not have a wife, she does not have a husband, though *I am saying either can remarry without committing adultery. He is saying one can and one cannot.*

How is this man to avoid fornication? 1 Corinthians 7:2, he is to have his own wife. Does he have divine permission to *remarry?* 1 Corinthians 7:27-28, "Art thou loosed from a wife?... if thou marry, thou hast not sinned." That is what God has to say about it. And that is all I know about it, is what God has to say. Now, we might introduce thousands of other witnesses. They might disagree with what God says.

The important thing is to get into our minds what God has to say on this matter. And when He has said that, we should accept it. We should never open the Bible and study it to try to prove what we think we know, what we suppose we know. We should open the Bible to ask, "Lord, what would you have me to know? Lord, what do you want me to know? Lord, what do you say in answer to my question?" And when we find the answer, we ought to be willing to accept that answer, and not try to put it away and argue against God. And that is exactly what many are guilty of today. They know, as well as anyone knows, what God said, but they say, "Now, Lord, you made a mistake there. That is not right." And so they bring in a lot of other witnesses to prove that God did not have enough sense, or did not know enough, to say what He meant and mean what He said. And that cannot be the case.

Our faith should rest in God, our faith should rest in the word of God. And that is how Paul wrote in 1 Corinthians 2, verse 1 through verse 5, that your faith should not stand in the wisdom of men, but in the power of God. And that would be my plea to you that through your study of the Bible, your faith would be produced by the word of God, Romans 10:17. That your faith would not stand in the wisdom of men, but it would stand in the power of God.

Third Evening
Halbrook's First Negative

Brother Freeman, brethren, moderators, ladies, and gentlemen, we are thankful for your presence tonight as we are studying this proposition and we want to notice the proposition on chart 2. My opponent's affirmation is, *"The Scriptures teach that a person who is divorced by his mate for committing fornication"* — for destroying a home, for violating God's law of marriage — *"is free to marry another."* Now, he affirms it, but there is *not a passage in all the Bible that teaches anything like it!* He speaks where the Bible is silent. Acts 15:24 says, "To whom we gave no such commandment," and it was forbidden to teach in that case. And 1 Peter 4:11 teaches that we must speak as the oracles of God, and there is *not one line* in all the oracles of God which teaches that proposition.

I want to notice my chart 4, clarifying *what is the issue*. Notice, my friend, we *agree* that the innocent mate can put away the fornicator and marry another. We agree on that in Matthew 19:9. We *disagree* in that *he would teach even that the fornicator could put away the innocent mate and marry another*. God's law, God's rule, is that the innocent can put away the fornicator and marry another. But this man will allow the fornicator to destroy the home, put away the mate, and go on and marry another. That is not God's law at all, and that is why we differ.

Then, we *agree* the put-away fornicator can marry again. He can remarry his first mate (Jer. 3:1-8). He can marry another when the first mate dies (Rom. 7:2-3). And that answers one of his questions. But we *disagree* when *he teaches the put-away fornicator can marry another while the first mate still lives*. There is no scripture in God's book that teaches that. We *agree* a Christian is enslaved to Christ alone and cannot give him up to meet the demands of unbelievers, according to 1 Corinthians 7 and other passages. *But, he teaches a Christian deserted by the unbeliever can marry another,* and there is no passage that teaches that anywhere! There are the differences between us tonight.

Keep in mind there are *three areas* where he will labor to prove his case. He will try to pervert Matthew 5 and Matthew 19, and get that exception clause to apply in the second part of the verse. We will study that more. He will have to twist 1 Corinthians 7, as he has done, and he will have to make false appeals to mercy and forgiveness.

Now, I would like to notice the questions that we have tonight. First of all,

Opponent Affirms

Passage   **Proposition**

? { "The Scriptures teach that a person who is divorced by his mate for committing fornication is free to marry another."

AFFIRM: Jack Freeman
DENY: Ron Halbrook

Because Proposition Speaks Where The Bible Is Silent
(Heb. 7:14; Acts 15:24; 1 Pet. 4:11; Matt. 15:9)

2

What Is The Issue?

We Agree:	We Disagree:
1. Innocent mate may put away fornicator & marry another (Matt. 19:9)	1. Fornicator may put away innocent mate & marry another (No Scripture)
2. Put-away fornicator can marry again: a. Remarry 1st mate (Jer. 3:1-8) b. Marry another when 1st mate dies (Rom. 7:2-3)	2. Put-away fornicator can marry another while 1st mate lives (No Scripture)
3. A Christian is enslaved to Christ alone & can't give Him up to meet demands of unbelievers (1 Cor. 7:15, 23)	3. A Christian deserted by unbeliever can marry another (No Scripture)

4

number one. *"Cite the exact words where Thayer used any of the following terms in his comments on 'bondage'"* [pointing to "Marriage," "Husband," "Wife" on chart]. Now, last night he said, and I quote as I took it down, "Thayer said it meant marriage." You did not suggest that there was an implication in Thayer that it could apply to marriage. No sir, you did not. You said, quote, "Thayer said it meant marriage." And you invited people to come down here and see *Thayer's Greek-English Lexicon.*

Now, my friends, on my chart 157-A, I am going to show you *Thayer's.* I am going to show you *Thayer's,* and let's just see if *Thayer* said it meant marriage, or even implied it. Alright, now notice. Here is your primary definition of DOULOO, that is used there, "to make a slave of, reduce to bondage." As a metaphor, to "give myself wholly to one's needs and service, make myself a bondman to..., wholly given up to, enslaved to" something, like enslaved to wine. And then he said, "to be under bondage, held by constraint of law or necessity, in some manner, 1 Corinthians 7:15."

The word *"marriage"* is *not* there, brother Freeman. *No sir, it is not!* You misled this good audience. Now, my friend, the meaning is: not "under bondage" to give up your faith, not "held by constraint" of your husband, the demand of

---

QUESTIONS - MAR. 1, 1990

1. Cite the exact words where Thayer used any of the following terms in his comments on "bondage" (DOULOO, 1 Corinthians 7;15):
   "Marriage," "Husband," "Wife."

2. Which verses in 1 Corinthians 7 address the put-away fornicator to tell him he can "marry another:"
   a. _____ v. 1-2   c. _____ v. 10-11   e. _____ v. 27-28
   b. _____ v. 8-9   d. _____ v. 15

3. Repentance requires severing which of the following sinful relationships:
   a. _____ homosexual marriages   d. _____ incestuous marriages
   b. _____ polygamous marriages   e. _____ man-beast marriages
   c. _____ adulterous marriages   f. _____ man married 100 times

4. Did Paul or other apostles ever tell anyone to remain unmarried in order to get to heaven?
   a. _____ Yes   b. _____ No

5. Jack Freeman believes that the marriage of Herod and Herodias would become lawful if Philip would say he put her away.
   a. _____ True   b. _____ False

Q3-1-90

> **THAYER'S GREEK - ENGLISH LEXICON OF THE NEW TESTAMENT**
> **158**
> δουλόω, -ῶ : fut. δουλώσω ; 1 aor. ἐδούλωσα ; pf. pass. δεδούλωμαι ; 1 aor. pass. ἐδουλώθην ; (δοῦλος) ; [fr. Aeschyl. and Hdt. down] ; *to make a slave of, reduce to bondage* ; a. prop. : τινά, Acts vii. 6 ; τούτῳ καὶ [yet T WH om. Tr br. καὶ] δεδούλωται to him he has also been made a bondman, 2 Pet. ii. 19. b. metaph. : ἐμαυτόν τινι give myself wholly to one's needs and service, make myself a bondman to him, 1 Co. ix. 19 ; δουλοῦσθαί τινι, to be made subject to the rule of some one, e. g. τῇ δικαιοσύνῃ, τῷ θεῷ, Ro. vi. 18, 22 ; likewise ὑπό τι, Gal. iv. 3 ; δεδουλωμένος οἴνῳ, wholly given up to, enslaved to, Tit. ii. 3 (δουλεύειν οἴνῳ, Liban. epist. 319) ; δεδούλωμαι ἔν τινι, to be under bondage, held by constraint of law or necessity, in some matter, 1 Co. vii. 15. [Comp.: κατα-δουλόω.]*
>
> 157 A

your husband, the law of your husband, in order to sacrifice your faith. And do you see there is not one thing in *Thayer's* definition that conflicts with what I have affirmed about 1 Corinthians 7:15. He wholly misled you.

2. *"Which verses in 1 Corinthians 7 address the put-away fornicator to tell him he can 'marry another'* [pointing to choices on chart]?" And I put the term "marry another" in quotation marks just as it appears in the Scriptures. Well, he said in verses 1 and 2, verses 8 and 9, verses 27, 28. Let's see. Look at my chart 122-A. My friends, open your Bibles and see. He can find "marry another" in 7:15, not the put-away fornicator in that case, but remember how he answered that the other night. He can find it in that passage and he can find "marry another" in these passages. And I am going to tell you his rule of interpretation. *"Marry another" is in every passage that does not say "marry another."* And so every passage in the Bible that does not say "marry another" is the passage that authorizes the put-away fornicator to marry another! See how simple it is to understand the Bible?

Now, look at verse two, "every man have his own wife," brother Freeman. Brother Freeman, not this: "Every man who wrecks his marriage, throws away his wife, defies the God of heaven by fornication and unscriptural divorce, gets another wife. *Go get another wife."* That is not what it says. Oh, but, you said that teaches the put-away fornicator

Does 1 Cor. 7 Authorize The Put-Away Fornicator To Marry Another?	
Text Says This:	**Not This:**
Vs. 2 "Every man have his own wife"	Every man who wrecks his marriage & throws away his own wife by fornication or unscriptural divorce, gets another wife!
Vs. 9 "Unmarried...widows... better to marry than to burn"	Unscripturally divorced & put-away fornicator... better to commit adultery than fornication!
Vv. 27-28 A man "loosed from a wife" (free, never married) and "a virgin" (free, never married) may marry.	A man unscripturally divorced or a divorced fornicator may marry a woman in the same condition!

122 A

can "marry another." There is *no* "marry another" in that, and *the fornicator is not even addressed.*

In verse 9, to the unmarried and widows, Paul said, "It is better to marry than to burn." Paul did not address the unscripturally divorced and the put-away fornicator and tell them, "It is better to commit adultery than fornication." Friend, I am showing you the text. And this man says "marry another" is *in* this text somewhere. Can you find it? Can you see it?

In verses 27 and 28, *the man who is "loosed from a wife"* (free, never married) *and "a virgin"* (free, never married) *may marry*. But this man can find a put-away fornicator in there marrying another. When the Bible means *marry another*, it says *"marry another."* But this is talking about the marriage of those who have never married.

3. *"Repentance requires severing which of the following sinful relationships"* [pointing to choices on chart, p. 170]? And so he just dismissed all of these human marriages that certainly do take place. I know God does not bind them, but they are marriages and the Bible even calls them marriages. In Mark 6, Herod married her, didn't he? That is what the Bible says. There is a human relationship and *he would not even say that people had to sever those sinful relationships*. He made his little play that these are not really marriages, just as though he was embarrassed to say that if you are in a homosexual marriage you have got to *get out* of it.

If you had given me this question, I would have said *get out* of the homosexual marriage, *get out* of the polygamous marriage, *get out* of the adulterous marriage, *get out* of the incestuous marriage, *get out* of the marriage of man to the beast, and the man married a hundred times to *get out* of that mess. But here sits the man that would not come up and say that. Imagine it! If I asked you the question, could you answer it? Ah, my friend, what a shame and a disgrace! Do you see that he is perverting and overturning the meaning of *repentance* in the word of God?

Alright, now he said on that man married a hundred times, *"What is the difference anyway between being married two times and a hundred times?"* Exactly, brother Freeman, oh exactly, brother Freeman! Your doctrine which allows just that second marriage opens the door to a hundred just like it. This perverts the will of God concerning marriage.

4. *"Did Paul or other Apostles ever tell anyone to remain unmarried in order to get to heaven?"* I took this question off of his chart. I just fed it back to him. And lo and behold, he answered it correctly! Now, my friend, notice my chart 140-X [1 Cor. 7:10-11]. Here is the text, 1 Corinthians 7:10-11. Here is an

inspired Apostle, the Apostle Paul, and what does he say to those that have violated the rule that they are not to depart? He says, "Let her remain unmarried or be reconciled to her husband." Do you see that? Now, my friend, if there is no reconciliation, what does that leave? That leaves "remain unmarried," doesn't it? And an Apostle told someone to remain unmarried in order to do what, brother Freeman? Do you suppose it was in order to go to heaven? I just think it might have been.

5. *"Jack Freeman believes that the marriage of Herod and Herodias would become lawful if Philip would say he put her away."* Now, you made a comment about it not being lawful as it was, but I said, "become lawful." You talk about dodging and dancing around questions. But in order to make your little dodge run, you said you were going to mark it *"false."*

Thank you, brother Freeman, you have *surrendered your proposition!* Put the proposition up here. Let me show you. He surrendered it. He just gave it up. He just gave it up, my friend. "The Scriptures teach that a person divorced by his mate for committing fornication is free to marry another." So, I gave him the case that Philip put away Herodias, did not want her anymore, and this man says now *she is unmarried, unattached, loosed, divorced,* as he will express it, *but she cannot be married to Herod.* Thank you, brother Freeman. Thank you, sir, you *surrendered your proposition* when you answered it that way.

The truth is the other night on 1 Corinthians 7:10-11, about that person that violated it and got in another marriage and had no right to it, he said that the first mate could say, "I do not want you back," and put them away anyhow. Well, then, *why couldn't Philip do that?* And why won't that work for Herodias? Do you see the fix he is in? I would not trade places with him for anything.

Now his questions to me. 1. *"What is the meaning of 'adultery' in Matthew 19:9?"* Look at my chart 72 [text, Matt. 19:9], the text, Matthew 19:9. Jesus said, "Whosoever shall put away his wife, except it be for fornication, and shall marry another, comitteth adultery; and whosoever marrieth her that is put away doth commit adultery." Now, my friend, the meaning of adultery here is immorality — it is *an unscriptural, unlawful, adulterous marriage and relationship*. And I want you to notice, brother Freeman, *whoever* marries her. That *"whoever"* there that marries the put-away one, they are going to get into *adultery*. That could be even someone never married before. But they are going to get into adultery.

Whom do they commit it against? You are always asking me, "Whom is it against?" Make a note of that. This "whosoever" is a single person, as I am giving you the case. O.K., sir, if she marries this one put away, I want to know *whom did she commit adultery against?* And if you will study on that, you will get the right definition of this word.

Notice my chart 85. "Adultery" is defined by usage, my friend. *It is unlawful sexual intercourse involving someone under constraint of God's marriage law.* In that case I just gave you, the person entered into a relationship with one who was under constraint of God's marriage law, and it results in *adultery.* Or, the married man with another man's wife. Or, a man puts away his wife without cause and marries another. Now, call for this chart. It is the answer to your questions.

Adultery Defined By Use:
Unlawful Sexual Intercourse Involving Someone Under Constraint Of God's Marriage Law

1. Married man with another man's wife (Jn. 8:4)
2. Man puts away wife w/o cause and marries another (Matt. 19:9; Mk. 10:11-12; Lk. 16:18)
3. Woman put away w/o cause marries another (Matt. 5:32; 19:9)
4. Put-away fornicator marries another (Matt. 5:32 & 19:9 read with exception)

85

Do not get up here and say I did not give a definition. You said I did not answer some of those questions the other night. I did answer them. Even the one I did not understand, I gave you my best understanding of it, answered that, and you have never made a reference to it. I am not going to take up my time repeating that all over again.

Now, look at the definition of adultery. It includes *a woman put away without cause who marries another,* and *a put-away fornicator who marries another.* There is your answer. Adultery is defined by the use, and our Lord made that use of it.

2. *"Under what conditions, if any, may the one guilty of adultery, and divorced for that reason, scripturally remarry?"* He may be reconciled to the first mate, Jeremiah 3, or marry another upon the death of the first mate. I gave you that on my chart 4 on what our real difference is.

Alright, let's go on to 3. *"If the husband is guilty of adultery, may his wife scripturally remain married to him?"* Yes.

4. *"Can you give a passage where those guided by the Holy Spirit to preach the gospel told anyone that she must remain unmarried?"* See my chart 140-X, 1 Corinthians 7:10-11. If there is no reconciliation, then they will have to remain unmarried the rest of their life — *if that mate does not die,* and *there is no reconciliation.*

5. *"Can you give a passage that told anyone to put away the husband or wife in order to be saved?"* If it is an *unlawful* marriage, every passage that mentions that word *repentance*. If it is a *lawful* marriage, Jesus said, "What God hath joined together, let not man put asunder."

Now, then, I want to notice tonight my chart number 15. Here is the basic principle involved in this debate that we are having. Notice, my friend, Jack Freeman at the time of living in San Pablo, California, now of Las Vegas, Nevada, said that things "not authorized...are...sinful." *If there is no passage to prove it,* then it is *wrong* and it is *sinful.* He believed that when he wrote it, and he wrote it in 1960, and it was published in the *Gospel Guardian.* And he has never yet confessed his error of calling me a liar for referring to him as the author of this. I am sorry for that; I am sorry it got on the record of this debate. I still beg and plead for him to get that off the record of this debate. But, my friend, the principle is true and the principle is right: *there is no clear passage authorizing the put-away fornicator or the deserted believer to marry another.* So, by Jack Freeman's biblical argument, such marriages are *sinful!*

> **Not Authorized = Sinful**
>
> 1. Things "not authorized within the doctrine of Christ are not only non-essential but sinful as well."
> 2. An author defended sponsoring church but had "no passage of Scripture to show that such a plan is authorized by the Lord" (Jack Freeman, Gospel Guardian, 28 April 1960, pp. 8-9).
> 3. No clear passage authorizes put-away fornicator or deserted believer to marry another.
> 4. Conclusion: such marriages are sinful!
>
> 15

And then we notice my chart 54, how do you know? How do we know? "The Bible tells me so." How do we know we can remarry? If a mate dies, Romans 7:2-3, it says marry "another." If you put your

> **How We Know**
>
> Simplicity Of Truth: "Yes, Jesus loves me, the Bible tells me so" (Rom. 4:3; Eph. 3:4)
>
> **Know We Can Remarry:**
>   1. If mate dies (Rom. 7:2-3)
>   2. If put away mate for fornication (Matt. 19:9)
>
> **Where Does The Bible Authorize These To Remarry:**
>   1. The put-away fornicator?
>   2. Those unscripturally divorced?
>
> 54

mate away for fornication, it says "marry another." Now, where does the Bible say "marry another" for *the put-away fornicator*, and *the unscripturally divorced?*

Notice my charts 59-B [text, Rom. 7:2-3] and 72 [text, Matt. 19:9]. I want you to see the text. I make my appeal to the text. Here is Romans 7: "if her husband be dead, she is free," so that she can be married. See it? *"Married to another."* That is that term brother Freeman can find all through 1 Corinthians 7. So remember, if a passage does not mention it, it means "marry another." That is the way you understand the Bible. And then on my chart 72, Matthew 19. Now, notice, if you put your mate away for fornication, then in that case you can "marry another" without committing adultery. And it said *"marry another." "Marry another."* That is how we know!

Now, my chart 37, my friend. The Bible ground is the unity ground. The Bible ground is the ground of unity. The Bible unites us on immersion, but human theories divide — sprinkling a baby. *We agree the innocent can put away the fornicator and marry another,* but brother Freeman teaches that others can remarry, and so the human theories divide us tonight.

Unity In Truth
(John 17:17-21)

Divine Truth Unites All Agree:	Human Theory Divides Men Differ:
1. Immerse (Acts 8:38)	1. Sprinkle Baby (Acts 16:15?)
2. Lord's Supper 1st Day (Acts 20:7)	2. Any Day (1 Cor. 11:26?)
3. Sing (Eph. 5:19)	3. Play (Rev. 5:8?)
4. Preach (1 Tim. 3:15)	4. Meal, Party, Gym (Jude 12?)
5. Hope - Heaven (1 Pet. 1:4)	5. 1,000 Years On Earth (Rev. 20:4?)
6. Innocent Put Away Fornicator & Remarry (Matt. 19:9)	6. Others Remarry (1 Cor. 7?)

37

Now, notice my chart 51, error makes common cause in departure, in digression, and in division. Spin the theory wheel and win instrumental music every time. Some will jump from the argument that *David used it,* to *it is used in heaven,* to *psallo,* but they all end up with the same answer, even contradicting one another.

Now, my chart 51-A, you have the same problem here on this matter. Spin the theory wheel and win an unscriptural mate every time. Those who become enemies of truth, even though conflicting among themselves, can unite one with the other in order to oppose us in the truth. *The fornicator can remarry,* brother Freeman affirms, and *the unbeliever leaves and you can marry,* and the *kingdom law* theory, and the *baptism* theory, and *redefining adultery,* and all of that, *but they all come out at the same place.* Oh, he insists he does not believe the

Third Evening: Halbrook's First Negative

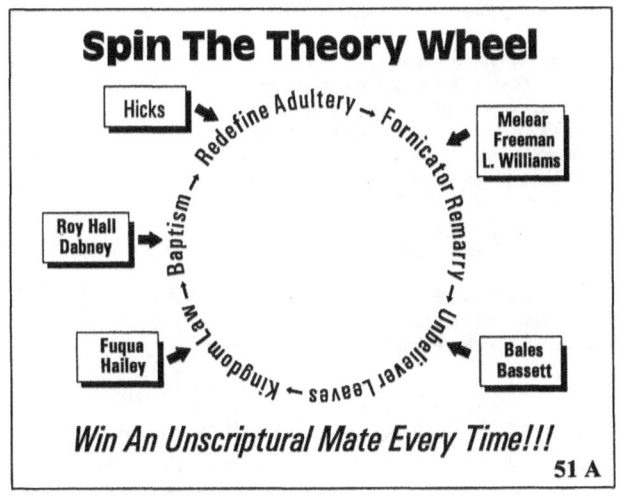

kingdom law theory, but you come right out at the same place, brother Freeman. Yes, you do! Yes, you do!

Now, he covered 13 of my 45 charts Tuesday night. For a man so anxious to study 1 Corinthians 7, acting like he had to prod me into it, he sure got off of it like a hot seat or something. Now, tonight, we are going to follow his charts and arguments. His chart 30 concerning the noun and the pronoun in Matthew 19, notice his chart 30,

---

NOUN & PRONOUN IN MATT. 19:9

WHOSOEVER SHALL PUT AWAY HIS <u>WIFE</u>, EXCEPT IT BE FOR FORNICATION,
WHOSO MARRIETH <u>HER</u> WHICH IS PUT AWAY DOTH COMMIT ADULTERY.

MAN WHO PUTS AWAY HIS WIFE FOR FORNICATION HAS NO WIFE,

<u>**CAN REMARRY.**</u>

WOMAN PUT AWAY FOR FORNICATION HAS NO HUSBAND,

<u>**CAN REMARRY.**</u>

30

---

my friend. Here is his chart trying to make the claim that you can *marry another* if you have been put away for fornication because you do not have a mate.

Divorced People Remain Under Constraint Of Law

1. Deut. 24:1-4 Divorce wife but can't have her back after her 2nd marriage
2. Deut. 24:1-4 Divorcee marry another but then can't ever return to 1st mate
3. Lev. 21:7, 13-14 Divorcee free from marriage but can't marry a priest
4. Matt. 5:32; 19:9 Pure divorce impure and marry another (new mate can't be one put away for fornication or other cause)
5. Matt. 5:32; 19:9 Not authorize a put-away person (whether put away for fornication or other cause) to marry another
6. 1 Cor. 7:10-11 If 2 Christians divorce, must remain unmarried or reconcile
7. 1 Cor. 7:12-15 Believer not give up Christ to keep unbeliever (no authority for either to marry another)

CONCLUSION:
1. Unscriptural divorce releases neither party from marriage!
2. Scriptural divorce releases both parties from marriage, but not from the constraint of the law!

101

Now, notice my chart number 101. And he said one who has no mate can marry someone who has no mate. He is talking about these who have been divorced. *Divorced people remain under the constraint of law*, brother Freeman. We have already studied this chart, and I would ask you to call for this and answer this. You have not yet, and you need to answer this. Unscriptural divorce releases neither party. God rules over all cases of divorce and remarriage. That was true in the Old Testament and is true in the New. Now, here are some people free from marriage in Leviticus [pointing to point 3 on chart]. A divorcee was free from marriage but could not marry a priest. God rules over it. Your little saying that one who has no spouse can marry one who has no spouse will not work in the Bible. It just

Third Evening: Halbrook's First Negative

> **My Opponent's Double-Talk**
>
> 1. He speaks of all "single" people having a right to marry. He puts all of these in the "single" category:
>   a. Never married } Right to marry
>   b. Widow   } (1 Cor. 7:8-9)
>   c. Divorced fornicator } No right to marry
> 2. He claims there is no such thing as the "guilty party" in a divorce for fornication once God forgives the sin. He confuses two separate issues:
>   a. The issue of spiritual status with God. } God forgives,
>   b. The issue of marital status in view of the } not change
>   constraint of the marriage law.   } marital status
> 3. He claims there is only one marriage law but makes adultery in 1 Cor. 7:11 case not adultery in vs. 15.
>
> 324

will not work, brother Freeman.

And then we notice my chart 324. I want you to notice my opponent's double-talk. He speaks of all *single* people — one having no spouse — having a right to marry. He puts *all* of these in the "single" category: the never-married, the widow, and *the divorced fornicator*. Now, my friend, in 1 Corinthians 7, the never-married and the widow are specifically told they *can* marry. *Where is the divorced fornicator told that?* He is *not* told that, but you just throw them all in the same basket, brother Freeman.

Then, brother Freeman claimed that there is no such thing as the guilty party in a divorce for fornication once God forgives the sin. Now, I want you to notice he confuses *two separate issues*. There is the issue of *our spiritual status with God*. God forgives, yes, but there is the issue of *marital status* in view of the constraint of the marriage law. And when God forgives, it does not change the marital status, brother Freeman. That is the thing that you are confusing.

You claim there is only one marriage law, but you make *adultery* in 1 Corinthians 7:11 *not adultery* in verse 15.

Notice his chart 31 please. Now, he is con-

> **NOUN & PRONOUN IN MATT. 19:9**
> (Cont)
>
> <u>GOD SAYS</u> --- "ART THOU LOOSED FROM A WIFE.."
> 1 COR. 7:27-28
>
> "...IF THOU MARRY, <u>THOU HAST NOT SINNED</u>".
> MAN WHO PUTS AWAY HIS WIFE FOR FORNICATION HAS NO WIFE,
>
> MY OPPONENT SAYS --- "IF HE MARRIES HE SINS"
>
> **GOD vs. HALBROOK**
>
> 31

tinuing his Matthew 19 argument, this time going to 1 Corinthians 7; if you marry "thou hast not sinned" because you are "loosed." Alright, look at my chart 191-A. We studied this Tuesday night, but he did not call for my charts; he did not call for 191-A. Would you like to catch up tonight? You did not call for 196, you did not call for 198. I have answered all of this. The never-married man is loosed from a wife, and the female counterpart is a virgin. If the loosed man in that passage is *divorced*, the virgin is a *divorcee!*

See my chart 196. Do you remember the Greek writers who used the expression "unbinding hair" and, then, with "unbound hair"? Is your hair tied up, do not unbind it. Is your hair *unbound*, do not tie it up. Now, my friend, the one who had hair unbound there does not mean it had been previously bound and then unbound. You see? Many dogs run *loose* in this community. Does this mean they first had been tied up, brother Freeman?

Next, consider my chart 198. Gordon Fee in his commentary points out that the Holy Spirit here "chose a word that could express 'being loosed' (= divorced) for the married, whose corresponding verb could mean to 'be free from' (= never married)." That is the truth on it.

Now, brother Freeman presented chart 56 on Alford. He uses Alford and we will use my chart 114 to follow this. This is from *Alford's Greek Testament*, I think that is volume one, and the argument is that the part "b" of Matthew 19:9 cannot include the put-away fornicator. Alright, give me my chart 114 [next page]. After all your storming against reference books, I just suspected you were

---

**1 Corinthians 7:27-28
Divorced People?**

Never married man is "Loosed from a wife"	His female counterpart is "A virgin"
IF "Loosed" man is Divorced	THEN "A virgin" is a Divorcee

191 A

Loose: Same Latitude in Greek & English
Can Be Simple State Of Freedom

1. Bion (200 B.C.): "unbinding her hair" (Liddell & Scott, 1068)
   Hermas (A.D. 140): "with unbound hair" (Arndt. & Ging., 484)

2. Is your hair tied up? Don't unbind it.
   Is your hair unbound? Don't tie it up.

3. "Free from a state of confinement, restraint, or obligation" (Webster)

Many dogs run **LOOSE, FREE** -
Context tells if they were ever tied up!

196

LOOSED = NEVER MARRIED
1 Cor 7:27

Gordon Fee, <u>1st Epistle to Corinthians</u>:
1. "Vv 25-38 take up the issue of the never-before married" (p. 288)
2. Vs 27 Paul "chose a word that could express 'being loosed' (= divorced) for the married, whose corresponding verb could mean to 'be free from' (= never married) for the case in hand" (p. 331)
3. "It lies totally outside the present context to suggest that the two questions address the married & the divorced" (p. 331 n.38)

198

Here is what I believe to be a correct diagram of Matthew 19:9, as it appears in the Greek text. You will note that *me epi porneia* is found a second time on dotted lines to indicate that it is understood to modify *apolelumenan*. In the paragraph following the diagram, Dean Alford is quoted in justification of this action in both Matthew 5:32 and 19:9.

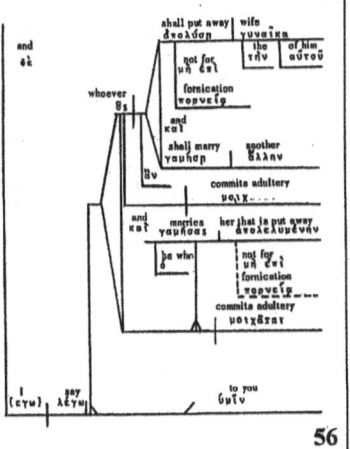

56

going to bring them up. Now, notice, Dean Alford does say "her that is divorced," "her which is put away," does not include the one put away for fornication, but he does *not* affirm a fornicator can remarry. No, Alford did not affirm your case at all; he does not mean by this what you mean. He said neither the innocent *nor the guilty* can remarry. He said 1 Corinthians 7:15 is *not grounds for remarriage,* brother Freeman.

> **Dean Alford "APOLELUMENEI"**
>
> ("Her that is divorced," "her which is put away" Matt. 5:32; 19:9) Does not include one put away for fornication (Alford's Greek Testament, I:194, cf. I:50)
>
> 1. But does not affirm a fornicator can remarry.
> 2. Says neither innocent nor guilty can remarry (I:50).
> 3. Says 1 Cor. 7:15 is not grounds for remarriage (II:525, I:50).
> 4. Pulpit Commentary says Alford is wrong - "apolelumenei" includes "one separated for porneia" (Matt., pg. 245).
> 5. If Alford is right on apolelumenei, still no positive authority for the fornicator to remarry!!
>
> 114

The *Pulpit Commentary* points out Alford's error; *"apolelumenei"* includes "one separated for *porneia."* Yes, it includes it, my friend. And so, *down goes his reference.*

> JANUARY 10, 1990
> TO WHOM IT MAY CONCERN:
>   SINCE I HAVE BEEN ASKED A QUESTION ON ENGLISH GRAMMAR, LET ME STATE MY BACKGROUND IN THE FIELD. I GRADUATED FROM NORTH TEXAS UNIVERSITY WITH A MAJOR IN ENGLISH AND TAUGHT ENGLISH FOR 32 YEARS IN TEXAS. I HAVE A SPECIAL INTEREST IN GRAMMAR AND THE DIAGRAMMING OF SENTENCES.
>   I HAVE BEEN ASKED WHETHER "SAVING FOR THE CAUSE OF FORNICATION" IN MATTHEW 5:32 HAS ANY GRAMMATICAL FORCE OR APPLICATION IN THE PART OF THE SENTENCE WHICH SAYS, "WHOSOEVER SHALL MARRY HER THAT IS DIVORCED COMMITTETH ADULTERY." THE ANSWER IS NO. MATTHEW 5:32 IS A COMPOUND-COMPLEX SENTENCE. IT INCLUDES TWO INDEPENDENT CLAUSES JOINED BY THE CONJUNCTION "AND." IN ORDER FOR THE ADVERBIAL PHRASE "SAVING FOR THE CAUSE OF FORNICATION" TO HAVE FORCE OR APPLICATION IN THE SECOND PART OF THE SENTENCE, IT WOULD BE NECESSARY TO REPEAT OR INSERT THE PHRASE IN THE SECOND PART.
>   I HAVE BEEN ASKED THE SAME QUESTION CONCERNING THE USE OF "EXCEPT IT BE FOR FORNICATION" IN MATTHEW 19:9. THIS TEXT IS ANOTHER COMPOUND-COMPLEX SENTENCE. THE ADVERBIAL PREPOSITIONAL PHRASE "EXCEPT IT BE FOR FORNICATION" FOUND IN THE FIRST PART OF THE SENTENCE MUST BE REPEATED IN THE SECOND PART IF IT IS TO HAVE FORCE OR APPLICATION THERE.
>   I AM SUBMITTING DIAGRAMS OF BOTH SENTENCES WHICH SHOW THE PROPER PLACEMENT AND FUNCTION OF THE ADVERBIAL PHRASES IN QUESTION.
>   SINCERELY,
>   MRS.. ANN ALEXANDER
>   307 LAKE DR., W. COLUMBIA, TX 77486
>
> 110

And the text will answer it on my chart 72 [text, Matt. 19:9]. Notice on chart 72, "Whosoever shall put away his wife, except it be for fornication, and shall marry another, committeth adultery." There are two possible causes of putting one away. You put them away *without cause,* or you put them away *with cause.* Here is your second independent clause: "Whoso marrieth her which is put away doth commit adultery." Alright, now notice my charts 110 and 110-A on this. Here you have where I submitted a question to one who has been an English teacher for 32 years in Texas, and now notice the enlargement:

"I have been asked whether the clause 'saving for the cause of fornication'

> **Grammar of Matthew 5:32 & 19:9**
>
> I HAVE BEEN ASKED WHETHER "SAVING FOR THE CAUSE OF FORNICATION" IN MATTHEW 5:32 HAS ANY GRAMMATICAL FORCE OR APPLICATION IN THE PART OF THE SENTENCE WHICH SAYS, "WHOSOEVER SHALL MARRY HER THAT IS DIVORCED COMMITTETH ADULTERY." THE ANSWER IS NO. MATTHEW 5:32 IS A COMPOUND-COMPLEX SENTENCE. IT INCLUDES TWO INDEPENDENT CLAUSES JOINED BY THE CONJUNCTION "AND." IN ORDER FOR THE ADVERBIAL PHRASE "SAVING FOR THE CAUSE OF FORNICATION" TO HAVE FORCE OR APPLICATION IN THE SECOND PART OF THE SENTENCE, IT WOULD BE NECESSARY TO REPEAT OR INSERT THE PHRASE IN THE SECOND PART. I HAVE BEEN ASKED THE SAME QUESTION CONCERNING THE USE OF "EXCEPT IT BE FOR FORNICATION" IN MATTHEW 19:9. THIS TEXT IS ANOTHER COMPOUND-COMPLEX SENTENCE. THE ADVERBIAL PREPOSITIONAL PHRASE "EXCEPT IT BE FOR FORNICATION" FOUND IN THE FIRST PART OF THE SENTENCE MUST BE REPEATED IN THE SECOND PART IF IT IS TO HAVE FORCE OR APPLICATION. (A. Alexander, English teacher for 32 years)
>
> 110 A

in Matthew 5:32 has any grammatical force or application in the part of the sentence which says, 'Whosoever shall marry her that is divorced committeth adultery.' The answer is no....To have force or application in the second part..., it would be necessary to repeat or insert the phrase in the second part."

Now then, he has his "doctrine of demons" charge—that if we teach someone is not to marry another, it is the "doctrine of demons." But here sits the man who said on my question number 4 tonight that the person in 1 Corinthians 7 *could not marry*. Now, we notice my chart 314. Do we forbid marriage and meats as in 1 Timothy 4:3? No. Would my opponent *forbid food* to the lazy? Yes, he would. He had better do it if he obeys what the passage said. He forbids Herod to Herodias. How does he *forbid marriage?* He for-

> **Do We Forbid "Marriage" & "Meats" As In 1 Timothy 4:3?**
>
> Would Opponent Forbid...
> 1. Food to the Lazy (2 Thess. 3:10)?
> 2. Herod to Herodias (Mark 6:17-18)?
> 3. "Whosoever" to "another" (Matt. 19:9)?
> 4. Man to wives (Matt. 19:4-6)?
> 5. Man to man (Matt. 19:4-6)?
> 6. Man to beast (Matt. 19:4-6)?
> 7. Woman of 1 Cor. 7:11 to new mate?
> 8. Widow of 1 Cor. 7:39 to unbeliever?
> 9. Fornication, Murder -- New Mate (Gen. 9:6; Rom. 13:4)?
> 10. Eat at Idolatrous feast or before the weak (1 Cor. 8-10)?
>
> 314

bids "whosoever" to marry "another." Now, my friend, we are not forbidding marriage. We are forbidding *wrecking your marriage* and going to get *another* one. That is it!

Notice my chart 315. My opponent says that if we forbid marriage we are apostate. No, we forbid *unlawful marriage* as he forbids *unlawful eating* at an idol's feast. And, was John apostate in Mark 6? You say you agree with him. That would make *you* an apostate. Apostates defend unlawful marriages as right. And, here the Catholic writer claims the so-called Pauline privilege in 1

Corinthians 7:15 that you claim. So, you embrace a Roman Catholic theory and that will make *you* apostate, won't it, brother Freeman? My friends, I want you to get the seriousness of these matters.

Now, on his chart number 22 he has a man living in sin, and who commits adultery, and he wants to know what part of this I will agree with. I

> **OPPONENT SAYS IF FORBID MARRIAGE APOSTATE PER 1 TIM 4:1-3**
>
> 1. NO, We Forbid Unlawful Marriage As He Forbids Unlawful Eating (1 Cor 10:21).
> 2. Was John Apostate? (Mk 6:17-18)
> 3. Apostates Defend Unlawful Marriages As Right (Matt 19:3-9).
> 4. Jn. A. Hardin, S.J., <u>The Catholic Catechism</u>, p. 359, Claims "Pauline Privilege" In 1 Cor 7:15.
>
> 315

will show you on my chart 60 [text, Matt. 5:32] what part of it I agree with. My friend, Christ said, "Whosoever shall put away his wife, saving for the cause of fornication, causeth her to commit adultery: and whosoever shall marry her that is divorced committeth adultery." Now, that is the plain unvarnished truth about that. It will stand when the world is on fire. And it does not include the claim that the put-away fornicator can marry another. "Whosoever shall marry her that is divorced committeth adultery."

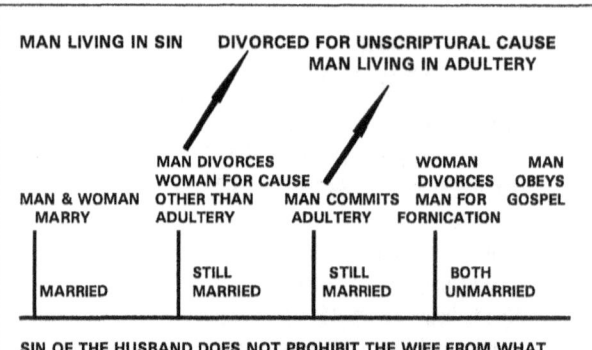

22

You can juggle the circumstances a hundred different ways. It all comes back to the same thing.

As shown on my chart 101, they are under restraint of law, brother Freeman. Yes, they are. They are under constraint of divine law. The pure can divorce the impure, the fornicator, and marry another. But the new mate cannot be one put away for fornication or other cause. And, he does not authorize the put-away person to marry another. They remain under that constraint.

Now, he made his appeal to mercy on his chart 28. Alright, he pleads for

> **Divorced People Remain Under Constraint Of Law**
>
> 1. Deut. 24:1-4 Divorce wife but can't have her back after her 2nd marriage
> 2. Deut. 24:1-4 Divorcee marry another but then can't ever return to 1st mate
> 3. Lev. 21:7, 13-14 Divorcee free from marriage but can't marry a priest
> 4. Matt. 5:32; 19:9 Pure divorce impure and marry another (new mate can't be one put away for fornication or other cause)
> 5. Matt. 5:32; 19:9 Not authorize a put-away person (whether put away for fornication or other cause) to marry another
> 6. 1 Cor. 7:10-11 If 2 Christians divorce, must remain unmarried or reconcile
> 7. 1 Cor. 7:12-15 Believer not give up Christ to keep unbeliever (no authority for either to marry another)
>
> **CONCLUSION:**
> 1. Unscriptural divorce releases neither party from marriage!
> 2. Scriptural divorce releases both parties from marriage, but not from the constraint of the law!
>
> 101

"mercy." We want our chart O-1 [page 186]. Yes, I believe the Bible teaches mercy, my friend. *But notice in Mark 6:17-18, John was preaching mercy to Herod and Herodias when he said your marriage is unlawful and you better get out of it if you want to go to heaven.* That is what he taught. Colossians 3:5-7 teaches the same thing. How do you preach mercy to those who are living in adultery? You teach them to *get out* of adultery. That is mercy! In 1 Corinthians 5, this man had his father's wife. You preach mercy by telling him to *get out* of it. In chapter 6:9-11, they had to *get out* of adultery. In 1 Corinthians 7:11, according to my opponent, when you violate that passage and there is no reconciliation, they must *remain unmarried*. Are you preaching mercy tonight or not? Now, what is mercy, my friend?

> **HOW DO WE KNOW?**
> **MERCY**
>
> **GOD THROUGH HIS MERCY:**
> REMITS SINS---------------ACTS 2:38
> BLOTS OUT SINS-----------ACTS 3:19
> WASHES AWAY SINS-------ACTS 22:16
> FORGIVES ALL TRESPASSES---COL. 2:13
> DESTROYS THE BODY OF SIN---ROM. 6:6
> REMEMBERS SINS NO MORE---HEB. 8:12
> BUT MY OPPONENT WILL ALWAYS REMEMBER THAT ONE HAS COMMITTED FORNICATION AND WILL ALWAYS DEMAND PENANCE, EVEN WHEN GOD HAS FORGIVEN.
> LET US BE THANKFUL WE DON'T DEPEND UPON "HALBROOK'S MERCY".
>
> 28

He says that I demand penance, but look at my chart 286 on mercy. Let's get another thought on that. Now, my friends, get this, *forgiveness does not remove the temporal consequences of sin*. The converted murderer cannot escape the death penalty. Paul said, "I refuse not to die if I did something worthy of death." You can be forgiven and yet die in the electric chair. The convicted thief does not escape his due reward. The converted prodigal cannot regain the money he wasted gambling. *The converted adulterer, brother Freeman, is not free to marry another, or to continue in the adulterous marriage.* That is a temporal consequence and has nothing to do with forgiveness and spiritual relationship in heaven. Forgiveness does not change your marital status one bit.

Now, my friends, this is one of the key points in this debate. Every time he says "mercy," "forgiveness," and all of that, you wonder if he is going to call for chart 286. You write it down, and then when he calls for it, you circle it so you will know he did. My friend, forgiveness does not remove the temporal consequences of sin. *When you throw away your wife and try to go get another, you are under the constraint of a law which will not permit you to do that.* That is the truth about it tonight. We are preaching mercy, but the temporal consequences are not removed.

FORGIVENESS NOT REMOVE TEMPORAL CONSEQUENCES
1. Converted Murderer Not Escape Death Penalty (Acts 25:11)
2. Convicted Thief Not Escape "Due Reward" (Lk. 23:40-43)
3. Converted Prodigal Not Regain Money Wasted Gambling (Lk 15:13)
4. Converted Adulterer Not Free To Marry Another Or Continue Adulterous Marriage (Matt 19:9)

286

Third Evening
Freeman's Second Affirmative

Brethren and friends, Mr. Moderators, brother Halbrook, I would like to take up where we left off, beginning first of all to notice something brother Halbrook had to say. He accused me of speaking where the Bible is *silent*. Did you notice the book, and the chapter, and the verse he gave you in answer to the last two questions I asked? Did an inspired person ever tell anyone to remain single the rest of their life? Did he give you book, chapter, and verse? Is that speaking where the Bible speaks? That is all I asked for was the verse. He did not give it, he cannot give it, and he knows it.

Let's look at his chart number 4. I want you to look at this chart, and he pointed out that when he was in the affirmative he had no obligation to answer any arguments I made in the negative. And so I do not have any obligation to answer anything he says in the negative. But, I am going to pay a little attention to that. Number 2, on the left side of the chart, *we agree that the put-away fornicator can marry again*. He can remarry the first mate and he cites an Old Testament passage as authority. He can remarry his first mate and, yet, what does he believe? If you marry a fornicator, you commit *adultery*. It is *an adulterous marriage*. Here is a put-away fornicator, one guilty of fornication, the put-away fornicator. We are not talking about just one who is guilty of fornication, but *one who has divorced, been divorced, because he was guilty of fornication*. He says here is someone that can marry him. His first mate. Why can the first mate and no one else? He is no longer married to the first mate. So, here is someone who can remarry the first one *without committing adultery*.

Do you see how inconsistent that is? Every time he comes to something, he changes it. Just change a little, changes here, a little change there, and after a

---

What Is The Issue?

We Agree:	We Disagree:
1. Innocent mate may put away fornicator & marry another (Matt. 19:9)	1. Fornicator may put away innocent mate & marry another (No Scripture)
2. Put-away fornicator can marry again: a. Remarry 1st mate (Jer. 3:1-8) b. Marry another when 1st mate dies (Rom. 7:2-3)	2. Put-away fornicator can marry another while 1st mate lives (No Scripture)
3. A Christian is enslaved to Christ alone & can't give Him up to meet demands of unbelievers (1 Cor. 7:15, 23)	3. A Christian deserted by unbeliever can marry another (No Scripture)

4

while he has rewritten the entire Bible. First, he tells us, "Under no circumstances," then he begins, "Well, *if his mate dies,"* then he says, "Or, *be reconciled to his first mate."* Those are the two conditions under which this one can remarry. According to his testimony for two nights in this debate, four nights in Las Vegas, any one who marries the put-away fornicator commits adultery. Now, that being the case, if he remarries, or goes back, or is reconciled to his first mate, that first mate is guilty of adultery. It becomes what he calls an adulterous marriage.

Further, as you notice on the right hand side, he said we *disagree* on whether a Christian deserted by an unbeliever can marry another. We are going to deal with this *"another"* in a minute. The fornicator may put away an innocent mate and marry another — Halbrook says "no scripture" for it. The put-away fornicator can marry another while the mate lives — again he says "no scripture." He says the put-away fornicator can marry *the one that put him away.* He makes a distinction God does not. He did not give any book, chapter, or verse for that. Did you notice that? He asked me to give a clear-cut passage where it says directly thus and so.

Now, he goes back to discussing a believer divorced by a non-believer, and that was to be included in the first proposition. He did not like to include it, but he finally got around to it both in North Las Vegas and here. Well, let's look at this *"another."* Brother Halbrook says if it does not say *"another,"* it does not mean a second marriage. Come over here to 1 Corinthians 7. He took you over there and said — let's read it — "That refers to people who have never been married," he says. Let's read it.

First of all, he wants us to read 1 Corinthians 7:2. "To avoid fornication, let every man have his own wife, and let every woman have her own husband." Let's go on down a little. Verses 8-9, "I say therefore to the unmarried and widows, it is good for them if they abide even as I." I want you to notice the word *"widows."* What is a widow? A woman who has been married, her husband is dead. Isn't that so? You know anymore about widows than that? You may know more about it than that, but that is all I know about widows. She is a woman who has been married, her husband dies. Now, what does he say to these widows and other unmarried. "If they cannot contain, let them marry another." No, he does not. The word "another" is not there, brother Halbrook.

He has insisted, unless it says "another," it is not a marriage. Whenever God authorizes a marriage, he always says "marry another." Now, I have pointed out repeatedly you cannot marry without *another* being involved. You cannot marry yourself. There have to be two people involved to make it a marriage. And here, too, one who had been married. He said you can marry and he did not put the word "another" in it. Now, maybe brother Halbrook wants to add it. He took the word "not" out of some passages. He added the word "not," put the word "not," in Matthew 19. Maybe he wants to put the word "another" here, the word "another." Now, he has *harped on that* four nights in North Las Vegas and this is the third night he has *harped on it* here. And, here it is right here before him, and it does not say "another." And, here is one who had been married. And if they get married, they necessarily will be *to another*. It will not be to the same one because that one is dead. It does not make any sense to me.

Now, he gets back on *Herod and Herodias*. The law, John says, did not allow him to have her. It is not lawful for you to have her. Period. I have not denied that. He said, "Well, what Jack Freeman says is that if he will just say, 'I put you away,' that he can keep her." I did not say that. The law did not allow Herod to have his brother's wife. Period. Incidentally, brother Halbrook, are we living under that law today? What law was John speaking of? You know there was a condition back in that same law, the law given through Moses, under which a man had to take his brother's wife. But, under ordinary circumstances he could not have her. Could not have her. But if his brother dies without leaving any seed, a son to carry on the family name, this brother had to take her and produce a child by her. Otherwise, he could not have his brother's wife.

And I want to remind you again I am not here to defend man's right to have the wife of another. Herod had another man's wife, but Herod had a right to his own wife. Now, what my opponent is saying, Herod had no right to marry period. John did not say, "You have no right to a wife." "It is not lawful for you to have her — *Herodias* — she belongs to your brother." We do not have to have a college degree to understand that. See, he wants to put something in there, "John said, 'It is not lawful for you to marry.'" John did not say that. John said, "It is not lawful for you to have her."

Look at his chart number 196. Now, notice, he says this person is *under constraint of law,* still bound by the law, but he will not tell us, I asked him, *what is he bound to?* What is he bound to by the law? They are still bound by the law, loosed from a mate. The fornicator, divorced, because he is guilty of fornication, is loosed from a mate. But they are *bound by the law*. To what? To whom? Not to their last mate. Well, what law is he talking about, if it is law pertaining to marriage? That is the law that binds husband and wife together. So, they are not bound together by the law. Romans 7:2-3 proves that. If the mate dies, she is no longer bound by him to the law, she is free from that law that bound her to him. And the one who is divorced scripturally is the same way.

No, he wants to talk about *loosed dogs* and *loose hair*. This has nothing at all to do with our subject. "Is your hair tied up, don't unbind it." What does that have to do with marriage? He quotes Webster. Many dogs run loose, but are free. But I used your own authority, your own witness to impeach you, where he said in 1 Corinthians 7 — that is the passage I had in mind, verse 27 — *the word loosed refers to divorce*. That is what your own witness had to say about it. This has nothing to do with the subject we are discussing [pointing to chart 196], and what does he do to prove that it does? Well, he introduces some more sectarian authors and then a man who writes a secular dictionary for us. The proposition, his and mine, reads, "The Scriptures teach."

> **Loose: Same Latitude In Greek & English**
> Can Be Simple State Of Freedom
>
> 1. Bion (200 B.C.): "unbinding her hair" (Liddell & Scott, 1068)
>   Hermas (A.D. 140): "with unbound hair" (Arndt. & Ging., 484)
> 2. Is your hair tied up? Don't unbind it.
>   Is your hair unbound? Don't tie it up.
> 3. "Free from a state of confinement, restraint, or obligation" (Webster)
>
> Many dogs run LOOSE, FREE -
> Context tells if they were ever tied up!
>
> 196

I am very well aware of what *Alford* had to say on one page, and then he contradicted himself on another. But why do you use a man who is a liar as a witness? Why do you use *Thayer*, who you do not agree with? He is *a liar*, according to you. He told the truth on one passage, did not tell the truth on another. Why introduce a liar, when you have these inspired men to introduce? Why call a liar to the witness stand, when you can call the Apostle Paul, or Jesus Christ, or some inspired man. He departs from that, why? Have you wondered that, when in one speech he referred to 14 commentaries, one dictionary, and a Catholic Catechism. Why? Because no inspired witness agreed with him, he called these to the witness stand. He knew they would not agree with him.

So, he had to go out there in the world to get sectarians. He said it is wrong to drink at sectarian wells. That is what he wants you to do, and that is what he has been doing. You know before brethren began to drink at sectarian wells, the doctrine he teaches was never heard of. But, when they began to drink from sectarian wells, they got it. They did not get it from the Bible — you know if they got it from the Bible, he would have set forth these inspired witnesses. He would have said, "Let's call Paul to the witness stand." You notice he never called him? Oh, he refers to some passages, but then, how do you know what they mean? We will turn over here and let this man tell us what Paul was talking about. We cannot know. Paul said, "I write so that when you read, you may understand my knowledge in the mystery of Christ."

Let's look at his chart number 314. *"Do We Forbid 'Marriage' and 'Meats'?"* He said, *"Would my opponent forbid food to the lazy?"* I have answered that in the first part of our debate. I introduced another passage along with it. If a man asked you, you do not forbid him, if he asks to borrow from you, do not turn him away. That is not a contradiction with 2 Thessalonians 3:10 at all. And God did not forbid marriage to Herod. He said you cannot have that woman. But my opponent is saying, you know what he is really saying? He says, "I teach the doctrine of devils, but Jack, you are just as guilty. Because you do this. You do this, you do this. And, therefore, I am no worse than you are." Now, that is not a way to prove anything, is it? That is like the pot saying to the kettle, "I am no blacker than you are." Or, the stove saying to the fireplace, "You're no hotter than I am." But "my opponent," mind, I am his opponent, I do not forbid food nor does God. He gives him conditions upon which he can eat.

Do We Forbid "Marriage" & "Meats" As In 1 Timothy 4:3?

Would Opponent Forbid...
1. Food to the Lazy (2 Thess. 3:10)?
2. Herod to Herodias (Mark 6:17-18)?
3. "Whosoever" to "another" (Matt. 19:9)?
4. Man to wives (Matt. 19:4-6)?
5. Man to man (Matt. 19:4-6)?
6. Man to beast (Matt. 19:4-6)?
7. Woman of 1 Cor. 7:11 to new mate?
8. Widow of 1 Cor. 7:39 to unbeliever?
9. Fornication, Murder -- New Mate (Gen. 9:6; Rom. 13:4)?
10. Eat at Idolatrous feast or before the weak (1 Cor. 8-10)?

314

And there was a condition upon which Herod could marry. He could have his own wife. And Matthew 19:9, you know he has already found an exception to it. I brought it out in my last speech. All of these — I am not forbidding what God allows. Why didn't he list a passage down here that said forbidding to marry? Have you wondered that? Why didn't he put number 11, forbidding to marry, period? Just forbidding to marry. That is what I have charged him with and he admits he is guilty. Now, notice it. He has not denied it. He admits that he forbids to marry. He forbids to marry. Who forbids to marry according to 1 Timothy 4:1-3? The doctrine of devils. The faith does not. My opponent admits he does. Why didn't he put down there, number 11, forbidding to marry?

Let's look at his next chart, 315. "Opponent Says If Forbid Marriage, Apostate Per 1 Tim. 4:1-3." He says no, we forbid *unlawful* marriage. Well, you go a little further than that. Not only do you forbid lawful marriage, you demand celibacy, remain single the rest of your life. John was not apostate, no, he was not, but John did not forbid marriage either. Just mark that down, read that passage, *Mark 6:17-18*. John did not say, "It is not lawful for you to have a wife." Now, that is the

> **OPPONENT SAYS IF FORBID MARRIAGE APOSTATE PER 1 TIM 4:1-3**
> 1. **NO, We Forbid Unlawful Marriage As He Forbids Unlawful Eating (1 Cor 10:21).**
> 2. **Was John Apostate? (Mk 6:17-18)**
> 3. **Apostates Defend Unlawful Marriages As Right (Matt 19:3-9).**
> 4. **Jn. A. Hardin, S.J., The Catholic Catechism, p. 359, Claims "Pauline Privilege" In 1 Cor 7:15.**
>
> 315

way he is reading it, "It is not lawful, Herod, for you to have a wife." "And even though you have got your brother's wife, it is not right." Now, John said because he had his brother's wife, it is not lawful for you to have her. He did not say it is not lawful for you to have a wife.

Oh, he twists, he squirms, he wants out of this. But I will tell you just as John implied and Jesus taught, *Herod and any other man had a right to have a wife, but no one had a right to have another man's wife.* I have never said in this debate or tried to affirm the right of a man to have another man's wife. That is not what this debate is about. All I am affirming is the right of those who are *unmarried,* those who are *single,* to have a wife. And women who are single, unmarried, to have husbands. That is all I am affirming. He twists and squirms, wants to make me out as a big bad boy. I am bad because I am in favor of all he is saying. That is not so, and don't you believe it. I do not defend unlawful marriages.

And he quotes the Catholic Catechism and the Pauline Privilege. I have not said anything about a Pauline Privilege either. I did not say anything about a Pauline Privilege in any part of this debate. As far as I know there is no such thing.

Let's look at my chart number 22. He never told us how far he agreed with this. I want him to step up here and say, now do you agree, are they still married over there? When he divorced his woman for a cause other than fornication, are they still married? When the man commits adultery, are they still married? When she divorces him for fornication, are they still married? When the man obeys the gospel, is he still guilty of any sin? Are they still married after this? Tell us. You would not do it. Why not? I do not see anything, it is not a trick

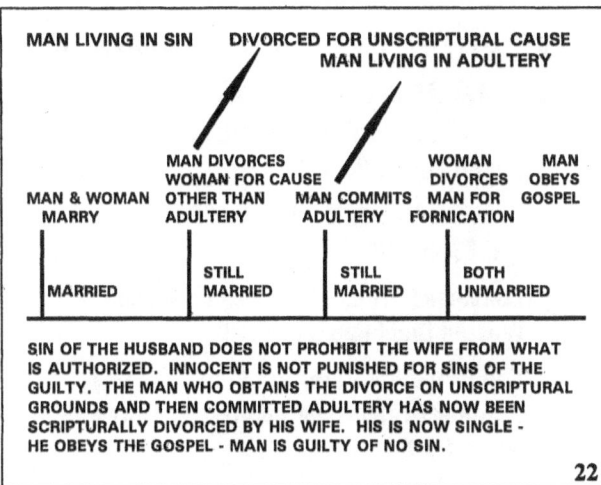

question, not a trick question, not a trick chart.

The sins of the husband do not prohibit the wife from what is authorized. You know, I heard about the man that finally got interested in salvation, and he went to the Baptist preacher. The Baptist preacher convinced him he could be saved by faith only. So, he went around claiming he was saved by faith only. About a year later, his wife got interested in salvation. She went to a gospel preacher. He said, "No, there is no way you can be saved because your husband did the wrong thing. You are going to have to suffer because of his sins." No, he did not tell him that. He said, "You repent and be baptized for the remission of sins." The wife could do the right thing even though the husband did the wrong thing. She was not punished because he committed sins.

And so the wife could obtain the divorce for a scriptural ground. The innocent is not punished for the sins of the guilty. The man who obtained the divorce on unscriptural grounds, *and then committed adultery,* has now been scripturally divorced by his wife. Incidentally now, we were not to be discussing some things one night, but we got on them anyway. All through this he has been determined to punish the guilty. That fornicator is a mean person. I have never tried to defend fornication. They are going to hell if they die in that condition. Now, that ought to be plain enough. You know where I stand. The adulterers are going to hell unless God forgives them. And they will be *living in that sin* and others until God forgives them. We will get to that later if we have time tonight, if not, tomorrow night. But, now he was out to punish the guilty, now he is out to punish the innocent. Why is he going to punish the innocent? Well, the adulterer he wanted to punish because they are mean. They have transgressed God's law. Well, the innocent has not transgressed God's law. But, he is going to punish them anyway.

Let's look at his chart number 286 *Now, how do you get out of the sin of adultery?* The same way you get out of the sin of theft. By receiving God's forgiveness. That is how you get out of any sin. *He says forgiveness does not remove the temporal consequences.* Where do these temporal consequences come from? You know, if we talk about legal consequences, we mean our civil law is so set up that if a man *steals* he is going to pay a certain penalty. If he *murders,* he may be put to

> **FORGIVENESS NOT REMOVE TEMPORAL CONSEQUENCES**
> 1. Converted Murderer Not Escape Death Penalty (Acts 25:11)
> 2. Convicted Thief Not Escape "Due Reward" (Lk. 23:40-43)
> 3. Converted Prodigal Not Regain Money Wasted Gambling (Lk 15:13)
> 4. Converted Adulterer Not Free To Marry Another Or Continue Adulterous Marriage (Matt 19:9)
>
> 286

death or get life in prison, or whatever the law demands. He talks about that. But God does not in our age under the new law put the death penalty in, even though he did in the Old Testament. That is up to civil law now. The convicted thief cannot escape [pointing to Halbrook chart 286]. Well, again, that is up to civil law. He cannot escape God, that is for sure. But he says he is talking about temporal consequences. Physical consequences.

Well, who put this physical consequence in there *that one divorced on grounds of fornication or adultery can never marry another?* Who put that temporal consequence in? Brother Halbrook went through his Bible, as many have. He decided God had been too lenient with fornicators and adulterers. That is just too easy. "Oh, it is alright, Lord, if you forgive murderers." You know, he does not like mercy, does he? "If you forgive murderers, that is fine; if you forgive thieves, that is fine. I will go along with you, Lord. But if you are going to forgive fornicators to the extent they can marry again, Lord, I am not going to stay with you. I will bring in my commentaries and my other books." I did not introduce them, he did. And, I brought them back to show that even they did not agree with him. The Bible does not and his own witnesses, sectarian witnesses, do not agree with him either.

So he has made up this temporal consequence. God did not make it up. *He claims it is found in Matthew 19:9.* And then, all you have to do is read that. *It is not talking about a person divorced on grounds of fornication.* It is talking about someone divorced on any other grounds than that.

Let's go back. Start with my next chart, number 34. The put-away fornicator. We introduced this in the last moment. He either has a wife or does not. Both of

Third Evening: Freeman's Second Affirmative 195

> **THE "PUT AWAY" FORNICATOR**
>
> FREE TO MARRY
>
> 1. HE <u>HAS A WIFE</u> (BOUND TO A WIFE)
>   OR
> 2. HE DOES NOT HAVE A WIFE (LOOSED FROM A WIFE)
> 3. WHAT IS THE MARITAL STATE OF THE PUT AWAY FORNICATOR?
>
>   A. DOES HE HAVE A WIFE? IF SO WHO IS SHE? WHERE IS SHE?
>   B. IF HE STILL HAS A WIFE, THE WIFE WHO PUTS HIM AWAY FOR FORNICATION CANNOT REMARRY, FOR SHE HAS A HUSBAND.
>   C. THE PUT AWAY FORNICATOR DOES NOT HAVE A WIFE.
>   1) HOW SHALL HE AVOID FORNICATION?
>   * 1 COR. 7:2 -- HAVE HIS OWN WIFE
>   2) DOES HE HAVE DIVINE PERMISSION TO REMARRY?
>   *1 COR. 7:27-28 -- "ART THOU LOOSED FROM A WIFE..."
>   IF THOU MARRY, THOU HAST NOT SINNED."
>
> 34

us agree. *Brother Halbrook and I agree that this put-away fornicator has no wife.* He is not bound to a wife. He does not have a wife, he is loosed from a wife. Well, what did Paul say to those who were loosed from a wife, 1 Corinthians 7:27-28. He said, "If thou marry, thou hast not sinned." What is his marital state? Unmarried. Well, if he is baptized for the remission of sins, as he arises from baptism, what is his spiritual state? Just as white as snow. My opponent says, "I will always remember he is guilty of fornication." God said, "I do not remember it." *Does he have divine permission to remarry?* In 1 Corinthians 7:28, he does. In 1 Corinthians 7:2, God says, "To avoid fornication, let every man have his own wife."

See my chart number 35. The put-away fornicator. Halbrook said, he could not have a wife to avoid fornication. He could not marry, even though loosed from a wife. But he said he cannot have a wife. But if Halbrook is right, God is wrong. If God is right, Halbrook is wrong. Now, who knows more about the right of a man to marry? Who knows? I am not going to tell you I know more than God does. I am not going to introduce a whole bunch, a whole stack, of sectarian commentaries, or their books, be they Greek scholars or otherwise, to try to prove to you what God says is wrong. What God says has to be right.

> **THE "PUT AWAY" FORNICATOR**
> (Cont)
>
> BUT <u>HALBROOK SAYS</u>:
>
> HE CANNOT HAVE A WIFE TO AVOID FORNICATION.
> HE CANNOT MARRY EVEN THOUGH LOOSED FROM A WIFE.
>
> IF HALBROOK IS RIGHT, GOD IS WRONG.
> IF GOD IS RIGHT, HALBROOK IS WRONG.
>
> WHO KNOWS MORE ABOUT THE RIGHT OF MAN TO MARRY?
>
> 35

Go to my chart number 36. The put-away, the right to put away. Matthew 19:9 does not give *the wife* the right to put away in so many words. It says to the husband, "Whosoever should put away her husband or his wife," showing it gives the wife the same, and my opponent agrees with this. "Whosoever shall put away *her husband*, except it be for fornication, and marry another, committeth adultery: and whosoever marrieth *him* which is put away doth commit adultery." Now, that is not in the text. It only refers to the man, and it often does in the New Testament. We know it applies to the woman also. *She has the same right the man does.* Well, does the man who puts away his wife, except for fornication, and marries another, commit adultery against her? In Mark 10:11 even though this phrase is not repeated in Matthew 19:9, it is not there, *"against her."* But we all agree, I am sure my opponent agrees, it belongs there.

Let's see my next chart please, 37. Put-away continued. If the husband *dies* without divorcing his wife who is guilty of adultery, *she may scripturally remarry*. We both agree there. But, if she commits adultery, in other words, *he does not have to put her away*. And then, he talked about the consequences of what I teach. I am not going to charge him with this direct consequence. I told someone today in the restaurant that I could charge him with this. I am not going to charge

> **Right To Put Away**
>
> *Matt. 19:9 - Does not give the wife the right to put away her husband for fornication and the right to remarry?
>
> *Is the following taught in Matt. 19:9:
>
>> "Whosoever shall put away her husband, except it be for fornication, and shall marry another, committeth adultery: and whoso marrieth him which is put away doth commit adultery."
>
> *Does the man who puts away his wife, except for fornication, and marries another, commit adultery (against her) Mk. 10:11 Even though this phrase is not repeated in Matt. 19:9?
>
> 36

> **PUT AWAY**
>
> (Cont)
>
> If the husband dies w/o divorcing his wife who is guilty of adultery, she may scripturally remarry, Rom. 7:2-3
> But she is still guilty of adultery and will be until GOD forgives her.
> The man who marries her will NOT be living in adultery.
>
> (But she will be)
>
> The marriage IS NOT adulterous.
>
> 37

him with it now, but here is a consequence. So, what you teach encourages all manner of sin. Well, read Romans 7:2-3, and you understand at least that *if your husband dies, without any question you can remarry*. But, you commit adultery and he finds out about it, and after awhile, he decides, "I am going to divorce her," and he tells you. You could hasten the death along, couldn't you? Not scripturally, of course, legally. And, you may be a murderer and get by with it. My opponent says, "God will forgive your murder, and you can marry again." *Is he encouraging murder?* I am not charging him with that. But you want to talk about consequence of a doctrine. Go out and murder your mate and then according to Romans 7:2-3, you are free. If they are dead, you are free.

But notice this. *If he dies without divorcing his wife who is guilty of adultery, she can scripturally remarry,* and he agrees with that. She is an adulterer, she is a fornicator. But, any man who wants to, who is unmarried, can marry her. And he will not call this an *adulterous* marriage, either. One is guilty, the other is not. One is living in fornication, the other is not. He will not call that an adulterous marriage. He has already admitted it in the debate that *any unmarried man can marry that woman*. Even though the husband did not divorce her, he planned to, but he *died* before he got around to it. *Now, if she is not guilty of adultery in getting remarried, the man who marries her would not be guilty of adultery.* She will be, therefore the marriage is not what he would call an adulterous marriage.

Let's go to my chart number 21. Contrasts. God said it is not good for man to be alone. Halbrook says some will have to be alone. God says it is better to marry than to burn. Halbrook says some will have to. Incidentally, he said now, by that, Mr. Freeman means that if your wife is insane, confined to an institution, or has AIDS, *rather than burn with passion, you have the right to remarry.* I did *not* say that. He is still married, he has a wife. I am talking about the man who has no wife, brother Halbrook. So, quit bringing charges against me. God says marriage is honorable; Halbrook says some cannot do that which is honorable. God says to

A CONTRAST:

GOD	HALBROOK
IT IS NOT GOOD FOR MAN TO BE ALONE	SOME WILL HAVE TO BE ALONE
IT IS BETTER TO MARRY THAN TO BURN	SOME WILL HAVE TO BURN
MARRIAGE IS HONORABLE	SOME CANNOT DO THAT WHICH IS HONORABLE
TO AVOID FORNICATION, MARRY	SOME CANNOT USE THIS MEANS TO AVOID FORNICATION
IF LOOSED, YOU DO NOT SIN WHEN YOU MARRY	SOME WHO ARE LOOSED DO SIN WHEN THEY REMARRY

WHO IS RIGHT?

21

avoid fornication, marry; Halbrook says there are some who cannot use this means to avoid fornication. God says if you are loosed, you do not sin when you marry. Halbrook says, "Well, Lord, you made a sad mistake. Some who are loosed, do sin when they marry."

Let's see my next chart please, 17. "Demanding the Impossible." How do we know? How do you know the one you are marrying, was never married before? How do you know the one you marry was not divorced because of adultery? How do you know the one you marry divorced a previous spouse on the grounds of fornication? How do you know the one you are marrying was not divorced for a cause other than fornication? How do you know that the Christian you marry was not divorced by an unbeliever? How do you know that the one you baptized and fellowship as a faithful child of God and for whom you perform a marriage ceremony was not previously married to a Christian? How do you know that — or not previously divorced for fornication? How can you know these things?

DEMANDING THE IMPOSSIBLE
HOW CAN YOU KNOW:

1. THAT THE ONE YOU MARRY WAS NEVER MARRIED BEFORE?
2. THAT THE ONE YOU MARRY WAS NOT DIVORCED BECAUSE OF ADULTERY?
3. THAT THE ONE YOU MARRY DIVORCED A PREVIOUS SPOUSE ON GROUNDS OF FORNICATION?
4. THAT THE ONE YOU MARRY WAS NOT DIVORCED FOR A CAUSE OTHER THAN FORNICATION?
5. THAT THE CHRISTIAN YOU MARRY WAS NOT DIVORCED BY AN UNBELIEVER?
6. THAT THE ONE YOU BAPTIZE AND FELLOWSHIP AS A FAITHFUL CHRISTIAN AND FOR WHOM YOU PERFORM A MARRIAGE CEREMONY WAS NOT PREVIOUSLY DIVORCED FOR FORNICATION?

17

Let's look at the next chart if there is time, number 18. "Demanding the Impossible." Well, what is true: the court records, the word of a friend, the word of the one you want to marry? Photographic evidence, seeing it with your own eyes? Ask brother Halbrook? He says if you do not know, the only safe way is not to marry. Oh

DEMANDING THE IMPOSSIBLE
(Cont)

WHAT PROOF WILL YOU DEMAND TO SHOW THAT ONE HAS BEEN GUILTY OF FORNICATION?

* COURT RECORDS?
* THE WORD OF A FRIEND?
* THE WORD OF THE ONE YOU WANT TO MARRY?
* PHOTOGRAPHIC EVIDENCE?
* SEEING IT WITH YOUR OWN EYES?
* ASK RON HALBROOK?

18

yes, he has an answer. Turn to brother Halbrook. He did not say, "Now, this is what the Bible says." He did not give us book, chapter, and verse. If you cannot be absolutely sure, having seen it with your own eyes, then you cannot be sure that the only safe thing is to remain single the rest of your life.

Oh yes, he is high on this doctrine of celibacy. Well, what proof is he going to demand? I have given you proof. He says I have not but I have given proof in every case. I have given the proof. I gave you book, chapter, and verse. Fornicators baptized, adulterers baptized, and what did God say to these people? To avoid fornication, have your own wife. He says, oh, he was not talking about them. Paul said he was. Read the chapter. He does not change positions. He does not say, "Now, I am not writing to you people anymore. This applies to someone over in Galatia, over in Asia." Well, maybe it did, but right there it applied to them. It certainly did apply to the people in Corinth, didn't it? He was addressing those at Corinth and it would have had to apply to them, even though it applies to us. It had to apply first of all to them.

Third Evening
Halbrook's Second Negative

Brother Freeman, gentlemen moderators, ladies and gentlemen, we are having a good discussion, a good spirit, testing arguments, and we bid you to stay with us as we continue to study. I want you to notice again the proposition. *"The Scriptures teach that a person who is divorced by his mate for committing fornication is free to marry another."* You keep listening tonight to find *the positive divine authority* for a put-away fornicator to marry another. You want a passage which is so simple and so plain about that, that you cannot misunderstand that that is what that passage teaches.

But, my friend, I want you to notice on my question five, *"Jack Freeman believes that the marriage of Herod and Herodias would become lawful if Philip would say he would put her away. True or False?"* Remember that question [chart Q3-01-90, p. 170]? He decided he will say "false" on that. Now, that *contradicts* what he said the other night about a person in just such a condition as that from 1 Corinthians 7:10-11, but I will take his latest answer. But he may change it again tomorrow; we will see.

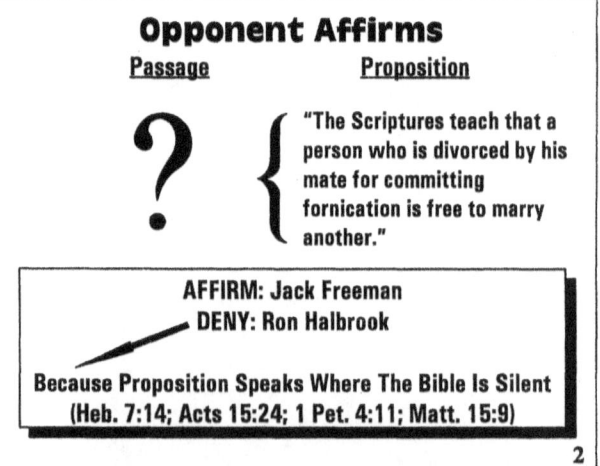

My friend, with his present answer, go back to the proposition. Now, watch it: *He has surrendered his proposition by the way he answers question five.* You see, "a person who is divorced by his mate for committing fornication." What did Herodias do when she went to Herod? Was that fornication? You agree it was, don't you? I agree it was. Yes, it was fornication, adultery, immorality. Now, Philip does not want her anymore. According to you, if Philip does not want her anymore, then she does not go back to Philip. *Now, where does she go? She goes to Herod.* If not, if not, you have surrendered your proposition! Yes, he has.

Alright, now then, we have been talking about his mercy chart and we go back to my chart 286. We have already seen his chart on that, 28. We look at 286, to start where we ended. *Forgiveness does not remove temporal consequences!* The converted murderer cannot escape the death penalty. You remember that. And, the convicted thief cannot escape his due reward. The prodigal cannot regain his money that he wasted. *And the adulterer is not free to marry another or to continue in an adulterous marriage.*

Now, he had somewhat to say about that chart 286, as I turn to my notes on that. He wanted to know who gave authority up here for putting this one to death [pointing to number 1 on chart]. In Romans 13, God gave the power to put them to death. God gave civil government the sword. And, it was the inspired Apostle who said, "I do not refuse to die." That is where the authority came from.

> **FORGIVENESS NOT REMOVE TEMPORAL CONSEQUENCES**
> 1. Converted Murderer Not Escape Death Penalty (Acts 25:11)
> 2. Convicted Thief Not Escape "Due Reward" (Lk. 23:40-43)
> 3. Converted Prodigal Not Regain Money Wasted Gambling (Lk 15:13)
> 4. Converted Adulterer Not Free To Marry Another Or Continue Adulterous Marriage (Matt 19:9)
>
> 286

Then, he wanted to know who gave this authority down here [pointing to number 4 on chart 286]. Let's just see my chart 72, *the text of Matthew 19:9*. I am going to show you the converted adulterer is not free. They can be forgiven of all their sins. It does not remove the temporal consequence. It does not change their marital status. They are forgiven, *but still divorced for fornication.* They are still in that marital status. Now, look at it. Here is the authority. *"Whosoever shall put away his wife, except it be for fornication, and shall marry another, committeth adultery."* Now, suppose you put her away for fornication. Well, then, you do not commit adultery.

Now, what about part "b" of the verse? *"Whoso marrieth her which is put away"*—that is, the put-away fornicator, then—*"doth commit adultery."* Now, that is who gave authority for that. And you cannot change the temporal consequence of a marriage just by being baptized. Even you have made the point that *baptism does not change the marital status.* That is exactly the point, my friend. That is right.

Now then, he said I demand penance. Let's look at my chart 241. Do I demand penance? Now, let's see. This is penance. The adulterer was excluded from the sacraments for 15 years according to one of the early canons during the apostasy. Here, you see, they are being excluded from participation in worship. Have I said anything like that? Is anything like that involved when I say that *temporal consequences do not change and marital status does not change?* You are *forgiven* of your sins. You can enter into singing, and praying, and the Lord's Supper, and be a Christian, and grow as a Christian. No, I am not teaching any penance doctrine.

> **Opponent Cries "Penance"**
>
> **This Is Penance:**
> 1. Adulterer "excluded from the sacraments for 15 yrs." (Canon 58 of Basil)
> 2. Penance removes both "external punishment" and "temporal" fruit of sin (<u>Catholic Concise Encycl.</u>, p. 271)
> 3. Opponent says BOTH removed for Divorced Fornicator!
>
> **This is Not Penance:**
> Forgiveness not remove temporal result of sin (Mk. 6:18; 1 Cor. 7:11; Matt. 19:9)
>
> 241

Now, *the doctrine of penance,* by the way, *removes both the "external punishment" and the "temporal" fruit of sin.* See the Catholic Encyclopedia on that. The doctrine of penance — are you listening to me? — removes *both the "external punishment" of sin* — there is your spiritual side — *and removes the temporal "fruit" of sin.* It looks like my opponent is teaching the doctrine of penance, doesn't it? Isn't this what *he* believes? This *is* what he believes: the external punishment is removed *and* the temporal consequence removed. You say *both* are removed for the divorced fornicator. There is your doctrine of penance.

Now, my friend, it is not the doctrine of penance when we said forgiveness does not remove the temporal consequence of sin. In *Mark 6:18,* Herod and Herodias could have been forgiven. They could *repent* of their sin, *be forgiven* of their sin, but could they *remain in that marriage?* See it? No, no. They are in the wrong marital situation. They have got to get out of that. They have been forgiven of all that adultery, haven't they? But they have got to get out of it. See *1 Corinthians 7:11.* If you violate it and you marry another, you can be forgiven, but you had better come back to what the passage says. See? To *remain unmarried* or *be reconciled* to your mate. I believe you can see it. I believe you can see it tonight. No, we are not teaching any penance doctrine.

See my chart 234, my friend. He is implying that we are punishing people. He said that. I want you to know that *repentance and the works meet for*

> **"REPENTANCE" & "WORKS MEET"**
> **Acts 26:20; 11:18**
>
> <u>Punishment OR Privilege?</u>
>
> 1) **Murderer Cease Murder**
>
> 2) **Thief Cease Stealing**
>
> 3) **Prodigal Cease Gambling**
>
> 4) **Adulterer Cease Adultery**
>
> 234

repentance are a privilege and not a punishment. Paul was preaching "works meet for repentance." And they rejoiced in Acts 11 that the privilege of "repentance" had been given "to the Gentiles." When the murderer must cease murdering, I want to know if that is his *punishment,* brother Freeman? Are *you* punishing him? You will not let him murder anymore. The thief will cease his stealing. Is that his *punishment?* No, indeed, it is his *privilege!* His sins are washed away. Now, both of them may have to stay in jail. That is the temporal consequence. That is not removed by forgiveness.

The prodigal ceases gambling. Is that his *punishment?* Do you feel sorry for him? Oh, he cannot go to the gaming table anymore. Oh, why are you *punishing* him? Why don't you forgive him and let him go to the gaming table?

Now, my friend, when you marry into adultery, you are going to have to cease that adultery. *It does not have a thing to do with punishment.* It is a matter of privilege that God will wash away your sins, and you bring the works meet for repentance. There is not any punishment to it.

Now, then, his charts 47 and 48. He used those together about Paul preaching to the alien and how that adultery was forgiven. Let's notice that. Paul preached to the alien, and they were washed and sanctified and justified. That is right. They were not guilty of sin if forgiven,

> **PAUL PREACHING TO ALIENS**
>
> ACTS 18:4 REASONED, PERSUADED
> <u>WHAT THEY DID:</u>
> ACTS 18:8 -- BELIEVED AND WERE BAPTIZED
> <u>WHAT GOD DID:</u>
> 1 COR. 6:11 ----- <u>WASHED, SANCTIFIED, JUSTIFIED</u>
> ACTS 2:47 ----- <u>ADDED TO THE CHURCH</u>
> <u>OF WHAT THEY HAD BEEN GUILTY OF BEFORE BAPTISM</u>
> 1 COR. 6:9-10 - SOME HAD BEEN GUILTY OF
> <u>FORNICATION AND ADULTERY.</u>
> <u>DID GOD ADD FORNICATORS TO THE CHURCH?</u>
> (ACTS 2:47 --- NO!)
>
> 47

but that does not remove temporal consequences.

Notice his chart 48 now, same thing again. Did Paul or other Apostles ever tell any woman to *leave her husband* in order to be saved? Did he tell anyone to *remain unmarried* in order to get to heaven? *My opponent said he did!* Remember, I asked him that in one of my questions.

PAUL PREACHING TO ALIENS
(Cont)

WHAT DID PAUL TELL THOSE WHO HAD BEEN FORNICATORS AND ADULTERERS TO DO TO AVOID FORNICATION?

1 COR. 7:2 - "LET EVERY MAN HAVE HIS OWN WIFE, AND LET EVERY WOMAN HAVE HER OWN HUSBAND."

*DID PAUL OR OTHER APOSTLES EVER TELL ANY MAN TO LEAVE HIS WIFE IN ORDER TO BE SAVED?

*DID PAUL OR OTHER APOSTLES EVER TELL ANY WOMAN TO LEAVE HER HUSBAND IN ORDER TO BE SAVED?

*DID PAUL OR OTHER APOSTLES EVER TELL ANYONE TO REMAIN UNMARRIED IN ORDER TO GET TO HEAVEN?

48

So the answer is yes, there, isn't it? Yes, my opponent said the answer is *yes!*

Now, notice my chart 0-1 overlay. Alright, now notice, my friend, here is what Paul told those who were in unlawful marriages, to get out to be saved. In

---

PAUL PREACHING TO ALIENS
(Cont)

MK 6:17-18
Col 3:5-7
1 COR. 5:6-7 ff
1 COR. 7:11

WHAT DID PAUL TELL THOSE WHO HAD BEEN FORNICATORS AND ADULTERERS TO DO TO AVOID FORNICATION?

1 COR. 7:2 - "LET EVERY MAN HAVE HIS OWN WIFE, AND LET EVERY WOMAN HAVE HER OWN HUSBAND."

*DID PAUL OR OTHER APOSTLES EVER TELL ANY MAN TO LEAVE HIS WIFE IN ORDER TO BE SAVED?

*DID PAUL OR OTHER APOSTLES EVER TELL ANY WOMAN TO LEAVE HER HUSBAND IN ORDER TO BE SAVED?

*DID PAUL OR OTHER APOSTLES EVER TELL ANYONE TO REMAIN UNMARRIED IN ORDER TO GET TO HEAVEN?

48/01

Mark 6:17-18, not Paul but John anticipated the gospel. Matthew 3 says he was preaching in fact the good news of the kingdom. *Colossians 3:5-7* teaches the same principle. You cannot continue in sin. You must mortify and put to death the deeds of the flesh. And that means if you are married to someone unscripturally, if the put-away fornicator married another, since there is no positive authority for it, then he is in the wrong for that.

In *1 Corinthians 5,* the man had his father's wife. Now, mercy means that he can be forgiven. But if you forgive him, *can he keep her?* No, indeed! No, indeed! And so the Apostle is telling him to *get out of the relationship* and telling her to *get out of it.* Now, watch it. He was a Christian. That is who was disciplined by the church. He was a Christian and he had to get out of it. The woman was not disciplined by the church, you see. She was not a Christian, but she had to get out of it. Both had to get out of it. The Apostle speaks the same way to the aliens and to the believers. In *1 Corinthians 6:9-11*, they were washed, sanctified, and justified, yes, but he said *don't be deceived, you can still lose your soul if you practice these things*. And we have had *1 Corinthians 7:11*.

Now, Look at his chart 49, what is adultery? *Thayer* gives the primary definition, but *Thayer* does not give every case of adultery. That is the way it is in any of these lexicons, my friend. Yes, I understand that it is "to have unlawful intercourse with another's wife, to commit adultery." That is the primary definition, and we agree to that.

> **WHAT IS ADULTERY?**
> THAYER: page 417
>
> "TO HAVE UNLAWFUL INTERCOURSE WITH ANOTHER'S WIFE, TO COMMIT ADULTERY" MATT. 5:32, MATT. 19:9
>
> MAN DIVORCES FOR CAUSE OF FORNICATION <u>HAS NO WIFE</u>. IF HE MARRIES A WOMAN WHO HAS NO HUSBAND, HE <u>CANNOT</u> COMMIT ADULTERY WITH HER. (HIS OWN WIFE) ANY MAN WHO HAS NO WIFE MAY SCRIPTURALLY HAVE A WIFE.
>
> 49

But I want you to notice my chart 85. Adultery, like any other word is defined by the use. You start with your primary definition and the passages will give you the different usages. Now watch it. You have *unlawful sexual intercourse involving someone under the constraint of God's marriage law*. A man with another man's wife, that is called adultery in John 8:4. A man puts away his wife without cause and marries another. What does the Bible call that? Adultery. A woman is put away without cause and marries another — adultery. The put-away fornicator marries another — adultery. Now, *that* is the way the Lord used it. That is the way *the Lord* used it. My friend, *that will stand!*

> **Adultery Defined By Use:**
> **Unlawful Sexual Intercourse Involving Someone Under Constraint Of God's Marriage Law**
>
> 1. Married man with another man's wife (Jn. 8:4)
>
> 2. Man puts away wife w/o cause and marries another (Matt. 19:9; Mk. 10:11-12; Lk. 16:18)
>
> 3. Woman put away w/o cause marries another (Matt. 5:32; 19:9)
>
> 4. Put-away fornicator marries another (Matt. 5:32 & 19:9 read with exception)
>
> 85

Now notice my chart 72 [text, Matt. 19:9]. I want you to see the actual text. Chart 72 shows the text again. I am making my appeal directly to the text tonight. Whoever puts away his wife *for fornication,* and marries another, does *not* commit adultery. Whoever marries her which is put away *doth commit adultery.* Do you see how simple and plain that is?

Now, let's see his chart 32. You have one put away due to fornication. And his chart 33, the right to put away. Alright. Yes, they have a right to put them away. And he said to live in sin does not mean to be married to a sinner. But, again, you have *different cases of adultery.* Now, you can have one like this: supposing I committed adultery, my wife was clean and pure, and I continued to live with her. That does not make her an adulterer, that is right. But if I married another woman, *both of us are committing adultery, and we are both living in an adulterous relationship.*

PUT AWAY DUE TO FORNICATION

Matt. 19:9

Gives MAN/WOMAN the RIGHT to put away spouse for fornication

Must the innocent put away (divorce) the guilty?
If not, it is NOT sinful to be married to a fornicator.

The fornicator IS living in fornication.
The innocent IS NOT living in fornication.

To live in sin DOES NOT mean to be married to a sinner.

32

RIGHT TO PUT AWAY
(Cont)

* WHEN A MAN IS PUT AWAY FOR THE CAUSE OF FORNICATION, DOES HE HAVE A WIFE?
* WHO IS SHE?
* WHERE IS SHE?
* IF HE MARRIED A WOMAN WHO HAS NO HUSBAND, DOES HE COMMIT ADULTERY WITH HER?
* THE MARRIAGE IS NOT ADULTEROUS.

33

There are different cases of adultery as we have shown on our chart 83. In fact, just show chart 83. Let's show him the cases. This chart shows him the cases. In the simplest case, we find a man with another man's wife. That is a simple case. But we also find *sin* upon *sin.* A man *divorces his wife* — that is not the same case now — and *marries another.* It is still adultery. If the put-away fornicator remarries, that is another case, not the same case, but *the Bible still calls it*

> **Cases of Adultery**
>
> 1. **Simplest Case:** A married man with another man's wife (John 8:4)
> 2. **Sin Upon Sin:** A man divorces his wife and marries another (Matt. 19:9)
> 3. **Sin Upon Sin:** The put-away fornicator remarries (Matt. 5:32 read with exception)
>
> "The remarriage of a man after divorcing his wife, or the remarrying of the divorced woman, is tantamount to adultery (Matt. 5:32; 19:9)" [Kittel, TDNT, IV:733]
>
> Tantamount = "Equivalent in value, significance, or effect" (Webster's 7th New Colleg. Dict.)
>
> Effect = Gal. 5:19-21 (such things); Heb. 13:4
>
> 83

adultery.

Now, in the dictionary of New Testament words here, by Kittle [*Theological Dictionary of the New Testament,* IV: 73], "The remarriage of a man after divorcing his wife, or the remarrying of the divorced woman, is tantamount to adultery." Tantamount means it is *equivalent to.* Just like Galatians 5 listed various sins and said, *"and such things,"* broadening that thing out. Fornicators and adulterers "God will judge." Cases of adultery can vary and can differ as to the circumstance, but God will judge every one of them. They will lose their soul if they do not repent and get out of it.

Next, notice my chart 231. Now notice, my friend, we must *cease* sin and *leave* the sinful situation. That is necessary for "works meet for repentance," and necessary if we are "washed," "sanctified," and "justified." Here is the act of unlawfully taking life. Suppose you are a member of the Mafia, and say, "I will repent but just stay

> **Cease Sin - Leave Situation**
>
> "Works meet for repentance" (Acts 26:20)
> "Washed, sanctified, justified" (1 Cor. 6:9-11)
>
> | CEASE | LEAVE |
> |---|---|
> | 1. Act of unlawful taking life | Unscr. Organization (Mafia) |
> | 2. Act of unlawful taking goods | Shoplifting Ring |
> | 3. Act of unlawful sexual intercourse | Unscriptural Marriage |
> | 4. Act of unlawful taking gain | Casino Operation |
>
> 231

in the organization." No, get out of that *sinful situation.* Here are acts of unlawfully taking goods. You are in a shop-lifting ring, and say "Well, I have been washed, and sanctified, but I believe I will just *stay* in that situation." You cannot do it. Repentance will not allow it.

Now, here is the act of *unlawful sexual intercourse.* There is more than one way to be guilty of it. And you could be a married person having sex with somebody else, but you could enter into *a marriage that is condemned, an unscriptural marriage*. And if you repent, you are going to have to *leave* that situation, *get out* of it. Do you see the principle?

Now then, he had his chart 33 [page 206], the right to put away. Certainly we agree there is a right to put away. And he asked, "When a man is put away for the cause of fornication, does he have a wife?" No, he does not have a wife, but look at my chart 72 [text, Matt. 19:9]. He is still under constraint of law as we have shown repeatedly. Look at the passage again. He does not have a wife, but what about him? *Whoever marries her or him that is put away doth commit adultery!* He is under the constraint of divine law, my friend.

Now, he had chart 451 on 1 Corinthians 7:25-28. I am following *each* chart, *every* chart. He got about 13 out of my 40-some-odd charts, the other night. And I am taking his *one by one*. Now, you remember that *repentance demands that we cannot stay in sin*. There is no way that we can do that. Alright, now notice, "Halbrook says only virgins are discussed." Then, it says "virgins," and, "Art thou bound to

> **1 COR. 7:25-28**
>
> HALBROOK SAYS ONLY <u>VIRGINS</u> ARE DISCUSSED.
>
> *V.25 - VIRGINS
>
> *V.27 - ART THOU <u>BOUND</u> TO A WIFE?
> (DIVORCED)
> *V.27 - ARE THOU <u>LOOSED</u> FROM A WIFE?
> IF <u>THOU</u> MARRY, <u>THOU</u> HAST NOT SINNED.
>
> -- AND --
>
> *V.28 - IF A VIRGIN MARRY SHE HATH NOT SINNED.
>
> 451

a wife?" Yes, we understand that to be a case of marriage, we realize that. That is *in contrast to* the virgins.

But then he says, "Art thou loosed from a wife?" "Loosed from a wife" is *the man*. Now, that is not the woman there. A woman is not loosed from a wife, brother Freeman. Now then, "Art thou loosed from a wife," *there is the man*, "if you marry, you have not sinned; and if a virgin marries, she has not sinned."

No, "loosed from a wife" does not mean divorced. Look at my chart 191-A. It just does not mean divorce. Now, he can insist on it all he wants to, but you look at your Bible. Here you have a never-married man, "loosed from a wife," and his female counterpart is the virgin. If the loosed man is divorced, then the *virgin* is a *divorcee!*

Look at my chart 196. "Loosed" is not talking about divorced people. Oh, he said, "I do not even know what this chart has to do with it." You are

> **1 Corinthians 7:27-28**
> **Divorced People?**
>
> Never married man is "Loosed from a wife" } { His female counterpart is "A virgin"
>
> IF "Loosed" man is Divorced } { THEN "A virgin" is a Divorcee
>
> 191 A

floundering around, brother Freeman. Read the chart. *Loosed* is the word we are discussing. Do you know what *1 Corinthians 7* has to do with it? You introduced it tonight. Now, that word has the same latitude in the Greek and the English. It can be *a simple state of freedom*. And he wanted to say, "Oh, what do these quotations have to do with it?" These are *Greek* writers. Did you know the New Testament was written in *Greek*? It was written during the *same time period* of these quotations which use the *same word* that is in 1 Corinthians 7:27. Are we getting warm? Are you seeing what this is all about, and why it is in there? You said you did not know what it had to do with anything.

Now, stay with me. "Unbinding her hair." See? Is your hair tied up? Don't unbind it. You have that usage of this

> **Loose: Same Latitude In Greek & English**
> Can Be Simple State Of Freedom
>
> 1. Bion (200 B.C.): "unbinding her hair" (Liddell & Scott, 1068)
>   Hermas (A.D. 140): "with unbound hair" (Arndt. & Ging., 484)
>
> 2. Is your hair tied up? Don't unbind it.
>   Is your hair unbound? Don't tie it up.
>
> 3. "Free from a state of confinement, restraint, or obligation" (Webster)
>
> **Many dogs run LOOSE, FREE - Context tells if they were ever tied up!**
>
> 196

word *"loosed"* that is in 1 Corinthians 7:27, see: "Seek not to be *loosed.*" Alright, but on the other hand, here was one "with unbound hair." That word "loosed" is used like that. "Is your hair *unbound?*" would be the parallel, see? Is your hair unbound — *are you unbound, are you loosed* — do not tie it up — *do not get married*. But if you marry, you have not sinned. Paul was giving advice there. But you see it is *freedom from a state of confinement*. He said, "I do not know what the dogs have to do with it." It is the word *"loosed."* Do you know what the word *"loosed"* has to do with it, brother Freeman? Now, call for it again,

Also, consider my chart 198. I think this audience knows what this has to do with it. *Loosed means "never married."* Gordon Fee, I gave you that. Paul "chose a word that could express 'being loosed'" or "divorced," see? And that was *for the married* in that passage. But, "the corresponding verb, could mean to 'be free from' (= never married) for the case in hand."

Now, see Freeman's chart 57. He has *Thayer* on *lusis,* "a loosing of any bound, as of marriage." And so when he has, "Art thou *loosed* from a wife, seek not a wife," he has *lusis* there.

> **LOOSED = NEVER MARRIED**
> **1 Cor 7:27**
>
> **Gordon Fee, <u>1st Epistle to Corinthians</u>:**
> 1. "Vv 25-38 take up the issue of the never-before married" (p. 288)
> 2. Vs 27 Paul "chose a word that could express 'being loosed' (= divorced) for the married, whose corresponding verb could mean to 'be free from' (= never married) for the case in hand" (p. 331)
> 3. "It lies totally outside the present context to suggest that the two questions address the married & the divorced" (p. 331 n.38)
>
> 198

Now, *lusis* is a noun. The noun is used in the first part of the verse. See, when you are bound to a wife, seek not to be *loosed.* Not to be in a loosed condition, that is *lusis.*

But, brother Freeman, in 1 Corinthians 7:27b, you have the verb *luo* there, see? You are confusing *Thayer's* quotation referring to part "a" of the verse with part "b" of the verse. *Lusis* is used only *one time* in all the New Testament. *Luo* is used many times and has a wider breadth of meaning. You are about to

> **THAYER**
> **page 384**
>
> LUSIS - "A LOOSING OF ANY BOND, AS THAT OF MARRIAGE; HENCE <u>ONCE</u> IN THE NEW TESTAMENT OF DIVORCE",
>
> *1 COR. 7:27 - THUS, "ART THOU <u>LOOSED</u> FROM A WIFE" "ART THOU <u>DIVORCED</u> FROM A WIFE"
>
> *1 COR. 7:28 - "BUT AND IF THOU MARRY, <u>THOU HAST NOT SINNED</u>..."
>
> 57

convince me that *some people* ought not to use reference works. You are not using them very carefully, brother. He has perverted that.

Now, to Freeman's chart 452. Bound, bound by law, and then finally loosed from law. He is trying to make this point over and over, that if you have been put away for fornication that you are no longer bound. Now, he says she is "bound

> **ROM. 7:2-3**
>
> "BOUND BY THE LAW TO HER HUSBAND"
> BUT
> "IF THE HUSBAND BE DEAD, SHE IS LOOSED FROM THE LAW"
>
> *V.3 - "IF HER HUSBAND BE DEAD, SHE IS FREE FROM THAT LAW"
>
> - BOUND VERSUS LOOSED.
> - BOUND VERSUS FREE.
>
> 452

by the law to her husband," but "if the husband be dead, she is loosed from the law." "If her husband be dead, she is free from that law."

Now, look at my chart 101. Alright, here you have the constraint. *Divorced people remain under constraint of law.* Get that point. In Deuteronomy 24, you could divorce your wife, but you could not get her back after the second marriage. Well, supposing that man put her away, well, you still cannot get her back! Under constraint of law. According to my opponent, they are "single." If they are "single," as he calls it, why then, they could have married; but God says they could *not*.

Now, maybe in your human wisdom you cannot see *why* God made it that way, but, friend, you are just going to have to acknowledge *God made it that way*. We are the creatures. We are the

> **Divorced People Remain Under Constraint Of Law**
>
> 1. Deut. 24:1-4 Divorce wife but can't have her back after her 2nd marriage
> 2. Deut. 24:1-4 Divorcee marry another but then can't ever return to 1st mate
> 3. Lev. 21:7, 13-14 Divorcee free from marriage but can't marry a priest
> 4. Matt. 5:32; 19:9 Pure divorce impure and marry another (new mate can't be one put away for fornication or other cause)
> 5. Matt. 5:32; 19:9 Not authorize a put-away person (whether put away for fornication or other cause) to marry another
> 6. 1 Cor. 7:10-11 If 2 Christians divorce, must remain unmarried or reconcile
> 7. 1 Cor. 7:12-15 Believer not give up Christ to keep unbeliever (no authority for either to marry another)
>
> **CONCLUSION:**
> 1. Unscriptural divorce releases neither party from marriage!
> 2. Scriptural divorce releases both parties from marriage, but not from the constraint of the law!
>
> 101

clay. God is the maker. God is the creator. And we are going to have to *submit to His* law. And the only authority we have is to put away the adulterer, the fornicator, and marry another, but *we do not have any positive divine authority for the fornicator to marry another*. It is just not there.

Now, let's see Freeman's chart 453 on 1 Corinthians 7:27, again. And, he says "loosed" here is the same as in Romans 7:2. Now, I am sorry again, but you need to go back and study your words. *It is not the same term.* No, it is *not* the same "loosed." Where 1 Corinthians 7:27 says "loosed from a wife," it is not the same word in Romans 7:2. It is just not. It is just not the same word, brother Freeman. And, so your whole argument is based on a fallacy.

Now, he had his charts 34, and 35, and 36 series about *the put-away fornicator*. We want to notice that we have already discussed this in dealing with the constraint of law. We covered all of this. Yes, they are put away, and what is their marital state? They do not have a mate when they are put away. I understand that well enough. Chart 35, repeats the same point — he just repeats as he follows up on it, and that is fine. I understand what he is arguing here well enough. Alright, they do not have a mate. Now, he says I teach a person cannot marry even though loosed from a wife. Friend, he has got to have *positive divine authority* to marry another. And that is what you have *not* found.

---

1 COR. 7:27

"**BOUND** UNTO A WIFE"
(SAME WORD AS ROM. 7:2)

"**BOUND** BY THE LAW TO HER HUSBAND"
1 COR. 7:27

"**LOOSED** FROM A WIFE"

"**LOOSED** FROM THE LAW" (**FREE FROM THAT LAW**)
REV. 1:5

- BOUND VERSUS LOOSED.
- BOUND VERSUS FREE.

453

THE "PUT AWAY" FORNICATOR

FREE TO MARRY

1. HE **HAS A WIFE** (BOUND TO A WIFE)
   OR
2. HE **DOES NOT HAVE A WIFE** (LOOSED FROM A WIFE)
3. WHAT IS THE MARITAL STATE OF THE PUT AWAY FORNICATOR?

  A. DOES HE HAVE A WIFE? IF SO WHO IS SHE? WHERE IS SHE?
  B. IF HE STILL HAS A WIFE, THE WIFE WHO PUTS HIM AWAY FOR FORNICATION CANNOT REMARRY, FOR SHE HAS A HUSBAND.
  C. THE PUT AWAY FORNICATOR DOES NOT HAVE A WIFE.
    1) HOW SHALL HE AVOID FORNICATION?
       * 1 COR. 7:2 -- HAVE HIS OWN WIFE
    2) DOES HE HAVE DIVINE PERMISSION TO REMARRY?
       *1 COR. 7:27-28 -- "ART THOU LOOSED FROM A WIFE..."
       IF THOU MARRY, THOU HAST NOT SINNED."

34

And let's look at my chart O-1, overlay 1 there. Remember those passages that we listed for you? Remember those passages, my friend? God's law for Herod — *he could not have her*. Colossians 3 — if you are in a state like that, *you cannot have her*. 1 Corinthians 5 and chapter 6 — *we cannot live that way today*. 1 Corinthians 7:11 — *see it?* Now, I believe you can see it.

Next, he had his chart 22 about living in sin, and he said I did not answer it. I did answer it. I gave you *Matthew 5:32*. He has the waiting game on that chart.

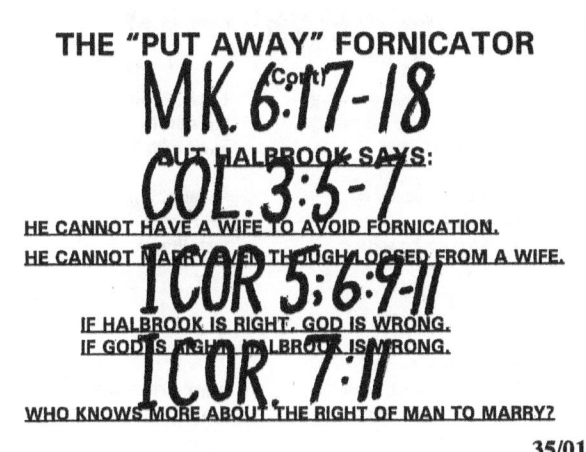

That is the one with all the lines and all of that. *He has got a waiting game situation and Matthew 5:32 forbids the waiting game.* It just forbids it!

And then on my chart 4 [next page], *what is the issue?* He said he agreed with point number 2, but I had cited Jeremiah 3 and he did not know why I was citing that. I cited it because it reflects Genesis 2:24. God had put Israel away as the guilty fornicator, and took them back. But according to you, they can marry another, so I guess Israel can go marry Chemosh. Is that it, brother Freeman? Tell us about it again. Tell us about it again.

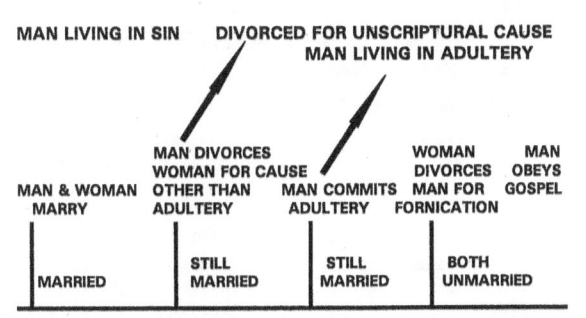

And then on point 2 over here, about the put-away fornicator marrying another while the first mate lives, brother Freeman says that *Ron says the fornicator can marry*. The point is to marry *another*. Yes, I said he could marry, *be reconciled,* just like Israel was reconciled to God. I think you can see that, my friend. But not to *another*.

And then on his view of 1 Corinthians 7, let's go to my chart 122-A. Alright, remember this: let every man have his own wife, *but not* every man can wreck his marriage, throw away his own wife for fornication, get an unscriptural divorce, and get *another*. That is where he misses it every time he goes through this! He does not call for this and refer to that point. The unmarried and the widow: better to marry than to burn. Unscripturally divorced and put-away fornicator: better for them to get in an unscriptural, unauthorized marriage. Is that the point of it? Alright, notice *the widows,* my friend, *the widows* — since brother Freeman talked about marrying *another* — that is parallel to Romans 7:2-3 which says she marries *"another."* Now, I want to know where the fornicator is in this chapter, and I want you to parallel it to a passage that says marry *another*. You cannot find it. It is just not there.

What Is The Issue?

We Agree:	We Disagree:
1. Innocent mate may put away fornicator & marry another (Matt. 19:9)	1. Fornicator may put away innocent mate & marry another (No Scripture)

2. Put-away fornicator can marry again:
  a. Remarry 1st mate (Jer. 3:1-8)
  b. Marry another when 1st mate dies (Rom. 7:2-3)
	2. Put-away fornicator can marry another while 1st mate lives (No Scripture)

3. A Christian is enslaved to Christ alone & can't give Him up to meet demands of unbelievers (1 Cor. 7:15, 23)	3. A Christian deserted by unbeliever can marry another (No Scripture)

4

Does 1 Cor. 7 Authorize The Put-Away Fornicator To Marry Another?

Text Says This:	Not This:
Vs. 2 "Every man have his own wife"	Every man who wrecks his marriage & throws away his own wife by fornication or unscriptural divorce, gets another wife!
Vs. 9 "Unmarried...widows... better to marry than to burn"	Unscripturally divorced & put-away fornicator... better to commit adultery than fornication!
Vv. 27-28 A man "loosed from a wife" (free, never married) and "a virgin" (free, never married) may marry.	A man unscripturally divorced or a divorced fornicator may marry a woman in the same condition!

122 A

Alright, then, on his comments about my chart 196, we covered that, when he said it had nothing to do with our subject. He added the thing about Alford being *a liar* according to me. I do not know why you have to use that kind of language. The man is examining evidence and putting it before us. We sift the evidence, we go back to the text. This is the nature of study, and *you are the one that introduced Alford tonight.* That is fine. I am not complaining. I did not say you threw away your Bible because you introduced something that helps us to weigh out the evidence. Now, you introduced Alford yourself.

Now, on this, do we forbid marriage? Let's see my chart 316. Now, he said the point I made earlier was the *Ron teaches the doctrine of devils,* and *Jack does too,* and so we are *both wrong.* No, I am showing you *pervert* the passage that talks about forbidding to marry. In Matthew 12:27-28, Jesus said, "If I cast

> **Do We Forbid "To Marry"?**
>
> 1. NO! Everyone has a right to marry and a responsibility to obey God's marriage law (Gen. 2:24; Matt. 19:9; 1 Cor. 7:2).
> 2. God's law forbids divorce without cause of fornication and marriage to another again and again and again (Matt. 19:9).
> 3. God's law forbids a man to commit adultery, be divorced, marry another and do it all over again and again and again (Matt. 19:9).
>
> 316

demons out by *Beelzebub,* by whom do your children?" Was Jesus admitting that he did it by *Beelzebub?* Was he? No, he was not! I am just showing you that you are perverting the passage.

Now, notice, do we forbid to marry? No, everyone has a right to marry and a responsibility to obey God's marriage law. God's law forbids divorce without the cause of fornication, and marriage to another, again and again and again. God's law forbids a man to commit adultery, be divorced, marry another, then do it again, do it again, do it again. That is the thing we are objecting to tonight.

I want to see his chart 37. He talked about this matter of murder. And, that you could hurry up death by murder since Romans 7 said you could free them by death. Do you remember that? Remember his point on that? He had Romans 7, and we agree that if your mate dies, you can marry another, and so he said that Ron is encouraging murder.

Let's look at my chart 250. Let's see about that. He is *encouraging fornication.* I could commit fornication against my wife in order to get

> **PUT AWAY**
>
> (Cont)
>
> If the husband dies w/o divorcing his wife who is guilty of adultery, she may scripturally remarry, Rom. 7:2-3 But she is still guilty of adultery and will be until GOD forgives her.
> The man who marries her will NOT be living in adultery.
>
> (But she will be)
>
> The marriage IS NOT adulterous.
>
> 37

put away, you see, by the doctrine he is teaching. So, my opponent says my proposition allows a woman or a man to murder and remarry. You *misunderstand* and *misrepresent* truth like the opponents of Jesus did. God ordained the death penalty for the murderer, and gave civil government the sword to execute wrath upon him. That is the truth about that!

Now, notice my chart 252. You check who can marry, brother Freeman. Only the innocent mate who puts away the fornicator? The man who commits fornication? The man who murders his mate? Now, you talked about hurrying death up. I want to know, when that man who murdered his wife comes *to you* — and maybe both of them committed fornication and then he murdered his mate — *will you say the marriage ceremony for him to get the next one? I will not! I will send him to you, brother Freeman.* I will just send him to you. No, he does not have any such right.

Notice, my chart 254. Now, you look at it, *why did God not give the murderer the right to live?* Divine law established moral order and justice. To restrain the evil, God made it so that *man cannot murder again,* if people would only carry out the law God ordained. That is a warning to others and that is to protect the good. One victim is enough, brother Freeman. *When a man commits murder, one victim is enough.* You wanted to know *who* ordained putting them to death. *God ordained it!* One victim is enough.

Now, *why did God not give the fornicator the right to remarry?* I do not know everything about God's wisdom and why He did things as He did, but I can make the same observations on this. Divine law establishes an order and a justice in

---

Opponent Says My Proposition Allows A Man To Murder & Remarry

1. My opponent misunderstands & misrepresents truth like the opponents of Jesus (John 2:19; Matt. 26:61).

2. God ordained the death penalty for the murderer and gave civil government "the sword" "to execute wrath upon him" (Gen. 9:6; Rom. 13:4).

250

Check Who Can Remarry:

___ Only the innocent mate who puts away the fornicator (Matt. 19:9)

___ The man who commits fornication

___ The man who murders his mate

___ The man who commits fornication & murders his mate

252

Why Did God Not Give The Murderer The Right To Live? (Gen. 9:6; Isa. 6:3; Rom. 13:4)	Why Did God Not Give The Fornicator Right To Remarry? (Gen. 2:24; Isa. 6:3; Mt. 19:4-9)
1. Divine Law Established Moral Order & Justice	1. Divine Law Established Order & Justice
2. Restrain Evil - Can't Murder Again - Warn Others	2. Restrain Evil - Can't Repeat Sin - Warn Others
3. Protect The Good - One Victim Is Enough	3. Protect The Good - One Victim Is Enough

254

the universe that must prevail, whether we understand God's wisdom and God's beneficence or not, my friend. God will restrain the evil, and *God fixed it where the fornicator cannot repeat that sin again, and wreck another home, and wreck another marriage.*

You look at the statistics on those people. It has been recently published in the magazines and the news. When they go to these second marriages, the biggest percentage of them fail again. What happens? *They repeat the sin.* Just like we are not respecting God's law on capital punishment, and *murder is running rampant,* even so we are not respecting God's law on marriage and divorce, and *divorces, unscriptural divorces and destruction of homes, are running rampant.* God intends to protect the good and the right and the true and the innocent and the pure. And one victim is enough, brother Freeman! One victim is enough. I can see that in God's law. Can you see it?

Indeed, who authorized it, who authorized capital punishment? *God did!* Then, who authorized certain constraints of law in this case [pointing to right side of chart 254]? *God did!* You act as though it is a punishment if we *respect* those constraints. It is not a punishment. It is God upholding the order and justice of the universe. It is God putting restraints upon evil, so that it will not run rampant. It is God protecting the good, the pure, and the innocent. One victim is enough, brother Freeman, and so let us respect God's law in this matter. *If we do not, the destruction of homes is going to continue to roll like a flood, and it will destroy our nation and the church if it continues like that.*

Rebuttals:
Third Evening
Freeman's Third Affirmative

Thank you for your patience. I have a ten minute speech, and then will be followed by Ron with a ten minute speech, and then we go home. I hope you come back tomorrow night.

I would like to say one thing in addition to what we were talking about on *Thayer*. I did not introduce any of these. I did not introduce *Alford*. *Alford* was introduced by brother Halbrook last night. I only introduced the witnesses he introduced and showed where they do not agree with his position. *Thayer* — since he brought him up again, about the word "loosed" in 1 Corinthians 7:27-28 — says in regard to the *second word* translated loosed that it can refer to either a divorced person or to one who has never married. Again, that is your own witness. I can refer to either. The first he says refers to a divorced person. The second loosed, from a different Greek word, is a shorter form of the same Greek word and can refer to either.

Now, as far as calling a man a liar, you are the one who called the witness, you are the one who said *Thayer* was wrong and had to be corrected by someone else, he turned out to be a liar. I have urged you to introduce these witnesses [indicating the Bible] and we will not have to get someone to come around and correct them. If you use these witnesses, you are on safe ground. No one had to come along and correct these inspired men. But maybe every uninspired man who wrote needed to be corrected. But if we will stay with those who were, we pointed out there is a lawful use to make of books written by sectarians and others, but it is not an effort to prove anything.

While God did approve and even demand the death penalty in the Old Testament, I am convinced and am highly in favor of it now, but He does not *demand* it now. I wish we were more strict in our law, just as brother Halbrook does. If I were a part of it, had anything to do with it, I would try to put some more teeth in our civil law to cut down on crime, but *God does not demand the death penalty*. According to the chart you used, you make it a necessary temporal consequence — the death penalty for murder. You make it necessary.

That means that our nation *sins* by not putting those who kill to death. [Halbrook said "Amen," from his seat.] Some they put to death. Well, you take it up with the government then [referring to Halbrook's "amen."]. And when you vote, try to put someone in who is in favor of it. God does *not* demand the death penalty. Our civil law does actually. God does not demand 55 miles an hour or 35 miles an hour. That is up to us. And if you do not like what it is, you elect someone who will properly represent you and perhaps get the speed limit you want. But you have made this a *necessary punishment*. Brother Halbrook, why haven't you gone out and tried to enforce this law yourself if it is God's will and has to be done? When the nation will not execute the murderer, why don't you go out and do it? You can do it with God's approval, you are saying. Just hop to it and you will be right in there with them. Maybe they will execute you.

Let's have my chart number 59. If we have time in these few minutes, we want to say a little about repentance. A man steals. He made this chart first of all, but he had a little different order. He had the woman as I recall over here. We have a man who steals another's wife, another's watch, another's car. Now, repentance certainly demands something. He will have to *return* the wife, *return* the watch, and *return* the car. *Agreed*. But he goes further, he says he can never have *his own wife*. He will have to remain celibate the rest of his life. If that is so, he can

A MAN STEALS

ANOTHER'S WIFE   ANOTHER'S WATCH   ANOTHER'S CAR

REPENTANCE DEMANDS: RETURN THE WIFE, THE WATCH, THE CAR

AND NEVER HAVE:

YOUR OWN WIFE----YOUR OWN WATCH----YOUR OWN CAR
(IF THIS IS TRUE)   (SO IS THIS)   (AND THIS)

BUT

IF AFTER REPENTANCE, A MAN CAN HAVE HIS OWN WATCH AND HIS OWN CAR; HE CAN HAVE HIS OWN WIFE!

59

never have his own watch, he can never have his own car. If he can never have his own wife, it has to be true by the same argument, he cannot have his own watch ever, and has to remain the rest of his life without his own car. But if after repentance he can have his own watch, he can have his own car, he can also have his own wife.

Look at my chart number 15. God versus Halbrook. I pointed out before that if you come up with false doctrine, you have got to come up with *a new plan of salvation*. Yes, you have a new plan of salvation. *He said you have got to have book, chapter, and verse where it really says that you fornicators have the right to remarry*. Well, I am asking you for the same type of scripture here. Where is it? Where does it say, "Repent, put away your spouse, be baptized, and remain single?" Well, he says, repentance infers it. Where does it plainly state it? If I have got to plainly state it, you find a scripture that plainly states it. God says repent and be baptized for the remission of sins. You add to it. For some people, repent, put away your spouse, be baptized, and remain single the rest of your life.

Incidentally, in 1 Corinthians 7:10-11, no one is going to remain single the rest of their life. When the woman was commanded to remain unmarried, that did not mean *the rest of her life*. Her mate could die. She could obtain a scriptural divorce at a later time. The Bible did not say or infer she had to remain single the rest of her life. When it says to *stay unmarried,* that did *not* mean necessarily the rest of your life.

Well, concerning the sinful member of the church, God says repent and pray, confess your sins in 1 John 1:9. 1 John 1:9 shows the results, God will forgive us. Brother Halbrook says to some sinful members of the church, "Now, you are a little different, you are in a different category over here. To you, now, these passages do not apply to you but here is one that does I have written up: 'Repent,' still to others, 'and remain unmarried the rest of your life.'" You do not find that in the Bible, but you find it maybe in one written by brother Halbrook.

Let's see my chart number 25. *Does repentance demand stopping sin? It certainly does.* If you are worshipping idols, you have to *stop*. Does that mean you can

---

GOD VS. HALBROOK

GOD TO:	HALBROOK TO:
ALL ALIENS "REPENT, AND BE BAPTIZED EVERY ONE OF YOU IN THE NAME OF JESUS CHRIST FOR THE REMISSION OF SINS..." SCRIPTURE: ACTS 2:38	**SOME ALIENS** "REPENT, PUT AWAY YOUR SPOUSE, BE BAPTIZED AND REMAIN SINGLE THE REST OF YOUR LIFE". SCRIPTURE: _____
SINFUL MEMBERS OF THE CHURCH "REPENT AND PRAY..." ACTS 8:22 CONFESS OUR SINS" 1 JNO. 1:9	**SOME SINFUL MEMBERS OF THE CHURCH** "REPENT, PUT AWAY YOUR SPOUSE, REMAIN UNMARRIED THE REST OF YOUR LIFE". SCRIPTURE: _____
"GOD IS FAITHFUL AND JUST TO FORGIVE US OUR SINS, AND TO CLEANSE US FROM ALL UNRIGHTEOUSNESS" 1 JNO. 1:9	"REPENT, REMAINED UNMARRIED THE REST OF YOUR LIFE". SCRIPTURE: _____

15

DOES REPENTANCE DEMAND:

STOP SIN?	LIVE REST OF LIFE W/O DOING THAT WHICH IS RIGHT?
WORSHIP IDOLS	WORSHIP THE TRUE GOD 1 THES. 1:9
FORNICATION	SEX WITHIN MARRIAGE 1 COR. 7:2
STEALING MONEY	HONEST LABOR EPH. 4:28
ADULTERY	MARRIAGE HEB. 13:4
HAVE ANOTHER MAN'S WIFE	HAVE OWN WIFE 1 COR. 7:2
YES!	NO!

25

never go back to worshipping the true God? Well, must I give up fornication in repentance? *Yes.* Does that mean I can never have sex within marriage? *No.* I must quit stealing. *Yes.* Does that mean I could never work at honest labor again? *No.* I have given scripture over here for these. Adultery? Yes, *I have to give it up in repentance.* That does not mean I can never remarry. I must give up the other man's wife. Yes. That does not mean I can never have *my own.*

And he keeps getting back to Herod, back to Herod. *Herod has nothing to do with this discussion.* And the law about which that he is talking was not the gospel of Christ. And I do not know what brother Halbrook would tell him today. I do not know if he ever lived to be under the gospel of Christ. Incidentally, I wonder when what brother Halbrook preaches became effective? One man in his debate said it did not start in Acts 2. It did not start in that generation. When did they begin to tell people what you are telling people tonight? "Repent, be baptized, put away your spouse, remain single the rest of your life." When did Peter begin to tell people to do that? When did Paul tell people that? Go through the book of Acts in the accounts in this book of their conversion, you will not find it there. Yes, we will have to give this up, but we do not have to quit doing what is right.

Let's see the next chart please, my number 43 on Colossians 3:5-7. "Living in" means "walking in." "Walking in" means guilty of, but does not mean *married to*. But if "living in" fornication means being *married to a fornicator,* then "living in uncleanness," it is the same passage, means being *married to an unclean person;* "living in inordinate affection" means being *married to one with inordinate affection;* "living in evil concupiscence" would mean being *married to one who is guilty of the same.* "Living in covetousness" or idolatry would mean *being married to an idol worshipper.* And, no, we know that is not so. "Living in" — and he has admitted that now, one person can be living in sin when the other marries, and he may not even know anything about it. Even if they do, they are

COL. 3:5-7
LIVING IN - WALKING IN = GUILTY OF
(DOES NOT MEAN MARRIED TO:)

MEANS:	IF:
LIVING IN FORNICATION	*BEING MARRIED TO A FORNICATOR
	THEN:
LIVING IN UNCLEANNESS	*BEING MARRIED TO AN UNCLEAN PERSON
LIVING IN INORDINATE AFFECTION	*BEING MARRIED TO ONE WITH INORDINATE AFFECTION
LIVING IN EVIL CONCUPISCENCE	*BEING MARRIED TO ONE WHO IS GUILTY OF EVIL CONCUPISCENCE
LIVING IN COVETOUSNESS (IDOLATRY)	*BEING MARRIED TO AN IDOL WORSHIPPER

43

not connected with it. They are not charged with sin because they are *married to the sinner*. And he admitted that is true even in regard to the fornicator. You can be married to a fornicator, but God does not automatically charge you with it. You are not living in it because your mate is. If that is so, a lot of people would perhaps be living in it, and not know anything about it. The mate may have committed fornication several times. They do not know anything about it — still living with them, still married to them, very happily so. If they find out about it, they might still plead with them to remain.

Living and walking, and let's see my chart that goes along with this, number 44. The clean person does not become guilty of uncleanness by *marrying* an unclean person. An honest person does not become a thief *by marrying a thief*. Within marriage, one can be guilty of living in any sin, without causing the spouse, her husband or his wife, to be guilty of that sin. Let's think about sin for a moment. I want you to know

> **COL. 3:5-7**
> (Cont)
>
> * THE CLEAN PERSON DOES NOT BECOME GUILTY OF UNCLEANNESS BY MARRYING AN UNCLEAN PERSON.
>
> * AN HONEST PERSON DOES NOT BECOME A THIEF BY MARRYING A THIEF.
>
> * WITHIN MARRIAGE, ONE CAN BE GUILTY OF (LIVING IN) ANY SIN WITHOUT CAUSING THE SPOUSE TO BE GUILTY OF THAT SIN.
>
> 44

I do not make light of sin nor does the Bible. Perhaps I can make it this simple. You children listen. You adults too. If you have ever stolen a penny, and God has not forgiven you, you are a thief and you are living in theft. So much as one penny, if you have stolen anything, if you have picked up a penny worth of candy, if they have such things now in the store, for which you did not pay, you are living in theft till God forgives you. No one else may be living with you, involved with you, but you are living in sin. That is how serious sin is. And if you die guilty of that sin, you will surely go to hell. I think my opponent will agree with that. So, how are we going to get out of that? By receiving God's forgiveness.

He said that *baptism does not wash away a marriage*. I never said it did. But I am trying to get him to agree that it does wash away sin. Even fornication. Even murder. Adultery. Theft. Idolatry. Now, it is up to God. Now, if we will just leave God up in heaven and leave ourselves down here, and quit trying to become little gods down here, setting up laws for people to live by and say, "Lord, you tell us what the punishment is for this person." Oh, he could set a whole list of temporal consequences punishment, but God knows nothing about that.

That is how serious sin is now. If you commit sin, number one, you are living in it. If you die in it, you are going to hell. What are you going to do about it? Obey the gospel of Christ. God in his mercy will forgive you. That is what God's mercy is all about. That is why He is merciful. He loves us so much that He sent His son to die for us.

See my chart number 426. Halbrook says, how do I know? Well, I know because I can quote 14 commentaries, as he did in one speech, one historian, and one Catholic Catechism, yet he claims his proposition is proved by the 66 books of the Bible. Freeman, I have quoted the Bible, I have referred to these others, but he brought them up. I brought them back just to show that they do not even agree with him. He does not agree with God, he does not agree with Christ, he does not agree with John the Baptist, he does not agree with Paul. And he does not agree with the witnesses he brought up. Now, you may agree with him, but I doubt that you agree with him on every point. He does not agree with his witnesses on every point. So, how do I know, now, if the Bible told him so, why did he introduce these things? I did not introduce them, he did. So, he has many commentaries, which at the same time disagree with Halbrook. He admits that. That is why he picked out the ones that agreed with him. And he will admit I could probably put a big stack over here that would agree with me. But what would that prove? Nothing. You know, this is the book I am recommending to you, the gospel of Jesus Christ.

HOW DO I KNOW?

HALBROOK	FREEMAN
*14 COMMENTATORS	
*1 HISTORIAN	THE BIBLE TELLS ME SO!
*1 CATHOLIC CATECHISM	

MANY COMMENTARIES DISAGREE WITH HALBROOK!

426

Rebuttals:
Third Evening
Halbrook's Third Negative

Brother Freeman, gentlemen moderators, ladies and gentlemen, do not mistake this strong clash of views for bitterness. We do not hate one another. We are testing arguments. This is to our good. This is how we study and learn. And I commend him for entering into this study.

I want us to remember again my chart 2, on the proposition. You remember that as to the idea that the marriage of Herod and Herodias could become lawful if Philip would say he put her away, my opponent in principle said *yes,* the other night. *But he definitely wants to say false now, so you remember his proposition went down world without end!* Here is the case of Philip. He puts her away, but Herod cannot marry her

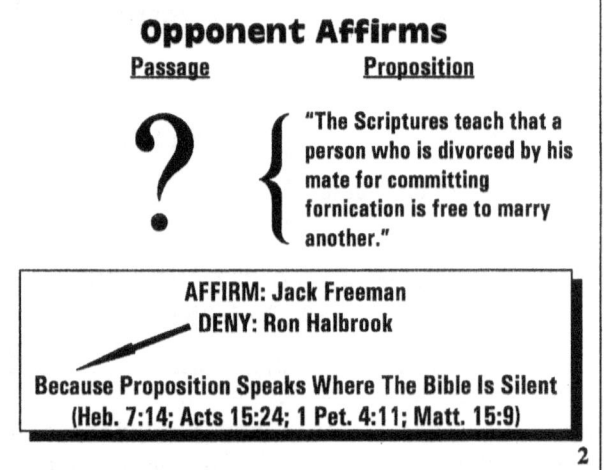

and she cannot marry Herod. There is "no mercy" in it, it is "the doctrine of demons," and, "How do you know?" On all those arguments, you just apply them *yourself,* brother Freeman.

Now then, he had his chart 21 on *1 Corinthians 7.* I am not going to show it. It is simply where he was pressing his point that you should not bind celibacy —these people are allowed to marry. I want to look at my chart 133 on that point. I want to pay attention to the principle that he points out to us. On chart 133, my friend, and notice it with me, please. My opponent says the divorced fornicator cannot receive celibacy. Matthew 19:10-12 points out, read your text and see, that *we are not animals.* My friend, we can rise above the animal instinct. Yes, God gave us a strong sexual drive, but we are not like the animal world. We are capable of rising above that. And I want you to know that there are those in this text that would *never* marry.

Jesus insisted on *the constraints of law* in Matthew 19:9 and that is what

> **Opponent Says Divorced Fornicator Can't "Receive" Celibacy (Matt. 19:10-12)**
>
> 1. Text refers to those who have never married
> 2. Jesus' insistence on constraints of law provoked disciples' comment, "...not good to marry."
> 3. After one married, he can't escape constraints of law by claim he "cannot receive" such constraints!
> 4. Man's extremity = God's opportunity - Phil. 4:13; 1 Cor. 10:13
>
> 133

provoked the disciples to say, "It is not good to marry. It looks like it is just better not to get married, Lord, if the constraints of the law are as strong as you say they are." My friend, I want you to notice *after* one is married, he cannot escape the constraints of law by saying, "Well, I decided I cannot receive these constraints." My friend, you have already stepped through that door and you do not go back out again. You are under those constraints, but you remember man's extremity is God's opportunity, and God can help you to deal with that in such a way as to save your soul. And there are plenty of people that are doing so!

Now on his charts 17 and 18, we will not show them again, but that is where he asked, "How do you know?" and said Halbrook "demands the impossible." Please notice my chart 72 [text, Matt. 19:9]. I will tell you how I know, because *the Bible tells me so,* brother Freeman. Here is how I know. My Lord and Savior said, "Whosoever shall put away his wife, except it be for fornication, and shall marry another, committeth adultery." And that, sir, is *how I know.* The Bible says so! If my mate commits adultery, I can put her away. If I commit adultery, she can put me away. And all you are doing is *throwing smoke and dust over this passage,* and making it sound like we can never practice what this passage teaches! Well, how do you know that your wife did not have a sex change? Maybe you are married to a man, how do you know? Such foolish talk, foolishness. Foolish talk.

Now then, my friends, you remember that he makes his point on the matter of *capital punishment.* He says he favors it but it is *not necessary.* Look at 254 again. He says it is not necessary, and the God of heaven said that it was. You can just take your choice. In *Genesis 9:6* God said that it was necessary. And because violence was not restrained, God even had to bring *the flood* upon the world, you remember, earlier than that, but then men turned back to that kind of violence. You had better know, my friend, that *God ordained that.* In *Romans 13:4* God still provides for that. No wonder our nation is shaking and rocking and in danger of collapsing, because some people are just *kind of in favor* of it, but they do not think it is really *necessary*. He said, why don't I enforce it? I am a gospel preacher and not a policeman! God ordained two realms.

And then he had his chart 59. And I want my chart 235. You notice this matter about a man steals. He talks about this and

Why Did God Not Give The Murderer The Right To Live? (Gen. 9:6; Isa. 6:3; Rom. 13:4)	Why Did God Not Give The Fornicator Right To Remarry? (Gen. 2:24; Isa. 6:3; Mt. 19:4-9)
1. Divine Law Established Moral Order & Justice	1. Divine Law Established Order & Justice
2. Restrain Evil - Can't Murder Again - Warn Others	2. Restrain Evil - Can't Repeat Sin - Warn Others
3. Protect The Good - One Victim Is Enough	3. Protect The Good - One Victim Is Enough

254

says, "Well, he can get his *car* back, and he could have the *watch* back." Now, my friend, the parallel would be, if he gets *that woman* back again, the *same* woman. He gets the *same* watch back, doesn't he, brother Freeman? He gets the *same* car back, doesn't he? He gets the *same* woman back! Not another watch, another car, another woman. How do you show repentance? If you steal a man's watch, you give it back. The same watch. If you steal his car, you give it back. And if you steal

A MAN STEALS

ANOTHER'S WIFE   ANOTHER'S WATCH   ANOTHER'S CAR

REPENTANCE DEMANDS: RETURN THE WIFE, THE WATCH, THE CAR

AND NEVER HAVE:
YOUR OWN WIFE----YOUR OWN WATCH----YOUR OWN CAR
(IF THIS IS TRUE)   (SO IS THIS)   (AND THIS)

BUT

IF AFTER REPENTANCE, A MAN CAN HAVE HIS OWN WATCH AND HIS OWN CAR; HE CAN HAVE <u>HIS OWN WIFE</u>!

59

the wife, do you *keep* her? Now, if the watch dies you can have another. If your car dies you can have another. If the wife *dies,* brother Freeman, the Bible says you can have *another.* But where does it say that we can have the put-away fornicator to marry another, or that I can take this woman without scriptural grounds and then keep her?

Now, my friends, consider unscriptural marriage and repentance on my chart 236. In Ezra 10, repent and *put away* those wives. My opponent would have to say, repent and *keep* them. In Mark 6:18, repent and *put away* the wife. Repent

How Do You Show Repentance?

If You Steal A Man's Watch	If You Steal A Man's Car	If You Steal A Man's Wife

You Give It Back!	You Give It Back!	You Keep Her?

Note: The offended party may concede a watch or car but can't give his wife the right to marry another (Acts 5:4; Matt. 5:32; 19:9)

235

Unscriptural Marriage & Repentance

1. Ezra 10 - Repent and put away wives.
2. Mk. 6:18 - Repent and put away wife.
3. Matt. 5:32; 19:9 - If violate, repent and put away wife.
4. 1 Cor. 5 - Repent and put her away.

1. Opponent: "Repent" and keep wives.
2. Opponent: "Repent" and keep wife.
3. Opponent: If violate, "Repent" and keep wife.
4. Opponent: "Repent" and keep her.

236

and *keep* her? What will he say? If you violate Matthew 5 and Matthew 19, repent and *put away* the wife. See the parallel? If you are in an unscriptural marriage, *get out*, just like in 1 Corinthians 5.

Alright, we notice his chart 15 — I am covering every one of his charts — chart 15 on God versus Halbrook. He wants to know where is the passage that says that repentance demands that these people get out of these unscriptural marriages. See my chart O-1, overlay. Here are the passages, we have covered them already: *Mark 6, Colossians 3, 1 Corinthians 5 and 6*, and then also in *chapter 7*.

Now, see my chart 108. He talks about God versus Halbrook. I want to show you this simple parallel. It is *God versus Satan*. God said if you eat, you will surely die. Satan said if you eat, you will *not* surely die. God said if you believe and are baptized, you shall be saved, but Satan said, if you believe and are *not* baptized, you will be saved. Now watch it, God clearly said, "Whosoever marrieth her which is put away doth commit adultery." My opponent says, "Whoso marrieth her which is put away doth *not* commit adultery." There is your difference!

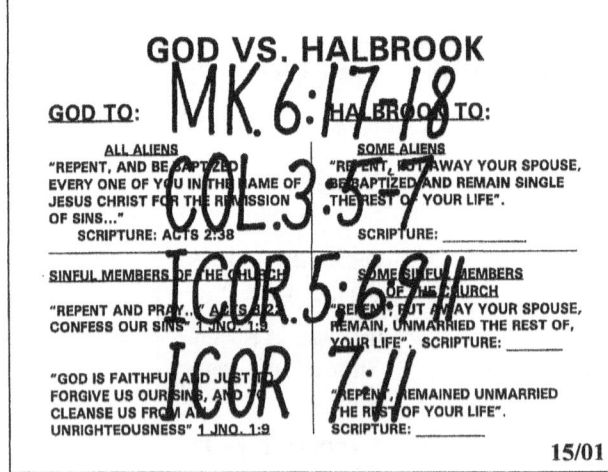

Now on his charts 43 and 44, we will not take the time to show them, he makes the point that if you marry an idolater or a thief, that does not make you one. Right. But if it said, "Whosoever marries a thief commits fraud," the only

God -vs- Satan

1. If you eat, "surely die" (Gen. 2:17)	1. If you eat, "NOT surely die" (Gen. 3:4)
2. Believe & "Baptized shall be saved" (Mk. 16:16)	2. Believe and NOT baptized shall be saved
3. "Whoso marrieth her which is put away doth commit adultery" (Matt. 5:32; 19:9)	3. Whoso marrieth her which is put away doth NOT commit adultery

108

way you can repent and get out of that sin is to get out of that marriage. "Whosoever marries an idolater commits idolatry." You would have to get out of that marriage. Now, notice my chart 72 [text, Matt. 19:9]. Here is what the Book does say. "Whosoever marrieth her which is put away doth commit adultery," and yes sir, brother Freeman, if you repent, you must *get out* of that. There is your difference. There is your difference.

And he talked about the commentators, "how do you know?" on his chart 426. We will just show our chart 321-B on that. Yes, I use commentators. We use them for the sake of study and they can be helpful and useful. But, I will tell you, *he has been on both sides of that throughout this debate.* He is on the fence. Why, even out there in Las Vegas he was castigating me for using scholars, but he used 354 scholars in one speech! Yes, he did. Did you know translators are

scholars? They are not inspired. They are uninspired men, and he listed 354 of them, and then, "But," he said, "you *cannot* use them." But *he uses* them, but you *cannot;* but *he uses* them, but you *cannot*! I would not say any more about that if I were you, brother Freeman. Now, my friend, *my appeal has been to the text*! We have gone through the passages and we have seen these passages time and time again.

Now, my friend, I want us to notice my chart 15. You remember the principle that *things not authorized are sinful*. If there is no passage of scripture for it, it is wrong. There is no passage for the put-away fornicator to marry another.

Also, look at my chart 35. When we compromise that principle of authority, we try to receive people on the basis of Romans 14. Then, we are going to have the church full of premillennialism, tongue speaking, abortion, polygamy, and *all* of these theories on marriage. *It is a breakdown of the authority principle!*

But furthermore, see my chart 59-X [text, Mk. 6:17-18]. *It destroys the purity of the church.* Now, you look at Herod. He took his niece. Now, my friend, suppose I take my niece, or somebody else in the church takes his niece, and then you have got preachers and elders and Bible class teachers and song leaders in that shape. What about it? *Are we ready for it?*

Now, my friend, the appeal of the flesh opens the door to sin with all of its sorrows. See my chart 175. Notice, my friend. *The misuse of 1 Corinthians 7 as he misuses it,* the historians have shown, *is an entrance wedge to increased looseness on divorce and remarriage.* These who try to say that "not under bondage" allows the liberty to contract a new marriage *open the door to all kinds of cases of divorce and remarriage.*

Not Authorized = Sinful

1. Things "not authorized within the doctrine of Christ are not only non-essential but sinful as well."
2. An author defended sponsoring church but had "no passage of Scripture to show that such a plan is authorized by the Lord" (Jack Freeman, Gospel Guardian, 28 April 1960, pp. 8-9).
3. No clear passage authorizes put-away fornicator or deserted believer to marry another.
4. Conclusion: such marriages are sinful!

15

Romans 14 - OR - 2 John 9-11

Receive Him	Receive Him Not
Instrumental Music	Women Preachers
Church Supported Missionary & Benevolent Societies	Modernism
Church Suppers, Ball Teams, Gyms	Evolution
Premillennialism	Abortion On Demand
Church Hospitals	Polygamy
A.D. 70 World Ended, Resurrection, Etc.	Domestic Partners
Choirs & Quartets	New Law On Marriage & Divorce: "Kingdom Law"
Interdenominational Services	Baptism Removes Marriage
Boston Church Schemes	Redefine "Adultery"
Tongue Speaking	Fornicator Remarry
Open Membership	2nd Exception - Desertion
Fellowship With The Christian Church	Homosexual Marriage

35

Misuse Of 1 Cor. 7:15

"An entrance-wedge" to "increased looseness" on divorce and remarriage.
Survey history of movement from "one cause of separation with remarriage"
to looser practices ("Divorce," McClintock & Strong,
<u>Cyclopedia of Bibl.</u>, Theol., & Eccl. Lit., II:839-844)

1. "'Not in bondage' to keep company with unbeliever at all events" but no "remarriage."
2. Later claim it gives "Liberty to contract a new" marriage - "Had wide effects."
3. "Entrance-wedge" for remarriage in any case of "malicious desertion."
4. RESULT: Much "Increased looseness" & "Shocking facility of divorce ... flowed from this source."

175

I.S.B.E. Article Warns

If use 1 Cor. 7:15 as right to remarry,
"The flood gates are open" (II:865-866)

Steps of Progression:

"If your husband deserts you, you may have another. If he is cruel, you may have another. If he fails to support you, you may have another. If he is drunken, you may have another. If he is incompatible or makes you unhappy, you may have another" - and yet others beyond these.

Results: Careless Marriages, Divorce For Any Cause, Multiplied Miseries!

176

Now, consider my chart 176. The historians point out that *that is the very thing which happened*. The floodgates are open because of that. If your husband deserts you, you can have *another*. If he is cruel, have *another*. If he fails to support you, have *another*. If he is drunken, have *another*. And so on. And the result is careless marriages, divorce for any cause, multiplied miseries, and our own children are involved in it in many cases.

Next, notice my chart 333. *The remarriage of the guilty party invites sin.* You talk about inviting sin, this encyclopedia points out that when the courts allow remarriage to the "guilty and innocent alike," "we invite the very evils we seek to remedy. We make it the interest of a dissatisfied party to create" the grounds that "free" him to marry another. Let me tell you, the law of Christ opens no such door to invite sin!

> **Remarriage Of Guilty Party Invites Sin!**
>
> I.S.B.E. article (II:865-866) warns that when courts allow remarriage to "guilty and innocent alike," "We invite the very evils we seek to remedy. We make it the interest of a dissatisfied party to create" the grounds that "free" him to marry another.
>
> The Law of Christ opens no such door to invite sin!
>
> 333

If we love our children, let us insist on what Jesus said in *Matthew 5*, what Jesus said in *Matthew 19*, what you can read in *Romans 7*. How do we know? *The Bible tells us so*. But, when you open the door, you invite sin, and you invite the destruction of homes, and you invite sorrows and multiplied miseries. And you invite the very condition our nation is in. It is being eaten up from the inside, rotting morally on the inside. Divorce and marry another, divorce and marry another, divorce and marry another. Where will it end? The Bible gives but *one* ground, my friend. We must maintain the purity of the church, and the purity of the home, and even try to protect our nation. I thank you very much.

Fourth Evening
Freeman's First Affirmative

[Proposition: The Scriptures teach that a person who is divorced by his mate for committing fornication is free to marry another.]

Brethren, Mr. Moderators, brother Halbrook, as we enter into the last night of this Bible study, I would like to join brother Walker in expressing appreciation to the elders here for arranging for this series of Bible studies. I want to express appreciation to those who have attended. I would like to thank especially those who have come to let me know that they stand with me in upholding the word of God. We look forward to other discussions. It has been pointed out that we should not enter into future discussions in this building, but if you would care to enter into future discussions, you can contact me by mail or shortly after services. I might point out that we are going to be leaving very early tomorrow morning and so we will not be here very long tonight. We need a little sleep. We are going to be leaving very early in the morning to go back home. It has been a pleasure to be with you. Perhaps we can be together under other circumstances at a later time.

Before defining the proposition, I want to read and answer the questions presented to me by Ron tonight. Question 1. *"If a man divorces his mate without cause and she later commits fornication, does her fornication give him the right to marry another?"* Answer: Fornication alone gives no one the right to marry another, but when the two are no longer bound in the sight of God, when the bond is broken, *both* can marry. If a man divorces his wife without scriptural cause and she dies, the bond is broken, certainly he can marry. Whenever the bond is broken. That is what this debate has been about. I believe that when the bond is broken, when man or woman is no longer married in the sight of God, they have the right to a spouse. They have none at that time.

2. *"On January 18th, 1990, you said, regarding an unscriptural divorce and remarriage, repentance would require giving up the mate, but you also said, such people* CAN CONTINUE *in the marriage. What will you say now?"* The marriage after an unscriptural divorce constitutes adultery and gives the innocent the right to divorce on that ground and remarry. She might not choose to divorce her husband.

3. *"Was Paul 'demanding celibacy,' teaching 'the doctrines of demons,' 'departing from the faith,' and showing 'no mercy,' when he said, 'REMAIN*

UNMARRIED' *in the event reconciliation is impossible (1 Corinthians 7:10-11)?"* No, he was not, and no other Bible passage does. The two were still husband and wife in the sight of God. My opponent has admitted that. They were still married in the sight of God. He had a wife, and she had a husband. Neither one is commanded to remain celibate. To remain unmarried meant not to contract *another* marriage. They were already married to one another, still married in the sight of God, but unmarried legally. A divorce had been obtained, but not in the sight of God. I have said this throughout every night of this debate. And I will say it tonight, but it has been in other speeches also. I think that you have no difficulty in understanding what I am affirming, but I will get into it a little deeper later.

4. *"When God* FORGIVES *a penitent sinner, what* PASSAGE *teaches that he removes the temporal consequences?"* Well, I would counter this with, what passage teaches that God put the temporal consequences there? What passage teaches that God put the temporal consequences there? We are talking about New Testament law. There is no passage that teaches that man is not allowed to return to do that which is right because he did once that which was wrong or more than once that which was wrong. You always have the right, a God-given right, to return to do that which is right. Including marriage which is honorable.

Question 5. *"Jack Freeman believes that if the events reflected in Mark 6:17-18 happened* TODAY, *the marriage of Herod and Herodias would* BECOME *lawful if Philip would say he put her away. True or false?"* No marriage becomes lawful just because a man says to his wife, "I put you away." I have told you before, I told you every night, and I am telling you again, that *this marriage* according to John the Baptist who spoke out and whose language is quoted there *was not lawful.* John said Herod could not lawfully have that woman. I am not defending his right to have her. But John did not say you must remain celibate, you cannot have a wife. He had the right to a wife, but he had the wrong wife. He had another man's wife.

If you desire to reach and preach the truth on this subject, why do we go back and discuss Herod? Why don't we begin with what the Apostles taught in Acts 2, knowing that in Luke 24 Jesus opened their understanding that they might understand the Scriptures. They understood what Jesus taught in Matthew 19 and all the other passages. They also understood the truth unto which they were guided by the Holy Spirit (Jn. 16:13) and preached it. They wrote as Paul said in Ephesians 3:3-4 so that when you read, you can understand it. So we can understand it. They did.

Some questions presented to brother Halbrook. 1. *"When a man is divorced*

Fourth Evening: Freeman's First Affirmative

by his wife for fornication and has not remarried, is he bound to a wife or loosed from a wife?" I want you to notice the difference between the questions. In this debate, and this is the eighth night, every question presented to me by brother Halbrook has been *a trick question*. Mine have been clear and simple, no tricks intended, no tricks could you find with them. I believe that is the way a question should be. 2. *"In what Bible passage is any marriage called an 'adulterous marriage?'"* You see how simple that is. If you want to, write it down. 3. *"Is a person living in fornication because of being married to one who is guilty of fornication?"* 4. *"If a man who is guilty of adultery and divorced for that cause obeys the gospel, of what sin is he guilty as he is raised up from baptism?"* 5. *"If a man who is guilty of adultery divorces his wife for a cause other than fornication, can she then scripturally remarry?"*

I come now to my responsibility to define the proposition under discussion tonight. By *"the Scriptures,"* I mean the sixty-six books of the Bible. By *"teach,"* I mean to give instruction or to impart information. By the expression, *"that a person,"* I mean that one who has been a husband or a wife, *"who is divorced,"* who has been put away. A man and a woman joined together by God have been put asunder. They are no longer married, not bound to a spouse. *"By his mate,"* by the one to whom he has been married, to whom he has been married. *"For committing fornication,"* for engaging in sex with someone other than his or her spouse. *"Is free,"* that means loosed, not bound by the law to his spouse, has no spouse, is not married, has God's authority *"to marry another,"* to be scripturally and legally joined to another in marriage.

Again, I want to state on the negative point what I am not defending in this debate. Debaters may be charged with many things, as I have, but I want to make it clear. I am not defending a man or a woman who plans or premeditates murder or adultery as a means of getting out of marriage. I am not defending homosexuals or lesbians. I am not defending Herod to have his brother's wife. I am not defending the fornicator who had his father's wife, 1 Corinthians five. But I am defending the right of those who are unmarried in God's sight to have a spouse. That is all I am defending, all I have been defending throughout this debate, and when we conclude it tonight, I am still defending that, that is all. The right of any person who is unmarried in the sight of God to have a wife or a husband, that is what this debate is about.

Now, we both agree that one can scripturally marry a fornicator without living in fornication. One is guilty of living in fornication, the other is not. We both agree that you can scripturally marry a fornicator. The difference is that brother Halbrook takes the position that if the man who is married to the fornicator gets a divorce first, gets a divorce first, then the one guilty cannot remarry. So, what this really hinges on is the seriousness of divorce. Keep in mind the guilty party, as people refer to him, the adulterer, the fornicator, is the one who obtains the divorce. If getting the divorce is sinful, you will have to place that burden upon the one you call the innocent party. The guilty commits the fornication. The innocent party gets a divorce. But unless there is a divorce you can remain married to them; he even admits that. And if they die without getting a divorce, they can remarry, even if they plan to get a divorce and do not get around to it before they die. Then, you can still remarry, though you are a fornicator. Their death does not remove your guilt. Only God's forgiveness does that.

Let's look at chart number one. If we could end this discussion tonight, *how do we know what false doctrine is, what the truth is?* God anticipated false doctrine, spelled it out clearly enough for all to understand in 1 Timothy 4, the first three verses. "The Spirit speaketh expressly, that in latter times some shall depart from the faith, giving heed to seducing spirits, and doctrines of devils." Among other things, *forbidding to marry*. The faith, according to this passage, does not forbid

> **HOW DO WE KNOW?**
> **GOD ANTICIPATED FALSE DOCTRINE**
>
> 1 TIM. 4:1-3
> "...<u>SOME SHALL DEPART FROM THE FAITH</u> GIVING HEED TO SEDUCING SPIRITS AND <u>DOCTRINES OF DEVILS, FORBIDDING TO MARRY</u>..."
>
> WHO IS DEMANDING CELIBACY?
> WHO IS FORBIDDING TO MARRY?
>
> <u>DO YOU WANT THE DOCTRINES OF DEVILS</u>
> OR
> <u>THE FAITH ???</u>
>
> 1

people to marry, but something does: the doctrine of devils. And so, we have a choice to make. Will we accept what the devils teach? Will we accept what the faith teaches? The faith, the gospel. The faith does not forbid a man to have a woman, does not forbid a woman to have a husband, but someone does. And Paul was guided by the Holy Spirit to reveal that this was the doctrine of devils. Who is demanding celibacy? Who is forbidding to marry? The faith does not. Brother Halbrook does and he admits that he does.

Now, brother Halbrook, I am really glad my wife was not here last night. I do not think you were directing this question directly at me, but if you were, I am going to answer it for you. *How can you know that your wife did not have a sex change?* That is a question you asked. Now, can you know your wife did not have a sex change? That is a question you asked. How can you know your wife did not have a sex change? I will have you know, I know. Maybe you do not. I do not think you meant to insult anyone by that, I think it was a *general* question. [Halbrook indicated from his seat that it was only general.] I am sure of that, okay, I will take your word for it. But, I will tell you in my case, I know, because I have known my wife all of her life. We were raised together, went to school together. She was my childhood sweetheart. We married, and we just celebrated last Friday our forty-fourth wedding anniversary. So, I *know*. But suppose you cannot know. Is God going to condemn you if you live your life with someone who has under-

DEMANDING THE IMPOSSIBLE
HOW CAN YOU KNOW:

1. THAT THE ONE YOU MARRY WAS NEVER MARRIED BEFORE?
2. THAT THE ONE YOU MARRY WAS NOT DIVORCED BECAUSE OF ADULTERY?
3. THAT THE ONE YOU MARRY DIVORCED A PREVIOUS SPOUSE ON GROUNDS OF FORNICATION?
4. THAT THE ONE YOU MARRY WAS NOT DIVORCED FOR A CAUSE OTHER THAN FORNICATION?
5. THAT THE CHRISTIAN YOU MARRY WAS NOT DIVORCED BY AN UNBELIEVER?
6. THAT THE ONE YOU BAPTIZE AND FELLOWSHIP AS A FAITHFUL CHRISTIAN AND FOR WHOM YOU PERFORM A MARRIAGE CEREMONY WAS NOT PREVIOUSLY DIVORCED FOR FORNICATION?

17

gone a sex change? If it is impossible for you to ever know about it? You live with them, die with them. Is God going to condemn you because of that?

Notice this, how can you know that the one you married was never married before? I am using this chart, these statements, these questions, to show that my opponent is demanding that which is impossible, that which you cannot actually know for sure. His answer to this is, if you cannot know it for sure, the only safe thing is never marry. You know that would apply to most people. Never marry. How do you know that the one you marry was not divorced because of adultery? That the one you marry divorced a previous spouse on grounds of fornication? That the one you marry was not divorced for a cause other than fornication? You know I have asked a lot of members of the church who revealed to me that they had been married before, *"Well, did you put away your spouse for fornication?"* They have all said, "Yes." Must I hire a detective agency? How am I going to know whether or not they are telling the truth? How can you know that the Christian you marry was not divorced by an unbeliever? That the one you baptized, and fellowship as a faithful Christian, and for whom you perform a marriage ceremony, was not previously divorced for fornication?

Let me ask a question of the congregation here through brother Halbrook, directed to him. How do you know when people come here to be identified with this congregation from elsewhere? Do you question their marriage relationship? If you do and they say, *"Well, I was married before and I am married again, but I put away my first spouse for fornication,"* do you accept their word for it, or do you go into some investigation?

Let's see the counterpart of this on my chart number 18. It just finishes up, "demanding the impossible." *What proof would you demand that one has been guilty of fornication?* Court records. You cannot depend on them. In Nevada they will not write it on the court records. A lawyer will not take the case. The judge does not want it. The lawyer gets his money for doing nothing that way. And if you divorce on grounds of fornication, you have got to have actual evidence. But even if they allowed it and it was on the court record, you could never be sure that was correct. What about the word of a friend? Or the word of the one you want to marry? Photographic evidence? That can be faked. Seeing it with your own eyes? Well, I suggest you ask brother Ron Halbrook, and we have, and he has replied in the cases where you cannot know, the only safe course is to remain unmarried.

I want my chart number 30 on the noun and the pronoun. In Matthew 19:9, *"Whosoever shall put away his wife, except it be for fornication,"* and, *"Whoso marrieth her that is put away doth commit adultery."* We have the noun *wife*, we

---

DEMANDING THE IMPOSSIBLE
(Cont)

WHAT PROOF WILL YOU DEMAND TO SHOW THAT ONE HAS BEEN GUILTY OF FORNICATION?

* COURT RECORDS?
* THE WORD OF A FRIEND?
* THE WORD OF THE ONE YOU WANT TO MARRY?
* PHOTOGRAPHIC EVIDENCE?
* SEEING IT WITH YOUR OWN EYES?
* ASK RON HALBROOK?

18

NOUN & PRONOUN IN MATT. 19:9

WHOSOEVER SHALL PUT AWAY HIS WIFE, EXCEPT IT BE FOR FORNICATION,
WHOSO MARRIETH HER WHICH IS PUT AWAY DOTH COMMIT ADULTERY.

MAN WHO PUTS AWAY HIS WIFE FOR FORNICATION HAS NO WIFE,

CAN REMARRY.

WOMAN PUT AWAY FOR FORNICATION HAS NO HUSBAND,

CAN REMARRY.

30

Fourth Evening: Freeman's First Affirmative

have the pronoun *her*. The pronoun her, by rules of language, whether German, Japanese, or English, has to refer to the noun preceding, wife. *"Whosoever shall put away his wife, except it be for fornication, and shall marry another, committeth adultery: and whoso marrieth her that is put away doth commit adultery."* The *her* in the second clause is *the wife* of the first clause. Incidentally, we have pointed out repeatedly Matthew 19:9 does *not* discuss a divorce on the grounds of fornication. *It only infers*. It discusses a divorce for reasons other than fornication. If you doubt that, put the first phrase together. If you put your wife away, except it be for fornication, and marry another, you commit adultery. *But we both believe he could put her away for fornication and marry another, and you do not commit adultery*. So, this is discussing divorces on the grounds other than fornication. The whole verse. Well, the man who puts away his wife for fornication has no wife. We both agree there. I say he can remarry. *The Bible says he can remarry*. My opponent says he cannot. The woman put away for fornication has no husband, she can remarry; my opponent say she cannot.

On my chart 31, continue "the noun and pronoun." God says, "Art thou loosed from a wife," 1 Corinthians 7:27-28, "if thou marry, thou has not sinned." My opponent says if he marries he sins. God says he does not. So, you choose to accept the word of God, or the word of Halbrook. You can have your choice.

Let's look at my chart 25. Let's talk about repentance. *Does repentance demand that we stop sinning? It certainly does*. But, does repentance demand that we live the rest of our life without doing that which is right? No, it does *not*. In regard to worshipping idols, must I give up idolatry when I repent? Yes, certainly so. But does that prohibit me, make it impossible for me, to ever worship God again? Must I live the rest of my life without ever worshipping the true and living God? The Thessalonians had worshipped idols. They turned to serve and worship the true and living God.

NOUN & PRONOUN IN MATT. 19:9
(Cont)

GOD SAYS --- "ART THOU LOOSED FROM A WIFE.."
1 COR. 7:27-28

"...IF THOU MARRY, THOU HAST NOT SINNED".
MAN WHO PUTS AWAY HIS WIFE FOR FORNICATION HAS NO WIFE,

MY OPPONENT SAYS --- "IF HE MARRIES HE SINS"

GOD vs. HALBROOK

31

What about fornication? Yes, repentance demands that I give up fornication, but does that mean I can never enjoy sex within marriage? 1 Corinthians 7:2, *"Let every man have his own wife,"* to avoid fornication. *"Let every woman have her own husband."* If I have become a thief, I have stolen money or anything else. Does repentance demand that I return the money? *Yes.* But does that mean that I cannot engage in honest labor? Paul told the man who had been a thief, do not steal anymore, but work with your own hands that which is right (Eph. 4:28). Well, if I have committed adultery, must I repent? *Yes.* But, does that mean I can never engage in marriage? Marriage is that which God calls honorable (Heb. 13:4). *Well, if I have another man's wife, must I give her up? Yes.* That is exactly right. Does that mean I cannot have my own? *No.* To those who have no wives, no husbands, Paul said in 1 Corinthians 7:2, "Let every man have his own wife, and let every woman have her own husband."

Next we go to my chart 43. We want to deal further with repentance. As we get into Colossians 3:5 and 7, he used Colossians 3:5 and 7 and other statements, an overlay on one of my charts. According to Colossians 3:5 and 7, the Apostle Paul mentions among other sins fornication and adultery, and he says, "in the which ye also walked..., when ye lived in them." Some say you cannot live in sin. The Bible says you

DOES REPENTANCE DEMAND:

STOP SIN?	LIVE REST OF LIFE W/O DOING THAT WHICH IS RIGHT?
WORSHIP IDOLS	WORSHIP THE TRUE GOD 1 THES. 1:9
FORNICATION	SEX WITHIN MARRIAGE 1 COR. 7:2
STEALING MONEY	HONEST LABOR EPH. 4:28
ADULTERY	MARRIAGE HEB. 13:4
HAVE ANOTHER MAN'S WIFE	HAVE OWN WIFE 1 COR. 7:2
YES!	NO!

25

COL. 3:5-7
LIVING IN - WALKING IN = GUILTY OF
(DOES NOT MEAN MARRIED TO:)

MEANS:	IF:
LIVING IN FORNICATION	*BEING MARRIED TO A FORNICATOR
	THEN:
LIVING IN UNCLEANNESS	*BEING MARRIED TO AN UNCLEAN PERSON
LIVING IN INORDINATE AFFECTION	*BEING MARRIED TO ONE WITH INORDINATE AFFECTION
LIVING IN EVIL CONCUPISCENCE	*BEING MARRIED TO ONE WHO IS GUILTY OF EVIL CONCUPISCENCE
LIVING IN COVETOUSNESS (IDOLATRY)	*BEING MARRIED TO AN IDOL WORSHIPPER

43

Fourth Evening: Freeman's First Affirmative 241

can. But *living in* and *walking in* is equal to *being guilty of.* That does not mean married to. Now, if walking in adultery means married to an adulteress, and walking in or living in fornication means *married to* a fornicator, then examine the rest of the verse there. These other things are also listed in Colossians 3:5-7. Living in uncleanness would mean being *married to* an unclean person. Living in inordinate affection would mean being *married to* one with that type of affection. Living in concupiscence would mean being *married to* that type of person. Living in covetousness or idolatry would mean being *married to* an idol worshipper. We both agree that you could be married scripturally to a person who worships idols. You could be married to a person that had evil desires. You might not even know it.

But we are not recommending, either one of us, that you engage in such a marriage. But, if a person is unclean, you may never know it. They may have affections you do not know anything about. That does not mean you cannot be married to them without being guilty of theft as he is. There are circumstances. If you aid and abet the crime, or course, the courts of our land would hold you equally guilty, and so would God. But, here just because you marry a thief, you may know nothing about it. That does not mean you have inherited his theft. You talk about inherited sin. That is not a doctrine taught upon the pages of the Bible.

Let's turn to my chart number 44. The clean person does not become guilty of uncleanness by marrying an unclean person. An honest person does not become a thief by marrying a thief. Within marriage, one can be *guilty of* or *living in* any sin without causing the spouse to be guilty of that sin, including fornication. And we both agree that if one is guilty of fornication, not divorced for that, we both agree

---

COL. 3:5-7
(Cont)

* THE CLEAN PERSON DOES NOT BECOME GUILTY OF UNCLEANNESS BY MARRYING AN UNCLEAN PERSON.

* AN HONEST PERSON DOES NOT BECOME A THIEF BY MARRYING A THIEF.

* WITHIN MARRIAGE, ONE CAN BE GUILTY OF (LIVING IN) ANY SIN WITHOUT CAUSING THE SPOUSE TO BE GUILTY OF THAT SIN.

44

---

that if no divorce has occurred, but if the mate does, or if they are single and never been married, *you can marry that fornicator scripturally*. God joins you together to a fornicator. My opponent believes that, and I believe it. And you are not guilty of fornication because you are married to a fornicator. But he goes further, and said, now if that fornicator is divorced, then you marry him, *you are living in adultery*. Why? They do not have a husband, they do not have a wife.

Let's see my chart number 59. Now, my opponent has a chart like this, except his woman was on the other side. Now, I think he misunderstood what was said last night. We are not concerned in this chart with the man who had a wife, first of all, and the man who owned a watch, and the man who owned a car. We are concerned with a thief and what repentance demands of the thief. We are not concerned with

A MAN STEALS

ANOTHER'S WIFE   ANOTHER'S WATCH   ANOTHER'S CAR

REPENTANCE DEMANDS: RETURN THE WIFE, THE WATCH, THE CAR

AND NEVER HAVE:
YOUR OWN WIFE----YOUR OWN WATCH----YOUR OWN CAR
(IF THIS IS TRUE)   (SO IS THIS)   (AND THIS)

BUT

IF AFTER REPENTANCE, A MAN CAN HAVE HIS OWN WATCH AND HIS OWN CAR; HE CAN HAVE HIS OWN WIFE!

59

the right of the man, or his responsibility, the man as the owner, but we are concerned with the man who stole the things. *Well, he stole another man's wife.* He stole another's *watch,* and he stole another's *car. Does repentance demand that he return these things? Yes,* he must return the wife, he must return the watch, he must return the car. And even if the one from whom he stole the wife will not have her back, *he cannot have her.* But, he must make restitution in this matter as far as is possible to return. But does this mean that he can never have his own wife? Now, that is what my opponent teaches.

Now, last night answering this, he got up here and talked about the man who had the wife to start with. That is not what we are talking about. We are talking about the man who stole the wife. He stole the wife and he gives her back in repentance. My opponent says that means, repentance means he can never have his own wife. If that is so, when he turns the watch back, he can never have his own watch. And when he returns the stolen car, he can never have his own car. You know that which proves too much, *proves nothing.* But, if his chart proves anything at all, it proves this. If you are guilty of stealing a woman, *you give her back.* Well, that is *repentance* alright. You are saved, but you will have to remain *unmarried* the rest of your life. You steal a watch, you give it back, you will have to live the rest of your life without a watch. You steal a car, and give it back, you will have to live the rest of your life without owning a car. That is exactly what it amounts to. I do not think we have any

Fourth Evening: Freeman's First Affirmative 243

difficulty getting into and seeing what we are dealing with.

Next, go to my chart 47. Paul is preaching to aliens. Ron says I want the clear cut passage that tells me the fornicator can marry. Well, just put these passages together and you will see that he can, because you read in Acts 18:7 that Paul arrived over there in Corinth, and the Corinthians hearing, believed, and were baptized. But, verse 4 tells you he reasoned, he persuaded; verse 8, tells you that they believed

---

PAUL PREACHING TO ALIENS

ACTS 18:4 REASONED, PERSUADED
WHAT THEY DID:
ACTS 18:8 -- BELIEVED AND WERE BAPTIZED
WHAT GOD DID:
1 COR. 6:11 --- WASHED, SANCTIFIED, JUSTIFIED
ACTS 2:47 ----- ADDED TO THE CHURCH
OF WHAT THEY HAD BEEN GUILTY OF BEFORE BAPTISM
1 COR. 6:9-10 - SOME HAD BEEN GUILTY OF
FORNICATION AND ADULTERY.
DID GOD ADD FORNICATORS TO THE CHURCH?
(ACTS 2:47 --- NO!)

47

---

and were baptized. Verse 11 of 1 Corinthians 6 tells you that they, when they were baptized, they were washed, sanctified, and justified. Acts 2:47 tells us that such people were added to the church. Now, what had they been guilty of before baptism? 1 Corinthians 6, verses 9 and 10. Some of them had been guilty of *fornication* and *adultery*. Did God add such people to the church? Not fornicators and adulterers, no. Washed, sanctified, and justified, saved. God forgave them their sins, and He added *saved* people to the church. Well, this certainly shows that God can and will forgive fornicators and adulterers, and all other sinners, *if they meet his conditions*.

Let's see the following chart please, my number 48. Now, what did Paul tell those who had been fornicators and adulterers to do to avoid

---

PAUL PREACHING TO ALIENS
(Cont)

WHAT DID PAUL TELL THOSE WHO HAD BEEN FORNICATORS
AND ADULTERERS TO DO TO AVOID FORNICATION?

1 COR. 7:2 - "LET EVERY MAN HAVE HIS OWN WIFE,
AND LET EVERY WOMAN HAVE HER OWN HUSBAND."

*DID PAUL OR OTHER APOSTLES EVER TELL ANY MAN
TO LEAVE HIS WIFE IN ORDER TO BE SAVED?

*DID PAUL OR OTHER APOSTLES EVER TELL ANY WOMAN
TO LEAVE HER HUSBAND IN ORDER TO BE SAVED?

*DID PAUL OR OTHER APOSTLES EVER TELL ANYONE TO
REMAIN UNMARRIED IN ORDER TO GET TO HEAVEN?

48

---

fornication? He is still talking to the same people. Next chapter. Read it. He does not switch now and say he is talking to someone else, but is talking to the very same people. He said, "Nevertheless,...let every man have his own wife, and let every woman have her own husband." Let's go back a little. You know Paul begins this chapter by advising under those certain circumstances, as brother Halbrook has said, that *it is better not to marry*. Does that apply to fornicators and adulterers — "it is better not to marry"? I believe it did. Did it apply to ex-thieves? Yes. It applied to every person there who has not married. It was better not to marry. But he goes on. That was *advice*. Then he says, "Nevertheless, to avoid fornication, let every man have his own wife, and let every woman have her own husband." Now, my opponent would tell you that I believe that it is alright for a man who is burning with passion because his wife is away on a trip, or locked up in jail, or in an insane asylum, *to go marry another woman*. I do not believe it at all. He has *his own* wife. He has *his own wife. That is all God allows him to have*. Now if she dies, if she commits adultery, and he divorces her scripturally, then he has a right to a wife, because he has none.

Notice, the bottom part of this chart. And this is what we have repeatedly asked for. You know the only answer we have received? *Herod, Herod*. Herod was not allowed to have his brother's wife, and *so the fornicator is not allowed to have any wife*. The ex-fornicator is not allowed to have any wife. Herod truly had a right to *his own* wife. Well, did Paul or other Apostles ever tell any man *to leave his* wife in order to be saved? Any of you preachers do that? Before you baptize someone, do you tell them, "Now, I will not baptize you until you *leave* your wife. You cannot get to heaven without *leaving* your wife." Did Paul or other Apostles ever tell any woman to leave her husband in order to be saved? Just give us the passage. *He said, I want a clear cut passage where it says the fornicator can remarry. I want a clear cut passage here.* Did Paul or other Apostles ever tell anyone to remain unmarried in order to get to heaven? Those are the passages I would like to have dealt with, and just cite the passage. That will be simple enough.

Our next chart, number 32, on the person who is put away due to fornication. *God gives man or woman the right to put away a spouse.* He does

---

PUT AWAY DUE TO FORNICATION

Matt. 19:9

Gives MAN/WOMAN the RIGHT to put away spouse for fornication

Must the innocent put away (divorce) the guilty?
If not, it is NOT sinful to be married to a fornicator.

The fornicator IS living in fornication.
The innocent IS NOT living in fornication.

To live in sin DOES NOT mean to be married to a sinner.

32

not demand that. It is *not a command*. You have *the right*. Must the innocent put away, divorce the guilty? No. If not, it is not sinful to be married to a fornicator. And we agree on this. The fornicator is not living in fornication. He *is* living in fornication rather, *the innocent is not*. Now, they are married. Because one is guilty, that does not mean the other is living in the same sin. The fornicator is living in fornication, the innocent is not. To live in sin does not mean to be married to a sinner. Can you see that? To live in sin does not mean to be married to a sinner.

Go to my chart number 34. The put-away fornicator again is free to marry. He has a wife, is bound to a wife, or he does *not*. Which is it? Both Ron and I agree he had *no wife*. What is *the marital state?* He has no wife, what is his *spiritual* state? Ron will tell you he has no sin. As he arises from baptism he has no sin. Here is a single man without sin. My opponent says he is a fornicator, he cannot remarry. It is not what the Bible teaches. Is he married or single, is he bound to a wife or loosed from a wife? We all recognize, or brother Ron and I at least agree, he is loosed *from a wife. Well, what* is his marital state? He is unmarried. What is his spiritual state? If he has been baptized, at least as he arises from baptism, as you raise him up out of the waters of baptism, he is completely without sin. Just as free from sin as Adam and Eve were as created by God. As you were when you were baptized in the name of Jesus Christ for the remission of sins. Think about that. But my opponent says that is alright, I am going to remember this, the fact that this man some time ago committed fornication and there are some consequences he is going to have to bear, and one of them is, he can never remarry. The rest of his life he is going to have to live without a spouse. The Bible does not teach it. Never has. I have even read his own human books to show that this is a doctrine responsible for many sins in the world. This doctrine of forbidding to marry. But we did not need that to know what the truth is. The Bible says forbidding to marry is the doctrine of devils. It is not taught in the faith and that is why we cannot find it in the faith.

THE "PUT AWAY" FORNICATOR

FREE TO MARRY

1. **HE HAS A WIFE** (BOUND TO A WIFE)
   OR
2. **HE DOES NOT HAVE A WIFE** (LOOSED FROM A WIFE)
3. **WHAT IS THE MARITAL STATE OF THE PUT AWAY FORNICATOR?**

   A. DOES HE HAVE A WIFE? IF SO WHO IS SHE? WHERE IS SHE?
   B. IF HE STILL HAS A WIFE. THE WIFE WHO PUTS HIM AWAY FOR FORNICATION CANNOT REMARRY. FOR SHE HAS A HUSBAND.
   C. THE PUT AWAY FORNICATOR DOES NOT HAVE A WIFE.
      1) HOW SHALL HE AVOID FORNICATION?
         * 1 COR. 7:2 -- HAVE HIS OWN WIFE
      2) DOES HE HAVE DIVINE PERMISSION TO REMARRY?
         *1 COR. 7:27-28 -- "ART THOU LOOSED FROM A WIFE..."
         IF THOU MARRY, THOU HAST NOT SINNED."

34

Fourth Evening
Halbrook's First Negative

Brother Freeman, gentlemen moderators, ladies and gentlemen, I want us to notice tonight the proposition on chart 2 that we are discussing. My opponent affirms, *"The Scriptures teach that a person who is divorced by his mate for committing fornication is free to marry another."* This proposition *speaks where the Bible is silent!* Where the Bible is silent, we dare not speak and we dare not act. This is *the real difference* between us tonight. As to the fact that a man can claim that he has a passage, the Roman Catholics claim that they have a passage for Peter to be the first pope. But you have to examine those passages and you see that they are not valid. Then, they are *acting in silence,* and that is the problem he has tonight.

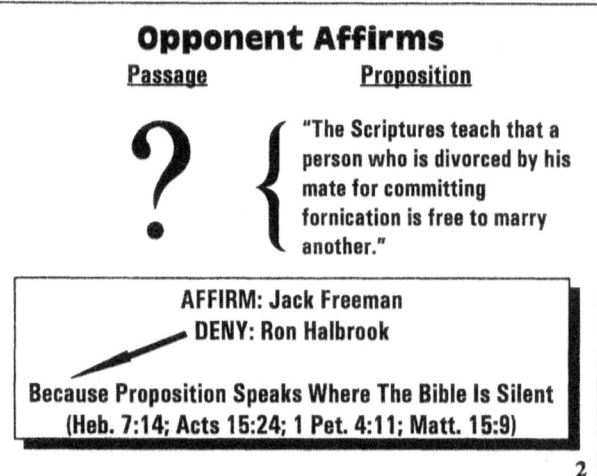

Now, we notice the questions that we are discussing, that we have handed to one another. He said that I had asked trick questions night after night, and he has made that little jab several times. Now, brother Freeman, I learned about questions from my Lord and Savior Jesus Christ in Matthew 21:25, that after they asked by what authority you do these things, he asked them a question, "The baptism of John, whence was it, *from heaven* or *of men?"* He offered them the *horns of a dilemma.* Was that a trick question, brother Freeman? Do you charge my Lord with lacking in integrity, trying to trick people? I want you to know *the false teachers in that day thought it was a trick question.* And, therefore, they dodged.

You know why it *appears* to be a trick question? When it has the power and force of truth and *you do not have the truth,* you can see you are about to be in hot water. When you are about to be in trouble, it looks like a trick to you. And do you know how they answered him? They said, well, we would just rather take the fifth amendment on this; we do not believe we want to answer this. Now, I think you must have learned to answer questions from *them,* by the way you danced around them and dodged them. No, there is no trick to it, if a man will just stand up and take the truth.

Now, he asks, *"When a man is divorced by his wife for fornication, and has not remarried, is he bound to a wife or loosed from one?"* Matthew 19:9 teaches that God released the marriage bond, my friend. But, notice my chart 101, still *under constraint of law.* As to the bond, yes, we understand that is loosed, as in 1 Corinthians 7:27, the "a" part of that verse. *Lusis,* which *Thayer* defines as divorce, is in that part of that verse. But the same *Thayer,* brother Freeman, in *7:27b,* referring to *luo,* speaks of single and never married people in connection with that term. So, do not get the two confused again like you did last night. *Now, the divorced people remain under the constraint of law.* These in Deuteronomy 24 are divorced and *you* would call them "single." You mix up "single," and "divorced," and "widowed," and all of these terms. The Bible does not do that. Here they are single according to you, but the Bible *restrained* them and *limited* them. I agree that when you are put away for fornication, you do not have a mate; but, my friend, you are under the constraint of law and there is no escaping that. *No escaping it!*

Divorced People Remain Under Constraint Of Law

1. Deut. 24:1-4 Divorce wife but can't have her back after her 2nd marriage
2. Deut. 24:1-4 Divorcee marry another but then can't ever return to 1st mate
3. Lev. 21:7, 13-14 Divorcee free from marriage but can't marry a priest
4. Matt. 5:32; 19:9 Pure divorce impure and marry another (new mate can't be one put away for fornication or other cause)
5. Matt. 5:32; 19:9 Not authorize a put-away person (whether put away for fornication or other cause) to marry another
6. 1 Cor. 7:10-11 If 2 Christians divorce, must remain unmarried or reconcile
7. 1 Cor. 7:12-15 Believer not give up Christ to keep unbeliever (no authority for either to marry another)

CONCLUSION:
1. Unscriptural divorce releases neither party from marriage!
2. Scriptural divorce releases both parties from marriage, but not from the constraint of the law!

101

Now, then, question two. *"In what Bible passage is any marriage called an 'adulterous marriage'?"* No passage used that exact term. *Such marriages are included in Colossians 3:5.* Now, brother Freeman, notice my chart 95. No passage used the term living in adultery, just exactly that term, but *you* use it. *You use it.* We agree that it represents *Bible teaching!* You say that we can "live in adultery," that is, we can use that expression, but you deny that we can speak of "adulterous relationships," and that is the "trick" to his question, that is the point to his question. I am not afraid to face it and I am not dodging it. I am telling you it is equal to the expression that you endorse, "live in adultery," my friend. *Living in adultery,* or *adulterous relationship,* which is it? Now, which is it, he does not know tonight.

He will *not say* when a married man has sex with a pretty little thing that *that is an adulterous relationship*. He will *not* say that. Why, my eighteen year old son knows that it is. A man divorces his wife not for the cause of fornication and marries a pretty little thing. Here is the man who *will not say that is an adul-*

> **FREEMAN'S SOPHISTRY TESTED**
> *"Live In Adultery"* Vs *"Adulterous Rel."*
> Can *"Live In Adultery,"* But Not In *"Adulterous Relationship."*
> (Freeman, Marriage Series, Fall 1988, #8)
> **LIVING IN ADULTERY OR ADULTEROUS REL.?**
> 1. Married Man Has Sex With "Pretty Little Thing."
> 2. Man Divorces Wife Not For Cause Of Forn. & Marries "Pretty Little Thing."
> 3. Man Keep Wife & Marry "Pretty Little Thing."
> *"LIVE IN ADULTERY"* = *"ADULTEROUS REL."*
> 95

terous relationship. Will you? I will give you a chance. I will take it back. Maybe he will. Brother Freeman, will you? Won't you? [Halbrook paused to give Freeman a chance to indicate his agreement, but Freeman chose not to do so.] No, sir, he will not say that is an adulterous relationship? Oh no, no, he says, it is just living in adultery. Now, so much for his adulterous relationship.

"Is a person living in fornication because of being married to one who is guilty of fornication?" If the two have no right to be married, they are *living in adultery*. Brother Freeman, same chart, be sure that you get that chart 95. That is the same as *an adulterous relationship,* you see, if the two have no right to be married. That is where they are.

4. *"If a man who is guilty of adultery and divorced for that cause obeys the gospel, of what sin is he guilty when he is raised up?"* None.

5. *"If a man who is guilty of adultery divorces his wife for a cause other than fornication, can she then scripturally remarry?"* Now, I do not care who gets the courthouse document. How many times have I answered that? The innocent party has the right to put away the guilty and marry another, and that is the *only* circumstance that God permits. That is not what this debate is about. He keeps wanting to bring up circumstances involving an *innocent* party, and what the *innocent* party can do, and can the *innocent* party do this, and what about the *innocent* party in this circumstance? I just wonder if he has forgotten the proposition? Our proposition is *the guilty party.* You need a passage on the *guilty* party! You need a passage and a scenario on the *guilty* party! He needs to read his proposition.

Then we had our questions. *"If a man divorces his mate without cause and she later commits fornication, does her fornication give him the right to marry another?"* Well, he said, not unless the bond is broken by putting away. So, in the case that *it is,* to which he knew I was referring, his answer is *yes.* Now, look at my chart number 60 [text, Matt. 5:32]. Here we have Matthew 5:32 describing the very case that you answered. A man divorces his mate without cause. Now, watch it. *"Whosoever shall put away his wife,"* — and it is not going to be for the cause, and I said she later commits fornication — *"causeth her to commit adultery."* Does her fornication give him *the right to marry another?* And, you say *yes.* But my Lord and Savior said that if you do this, you are *the cause* of it and you *do not have a right* to do anything. No, sir.

QUESTIONS - MAR. 2, 1990

1. If a man divorces his mate without cause and she later commits fornication, does her fornication give him the right to marry another?   a. _____ Yes   b. _____ No

2. On 18 January 1990 you said regarding an unscriptural divorce and remarriage, repentance would require GIVING UP the mate, but you also said such people CAN CONTINUE in the marriage. What will you say now?   a. _____ Give her up   b. _____ Continue in the marriage

3. Was Paul "demanding celibacy," teaching "the doctrine of demons," "departing from the faith," and showing "no mercy," when he said "REMAIN UNMARRIED" in the event reconciliation is impossible (1 Corinthians 7:10-11)?   a. _____ Yes   b. _____ No

4. When God FORGIVES the penitent sinner, what PASSAGE teaches that he removes the temporal consequences:
   a. murderer - death penalty
   b. convicted thief - prison   } Passage
   c. gambler - can't get wasted money back
   d. adulterer - threw away his own wife, } _____
   no authority to marry another

5. Jack Freeman believes that if the events reflected in Mark 6:17-18 happened TODAY, the marriage of Herod and Herodias would BECOME lawful if Philip would say he put her away.
   a. _____ True   b. _____ False

Q3-2-90

Look at my chart 65. Now, I want you to focus on *"not causing"* or *"not committing."* He has been confused on this throughout this debate. Be sure to get chart 65. In Matthew 5:32, does the exception refer to not *causing* adultery, or to not *committing* it? Now, get the exception. Whoever puts away his wife for fornication does *not cause* her to commit adultery. In other words, he is *not responsible for* her subsequent adultery. He does *not cause* it. But my opponent's interpretation is, whoever puts away his wife for fornication causes her to not commit something. *Causes her to not commit adultery.* He is responsible for her *not* committing adultery. And so, men, if you would like to be responsible for not causing your wife to commit adultery, *put her away,* and *get her in another marriage!* Now, that is *his* understanding of the passage. He has got it: The man causes her not to commit adultery when he puts her away and gets her in another marriage.

> **Matthew 5:32 Exception:
> Not Cause Or Not Commit?**
>
> | What Jesus Taught | -vs- | Opponent's Interpretation |
> |---|---|---|
> | Whosoever shall put away his wife **for fornication** does NOT CAUSE her to commit adultery (i.e. is not responsible for her subsequent adultery). | | Whosoever shall put away his wife **for fornication** causes her to NOT COMMIT adultery (i.e. he is responsible for her not committing adultery). |
> | **HE DOES NOT CAUSE HER ADULTERY** | -vs- | **HE CAUSES HER TO NOT COMMIT ADULTERY** |
>
> 65

2. *"On 18 January 1990, you said regarding an unscriptural divorce and remarriage, repentance would require* GIVING UP *the mate, but you also said such people* CAN CONTINUE *in it. What will you say now?"* He answered that just like they answered, "The baptism of John, whence was it, from heaven or of men?" I learned to *ask* questions from *the Lord.* He learned to *answer* them from the *enemies* of the Lord — *he did not answer it!* And I will show you why on my chart 242. Here is exactly why he did not answer. Here is why he did not answer, my friend. It has already gotten him into trouble before. If you have another man's wife he said, "Yes, you will have to give her up...That's repentance." And he repeated that tonight. But on another question, if an alien sinner in a second marriage following a divorce not for fornication desires to be acceptable to God, he "may" what? *"Continue in the marriage."* That is what my opponent said. "Continue in the marriage." Do you see why he did not want to answer that — do you see why he did not want to answer that question? And so he followed the path

> **Mark 6:17-18
> Contradictions of Error**
>
> 1. "If you have another man's wife, yes, you'll have to give her up ... that's repentance (Freeman, 18 Jan. 1990)
>
> 2. If an alien sinner in a second marriage following a divorce not for fornication desires to be acceptable to God, he:
>
>   FREEMAN: "May continue in the marriage" (18 Jan. 1990, answer to my question 3)
>
> 242

of the enemies of my Lord.

3. *"Was Paul 'demanding celibacy,' teaching 'the doctrine of demons,' 'departing from the faith,' and showing 'no mercy,' when he said 'REMAIN UNMARRIED' in the event reconciliation is impossible?"* And you said, *"No."* But, brother Freeman, they are unable to fulfill sexual passion. Unable to fulfill it. And you agree with Paul one time on this. You never know what he will say the next time; but as we see on my chart 145, he agreed one time. You answer on the violation of 1 Corinthians 7, he has *no right to another wife*. What will he have to do? "No right to wife number two." And we were discussing this very passage, this very matter. Well, if he has no right to her, he has got to *give her up*, and I suppose remain celibate. My, what a doctrine of demons! No mercy! And he remembers sin when God forgives it! So, he contradicts himself on that.

Freeman's Answer To Violation Of 1 Cor. 7:10-11

"He has no right to another wife. What will he have to do? Well, he already had a wife. That's the wife he belongs with. He has no right to wife number two."

(Debate, 16 Jan. 1990)

-Compare Mark 6:18

145

Notice my chart 146. He said of the Christian who violates this passage and marries another, when he repents, he has *"no right"* to her. But then, if an erring Christian does that very thing, he ended up saying he *"may continue in the marriage"* in case the first alienated mate may say, "I do not want her anymore, anyway." Remember he answered that way? So, there is his trouble, and he is in *deep* trouble.

4. *"When God FORGIVES the penitent sinner, what PASSAGE*

---

1 Cor. 7:10-11
Contradictions of Error

1. If a Christian violates 1 Cor. 7:10-11 by divorcing his mate and marrying another, when he repents, what must he do? (My chart #141)

   FREEMAN: "He has no right to wife #2" (16 Jan. 1990)

2. If an erring Christian in a second marriage following a divorce not for fornication desires to be acceptable to God, he:

   FREEMAN: "May continue in the marriage" (18 Jan. 1990, answer to my question 4)

146

teaches that He removes the temporal consequences?" And I gave him the case of the murderer, and the convicted thief, and the gambler, and the adulterer, and he said, "Well, the Bible does not teach that there are temporal consequences." Let's see my chart 286. Let's see if it does or not. He could not find the passage, could not imagine where it is from Genesis to Revelation. No temporal consequence to sin. Why, my friend, the *converted murderer* does not escape the death penalty, and Paul said that I do not refuse to die if I have done anything worthy of death. Why didn't he say, "You people ought to learn that God does not require a death penalty, and you do not have any right to put me to death anyway because my sins are forgiven"? The *convicted thief* admitted that he was receiving his due reward and Jesus said that man shall be with me in Paradise. Now, there is a man facing the temporal consequence, and when he was forgiven, he was not removed from the cross. There is where the Bible teaches it! He does not know where the Bible teaches it, but all of you do. The converted prodigal cannot get his money back. *The converted adulterer is not free to marry another or to continue in an adulterous marriage.* Yes sir, there are temporal consequences.

FORGIVENESS NOT REMOVE TEMPORAL CONSEQUENCES

1. **Converted Murderer Not Escape Death Penalty (Acts 25:11)**
2. **Convicted Thief Not Escape "Due Reward" (Lk. 23:40-43)**
3. **Converted Prodigal Not Regain Money Wasted Gambling (Lk 15:13)**
4. **Converted Adulterer Not Free To Marry Another Or Continue Adulterous Marriage (Matt 19:9)**

286

---

5. *"Jack Freeman believes that if the events reflected in Mark 6 happened TODAY, the marriage of Herod and Herodias would BECOME lawful if Philip would say he put her away."* Well, he said, but it was not lawful *then* and he went back to that approach. But I said TODAY! The question said *today!* Now, let's see my chart 243. And he said, "Why don't you go to Acts 2?" *That is what my question asked!* My question asked him to go to Acts 2, the covenant we are under, my friend. That is what I am asking him, and *what about a case like that?* Well, brother Lovelady can whisper the answer to you. He has answered it in the *Smith-Lovelady Debate,* quote: "How long is he guilty? Until his first mate says, 'I don't want to be bound to that adulterous partner.' That is when that man stops committing adultery."

Now then, notice the sequence. *Today,* brother Freeman. Do not get up here and tell about some time before this covenant. Now, *today,* Mr. Herodias leaves, Mrs. *Herodias, rather, leaves Philip,* goes down, and Herod marries her. There is the *adultery.* Philip says, out of the mouth of Lovelady, "I do not want to be bound to that adulterous partner." Now, as to Herod and Herodias, what about them? What about them? When you want to answer that question again, call for my chart 243 and you will have your answer out of the very pen of your own chart man. He said the

> **LOVELADY ON SIN OF ADULTERY**
> (Matthew 5:32; Matthew 19:9)
> *"HOW LONG IS HE GUILTY? Until his first mate says, 'I DON'T WANT TO BE BOUND TO THAT ADULTEROUS PARTNER.' That is when that man stops committing adultery."*
> (Glen Lovelady in Smith-Lovelady Debate. p.69)
>
> **CONCLUSION**
> 1. Herodias leaves Philip
> 2. Herod marries her -- adultery
> 3. Philip says, "I don't want to be bound to that adulterous partner."
> 4. Herod and Herodias -- marriage becomes lawful
> 243

marriage becomes *lawful.* What do you say? Maybe you two would like to debate it. The fact is you believe just what he believes and you are doing your best to hide it from this audience. The truth will come out. Yes, it will.

Now then, we notice his presentation tonight. He defined the proposition. I do not notice any objection there. He said he was not defending premeditated murder or fornication. But, my friend, the doctrine that he is teaching will lead people to commit fornication to get out of their marriage. He is not going to refuse to marry them. He is not defending homosexuals he said. *Well, I want the specific example where somebody got out of that.* That is the only way you seem to understand the subject. Give *a specific example* of someone getting out of it.

And then he said death does not remove the guilt, but it removes the constraint of law. It is a one *flesh* relationship, and in Romans 7 death removes the restraint of law. And he said, you can marry without *"living in,"* and then he said, an *"adulterous"* relationship. Yes, you did. I wrote it down exactly. Thank you. Thank you, brother Freeman.

Now, he has his chart number 1, "doctrine of demons." And you will remember we have seen that one over and over again, from 1 Timothy 4, and we want to respond to this matter with my chart 316. Now, he will not let the woman in 1 Corinthians 7:11 marry another, so *he* has got the "doctrine of demons." *But, do we forbid to marry? No, everyone has a right to marry and a responsibility to obey God's law.* But, my friend, we object to this matter of committing fornication, and then getting out of that marriage, and doing it again and again and again! That is what it is all about, exactly what it is all about.

Then, he has his charts 17 and 18, how do you know? He says he knows that his wife has had no sex change. I commend him for the fact that he does know, and it proves the fact that *you can know!* You learn God's will, and you know what is right, and you do it. *You can know!* Yet, we hear all this business about you *cannot* know. Matthew 19:9 says you *can* know!

Now, we turn to my charts 326 and 326-A, and this will answer his charts 1, 17, 18, 47, 48, and 28. My opponent *opposes himself* on all of those charts. What about these cases? Here is the *homosexual* and you are forbidding him *that marriage*. This is "the doctrine of demons," brother. And *mercy* ought to remit the sin, but you *remember* the sin. When Paul preached to aliens, where did he ever say leave husband or wife to be saved? I want a specific verse where he told the homosexual to get out of that relationship.

And *you* demand the impossible. "How do you know?" They might have had a *sex change,* and you are married to one in that condition. Now, what about *polygamy?* Same problem. *Unscripturally divorced?* Same problem. *Unscripturally remarried?* Same problem. So, you just answer your own charts! You have got the problem, brother Freeman.

Now, he said that when people come to be a member of the church, do we

---

Do We Forbid "To Marry"?

1. NO! Everyone has a right to marry and a responsibility to obey God's marriage law (Gen. 2:24; Matt. 19:9; 1 Cor. 7:2).

2. God's law forbids divorce without cause of fornication and marriage to another again and again and again (Matt. 19:9).

3. God's law forbids a man to commit adultery, be divorced, marry another and do it all over again and again and again (Matt. 19:9).

316

**DEMANDING THE IMPOSSIBLE
HOW CAN YOU KNOW:**

1. THAT THE ONE YOU MARRY WAS NEVER MARRIED BEFORE?
2. THAT THE ONE YOU MARRY WAS NOT DIVORCED BECAUSE OF ADULTERY?
3. THAT THE ONE YOU MARRY DIVORCED A PREVIOUS SPOUSE ON GROUNDS OF FORNICATION?
4. THAT THE ONE YOU MARRY WAS NOT DIVORCED FOR A CAUSE OTHER THAN FORNICATION?
5. THAT THE CHRISTIAN YOU MARRY WAS NOT DIVORCED BY AN UNBELIEVER?
6. THAT THE ONE YOU BAPTIZE AND FELLOWSHIP AS A FAITHFUL CHRISTIAN AND FOR WHOM YOU PERFORM A MARRIAGE CEREMONY WAS NOT PREVIOUSLY DIVORCED FOR FORNICATION?

17

Fourth Evening: Halbrook's First Negative 255

> **Opponent Opposes Himself
> (2 Tim. 2:25)**
>
> **What About These Cases?**
>
> 1. "Doctrine of Devils" if forbid marriage.   Homosexual (1 Cor. 6:9-11)
> 2. "Mercy" remits sin, but "opponent remembers sin."   Polygamy (Gen. 2:24)
> 3. "Paul preached to aliens," "not say leave husband or wife to be saved."   Unscripturally divorced (Matt. 5:28; 19:9; 1 Cor. 7:10-11, 15)
> 4. "Demands impossible," "how do you know?"   Unscripturally remarried (Mk. 6:17-18; Mt. 5:28; 19:9)
>
> 326

inquire about their marriage? Listen carefully and listen closely. *Not unless something creates a reason to ask.* But, brother Freeman, sound teaching brings it out — you know, that doctrine that is new in Las Vegas. When you preach *Matthew 19:9* and preach it like the Book has it, then they will come to you and say, "Look here, we are in that case." Then, you sit down, and godly elders deal with them and help, help them to work it out and save their soul. Now, when people come to us and they say they have been baptized, *"how do you know?"* Are you going to get the court records to see if they were baptized, or ask brother Freeman to see if they were baptized? No, we preach sound doctrine, and that solves it.

Then, his chart 30.

> **Opponent Opposes Himself**
>
> *"If you've got another man's wife, you've got to give her back" (Freeman, Debate, 16 Jan. 1990)*
>
> 1. "Doctrine of Devils" if forbid marriage.
> 2. "Mercy" remits sin, but "opponent remembers sin."
> 3. "Paul preached to aliens," "not say leave husband or wife to be saved."
> 4. "Demands impossible," "how do you know?"
>
> 326 A

Alright, on his charts 30 and 31, he again talks about this matter of Matthew 19:9, trying to show that the man who puts away his wife for fornication has no wife. And, he is trying to show then that the one who has been put away has no husband. But, *they are under constraint of law!* We have already covered that.

On his chart 31, he deals with 1 Corinthians 7:27 again. 1 Corinthians 7:27, remember that? And so, if you are loosed from a wife, you can marry, you have not sinned. Let's see my chart 191 [page 257] now. Alright, now notice, we clarify the passage by its context. 2 Corinthians 9:1 speaks of "ministering to the saints," and verse 13, said, "them and all." Two groups of saints: *"them,"* the

NOUN & PRONOUN IN MATT. 19:9

WHOSOEVER SHALL PUT AWAY HIS <u>WIFE</u>, EXCEPT IT BE FOR FORNICATION,
WHOSO MARRIETH <u>HER</u> WHICH IS PUT AWAY DOTH COMMIT ADULTERY.

MAN WHO PUTS AWAY HIS WIFE FOR FORNICATION HAS NO WIFE,

<u>CAN REMARRY.</u>

WOMAN PUT AWAY FOR FORNICATION HAS NO HUSBAND,

<u>CAN REMARRY.</u>

30

NOUN & PRONOUN IN MATT. 19:9
(Cont)

<u>GOD SAYS</u> --- "ART THOU LOOSED FROM A WIFE.."
1 COR. 7:27-28

"...IF THOU MARRY, <u>THOU HAST NOT SINNED</u>".
MAN WHO PUTS AWAY HIS WIFE FOR FORNICATION HAS NO WIFE,

MY OPPONENT SAYS --- "IF HE MARRIES HE SINS"

GOD vs. HALBROOK

31

Fourth Evening: Halbrook's First Negative   257

> **1 Corinthians 7:27**
> **Clarified By Context**
>
> | 2 Corinthians 9:1 | 1 Corinthians 7:25 |
> | Concerning Ministering To The Saints: | Concerning Virgins (Never Married): |
> |---|---|
> | Vs. 13 Them & All = Two Groups of Saints | Vv. 27-28 Loosed & Virgins = Two Groups Never Married |
> | 1. Them - Jerusalem Saints | 1. Free - Males Never Married |
> | 2. All - Other Saints | 2. Virgins - Females Never Married |
>
> 191

Jerusalem saints, and *"all,"* other saints. In 1 Corinthians 7:25 he said in setting the context, *"concerning virgins,"* referring to those never married. In verses 27-28 you have the *"loosed"* and the *"virgins"* — *two groups never married.* Context! These free, these loosed ones, *the males never married* match these virgins, *females never married.* Now, that is the truth about it, and that answers his chart.

Let's consider his chart 25 now, and we will notice 231 to follow it. Does repentance demand that we stop the sin, and then that you can never marry and so on? Well, look at my chart 231. It depends upon the constraint of law. It also involves this matter that if you are in an unscriptural organization, a shoplifting ring, or an unscriptural marriage, *repentance* means that you have to *get out of it*. Whether you can ever have a scriptural marriage or not will depend on whether you are

> | **DOES REPENTANCE DEMAND:** | |
> |---|---|
> | **STOP SIN?** | **LIVE REST OF LIFE W/O DOING THAT WHICH IS RIGHT?** |
> | WORSHIP IDOLS | WORSHIP THE TRUE GOD 1 THES. 1:9 |
> | FORNICATION | SEX WITHIN MARRIAGE 1 COR. 7:2 |
> | STEALING MONEY | HONEST LABOR EPH. 4:28 |
> | ADULTERY | MARRIAGE HEB. 13:4 |
> | HAVE ANOTHER MAN'S WIFE | HAVE OWN WIFE 1 COR. 7:2 |
> | **YES!** | **NO!** |
>
> 25

a put-away fornicator. It can depend upon whether your other mate dies, or whether there can be reconciliation. There can be any number of circumstances there. But when you are in an unscriptural situation, an unauthorized marriage, then, my friend, *repentance* means you must *get out of it*.

And then he had charts 43 and 44 that had the same argument. This thing about, if you are married to a sinner, does it make you a sinner; married to a thief, does it make you a thief; married to an idolater, does it make you an idolater;

married to an adulterer, does it make you an adulterer? Now, listen. If you are married to a fornicator, it does not make you one. That is true in some circumstances. If the two of you though are *married in an unlawful, unscriptural marriage*, then you are *both living in the same sin!* Now listen, "Whoever marries an idolater, commits idolatry." If the Bible said that, and you *repented,* would you have to *get out* of the marriage? Yes. And so when the Bible says, "Whoso marrieth her which is put away doth commit adultery," and if you marry her, then what must you do if you *repent?* You can see the point.

> ### Cease Sin - Leave Situation
> "Works meet for repentance" (Acts 26:20)
> "Washed, sanctified, justified" (1 Cor. 6:9-11)
>
> | CEASE | LEAVE |
> |---|---|
> | 1. Act of unlawful taking life | Unscr. Organization (Mafia) |
> | 2. Act of unlawful taking goods | Shoplifting Ring |
> | 3. Act of unlawful sexual intercourse | Unscriptural Marriage |
> | 4. Act of unlawful taking gain | Casino Operation |
>
> 231

Now, we consider his chart 59 about the man who steals, and he is to return the wife. This is where he was responding to our chart 235. He said the man who stole her can have a scriptural mate. That might be the case if he is not a put-away fornicator, brother Freeman. Let's look at our chart 235. Now, notice that the offended party could concede a watch or a car, but *cannot give his wife the right to marry another!* But according to your helper on the charts there [Glen W. Lovelady], you see, all that required is for the offended party to say, *"I do not want them anymore."* It will not work. It might work with a car or a watch, but it will not work with a wife. You do *not* have authority to do it, my friend, you do *not* have authority to do it.

A MAN STEALS

ANOTHER'S WIFE   ANOTHER'S WATCH   ANOTHER'S CAR

REPENTANCE DEMANDS: RETURN THE WIFE, THE WATCH, THE CAR

AND NEVER HAVE:
YOUR OWN WIFE----YOUR OWN WATCH----YOUR OWN CAR
(IF THIS IS TRUE)   (SO IS THIS)   (AND THIS)

BUT

IF AFTER REPENTANCE, A MAN CAN HAVE HIS OWN WATCH AND HIS OWN CAR; HE CAN HAVE <u>HIS OWN WIFE</u>!

59

How Do You Show Repentance?

If You Steal A Man's Watch — You Give It Back!

If You Steal A Man's Car — You Give It Back!

If You Steal A Man's Wife — You Keep Her?

Note: The offended party may concede a watch or car but can't give his wife the right to marry another (Acts 5:4; Matt. 5:32; 19:9)

235

And then, as to his charts 47 and 48, I have already answered on 326-A. He has got the problem.

Then we have his charts 32 and 34 about the one put away due to fornication. On charts 32 and 34, he uses there 1 Corinthians 7:2 and 7:27-28. Well, just go ahead and give us our chart 83. As to these people who are put away due to fornication, it depends on the circumstances — there are *different cases*. A man could be married, yet with another man's wife. That is *adultery*. A man divorces his wife and marries another, *adultery*. The put-away fornicator remarries, *marries another*, that is; my friend, that is *adultery*. The Lord defined it that way. "The remarriage of a man after divorcing his wife, or the remarrying of the divorced woman, is tantamount to adultery." That is the truth about it! That is the truth about it!

Then, look at my chart 122-A. He had used

Cases of Adultery

1. **Simplest Case:** A married man with another man's wife (John 8:4)
2. **Sin Upon Sin:** A man divorces his wife and marries another (Matt. 19:9)
3. **Sin Upon Sin:** The put-away fornicator remarries (Matt. 5:32 read with exception)

"The remarriage of a man after divorcing his wife, or the remarrying of the divorced woman, is tantamount to adultery (Matt. 5:32; 19:9)" [Kittel, TDNT, IV:733]

Tantamount = "Equivalent in value, significance, or effect" (Webster's 7th New Colleg. Dict.)

Effect = Gal. 5:19-21 (such things); Heb. 13:4

83

1 Corinthians 7:2, 27-28. That is on his chart 34. I am covering each and every chart. I remind you of the context of that passage. Notice the context. "Let every man have his *own* wife," does not mean, "Wreck your marriage, throw away your *own* wife by fornication, and then get *another.*" And in verses 27-28, we read of *a man* "loosed from a wife," free, never married, and *a virgin,* free never married; they may marry. It does not refer to a man who is a divorced fornicator, that he may marry a woman who is a divorced fornicator. No, indeed, it does *not*.

No, it does not.

Now then, we want to notice our 346 series. We have covered his charts, answered his arguments one by one. On Tuesday night I used 45 charts, and he called for only 13 of them. Now, notice our 346, the Elijah chart. In 1 Kings 18, Elijah probed and exposed the weaknesses of error — maybe your God is asleep or on a trip. He was showing the bloopers and the blunders and the weaknesses of error. I want to preface it by saying that *the weakness is not in this man. The weakness is in error.* When he has truth, he can be strong and be powerful. But he has error on this proposition.

My friend, *he never did admit he wrote the article.* He called me a liar and never made an apology. And he will not confess that same error at Las Vegas. Furthermore, as to *Mark 6,* he does not know what it has to do with this debate. *Except, if and only if* — he made such a mess out of that, I was recommended to give him five more minutes of my time to explain it again. And, *he cannot find the guilty fornicator in 1 Corinthians 7,* but he keeps using that passage over and over.

Volume II. Now, he says *you cannot know,* you cannot know. Well, why did the Lord say in Matthew 19:9 you could put her away for fornication? Apparently, you *can know* something!

He says *he knows* about his wife. Why does he know? He made a proper

Does 1 Cor. 7 Authorize The Put-Away Fornicator To Marry Another?

Text Says This:	Not This:
Vs. 2 "Every man have his own wife"	Every man who wrecks his marriage & throws away his own wife by fornication or unscriptural divorce, gets another wife!
Vs. 9 "Unmarried...widows... better to marry than to burn"	Unscripturally divorced & put-away fornicator... better to commit adultery than fornication!
Vv. 27-28 A man "loosed from a wife" (free, never married) and "a virgin" (free, never married) may marry.	A man unscripturally divorced or a divorced fornicator may marry a woman in the same condition!

122 A

THE ELIJAH CHART (1 Kings 18:27)
EXPOSING THE WEAKNESS OF ERROR
Bloopers and Blunders of the Weak

Volume I

1. Not admit wrote article
2. Called me a liar - no apology
3. Not confess the error at Las Vegas
4. Mark 6:17-18 not have anything to do with this debate
5. Except - if and only if
6. Can't find guilty fornicator in 1 Cor. 7

346

Volume II

7. Can't know: But Matthew 19:9
8. Can't know: What about polygamy, married 100 times, sex change marriage?
9. Newspaper ad: imply I did/did not want debate?
10. Deut. 24 allows divorce if burn biscuits
11. Matthew 19:9 "New" in Las Vegas
12. I lead people to hell by teaching Matthew 19
13. Didn't remember how to put questions in record
14. I put ONLY in Matthew 19 (except; only sing?)
15. Hasn't found fornicator can "marry another" in 1 Cor. 7

346 A

investigation, both of her upbringing and of the Bible teaching. And I commend him for being in a scriptural marriage. I assume that he is, from that remark, and I commend him for it. Apparently, he *can* know, and then *cannot* know.

If we *cannot* know, well then, what about *polygamy, married a hundred times, sex change marriage?* Well, my friend, maybe you are in that situation, and you just cannot know. Sound teaching will help you to know. And an honest heart can know. The Bible says God is not far from everyone of us. Don't you remember that, brother Freeman? There is a God who cares for people who are trying to get to heaven. And if they are in a mess like that, the God of heaven opens doors and makes opportunities for people to learn the truth. Just like He has opened the door for this community to hear this teaching, and even maybe for you to learn the truth, who knows?

And then, concerning *the newspaper ad*. He tried to explain that it did not really imply that I did not want to debate. Explain it again. I may just give him five more minutes on that too. Did it imply that I *did* want to debate? And when you were going to make it bigger and bigger and bigger each time, I guess it meant I wanted to debate more and more and more. Explain it again.

Deuteronomy 24 allows divorce if you burn the biscuits. Folks, he said that is what that pas-

Volume III

16. Won't forbid food to lazy
17. His answer on 1 Cor. 7:11, no mercy
18. Ditto - Doctrine of demons
19. Ditto - Penance
20: Ditto - No mercy
21. Ditto - Adulterous relationship
22. Ditto - No one told to leave
23. Ditto - No one told to remain unmarried
24. Ditto - Changed answer (can remain)

346 B

sage taught. He is too liberal for Christ and too liberal for Moses! It was for shameful indecency. Matthew 19:9 is *"new"* in Las Vegas — I lead people to hell by teaching it. He does not remember how to put a question in the record Monday night.

And then he said that I said put *"only"* in Matthew 19. No, sir, *the Lord* said, "Except it be for fornication." If and only if, my friend. And when the Bible says, "Sing," does brother Freeman put *"only"* in there? He has not found the fornicator marrying another in 1 Corinthians 7.

Volume III. He will not forbid food to the lazy. The Bible says he better. On *1 Corinthians 7:11* he said one time you have no right to wife number two. Why, that is *no mercy!* Why don't you show mercy? That is *the doctrine of demons*. You are demanding *penance* of that poor woman. How can she fulfill her sexual urge? Come up and tell us how she can do it. How will she ever do it? Oh, why are you demanding penance, no mercy? You have got them living in an adulterous relationship like you said tonight, but supposedly he does not believe there is any such thing. And then, no one was told to *leave*. No one was told to *remain unmarried*. But that passage does it. And he agreed with it one time, but then he changed his answer and said you can remain [i.e. in a second marriage].

Volume IV

25. Can be married 2 or 100 times!!!
26. 1 Cor. 7:15 says "marry another"
27. Thayer on 1 Cor. 7:15 says "marriage"
28. 1 Cor. 7:15 - Catholic Catechism
29. Ditto - 2 marriage laws
30. Ditto - cf. slaves (v.23)
31. Ditto - Entrance wedge
32. Ditto - Opens flood gates

346 C

Volume IV. You can be married two or 200 times, he said. That is right, and when you open the door to the *two*, you open the door to the *100*, my friend.

Now, we want to give him "The Blunder of the Weak Award." On *1 Corinthians 7:15,* he said it all week out in Las Vegas, he said it all week here, that it says *marry another*. You know it is not there, I know it is not there, but it is a secret to him! And then he claimed that *Thayer* on 1 Corinthians 7:15 says marriage in defining bondage, and we exposed the weakness of that. It is *not* so.

And then he has the same position as the *Catholic Catechism* on that passage. He said he did not know what a "Pauline privilege" is. Listen, a privilege is a right to do something. And Paul wrote the passage, and they are

Volume V

33. Ignores context - 1 Cor. 7:2, 8, 11, 15, 27
34. Commentaries - Both sides of fence
35. Thayer - On "loosed" (LUSIS) in 1 Cor. 7:27
36. Rom. 7:2-3 & 1 Cor. 7:27 - same word for "loosed"
37. Rev. 2:22 - "Except"
38. Death penalty not necessary for murder
39. Denied his proposition on Mark 6:17-18!!!

346 D

saying Paul meant that *if you are deserted, you can marry another*. Now, do you believe it? Want to nod your head? Yes, you *do* believe what the Catholic Catechism teaches, and that has got you into *two marriage laws!*

And, if you can understand *verse 23*, you can understand *verse 15*. And, this is the entrance wedge which opens the flood gates to more and more divorce and remarriage.

Volume V. He ignores the *context* in 1 Corinthians 7. He is on *both* sides of the fence about commentaries. He abused *Thayer* on loosed, *lusis,* in 1 Corinthians 7:27a, and said *Thayer* was defining loosed in part b, which *Thayer* was not. *Thayer* speaks of those who are single and those never married when he defines *luo* down there, in part b. On *Romans 7* and *1 Corinthians 7,* he says they use the same word for loosed; there is not a word of truth in it.

God -vs- Satan

1. If you eat, "surely die" (Gen. 2:17)	1. If you eat, "NOT surely die" (Gen. 3:4)
2. Believe & "Baptized shall be saved" (Mk. 16:16)	2. Believe and NOT baptized shall be saved
3. "Whoso marrieth her which is put away doth commit adultery" (Matt. 5:32; 19:9)	3. Whoso marrieth her which is put away doth NOT commit adultery

108

On *Revelation 2:22,* he introduced it, and we have not heard a word about it in a long time. It was supposed to show that "except" can go from one clause to another. Then, he said the *death penalty* is not necessary for murder. And then he denied his proposition on *Mark 6:17-18.*

Now, my friend, you remember the difference between us. God said whoever marries her that is put away *commits adultery*. He says whoever marries her which is put away doth *not commit adultery*. That is the difference between us tonight. Thank you for your good attention. Thank you, brother Freeman.

Fourth Evening
Freeman's Second Affirmative

Brethren moderators, brother Halbrook, I would like to say in the very beginning that Ron has said that I have not called for some of his charts in debates. Did you notice, right at the end, how he answers mine? I could answer all of his charts with one word. That is how he answered thirteen of mine. Ditto. Ditto. Ditto. That takes care of your charts, brother Halbrook.

I want to refer to something you said within some of the questions you answered. Let's look at your chart number 101. I asked, *"When a man is divorced by his wife for fornication and has not remarried, is he bound to a wife or loosed from a wife?"* Well, you said the marriage bond is released, but he is *still under constraint of law*. I would like for you to tell us, constraint of law to *what?* Bound by law to what? I asked that question last night. You have not answered it yet. This person who is divorced is under constraint of law, you said, *still under constraint of law,* but, bound by the law to what? You never have told us what the law bound him to. Now, it cannot be the mate that put him away for fornication. You have admitted that he is not bound to her. Well, to what is he bound? Be very interesting! Now, if you say the marriage law of Genesis 2:24 or Matthew 19:9, that applies to married people. You say this man is not married. He does not have a wife.

Well, he said, I just cannot give him the passage that says where people *lived in* or *walked in adultery*. I read it. I will read it to you again. Now, these words were used, brother Halbrook. You insist that we have got to have that express language. Open your Bible and read with me. Colossians chapter three, beginning with verse five, "Mortify therefore your members which are upon the earth; fornication, uncleanness, inordinate affection, evil concupiscence, and covetous-

---

Divorced People Remain Under Constraint Of Law

1. Deut. 24:1-4 Divorce wife but can't have her back after her 2nd marriage
2. Deut. 24:1-4 Divorcee marry another but then can't ever return to 1st mate
3. Lev. 21:7, 13-14 Divorcee free from marriage but can't marry a priest
4. Matt. 5:32; 19:9 Pure divorce impure and marry another (new mate can't be one put away for fornication or other cause)
5. Matt. 5:32; 19:9 Not authorize a put-away person (whether put away for fornication or other cause) to marry another
6. 1 Cor. 7:10-11 If 2 Christians divorce, must remain unmarried or reconcile
7. 1 Cor. 7:12-15 Believer not give up Christ to keep unbeliever (no authority for either to marry another)

CONCLUSION:
1. Unscriptural divorce releases neither party from marriage!
2. Scriptural divorce releases both parties from marriage, but not from the constraint of the law!

101

ness, which is idolatry: for which things' sake the wrath of God cometh on the children of disobedience: in the which ye also walked some time when ye lived in them." *Walking* and *living,* and he said it is not there. It is there. Now, he knows, whether it is there or not, that he is the one that brought this up, "You are living in adultery." And I was using this passage to show what living in adultery means. But, he brings this up, because he cannot give a specific passage for what I asked him. Now, I have given book, chapter, and verse for what he has asked me, including this. But, he cannot give book, chapter, and verse, like where did the Apostles ever tell a man to *leave* his wife "before I will baptize you," or, "You will have to *leave* your wife to get to heaven," or, "You will have to remain single the rest of your life in order to get to heaven." He has not come up with that, yet.

Incidentally, our proposition is not about the *guilty* person, as you call it. It is simply about a person who *was guilty*. He may be guilty, and may have been then, of many other things besides fornication, but I asked you what about this man, what is his spiritual state when he is raised from the waters of baptism? You said he has no sin. No sin. Well, tell us then, if he has no sin, is not guilty of anything, can he remarry? *He still says no*. So, the phrase guilty party is just a prejudicial phrase. You are just a mean old fornicator, we are going to get back at him, we are going to show him, we will never let him marry again. Well, that is his attitude, not God's. Now, why are we going to emphasize the guilt, when he says that he was without sins when he was raised from baptism? But, he still comes up with the same end, *he cannot marry* anyway. It does not make any difference to him whether he is innocent or guilty. He cannot marry. That is exactly what it comes back to.

Let's notice here his chart number 60 [text, Matt. 5:32]. This just shows a text, Matthew 5:32, and Ron you said this, we have your exact words. *"I say unto you, That whosoever shall put away his wife, saving for the cause of fornication, causeth her to commit adultery: and whosoever shall marry her that is divorced, committeth adultery."* And you said "He does not have the right to do anything." He does not have the right to do anything. Maybe you were carried away, but that is your exact statement. "He does not have the right to do anything." If he puts away his wife, he did not have the right. If he keeps her, he does not have the right. If he treats her good, he does not have the right. If he treats her mean, he does not have the right. Well, maybe he made it in the heat of the debate, I do not know.

On temporal consequences, let's look at his chart number 243. I would like to ask you, what is New Testament law in regard to having *your brother's wife?* What is the law in Texas in regard to intermarriage? Now, there was a case in Nevada not long ago where a man was arrested, put in jail, because he had fathered children by his own daughter. I do not know in Nevada how close you can get, to third cousin or whatever, I do not know. What is the New Testament law in regard to what you might call incest? The important thing is, we are dealing with the fact, we know what the New Testament law is in regard to having your brother's wife.

Now, if we are going to get Herod and Herodias over here on this side of Acts 2, *he could not have her because she was another man's wife*. The fornicator in 1 Corinthians 5 could not have *his father's* wife; Herod could not have *his brother's* wife. But both were permitted to have *their own* wives. Now, my opponent has a hard time acknowledging that. He will not allow some to have their own wives. He admits it. Some women cannot have *their own* husbands. And he will tell you *who* in no uncertain terms. Now, you are not allowed to have her, but he says, *"I want an example of those getting out of homosexuality."*

Let me give you one. I have already given it. You paid no attention to it. You said ditto, ditto, ditto. That is how he answers it. I want you to read about these who had been homosexuals. Paul is reminding them that they had been. 1 Corinthians 6, beginning with verse 9: "Know ye not that the unrighteous shall not inherit the kingdom of God? Be not deceived: neither fornicators, nor idolaters, nor adulterers, nor effeminate," — other translations show, use plainly, *homosexuals* — "nor abusers of themselves with mankind, nor thieves, nor covetous, nor drunkards, nor revilers, nor extortioners, shall inherit the kingdom of God. And such were some of you" — *find me a passage where it says how they got out of it* — "but ye are washed, but ye are sanctified, but ye are justified." That is how they *got out of it,* by receiving God's forgiveness.

We used the chart showing 1 Corinthians 6 and 1 Corinthians 7. Now, as to this homosexual, even if he were in the eyes of civil law legally married to another homosexual, it was not a marriage in God's sight. But now, one of them obeys the gospel. Oh, he cannot even legally be married to that homosexual.

LOVELADY ON SIN OF ADULTERY
(Matthew 5:32; Matthew 19:9)
"HOW LONG IS HE GUILTY? Until his first mate says, 'I DON'T WANT TO BE BOUND TO THAT ADULTEROUS PARTNER.' That is when that man stops committing adultery."
(Glen Lovelady in Smith-Lovelady Debate. p.69)

CONCLUSION
1. Herodias leaves Philip
2. Herod marries her -- adultery
3. Philip says, "I don't want to be bound to that adulterous partner."
4. Herod and Herodias -- marriage becomes lawful

243

Fourth Evening: Freeman's Second Affirmative

What is he going to do? He has sexual desires. He comes to the phone and says, "Now Paul, I have given up homosexuality, but I have sexual urges. I want to know what God tells me to do to avoid fornication." Brother Halbrook says, "No way, brother, not by God's way." God has a way for you. Paul speaks in 1 Corinthians 7:2. He is still talking about those married people who had been homosexual, who had been lesbians, who had been idolaters before. But they no longer were, and he says, "In order to avoid fornication, let every man have his own wife, and let every woman have her own husband." Now, that is what God says about it. That ought to be simple enough. *I have never taught that a person had the right to live in homosexuality or any other sin.*

Now, Jesus did not use trick questions. *When he says, "By whose authority?" there is no trick to that.* They knew it, but they did not want to answer because they have the reason. They gave the reason. If we answer this way, then we are in trouble with the people, because they think this person is a great man, Jesus. If we do not answer that, we are in trouble with someone else. Well, if you want to stay out of trouble with the people, that may be the way to move, but my concern is staying out of trouble with God. I am not concerned with staying out of trouble with brother Halbrook. He will write questions, and give you three or four choices, and none of them may be a scriptural answer, so I write down my own answer. What the Bible says. He does not like it. Because he writes these down, he thinks you have to chose one or the other.

Now, Jesus asked the questions where you had to chose one or the other. One was right. You know that. Was the baptism of John from heaven or men? Let me ask you, "Was the doctrine of celibacy from heaven or man?" That is the equivalent of what Jesus asked, a simple question, not a trick question. Is the doctrine of forbidding to marry from heaven or men? Jesus never taught it. The Apostles never taught it. My opponent teaches it. That is why Paul was guided by the Holy Spirit to call it the doctrine of devils.

Let's go back to my chart 34 and continue.

THE "PUT AWAY" FORNICATOR

FREE TO MARRY

1. HE HAS A WIFE (BOUND TO A WIFE)
   OR
2. HE DOES NOT HAVE A WIFE (LOOSED FROM A WIFE)
3. WHAT IS THE MARITAL STATE OF THE PUT AWAY FORNICATOR?

   A. DOES HE HAVE A WIFE? IF SO WHO IS SHE? WHERE IS SHE?
   B. IF HE STILL HAS A WIFE, THE WIFE WHO PUTS HIM AWAY FOR FORNICATION CANNOT REMARRY, FOR SHE HAS A HUSBAND.
   C. THE PUT AWAY FORNICATOR DOES NOT HAVE A WIFE.
   　1) HOW SHALL HE AVOID FORNICATION?
   　　* 1 COR. 7:2 -- HAVE HIS OWN WIFE
   　2) DOES HE HAVE DIVINE PERMISSION TO REMARRY?
   　　*1 COR. 7:27-28 -- "ART THOU LOOSED FROM A WIFE..."
   　　IF THOU MARRY, THOU HAST NOT SINNED."

34

And, brother Halbrook, if you do not want to deal with these, just leave them in the box and say, "Ditto."

Here, we are dealing with *the put-away fornicator*. He is *free to marry*. Why? He has a wife or he does not. Well, we know, and we both admit, he does not have a wife. What is his marital state? He does not have a wife. If he does, who is she, where is she? If he still has a wife, then the wife who put him away still has a husband. So, if she remarries, she would commit fornication. The put-away fornicator does not have a wife. How shall he avoid fornication? He may have his own wife.

Does he have divine permission to remarry? 1 Corinthians 7:27-28. Again, I want you to read that. My opponent said no one there but virgins, no one but a virgin. He said this in the debate in North Las Vegas. I do not know how anyone can reach this conclusion. *Verse 27:* "Art thou bound to a wife, seek not to be loosed." Were those virgins? Here is a man bound to a wife, who is commanded, "Don't you seek to be loosed." It does not sound like virgins to me, either the man or his wife. He said this husband and wife are virgins, all that Paul talks about from verses 25 to 28 are virgins. That is not so. In verse 27 he talks about married people, those who are bound, a man who is bound to a wife. Now, if nowhere else he does in that paragraph, he does there. Are you bound to a wife? *He is not talking to a virgin*. Now, if you are a virgin bound to a wife, or if you are a virgin bound to a husband, it is not what he is talking about. He is talking about married people, not virgins.

Let's go to my chart number 35 on the put-away fornicator. Halbrook says he cannot have a wife to avoid fornication. He cannot even marry, though loosed from a wife. If Halbrook is right, God is wrong. If God is right, Halbrook is wrong. I asked you a simple question, not a trick question. Who knows more about the right of a man to marry than God? Who knows more about this right than God? I do not. Halbrook does not, either.

Let's continue next with my chart 37 on the

THE "PUT AWAY" FORNICATOR
(Cont)

BUT HALBROOK SAYS:

HE CANNOT HAVE A WIFE TO AVOID FORNICATION.
HE CANNOT MARRY EVEN THOUGH LOOSED FROM A WIFE.

IF HALBROOK IS RIGHT, GOD IS WRONG.
IF GOD IS RIGHT, HALBROOK IS WRONG.

WHO KNOWS MORE ABOUT THE RIGHT OF MAN TO MARRY?

35

PUT AWAY
(Cont)

If the husband dies w/o divorcing his wife who is guilty of adultery, she may scripturally remarry, Rom. 7:2-3
But she is still guilty of adultery and will be until GOD forgives her.
The man who marries her will NOT be living in adultery.

(But she will be)

The marriage IS NOT adulterous.

37

same thought. *If the husband dies without divorcing his wife who is guilty of adultery, she may scripturally remarry,* and brother Halbrook admitted it. She is still guilty of adultery and will be until God forgives her. *The man who marries her will not be living in adultery.* Now, he tried to say in some cases she would be, in some cases she would not. So, she could scripturally be married and you could scripturally marry her at least in some cases, he said. Here is a marriage. One walking in, living in, *guilty* of adultery, and the one married to her *innocent* of that sin. I think we need to understand that in marriages both husband and wife are guilty of sins in many cases. We are talking about, however, one particular sin and one particular right, the right to remarry. When you have committed the sin of fornication and you have been divorced on that ground, so the man who marries her will *not* be living in adultery, but *she will be.* That is how serious sin is.

My next chart, please, number 45, married to an adulteress. *Can one be married to an adulteress without the marriage being sinful?* He admits that is true. *Can one marry an adulteress without the marriage being sinful?* Of course, this is another way of saying the same question. He admits that is true. Matthew 19:9, the husband does not have to divorce his wife when she is guilty of adultery. So, that is *a right, not a command.* He also has the right to keep her. Some people have difficulty

MARRIED TO AN ADULTRESS

* CAN ONE BE <u>MARRIED TO</u> AN ADULTRESS WITHOUT THE MARRIAGE BEING SINFUL?
* <u>CAN ONE MARRY</u> AN ADULTRESS WITHOUT THE MARRIAGE BEING SINFUL?

<u>MATT 19:9</u> - HUSBAND DOES NOT HAVE TO DIVORCE HIS WIFE WHEN SHE IS GUILTY OF ADULTERY.

A. <u>A RIGHT</u> --- NOT A COMMAND
B. <u>THUS, HE CAN BE SCRIPTURALLY MARRIED TO AN ADULTRESS.</u>
C. SHE IS LIVING (GUILTY OF) IN ADULTERY, HE IS NOT.
D. <u>SHE WILL BE LIVING (GUILTY OF) IN ADULTERY UNTIL GOD FORGIVES HER.</u>
E. <u>THE MARRIAGE IS NOT AN ADULTEROUS MARRIAGE</u> AFTER SHE COMMITS ADULTERY.

45

with this. "I just could not forgive." Well, God can. But you have a right. You do not have to exercise it, but you have a right. He can scripturally be married to an adulteress. He does not have to put her away.

Well, what is wrong with being married to a fornicator or an adulterer? "Nothing," brother Halbrook says, "unless they have been divorced." It does not matter how many times they have committed a sin, if they committed it every day of their lives from the time they were physically able, that is alright, if they have never been divorced for it. If they have never been married, or if they have been married but never been divorced for it, that is fine. But once you have been divorced for that, you are doomed to celibacy for it the rest of your life. The Bible does not teach it. Again, he could scripturally be married to an adulteress. She is *living in* or *guilty of,* and we read of it in these scriptures, these passages — living in, walking in. She will be living in adultery until God forgives her. The marriage is not an adulterous marriage, then. He would have to agree with that. Because the sin is only on the part of one.

Next is my chart number 46, marriage to an adulteress, continued, Romans 7:2-3. A wife is bound by the law to her husband. Now, he said, when I made the "if and only if argument," to show how foolish, the foolish position I had placed him in, he could not understand it. He is tempted to give me five minutes. You notice he did not. Now, if he wants to give me five extra minutes tonight, I will explain it further. Notice, a wife is bound to her husband by the law as long as she lives. Now, what

---

MARRIED TO AN ADULTRESS
(Cont)

ROM. 7:2-3 -- WIFE IS BOUND TO HER HUSBAND BY THE LAW AS LONG AS HE LIVETH.

A. IF SHE COMMITS ADULTERY, HE CAN KEEP HER AS HIS WIFE.
B. SHE IS LIVING IN (GUILTY OF) ADULTERY, BUT HE IS NOT. (*THE MARRIAGE IS NOT ADULTEROUS*)
C. SHE WILL BE LIVING IN (GUILTY OF) ADULTERY UNTIL GOD FORGIVES HER.
D. IF HER HUSBAND DIES (WITHOUT DIVORCING HER), SHE CAN SCRIPTURALLY REMARRY.
E. SHE WILL STILL BE LIVING IN ADULTERY, BUT HER HUSBAND WILL NOT.
F. THE SECOND MARRIAGE IS NOT AN ADULTEROUS MARRIAGE.

46

---

does the law bind this woman to? I am going to answer his question for him, the one I asked him. He will not tell me. What does the law bind the woman to, the man to? The answer: *She is bound by the law to her husband.* The law binds her to her husband as long as she lives. Now, if she commits adultery, this is not discussed in Romans 7. But if she commits adultery, he could keep her as his wife, and brother Halbrook admits that. She is living in adultery, guilty of it, but he is not. The marriage is not adulterous. She will be *living in,* guilty of, *adultery*

Fourth Evening: Freeman's Second Affirmative

until God forgives her. If the husband dies, she is still living in adultery. His death does not remove her guilt. In the second marriage then, if he dies now without ever divorcing her, she is guilty of adultery. Brother Halbrook agrees with me, that is, if another man who is not the spouse of another can marry that woman, *she* is still living in, walking in adultery, guilty of it. *He* is not. And, he agrees with me on that. If not, he can come up and straighten it out. I do not mean to misrepresent him. I have understood him to say several times on this point we agree.

Go to my chart number 41 on God's way to avoid fornication. 1 Corinthians 7:2, *"let every man have his own wife."* Halbrook says, some cannot have their own wife. *"Let every woman have her own husband."* Halbrook says some women cannot have their own husband. 1 Corinthians 7:9, "it is better to marry than to burn." Halbrook said some will have to burn. Incidentally, he said, it is up to you to exercise self-control. You are able to do it. Let's go back and read 1 Corinthians 7:8-9.

GOD'S WAY TO AVOID FORNICATION	
GOD SAYS:	**HALBROOK SAYS:**
1 COR. 7:2 "LET EVERY MAN HAVE HIS OWN WIFE."	"SOME MEN CANNOT HAVE WIVES"
"LET EVERY WOMAN HAVE HER OWN HUSBAND"	"SOME WOMEN CANNOT HAVE HUSBANDS"
1 COR. 7:9 "IT IS BETTER TO MARRY THAN TO BURN"	"IT IS BETTER TO BURN THAN TO MARRY"
WHO IS TELLING THE TRUTH? GOD OR HALBROOK?	

41

"I say therefore to the unmarried and widows, It is good for them if they abide even as I. But if they cannot" — it does not say they will not make any effort — "if they cannot contain, let them marry: for it is better to marry than to burn." He says, "I will not let them marry. I will not let them marry. It is up to them to exercise self-control, that they can live like eunuchs, without castration." He thinks they can exercise such self-control, that they could live that kind of life. God knew, because He made man, that some would not have that much self-control and so He said, "If you cannot have that much self control, if you cannot contain, then marry. Let them marry." Halbrook says, "I will not let them do it."

Let's go back for a minute or two to Herod. He keeps bringing up about Herod and Herodias. We have answered it, we have dealt with it, *it has nothing to do with this debate*. But if you bring that position over here, he had his brother's wife. Well, the Bible says, "Let him have his own wife." He still could not have her, but let him have his own wife, with still having no right to his brother's wife, or any other man's wife.

Let's continue with my next chart, please, chart number 16. In Mark 16:15, Matthew 28:19-20, Jesus commanded the Apostles to preach the gospel throughout the world. Paul said they had done it in Colossians 1:6 and 23. Okay, here is the gospel preached to every creature, all nations. You go back and begin, to the beginning of this preaching, Acts 2, and read all the way throughout, not just the book of Acts, all the way through the book of Revelation. *Find one passage where one person was ever told to leave a husband or a wife to be saved,* or one person was ever told to remain *single* for the rest of his life in order to get to heaven. People were saved, we know that. In Acts 2, they were added to the church. They had the hope of eternal life. Who needs the doctrine of Halbrook? See that? Now, I said the other night, and I did not invite you down to wrangle with me, if you have a passage where one inspired man said this after Acts 2, "You will have to *leave* your wife before I will baptize you; you will have to *leave* your wife to get to heaven; or, you will have to remain *single* the rest of your life to get to heaven," I invited you to give it to me. I am inviting you the same tonight. As I walk out, just give me that passage. I will appreciate it very much. I have not found it. Halbrook has not found it. He cannot find it, because forbidding to marry according to Paul is the doctrine of devils. It is not the faith.

Let's go to my next chart, please, number 15, God versus Halbrook. God said to aliens, through Peter, "Repent, and be baptized every one of you in the name of Jesus Christ for the remission of sins." That included every alien in the audience there. Thousands of people, from 17 different nations were identified. Peter said to all of them — after they cried out, "Men and brethren, what shall we do?"—*"Repent, and be baptized."* Halbrook says, "Repent, put away your spouse, be baptized, remain *single* the rest of your life."

Well, I asked him last night to tell me when what he preaches began. Did it begin in Acts 2, when the gospel was first preached in fact? Did it begin over

---

MK. 16:15 - MATT. 28:19-20 - COL. 1:6, 23

GOSPEL PREACHED TO EVERY CREATURE - ALL NATIONS

*NOT ONE PERSON WAS TOLD TO LEAVE HUSBAND OR WIFE.

*NOT ONE PERSON WAS TOLD TO REMAIN SINGLE FOR LIFE.

*BUT PEOPLE WERE SAVED - ADDED TO THE CHURCH AND HAD HOPE OF ETERNAL LIFE.

WHO NEEDS HALBROOK'S DOCTRINE?

16

Fourth Evening: Freeman's Second Affirmative 273

GOD VS. HALBROOK

GOD TO:	HALBROOK TO:
ALL ALIENS "REPENT, AND BE BAPTIZED EVERY ONE OF YOU IN THE NAME OF JESUS CHRIST FOR THE REMISSION OF SINS..." SCRIPTURE: ACTS 2:38	**SOME ALIENS** "REPENT, PUT AWAY YOUR SPOUSE, BE BAPTIZED AND REMAIN SINGLE THE REST OF YOUR LIFE". SCRIPTURE: _____
SINFUL MEMBERS OF THE CHURCH "REPENT AND PRAY..." ACTS 8:22 CONFESS OUR SINS" 1 JNO. 1:9	**SOME SINFUL MEMBERS OF THE CHURCH** "REPENT, PUT AWAY YOUR SPOUSE, REMAIN UNMARRIED THE REST OF YOUR LIFE". SCRIPTURE: _____
"GOD IS FAITHFUL AND JUST TO FORGIVE US OUR SINS, AND TO CLEANSE US FROM ALL UNRIGHTEOUSNESS" 1 JNO. 1:9	"REPENT, REMAINED UNMARRIED THE REST OF YOUR LIFE". SCRIPTURE: _____

15

there in Corinth when Paul went there? Just where did what you call the marriage law become binding? If it became binding here, you might read, well, maybe in that 3,000, there is surely one. But I will not even say that. I *know* that when Paul preached at Corinth, he found some fornicators. He found some adulterers. And he told them, or they, when they heard what he preached, they believed and were baptized. There is no indication that anyone left his wife, or left her husband.

Well, to the sinful member of the church, God says, repent and pray (Acts 8:22). Confess your sins, (1 John 1:9). And he tells us what this will accomplish, God will forgive us. To some sinful members of the church Halbrook says, "Repent, put away your spouse, remain unmarried the rest of your life." Where is the scripture? Where is the scripture? To others he says, "Repent and remain unmarried the rest of your life." Do you know why this doctrine had to be brought up? Over here on the right of this chart. Well, because we came up with another new doctrine, celibacy, forbidding to marry. So, we have got to come up with a new plan of salvation to take care of those who break it. A new plan of salvation. Any time you come up with a new doctrine violating God's will, it is going to call — one false doctrine will call for another.

Go to my chart number 21, a contrast, God verses Halbrook. God said, "It is not good for man to be alone." Hal-

A CONTRAST:

GOD	HALBROOK
IT IS NOT GOOD FOR MAN TO BE ALONE	SOME WILL HAVE TO BE ALONE
IT IS BETTER TO MARRY THAN TO BURN	SOME WILL HAVE TO BURN
MARRIAGE IS HONORABLE	SOME CANNOT DO THAT WHICH IS HONORABLE
TO AVOID FORNICATION, MARRY	SOME CANNOT USE THIS MEANS TO AVOID FORNICATION
IF LOOSED, YOU DO NOT SIN WHEN YOU MARRY	SOME WHO ARE LOOSED DO SIN WHEN THEY REMARRY

WHO IS RIGHT?

21

brook says, "Some will have to be alone." God said, "It is better to marry than to burn." Halbrook says, "Some will have to burn." God says, "Marriage is honorable." Halbrook says, "Some cannot do that which is honorable." And I am not saying that anyone has the right to two wives, or anything like that. *One man* has a right to *one wife*. That is what God said. *One woman* has a right to *one husband*. He said, "No, not all people, not all women, not all men." God said, "To avoid fornication, marry." Halbrook says, "Some cannot use this means to avoid fornication." God says, "If loosed, you do not sin when you marry." My opponent says, "Some who are loosed sin when they marry." Well, who is right? On the left of this chart, we have God, and that properly represents God. We have not misrepresented Halbrook. He is properly represented over here. If he is not, let him tell us. Well, they are exact opposites. Who is right? Who are you going to accept?

Let's see my next chart, please, number 22, man is living in sin. We used this, and I asked brother Halbrook last night, just step up here and tell us, how far do we agree? Now, if it is *here* tell us, if it is over *there,* tell us. You never did. You beat around the bush about it. Well, tell ditto. Just say, "Ditto, ditto," when you call for this chart. The man or woman are married, they are married. I believe we agree there. I do not know when we have ceased to agree. That is what I want to know. How close are we to being in agreement? Maybe closer than we think.

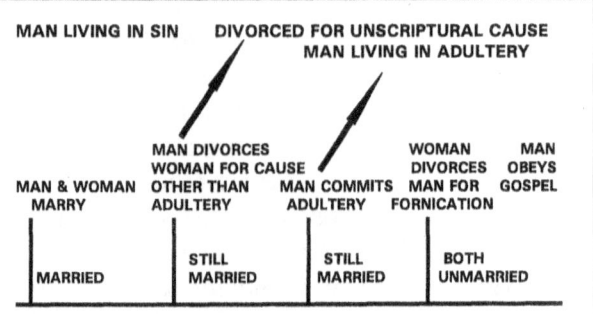

Well, this man divorces his wife for a cause other than fornication. According to you and me, and I believe the Bible, they are still married in God's sight, even though they have a civil divorce. You said the courthouse record is meaningless, proves nothing. Then, they are still married in God's sight. Now, the man commits adultery. Now, these two are still married. The woman against whom adultery has been committed can divorce her husband on scriptural grounds. If you do not believe this, say so. She now divorces him on scriptural grounds. Now, they are both unmarried. If you do not believe that, say so. Now,

Fourth Evening: Freeman's Second Affirmative

if the man obeys the gospel, I remind you on the other chart, when he obeys the gospel my opponent said that man who obeys the gospel arises from baptism without the guilt of any sin. Now, the sin of the husband does not prohibit the wife from doing what is authorized. The innocent is not punished in this case for the sins of the guilty. The man who obtained the divorce for unscriptural grounds, and then committed adultery, has now been scripturally divorced by his wife. He is single, he obeys the gospel, the man is guilty of no sin.

But notice up here at the top. When he commits the first sin mentioned here, he *divorces* his wife for a cause other than fornication, he is living in sin. That sin. When he commits *adultery,* he is living in that sin. Now, he is living and walking in two sins and perhaps many others as well. But the fact is, when he obeys the gospel, at least when he is raised from baptism, if at no other time, after that, at least at that time *he is altogether without sin, free from sin.* And my opponent admits that. And he is unmarried. My opponent admits that, but he still says that even though he is not a sinner, not guilty of any thing, not guilty of one sin, and he is not married to anyone, my opponent says, *"I still forbid him to marry."*

See my next chart, number 452. Romans 7:2, bound by the law to what? To her husband. You ask me, under constraint of law to what, bound by the law to what? I am going to tell you just what the Bible says. To her husband, or to his wife. If the husband be dead, she is loosed from the law. What does loosed mean? No longer bound by the law. No longer bound by the law to her husband. Well, if she is bound by the law, *to what?* If her husband be dead, she is free from that law. Bound versus loosed, bound versus free. No difficulty understanding that.

ROM. 7:2-3

"BOUND **BY** THE LAW **TO** HER HUSBAND"

BUT

"IF THE HUSBAND BE DEAD, SHE IS LOOSED FROM THE LAW"

*V.3 - "IF HER HUSBAND BE DEAD, SHE IS **FREE** FROM THAT LAW"

- BOUND VERSUS LOOSED.
- BOUND VERSUS FREE.

452

Next is my chart 453. 1 Corinthians 7:27, bound unto a wife, the same word as Romans 7:2. Now that is what I said, the word *bound.* 1 Corinthians 7:27, the same as that found in Romans 7:2. And you read from your own Greek authorities. Now, you agreed to that before. And I think you will agree, just think about it. The word bound in Romans 7:2 and 1 Corinthians 7:27 is the same word. "Art thou bound unto a wife?" Bound by the law to her husband, 1 Corinthians 7:27. Loosed from a wife. Well, loosed from the wife, then you are free from that law. Bound versus loosed. Bound versus free. These are opposing terms. If you

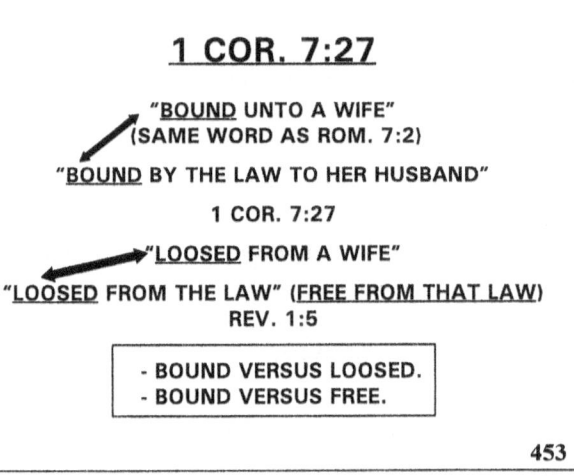

are not bound, you are loosed. If you are not bound, you are free.

Let's look at the next chart if we have time. Now Halbrook says that his inspired, uninspired witnesses show that what Jack Freeman teaches causes people to sin. His own witness tells about the evils brought into the world by forbidding to marry. I am beginning to quote that witness. "With what impunity, fornication rages among them, is unnecessary to remark. Emboldened by their polluted celibacy, they have become hardened by every crime. In the first place, it was on no account lawful for men to prohibit that which the Lord left free."

Next chart, 749. "Secondly, that God has expressly provided in His word that liberty should not be infringed is too clear to require much proof. When an institution has been tried a dozen centuries in all parts of the world, and has uniformly been found productive of the same evil effects, there could not be a doubt that sentence ought to be passed on it. Cut it down. The Apostle Paul denominates that a doctrine of devils forbids marriage."

Next chart, 750 [page 278]. Just continue the same witness. "It was an evil law, it was not the law of God, it was against the necessity of nature. It was unnatural, unreasonable. It was not for the edification of the church. It had no advantage of spiritual life. It is a law therefore that is against public honesty, because it did openly and secretly introduce dishonesty. It had no consideration of human frailty, nor of human comfort. It was neither necessary or profitable, nor innocent — neither fitting to time, nor place, nor person." His witness, McClintock. You know, he read from that witness what I teach. This brings it over to his own witness. His own witness. I am not introducing this to prove anything.

Fourth Evening: Freeman's Second Affirmative   277

> **WITNESS**
>
> * HALBROOK SAYS THAT HIS UNINSPIRED WITNESS SHOWS THAT WHAT JACK FREEMAN TEACHES CAUSES PEOPLE TO SIN.
>
> * HALBROOK'S OWN WITNESS TELLS ABOUT THE EVILS BROUGHT INTO THE WORLD BY FORBIDDING TO MARRY:
>
> "WITH WHAT IMPUNITY FORNICATION RAGES AMONG THEM IT IS UNNECESSARY TO REMARK; EMBOLDENED BY THEIR POLLUTED CELIBACY, THEY HAVE BECOME HARDENED TO EVERY CRIME."
>
> "IN THE FIRST PLACE, IT WAS ON NO ACCOUNT LAWFUL FOR MEN TO PROHIBIT THAT WHICH THE LORD LEFT FREE."
>
> 748

We will reserve this, just briefly refer to it, while we still have time. He says he is merciful. Well, God says in His mercy, "I will remember their sins and iniquities no more." I will tell you about my opponent. If the sin is fornication, Halbrook will remember it. And you come to here, and you say to brother Halbrook "Can I remarry?" He says, "No, I remember back there, 10, 15, 20 years ago, you committed fornication and someone divorced you for it."

> **WITNESS**
> (Cont)
>
> "SECONDLY, THAT GOD HAS EXPRESSLY PROVIDED IN HIS WORD THAT LIBERTY SHOULD NOT BE INFRINGED, IS TOO CLEAR TO REQUIRE MUCH PROOF."
>
> "WHEN AN INSTITUTION HAS BEEN TRIED A DOZEN CENTURIES IN ALL PARTS OF THE WORLD, AND HAS UNIFORMLY BEEN FOUND PRODUCTIVE OF THE SAME EVIL EFFECTS, THERE CANNOT BE A DOUBT WHAT SENTENCE OUGHT TO BE PASSED ON IT. CUT IT DOWN."
>
> "THE APOSTLE PAUL DENOMINATES THAT A DOCTRINE OF DEVILS <u>FORBIDS MARRIAGE</u>."
>
> 749

WITNESS
(Cont)

"IT WAS AN EVIL LAW... IT WAS NOT THE LAW OF GOD; IT WAS AGAINST THE NECESSITIES OF NATURE; IT WAS UNNATURAL AND UNREASONABLE; IT WAS NOT FOR THE EDIFICATION OF THE CHURCH; IT WAS NO ADVANTAGE TO SPIRITUAL LIFE; IT IS A LAW THEREFORE THAT IS AGAINST PUBLIC HONESTY, BECAUSE IT DID OPENLY AND SECRETLY INTRODUCE DISHONESTY... IT HAD NO CONSIDERATION OF HUMAN FRAILTY NOR OF HUMAN COMFORTS; IT WAS NEITHER NECESSARY OR PROFITABLE, NOR INNOCENT --- NEITHER FITTED TO TIME, NOR PLACE, NOR PERSON."

750

HOW DO WE KNOW?
MERCY

GOD THROUGH HIS MERCY:

REMITS SINS--------------------------------ACTS 2:38

BLOTS OUT SINS---------------------------ACTS 3:19

WASHES AWAY SINS---------------------ACTS 22:16

FORGIVES ALL TRESPASSES------------COL. 2:13

DESTROYS THE BODY OF SIN-----------ROM. 6:6

REMEMBERS SINS NO MORE------------HEB. 8:12

BUT MY OPPONENT WILL ALWAYS REMEMBER THAT ONE HAS COMMITTED FORNICATION AND WILL ALWAYS DEMAND PENANCE, EVEN WHEN GOD HAS FORGIVEN.
   LET US BE THANKFUL WE DON'T DEPEND UPON "HALBROOK'S MERCY".

28

Fourth Evening
Halbrook's Second Negative

Brother Freeman, gentlemen moderators, ladies and gentlemen, brother Freeman says that I am not really calling for his charts and examining them, that all I do is holler, "Ditto, ditto, ditto!" Well, he seems to like that *"ditto."* Let's look at the 346 series of charts again. Let's let him look at "ditto." He does not seem to understand what that means. Brother Freeman, that means *you made a multitude of mistakes on the same subject.* We will get one of the "ditto" charts and let him see what that is all about. As to 1 Corinthians 7:15, he made about ten or twelve mistakes on it. That is what "ditto" means. Is that what you wanted to see again?

> **THE ELIJAH CHART (1 Kings 18:27)**
> **EXPOSING THE WEAKNESS OF ERROR**
> *Bloopers and Blunders of the Weak*
>
> **Volume I**
>
> 1. Not admit wrote article
> 2. Called me a liar - no apology
> 3. Not confess the error at Las Vegas
> 4. Mark 6:17-18 not have anything to do with this debate
> 5. Except - if and only if
> 6. Can't find guilty fornicator in 1 Cor. 7
>
> 346

Here is what *"ditto"* means. You said in *1 Corinthians 7:11*, there was no right to have that second wife. I charge you with teaching *the doctrine of demons!* That is what ditto means. I charge you with *the doctrine of penance* and *no mercy,* and you have got them in *an adulterous relationship*. And you say no one was ever told to leave, but *you told that woman to leave.* And you say no one was told to remain unmarried, but *you and Paul told that woman to remain unmarried.* And then, *"ditto"*

> **Volume III**
>
> 16. Won't forbid food to lazy
> 17. His answer on 1 Cor. 7:11, no mercy
> 18. Ditto - Doctrine of demons
> 19. Ditto - Penance
> 20. Ditto - No mercy
> 21. Ditto - Adulterous relationship
> 22. Ditto - No one told to leave
> 23. Ditto - No one told to remain unmarried
> 24. Ditto - Changed answer (can remain)
>
> 346 B

on the same passage, you changed your answer. That is what "ditto" is about.

1 Corinthians 7:15 says "marry another" — you have repeated that mistake throughout the debate. For that, you get *The Blunder of the Weak Award!* And 1 Corinthians 7:15 says, "marriage," see? Now, you are getting into the mire and the muck deeper and deeper on 1 Corinthians 7:15. And "ditto" means *deeper,* and *deeper,* and *deeper.* That is what it means. Yes sir, I *am* answering your charts and dealing with your material.

> **Volume IV**
>
> 25. Can be married 2 or 100 times!!!
> 26. 1 Cor. 7:15 says "marry another"
> 27. Thayer on 1 Cor. 7:15 says "marriage"
> 28. 1 Cor. 7:15 - Catholic catechism
> 29. Ditto - 2 marriage laws
> 30. Ditto - cf. slaves (v.23)
> 31. Ditto - Entrance wedge
> 32. Ditto - Opens flood gates
>
> 346 C

Now then, on questions, he says that on this matter about the trick question, Jesus used no trick questions. Indeed, that is very true, *but it seemed like a trick question to those who were trying to answer it.* See? *And they seem like trick questions to you when you are trying to answer these!*

And you have pointed out that they would be in trouble either way they went. Well, look at my chart 242 if you want to see why he does not answer questions. He is in trouble *either* way he goes, and he has gone *both* ways, and already found it out. And, now, I cannot get him to go *either* way, cannot get him to go *either way!* Remember, he said that they had *no right* to the second mate? We gave the quotation, and then he said they may *continue* in the marriage. See, that is like those people, if they said the baptism was *from heaven,* they were in trouble. If they said the

> **Mark 6:17-18**
> **Contradictions of Error**
>
> 1. "If you have another man's wife, yes, you'll have to give her up ... that's repentance" (Freeman, 18 Jan. 1990)
>
> 2. If an alien sinner in a second marriage following a divorce not for fornication desires to be acceptable to God, he:
>
>   FREEMAN: "May continue in the marriage" (18 Jan. 1990, answer to my question 3)
>
> 242

baptism was *from men,* they were in trouble. Well, do you see, brother Freeman made the mistake of trying *both* answers? Now, he will not answer it any more. So, that is the way that works.

Now then, he said on my chart 101, under constraint of law to what? I pointed out that they are under constraint of law in these cases where people are *unscripturally divorced,* and *the put-away fornicator.* Well, look at the chart and I will show you under constraint to what. Now take number three here, Leviticus 21. The divorcee is *free from marriage* but she *cannot* marry a priest. Why can't she? What law is she constrained by? What is she under constraint to? Well, you answer it, brother Freeman. *God Almighty* is the one who puts these constraints there. It is the constraint of *divine law* for those in a given marital status. That is what it is. Now, it is the same way, *the put-away person is not authorized to marry another.* You can holler, "To what are they bound in this constraint?" all you want to, but *God* put it there! And it will stand tonight, and it will stand tomorrow, it will stand when the world is on fire. God put the law there. That is what that constraint is all about.

> **Divorced People Remain Under Constraint Of Law**
>
> 1. Deut. 24:1-4 Divorce wife but can't have her back after her 2nd marriage
> 2. Deut. 24:1-4 Divorcee marry another but then can't ever return to 1st mate
> 3. Lev. 21:7, 13-14 Divorcee free from marriage but can't marry a priest
> 4. Matt. 5:32; 19:9 Pure divorce impure and marry another (new mate can't be one put away for fornication or other cause)
> 5. Matt. 5:32; 19:9 Not authorize a put-away person (whether put away for fornication or other cause) to marry another
> 6. 1 Cor. 7:10-11 If 2 Christians divorce, must remain unmarried or reconcile
> 7. 1 Cor. 7:12-15 Believer not give up Christ to keep unbeliever (no authority for either to marry another)
>
> **CONCLUSION:**
> 1. Unscriptural divorce releases neither party from marriage!
> 2. Scriptural divorce releases both parties from marriage, but not from the constraint of the law!
>
> 101

And then on his question number two to me, *where does the Bible speak of "adulterous marriage?"* He wanted to read Colossians three, and suggests to me that he could find "live in," but I did not just ask for the expression "live in." Let's look at my chart 94. I asked for the expression *"live in adultery,"* just like that. And you did not find that, see? He says you can say "live in adultery," and say it *just like that.* I took this off of his tapes. But, then, you cannot say *"adulterous relationship,"* and say it *just like that.* Now, brother Freeman, look. I want you to look. *Adulterous* means "characterized by adultery." *Relationship,* "two or more," as in "sexual intercourse." Now, *live,* the word you can let us use, "to conduct...one's life," "practice," or "cohabit." What does *cohabit* mean? "Live together as husband and wife." So now, the expression he uses, *"live in adultery,"* matches the definition of *"adulterous relationship,"* and *Colossians*

3:5 indeed speaks of it. Alright, now my friend, that is the answer to that. The exact expression is not there for *either* one, but the teaching is there for *both*.

Alright, now then, on my chart 60 [text chart] concerning Matthew 5:32 that we read, he said that I made some statement about that he could not do *anything*. The put-away fornicator *cannot marry another!*

> **FREEMAN'S SOPHISTRY EXPOSED**
> *"Live In Adultery" Vs "Adulterous Rel."*
> CAN "LIVE IN ADULTERY," BUT NO SUCH THING AS "ADULTEROUS RELATIONSHIPS"
> *(Freeman, Marriage Series, Fall 1988, #8)*
> 1. Adulterous - "Characterized by ... adultery" (Webster's Dict.)
> 2. Relationship - "2 or more ... taken together," as "sexual intercourse" (Webster)
> 3. Live - "To conduct ... one's life," "to practice," "to cohabit" (Webster)
> 4. Cohabit - "To live together as husband and wife" (Webster)
>
> **LIVE IN ADULTERY = ADULTEROUS REL.**
> 94

But at any rate, look at my chart 65. He did not say anything about this, but I want you to see the difference in his doctrine and in what Jesus taught. Here is the force of it. I think the debate will close, I predict it will, and he will never ask for this. Whosoever shall put away his wife for fornication does *not cause* her to commit adultery, is not responsible for her subsequent adultery. He does not cause her adultery. Now, here is your interpretation of it. See, he called for the passage, that was the lead into this, and then, like those who did not answer the Lord, he did not answer *the chart*, did not answer *the argument*. Now, your interpretation says, whosoever shall put away his wife for fornication *causes* her to NOT COMMIT adultery. So, all of you who want to cause your wife to *not* commit adultery, be sure and *put her away,* and *get her into another marriage!* He does not understand the passage. He is perverting the passage altogether.

Now then, he said the homosexual must *leave.*

> **Matthew 5:32 Exception: Not Cause Or Not Commit?**
>
> | What Jesus Taught | -vs- | Opponent's Interpretation |
> |---|---|---|
> | Whosoever shall put away his wife **for fornication** does NOT CAUSE her to commit adultery (i.e. is not responsible for her subsequent adultery). | | Whosoever shall put away his wife **for fornication** causes her to NOT COMMIT adultery (i.e. he is responsible for her not committing adultery). |
> | **HE DOES NOT CAUSE HER ADULTERY** | -vs- | **HE CAUSES HER TO NOT COMMIT ADULTERY** |
>
> 65

Now, wait a minute. Let's look at my chart 243 again. I was about to forget my *question five*. He believes that in the event, that if you have the events of Mark six today, the truth is *he believes that the marriage of Herod and Herodias would* BECOME *lawful if Philip would say he put her away*. But, he made the comment, well, he still could not have her because it is another man's wife. But you forgot, you called for this chart, then you *did not read it* and *make the application*.

> **LOVELADY ON SIN OF ADULTERY**
> (Matthew 5:32; Matthew 19:9)
> *"HOW LONG IS HE GUILTY? Until his first mate says, 'I DON'T WANT TO BE BOUND TO THAT ADULTEROUS PARTNER.' That is when that man stops committing adultery."*
> (Glen Lovelady in Smith-Lovelady Debate. p.69)
>
> **CONCLUSION**
> 1. Herodias leaves Philip
> 2. Herod marries her -- adultery
> 3. Philip says, "I don't want to be bound to that adulterous partner."
> 4. Herod and Herodias -- marriage becomes lawful
>
> 243

You could have the same circumstance *today,* couldn't you, brother Freeman? Sure you could. Now then, the man that is helping you there [referring to Glen W. Lovelady who handled Freeman's charts] says this thing is resolved when the first mate says, "I DON'T WANT TO BE BOUND TO THAT ADULTEROUS PARTNER." So, Philip says that. Now, I want to know why Herod and Herodias cannot have a lawful marriage *now?* What are you going to do, take up preaching the doctrine of demons? No mercy? God forgets, but you remember? Now, tell us about it again. "Why not go to Acts 2?" he said, That is what I am asking you — it is concerning *under Acts 2.*

Now then, he said that I asked for a *specific example* to prove the homosexual must leave. And, he gave us *1 Corinthians 6:9-11.* Well, my friend, if that will work for the *homosexual* mentioned there, and he must *leave,* it mentions the *adulterer* and *fornicator,* and both of us agreed that it could be *the put-away fornicator* there. So, what must he do, brother Freeman? Now, that passage means the homosexual must leave the relationship, you said. And then it mentions and includes at least *the put-away fornicator.* So, now if he repents, he must, he must *what?* [Halbrook cups his hand to his ear and leans toward Freeman, as if listening for an answer.] I cannot hear him. He must *leave,* by *your* argument! Thank you, sir. Thank you, sir.

Now, we have already answered his chart 34, we have already answered it. If we can get it up here again, we will look at it. (He says I do not answer his charts. I call for each one of them. And then I introduce *45* charts, how many does he call for? *Thirteen!* He might be getting close to twenty-five percent there.) Well, that is alright, if he cannot find it. Look at my charts 122-A and 198. This is the answer to it. This is the answer to it, my friend.

First show chart 122-A. On *1 Corinthians 7,* the text says, "Let every man have his own wife." It does *not* say, "Let every man throw away your wife by fornication, and I will just let you get *another.* And if you throw that one away, get *another.* And throw that one away, get *another.*"

"To the unmarried and widows,...it is better to marry than to burn." I was amused when he was reading that verse.

Does 1 Cor. 7 Authorize
The Put-Away Fornicator To Marry Another?

Text Says This:	Not This:
Vs. 2 "Every man have his own wife"	Every man who wrecks his marriage & throws away his own wife by fornication or unscriptural divorce, gets another wife!
Vs. 9 "Unmarried...widows... better to marry than to burn"	Unscripturally divorced & put-away fornicator... better to commit adultery than fornication!
Vv. 27-28 A man "loosed from a wife" (free, never married) and "a virgin" (free, never married) may marry.	A man unscripturally divorced or a divorced fornicator may marry a woman in the same condition!

122 A

He read that verse. And I heard those words, "unmarried and widows," and I was waiting for it to say, *"and put-away fornicators,"* but he left that out. Because Paul left it out and the Holy Spirit left it out! And you were trying to *insert* the put-away fornicator there, and God did not put it there. You have got the thing meaning it is better to commit adultery than fornication. That is the *result* of what you teach.

In verses 27 and 28, you have *a man "loosed from a wife"* (free and never married) and the *"virgin"* (free and never married), and you are trying to get from it the *divorced fornicator* can marry the *divorced fornicator.* My, my, brother Freeman, my, my.

THE "PUT AWAY" FORNICATOR
(Cont)

BUT HALBROOK SAYS:

HE CANNOT HAVE A WIFE TO AVOID FORNICATION.
HE CANNOT MARRY EVEN THOUGH LOOSED FROM A WIFE.

IF HALBROOK IS RIGHT, GOD IS WRONG.
IF GOD IS RIGHT, HALBROOK IS WRONG.

WHO KNOWS MORE ABOUT THE RIGHT OF MAN TO MARRY?

35

Then on his chart 35, I want to see his chart 35 if we can find it. And I know it is hard for these chart men, as fast as we move sometimes. I want to see the middle of that chart 35. See this middle section of it: "He cannot have a wife to avoid fornication. He cannot marry even though loosed from a wife." Now then, notice the key of his argument is, *"to avoid fornication."*

Look at chart 140-X [text, 1 Cor. 7:10-11]. God can have constraints of law, brother Freeman. And, in that case, He does it in *verses 10 and 11* here. Notice, "but and if she depart, let her remain" *what? "Remain unmarried."* Now, put his chart back up again. [See Freeman's chart 35 above.] Put his chart 35 back up again. I just may borrow that one from him. She *remains unmarried.* Now, you tell me, *how does she avoid fornication,* brother Freeman? *You* tell me, how does this woman avoid fornication? The way you argue in verse 8 and 9, if you burn with passion you have got to get *another mate,* whether it is authorized or not. And my friend, that woman is told to remain in that condition, *separated from her husband.* I want to know how she avoids fornication.

Now then, let's see his chart 37. You can be married to an adulterer without being one. I agree to that. I agree to that part of his argument. But the point is, friend, it could be that, but it could be *both living in an adulterous marriage,* see? That is the thing he is leaving out of this. Yes, it could be you are married to an adulterer, somebody going out to a prostitute, and you are not doing that. So, you are married to an adulterer. Does that make you an adulterer? No. But he is not covering all the cases.

PUT AWAY

(Cont)

If the husband dies w/o divorcing his wife who is guilty of adultery, she may scripturally remarry, Rom. 7:2-3
But she is still guilty of adultery and will be until GOD forgives her.
The man who marries her will NOT be living in adultery.

(But she will be)

The marriage IS NOT adulterous.

37

Notice my chart 83. My Lord described different and various cases, and you have not got all the cases up here. *A married man with another man's wife,* that is the case he wants. And, I agree that is adultery. But Jesus said, if *a man divorces his wife, and marries another,* that is adultery too. And, if *the put-away fornicator marries another!* Whoever puts away his wife for fornication does not cause her to commit the adultery that she commits in that second marriage. You are not responsible for it, but *what* did *she* commit? *The put-away fornicator* is going to be committing the sin of *adultery*. Whoever marries her that is put away, committeth *adultery*. And so, he is just not describing all the cases.

Then on his chart 46, he argues that if one is loosed the other is loosed, and so they can both get married. Now, that is simplistic, an over-simplification. He talked about being bound by law and so if you have a death, both of them are loosed. Well, *God said* you can *marry another*. That is the difference! But, my friend, in this matter of the put-away fornicator, and unscriptural marriages, when they *marry another*, they are going to be in *adultery*. And if you put one away for fornication, just because God releases *one*, it does not prove he does the *other*. We talked about the constraint of law. I will not show that again. We have shown it over and over and over.

> **Cases of Adultery**
>
> 1. **Simplest Case:** A married man with another man's wife (John 8:4)
> 2. **Sin Upon Sin:** A man divorces his wife and marries another (Matt. 19:9)
> 3. **Sin Upon Sin:** The put-away fornicator remarries (Matt. 5:32 read with exception)
>
> "The remarriage of a man after divorcing his wife, or the remarrying of the divorced woman, is tantamount to adultery (Matt. 5:32; 19:9)" [Kittel, TDNT, IV:733]
>
> Tantamount = "Equivalent in value, significance, or effect" (Webster's 7th New Colleg. Dict.)
>
> Effect = Gal. 5:19-21 (such things); Heb. 13:4
>
> 83

> **MARRIED TO AN ADULTRESS**
> (Cont)
>
> ROM. 7:2-3 -- WIFE IS BOUND TO HER HUSBAND BY THE LAW AS LONG AS HE LIVETH.
>
> A. IF SHE COMMITS ADULTERY, HE CAN KEEP HER AS HIS WIFE.
> B. SHE IS LIVING IN (GUILTY OF) ADULTERY, BUT HE IS NOT. (*THE MARRIAGE IS NOT ADULTEROUS*)
> C. SHE WILL BE LIVING IN (GUILTY OF) ADULTERY UNTIL GOD FORGIVES HER.
> D. IF HER HUSBAND DIES (WITHOUT DIVORCING HER), SHE CAN SCRIPTURALLY REMARRY.
> E. SHE WILL STILL BE LIVING IN ADULTERY, BUT HER HUSBAND WILL NOT.
> F. THE SECOND MARRIAGE IS NOT AN ADULTEROUS MARRIAGE.
>
> 46

Let's look at our chart 301. Now, I want you to see, does an illustration prove? Really, what he is doing is trying to insert *an illustration* and bring it in under *the text*. His illustration in his mind is that *if one is free, the other is*. You know, it is kind of like you are handcuffed. If you get free from the cuffs, you are totally free. You see? And so, here is brother Freeman's reasoning. You are divorced for fornication as the guilty party, and that leaves you totally free to remarry. He asked me, "Is the innocent party free?" Of course, I agree, and he

> **Illustrate = Prove???**
>
> Freed From Cuffs, } Divorced for fornication,
> Totally Free   guilty party totally free
>   to remarry
>
> Freed from cuffs,
> but must:
> 1. Post bond
> 2. Appear in court
> 3. Return for sentence
> 4. Report for parole   Divorced for fornication,
> 5. Not own gun   but the guilty party is
> 6. Obey injunction   not authorized to marry
> 7. Obey all laws   another!
> 8. Pay alimony,
>   child support
>
> 301

thinks he has won the war. He thinks that made the *other* free. If one is free, the other is free.

Now, watch it. You can be freed from cuffs. You see, you have been arrested and put in cuffs, but you are freed from it. And yet, you continue to be under constraint of law. You have got to post bond, but you are not in the cuffs. You have got to appear in court, return for sentence, and report for parole. You cannot own a gun. You must obey an injunction, and you must pay alimony and child support.

Now, my friend, notice the parallel. You can be divorced for fornication and, that is right, you are free from a mate. That is, you do not have one. But the guilty party is *not authorized to marry another,* brother Freeman. Now, that is the answer to it. That is the answer to it.

And then, he said again *concerning Herod that he could not figure out what that had to do with the debate.* Everybody else here knows it, but he has not learned it. We may have to give The Blunder of the Weak Award to that point!

And then, let's see on his chart number 16, *where was one told to leave to be saved?* Do you remember that? It is on chart 16. Remember that? Where was anyone told that they had to leave? Alright, let's look at our chart 326. You an-

> **MK. 16:15 - MATT. 28:19-20 - COL. 1:6, 23**
>
> GOSPEL PREACHED TO EVERY CREATURE - ALL NATIONS
>
> *NOT ONE PERSON WAS TOLD TO LEAVE HUSBAND OR WIFE.
>
> *NOT ONE PERSON WAS TOLD TO REMAIN SINGLE FOR LIFE.
>
> *BUT PEOPLE WERE SAVED - ADDED TO THE CHURCH AND HAD HOPE OF ETERNAL LIFE.
>
> **WHO NEEDS HALBROOK'S DOCTRINE?**
>
> 16

swer it, you answer it, brother Freeman. What about it? *Where was anyone ever told to leave?* I want a specific example where the homosexual was told to leave.

Now, you said *1 Corinthians 6:9-11*. Alright, because it mentioned the homosexual. It mentions a fornicator, which could include *a put-away fornicator*. If that was teaching that the homosexual had to leave, then so it is for the put-away fornicator! Thank you, brother Freeman.

And then, what about *polygamy?* You did not

> **Opponent Opposes Himself (2 Tim. 2:25)**
>
> **What About These Cases?**
>
> 1. "Doctrine of Devils" if forbid marriage. — Homosexual (1 Cor. 6:9-11)
> 2. "Mercy" remits sin, but "opponent remembers sin." — Polygamy (Gen. 2:24)
> 3. "Paul preached to aliens," "not say leave husband or wife to be saved." — Unscripturally divorced (Matt. 5:28; 19:9; 1 Cor. 7:10-11, 15)
> 4. "Demands impossible," "how do you know?" — Unscripturally remarried (Mk. 6:17-18; Mt. 5:28; 19:9)
>
> 326

find me a case of polygamy. I want a case of polygamy, where Paul ever preached to them, and said, "You have got to leave that one." Jerry Bassett and some others are publicly taking the position that they could not demand that you would have to leave a polygamous marriage in order to obey the gospel, but that sooner or later it would be good if you would learn that, and get out of that. We have material out at the back on that, and you need to read it. These brethren are trying to be consistent with their doctrine. It is pushing them further and further and further out from the truth of Almighty God. When you preach to people over and over that *you cannot find a passage where the put-away fornicator was told to leave* — you *cannot* find it, *cannot* find it — somebody is going to suddenly realize, *"Hey, there is no passage like that for polygamy, either. Now what?"* Now what, indeed! Maybe you and brother Bassett can debate it, or explain it. And also brother Freeman, *you* just answer it. *You* answer it.

And then, let's see his chart 15, God and Halbrook. Where is someone told to repent and put

> **GOD VS. HALBROOK**
>
> | GOD TO: | HALBROOK TO: |
> |---|---|
> | **ALL ALIENS** "REPENT, AND BE BAPTIZED EVERY ONE OF YOU IN THE NAME OF JESUS CHRIST FOR THE REMISSION OF SINS..." SCRIPTURE: ACTS 2:38 | **SOME ALIENS** "REPENT, PUT AWAY YOUR SPOUSE, BE BAPTIZED AND REMAIN SINGLE THE REST OF YOUR LIFE". SCRIPTURE: _____ |
> | **SINFUL MEMBERS OF THE CHURCH** "REPENT AND PRAY..." ACTS 8:22 CONFESS OUR SINS" 1 JNO. 1:9 | **SOME SINFUL MEMBERS OF THE CHURCH** "REPENT, PUT AWAY YOUR SPOUSE, REMAIN UNMARRIED THE REST OF YOUR LIFE". SCRIPTURE: _____ |
> | "GOD IS FAITHFUL AND JUST TO FORGIVE US OUR SINS, AND TO CLEANSE US FROM ALL UNRIGHTEOUSNESS" 1 JNO. 1:9 | "REPENT, REMAINED UNMARRIED THE REST OF YOUR LIFE". SCRIPTURE: _____ |
>
> 15

away the mate? And, I believe this is the one that had Acts 2:38 on it. That passage would work fine. Acts 2:38 will work fine. You have got the passage on it right there. See, he puts it on *this side,* just put it on this side [pointing to left and right sides of chart respectively]. *Repentance,* my friend, means that if you are in an unscriptural marriage, you have to *get out* of it. And he wants to make a little play on "remain single the rest of your life." It could be that. It could be that you are the put-away fornicator, and you cannot be reconciled, and your mate did not die first. Yes, you *could* be in that position. And, *the person in 1 Corinthians 7:11 could be in that position, couldn't he?* Yes, and grinning will not answer it. [Halbrook was referring to Freeman looking up and grinning when 1 Cor. 7:11 was mentioned.] Yes sir, brother, now that person could be in that condition.

Put my chart O-1 up here. He wants the passage, so I will cover him up with passages, just cover him up with passages. Here it is, friend. He wants the passage. In *Mark 6,* John was preaching the principle that *if you are in an unscriptural, adulterous marriage, you have got to get out of it.* John preached it, and *Colossians 3:5* teaches it, that you *cannot* live in an adulterous marriage. *1 Corinthians 5* teaches it, and chapter *6:9-11* teaches it for the homosexual and the put-away fornicator. Do not forget that. And *1 Corinthians 7:11* teaches it.

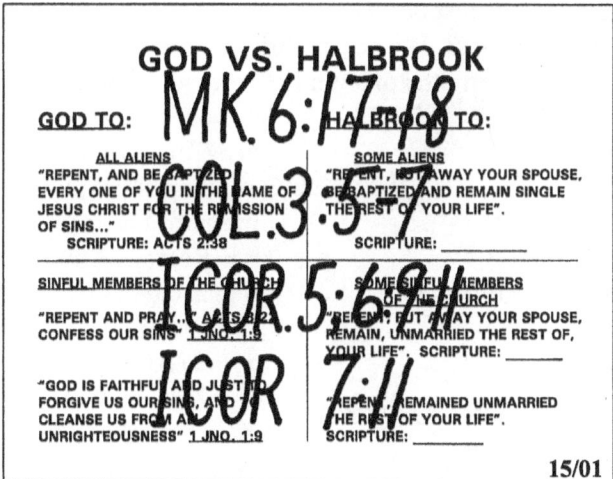

Now then, his charts, 21 and 22. We had those two before, on 1 Corinthians 7. I answered it in my other speech. He keeps using 1 Corinthians 7 and *perverting* it. He uses the thing about contrast: "it is better to marry than to burn." Look at our chart 122-A [page 284]. We may all go home and dream about 122-A. He just keeps using chapter 7, and he just keeps *perverting* it. "Let every man have his own wife," not, "Let every man throw away his wife for fornication and get another." "It is better to marry than to burn." That is what he had on his chart. Of course, I am not answering his charts, folks. I am not answering his charts tonight — you can see that. He has got this thing meaning that for the put-away fornicator, "It is better for you to commit adultery than fornication." What about it?

And then in verses 27 and 28, we read about a *man* "loosed from a wife" (free, never married) and then the *"virgin"* (free, never married). But he wants it to read that the *put-away fornicator* is marrying a *put-away fornicator.* It is

A CONTRAST:	
GOD	**HALBROOK**
IT IS NOT GOOD FOR MAN TO BE ALONE	SOME WILL HAVE TO BE ALONE
IT IS BETTER TO MARRY THAN TO BURN	SOME WILL HAVE TO BURN
MARRIAGE IS HONORABLE	SOME CANNOT DO THAT WHICH IS HONORABLE
TO AVOID FORNICATION, MARRY	SOME CANNOT USE THIS MEANS TO AVOID FORNICATION
IF LOOSED, YOU DO NOT SIN WHEN YOU MARRY	SOME WHO ARE LOOSED DO SIN WHEN THEY REMARRY
WHO IS RIGHT?	

21

just not there, brother Freeman! It is just not there!

Then, he had his charts 452 and 453. We do not differ on the 452, so show the one we differ on, 453. We have the matter of bound and loosed, where he says

1 COR. 7:27

"**BOUND** UNTO A WIFE"
(SAME WORD AS ROM. 7:2)
"**BOUND** BY THE LAW TO HER HUSBAND"
1 COR. 7:27

"**LOOSED** FROM A WIFE"
"**LOOSED** FROM THE LAW" (FREE FROM THAT LAW)
REV. 1:5

- BOUND VERSUS LOOSED.
- BOUND VERSUS FREE.

453

that you have the same word for bound in 1 Corinthians 7:27, which is the marriage bond, and it is in Romans 7, and it is the marriage bond. And by the way, *that is the word that is not in 1 Corinthians 7:15, brother Freeman.* Remember that? It is not the same word in that passage. But then he said of "loosed" here and "loosed" in 1 Corinthians 7, Romans 7 and 1 Corinthians 7, that the word "loosed" is the same term. They are *not* the same terms, they are just *not at all*. He is just perverting that. He can keep saying it all he wants to. Look at your interlinear. They are not the same terms. You are just about to convince me some people ought not to use reference books, the way you pervert the use of them, and even the word of God.

Now, brother Freeman quoted some material on his charts 748 and 749, which we will not have to show again. It said that forbidding of marriage has brought all of these horrible results. It was talking about the Catholic doctrine of celibacy. *It was not talking about the question of the guilty fornicator marrying another.* Brother Freeman, the material you quoted is *not* discussing this question *at all!* And I will show you what the historians have pointed out. His position on 1 Corinthians 7:15 and Matthew 19:9, teaching that the guilty party can marry another, broke down the restraints of the law of God on marriage and divorce, and brought about the mess we are in today. And, your quotation said that if a tree produced fruit like that, "cut it down." Amen and amen! Cut it down!

And then we had his "mercy" chart. We have really already answered that. *We have covered everything that he brought up. Item by item. Point by point.*

Now, I want you to notice with me our chart 317. *False teaching presses men into the kingdom of God by sacrificing the truth,* according to Luke 16. The Pharisees were not faithful in the use of material blessings. They were guilty of materialism. Our Lord said they could not receive the true riches of the coming kingdom, although they professed and pretended that kingdom was for them. They would not obey Moses' law, yet they thought they could press into the kingdom of God with its law. Well, my friend, the law of Moses would not yield to them and the new law was *even stricter.*

> **False Teaching Presses Men Into The Kingdom By Sacrificing Truth (Luke 16:1-18)**
> 1. Pharisees not faithful in use of material blessings - sin of materialism - can't receive "true riches" of coming Kingdom (vv. 1-13).
> 2. Not obey Moses' law but press into "Kingdom of God" (vv. 14-17).
> 3. Moses' law not yield to them and new law stricter! Illustrated with divorce & remarriage (vs. 18).
>
> 317

The Lord illustrated that with divorce and remarriage. Notice it on our chart 318. Look at what my Lord said. Under Moses, the Jews eventually dropped the death penalty for adultery. This is what some of the rabbis did. I want to show you what the rabbis did. They dropped the death penalty for adultery. They allowed divorce and allowed both to remarry. Do you see what they were doing? *Loosening up that law.* Then, they added additional bases for divorce and remarriage by *twisting Deuteronomy 24.* Hillel said it could be *any* cause, kind of *like my opponent.* See, my opponent is in the Hillel party. He said if she burned the biscuits, that is what Deuteronomy 24 could include. No sir. No sir. Now, that is the kind of reasoning that kept them out of the kingdom. Akibah said if a man sees a prettier woman, then that gives him the ground.

Now, watch it under Christ. You see, these people doing those things thought, "Oh, we want to press into this kingdom of the Lord!" My Lord and Savior said, "No, no, friend, you do not respect this law [pointing to Moses' law on the chart]. My law is even stricter yet." Under Christ *my opponent, like these rabbis of old, is loosening up the law that God gave. He allows the fornicator to marry another, and allows an additional basis for remarriage in 1 Corinthians 7:15.* And then some allow remarriage through the theory of two laws, and others by redefining adultery. Such perverting of God's word cannot get men into the kingdom. *It keeps them out.*

> **Sacrificing Truth On Marriage, Divorce & Remarriage**
>
> | Under Moses | Under Christ |
> |---|---|
> | 1. Drop death penalty for adultery - allow divorce & both remarry (Shammai) | 1. Allow fornicator to remarry |
> | 2. Add additional basis for divorce & remarriage by twisting Deut. 24. | 2. Add additional basis for remarriage by twisting 1 Cor. 7:15 |
> | a. Hillel - any cause | 3. Theory of Two Laws |
> | b. Akibah - sees prettier woman | 4. Redefine Adultery |
> | | 5. Baptism wash away wives |
>
> **Such Perverting of God's Word Can't Get Men Into The Kingdom - It Keeps Them Out!**
>
> 318

Next, observe our chart 330. My friends, the doctrine we are hearing from brother Freeman encourages sin. Now, Matthew 7 said that we have got to be fruit watchers. Somebody said, "Oh, I don't know about these 'watchdog brethren.'" *Well, read about them in Matthew 7.* A watchdog sounds a warning and gives protection. My friend, you watch this. Here is the doctrine of "once saved, always saved." And you know the people who follow it in many cases — they cheat, and lie, and curse, and get in unscriptural divorces and remarriages, and they say the grace of God will take care of it. What happens? *Their error*

> **Does He Encourage Sin?**
> Each Says "NO," But Watch Fruit!
> (Matthew 7:15-20)
>
> 1. "Once saved, always saved" - Followers not attend services, lie, cheat, curse, unscriptural divorce and remarriage, etc.
> 2. "Church support of missionary societies" - Lose personal zeal; apathy; decline of church, etc.
> 3. "Church support of benevolent institutions" - Lose personal interest; dump children on institution; 10 cents per member, etc.
> 4. "Worship with instrumental music" - Not participate in songs or sing weak; choir, solo, plays, dance, etc.
>
> 330

encourages the sin!

Church support of these human institutions creates apathy, and results in ten cents per member to help the poor, and such as that. Worship with instrumental music encourages sin as we become lazy about our singing, and they substitute the choirs and solos for congregational singing.

Now, let's see our next chart, 330-A. Consider the doctrine of *my opponent* and *those with him:* Those who teach the kingdom law theory, and that baptism washes away wives, and redefining of adultery, and then *my opponent's position.* You know, they all spin the theory wheel, *and they all get an unscriptural mate.* They all have a way to explain it. My friend, they are all encouraging sin! You watch the *fruit.* They accept into the congregations many that are in unscriptural marriages.

Does He Encourage Sin?
Each Says "No," But Watch Fruit!!!

1. Kingdom Law	1. Accept Many in Unscriptural Marriages
2. Baptism Wash Away Wives	2. High Divorce Rate
	3. Deacons Swap Wives
	4. Elders in 2nd, 3rd, 4th... Marriage
3. Redefine Adultery	5. Preachers in 2nd, 3rd, 4th... Marriage-
4. Fornicator Remarry	Run off with members wife, run off with niece, leave sick wife for "cute little thing"
5. Unbeliever Leaves	6. Children Of Elders & Preachers In 2nd, 3rd, 4th ... Marriage
	7. General Looseness in Moral Issues Gambling, social drinking, immodest dress, dance, etc., etc.

330 A

Many of these churches have a high divorce rate. You have deacons that swap wives, and yet, they are still serving as deacons. You may find elders in second, third, and fourth marriages.

Preachers have sometimes run off with a member's wife, or maybe run off with their own niece. They may leave a sick wife for some cute little thing, and they are still in the pulpits preaching. *Are you ready for it? Are you ready for it?* Are you ready to have such preachers? You say, "I know some dear brother who teaches this, and it is just hard for me to see why we need to draw a line about it." Well then, friend, you *get ready* not only to fellowship the dear brother, but also *to fellowship those the dear brother is bringing into the church.* You get ready to fellowship the preacher who is *in* a condition like that, and the children of elders and preachers in the same condition. Get ready for general looseness on other things.

Notice our chart 331, my friend, on error's appeal, how it allures through the lusts of the flesh. People justify abortion, the slaughtering of these innocent babies. *"Why? Why?"* you ask. They want the sin of fornication without the responsibility, and it blinds them even to natural affection. But I want you to see also why there are those among us who would justify dancing. What is the *appeal* behind it? Revelling. The appeal of the flesh. Some justify gambling. It is covetousness. We have got some in the church who will do it. "Yes," they will say, "I cannot see that it is all that bad and all that wrong." It is the appeal of covetousness. Pornography has the appeal of lasciviousness. Immodest dress has the same.

> **Error's Appeal**
> "Allure thru lusts of the flesh" (2 Pet. 2:18)
>
> | ERROR | APPEAL |
> |---|---|
> | 1. Justify abortion | Fornication w/o responsibility (Heb.13:4) |
> | 2. Justify dancing | Reveling (Gal. 5:19-21) |
> | 3. Justify gambling | Covet (Rom. 13:9-10) |
> | 4. Pornography | Lasciviousness (2 Pet. 2:14) |
> | 5. Intoxicating drink | Stages of intoxication (1 Pet. 3:4; 5:8) |
> | 6. Immodest dress | Lasciviousness (Gal. 5:19-21) |
> | 7. Unscriptural Divorce & Remarriage | Fornication & Adultery (Heb. 13:4) |
>
> **"Be not conformed to this world" (Rom. 12:1-2)**
>
> 331

Now, what is the *appeal* of this error on unscriptural divorce and remarriage? *It is the appeal of fornication and adultery.* That is the pure and unvarnished truth, and I do not know how to make it sound nice or look pretty. The Bible says, "Be not conformed to this world." Are we going to bring the standard of truth *down* to meet our weaknesses? Or, are we going to *fight* those weaknesses with the power of divine truth? What will it be? What will it be?

Are we going to teach like Jesus did, or are we going to teach like the scribes?

> **Our Teaching: Like Jesus or The Scribes?**
>
> 1. "In distinction from the scribes, who as lawyers give definitions and relativise the Divine commandment by assimilating it to the actualities of life, Jesus, as a ... teacher tries to make men realize how absolute is the divine requirement" (Kittel, T.D.N.T., IV:734)
>
> 2. False teachers still relativise God's law and assimilate it to the actualities of life!
>
> 336

In distinction from the scribes, who are always making the divine commandment relative and trying to bend it to the actual problems of life, Jesus tried "to make men realize how absolute is the divine requirement." False teachers are still trying to make God's law relative and are still trying to bend it, *trying to bend it to the weakness and the sin of man.* My friend, here sits the man who is teaching a doctrine that does that very thing!

Fifty years ago, this teaching could hardly be heard anywhere among churches of Christ. Why is it being heard today? My friend, it is because we are trying to make the commandments relative, to make them fit the problems among our people in this society. Now, *that* is where the problem is, my friend. That is where the problem is tonight.

I want you to remember that *somebody* is legislating. Let's just look at our chart 108. What is the basic problem and difference? God said, "If you eat, you will surely die." Satan said, "You will *not* surely die." God says we *must* believe and be baptized to be saved. But Satan says we can believe and *not* be baptized, and still be saved. Now, watch it. My Lord and Savior said — you know, the one who would not make it relative, the one who would not bend it to the weakness and sin of man — my Lord said, "Whosoever marrieth her which is put away doth commit adultery." But those who are bending it to the situations that we are facing today are teaching, "Whosoever marrieth her which is put away doth *not* commit adultery." *That,* brother Freeman, is what *you* are preaching. *You are bending the law of God and destroying the restraints that God put here to protect our children, our homes, and our families!*

God -vs- Satan

1. If you eat, "surely die" (Gen. 2:17)	1. If you eat, "NOT surely die" (Gen. 3:4)
2. Believe & "Baptized shall be saved" (Mk. 16:16)	2. Believe and NOT baptized shall be saved
3. "Whoso marrieth her which is put away doth commit adultery" (Matt. 5:32; 19:9)	3. Whoso marrieth her which is put away doth NOT commit adultery

108

Rebuttals:
Fourth Evening
Freeman's Third Affirmative

As I begin this last ten minute speech, which will to me at least go very quickly, I want to point out to brother Halbrook that the idea that brother Jerry Bassett believes in polygamy is *an outright lie*. He was there in North Las Vegas during our debate. He was in my home and someone asked him about it. They had heard the same report. And I was there and talked to him myself. He said, "I never have believed it, never have preached it." So, that charge is not the truth. As evil as fornication is, fornicators *and liars* are going to spend eternity together. I would like to say it is good to have debates on this or any other Bible subject. But, I would like to point out something else equally important. That is, the need to investigate before we start out character assassination. I was written up as a false teacher. No one contacted me to find out anything about it. It just came out in the paper [referring to article by Ron Halbrook, "Opportunities to Sound Out the Word," *Guardian of Truth*, 16 Feb. 1989, pp. 108-109]. And Jerry Bassett has been labeled here publicly as a false teacher. Have you ever asked him what he believes about it? You know, when I wanted to know what you believed, I asked you.

It is good to have debates on this subject, but there is something else that needs to be considered and that is this, and I think we can all agree, though maybe we have not thought of it. If the put-away fornicator believes what brother Halbrook preaches and remains single the rest of his life, he is still going to hell. Why? He is *still guilty of adultery*. What brother Halbrook teaches is not going to save his soul because it does not get rid of his sins. If he believes what I preach and marries, he is *still going to hell*, because that does not get rid of his sins. So, while it is well and good for you and me to get together and have these Bible studies, and we need more of them, when we go to the fornicator, a man, the alien, let's give him the part of the gospel he needs first. And, a lot of these and other questions will be solved. Let's teach to him what the Apostles did, when they first preached to those who needed remission of sins. What should we do then? Well, let's go to those who are lost and reveal to them from the Bible what they must do in order to be saved. And that will answer the majority of the questions that have been brought up in the course of this debate.

Let's see now my chart number 28. I know brother Halbrook does not like this chart on mercy and does not like the chart on false doctrine, but here it is,

> **HOW DO WE KNOW?**
> **MERCY**
>
> GOD THROUGH HIS MERCY:
> REMITS SINS----------ACTS 2:38
> BLOTS OUT SINS----------ACTS 3:19
> WASHES AWAY SINS----------ACTS 22:16
> FORGIVES ALL TRESPASSES----------COL. 2:13
> DESTROYS THE BODY OF SIN----------ROM. 6:6
> REMEMBERS SINS NO MORE----------HEB. 8:12
> BUT MY OPPONENT WILL ALWAYS REMEMBER THAT ONE HAS COMMITTED FORNICATION AND WILL ALWAYS DEMAND PENANCE, EVEN WHEN GOD HAS FORGIVEN.
> LET US BE THANKFUL WE DON'T DEPEND UPON "HALBROOK'S MERCY".
>
> 28

mercy. Before leaving that chart, I want to talk to you a little bit about mercy from the Bible. I wonder if we as Christians really accept God's mercy, really believe. You know Jesus said, "Be ye merciful as your Father in heaven is merciful." He said, "Blessed are the merciful: for they shall obtain mercy." I read in Acts 2 of three thousand murderers being forgiven by God, three thousand murderers being forgiven by God. In Acts 22, Saul the persecutor was forgiven by God as he arose, was baptized, and washed away his sins. I read in Acts 17 of idol worshippers in Athens being forgiven by God. In Acts 18, homosexuals and fornicators were forgiven by God. A sorcerer in Acts 8 was forgiven by God. Those who were dead in sin, Ephesians 2, verse 1, were forgiven by God. Those who were without God, without Christ, without hope, were forgiven by God.

Now, think about it. *How were they forgiven by God?* God is not showing partiality. The Gentile was offered salvation as well as were the Jews. That brings us to consider this chart about God's mercy. God through His mercy remits sins (Acts 2:38), when we repent and are baptized. Now, if a man is guilty of fornication or adultery, let's teach him. If he is not a member of the church, he needs to repent and be baptized. In Acts 3:19, through his mercy, God blots out sins. All these phrases are perhaps equivalent to one another, but as you look at them, one can perhaps give you a little better understanding or add a little force to another. Blots out sins. Washes away sins (Acts 22:16). Forgives all trespasses (Col. 2:13). God through His mercy destroys the body of sin (Rom. 6:6). God has said in Hebrews 8, verse 12, under this new covenant, their sins and their iniquities will I remember no more.

Now, just how far reaching is that? Well, it had to apply to three thousand murderers in Acts 2. It had to apply to Saul the persecutor in Acts 22. It had to apply to idol worshippers in Acts 17. It applied to homosexuals and fornicators in Acts 18. It applied to that old sorcerer over there in Acts 8. It applied to those who were dead in sin in Ephesus, those in Ephesus who were without Christ, without God, without hope. And it applied to liars, too. Yes, it applied to all of them.

Well, you say, *"That sounds mighty easy to me."* You know, *that is how God intended it to be.* God so loved the world that He gave His only begotten son. Brother and sister, you know that includes us. Long ago Jesus shed His blood, but he shed it for you and me. God knew that we would come along, we would sin, we would need forgiveness. Brother Halbrook is saying, "Well, there is one, yes, he is *forgiven,"* but he does *not really believe that* because he will hold it against that man the rest of his life. God says, "I will remember His sins and iniquities no more." None of them. Brother Halbrook says, "If it is fornication, I will never forget it. And I will see to it that he is punished. He will never be allowed to marry if I have my way about it." And you have seen that is what he preaches, not just tonight, but throughout these four nights here, and four nights in North Las Vegas, if you were there.

I want to make an appeal to you to appreciate God's mercy. Do not try to make yourself a god, and say now here is one man who cannot receive it. He meets the same conditions, but God is going to tack an extra punishment onto the end. You get rid of all of yours, but God is going to tack some punishment on him for this particular sin. When did we have the right to become gods, brethren? When did we have that right? We have never had it. And every time men have assumed it, they have stood condemned in the sight of God. Think about it. Murderers, persecutors, idol worshippers, homosexuals, fornicators, adulterers, sorcerers, those dead in sin, those without God, without Christ, without hope. In 1 Corinthians 6, all manner of sin is discussed. *"Such were some of you"* — all under the heading of unrighteousness. God freely forgave them when they heard, believed, and were baptized (Acts 18:8). That is the gospel I preach. And God never remembered any of their sins again.

Now, we get back to this. We get down to the fornicator we are discussing these last two nights. *This fornicator has been divorced because he committed fornication.* My opponent admits he is without sin when he is baptized. And he is *without a wife* when she divorces him for the sin of fornication. But, he is going to have to suffer anyway. God cuts His mercy off there. He grants remission of past sins, but there are some *consequences;* Halbrook calls them *"temporal."* He is going to have to bear these consequences the rest of his life. Who said so? Who said so? Who said the man is going to have to suffer these consequences? Who brought these consequences up? Brother Halbrook. Brother Halbrook. Is that God sitting over there? Is that what I expect? You know I did not come to Texas to meet God. I did not come to Texas to find God. I believe that God is with faithful brethren wherever they are. I did not have to leave Nevada to find God.

I find God every time I open the pages of this Bible, and I read of His mercy. Every day I thank God that I have His mercy available.

I do not have to depend on a man like brother Halbrook and his mercy, because he would hold something against me. Oh, they would be his worst sin in his estimation, he would draw something around it, and that is the worst sin you could ever commit, and, "I will never forget that. Oh, I will tell you I will forgive it, but you will bear the consequences of it as long as you live on this earth." And the consequence is he said, "You will never marry. I will see to that." Imagine a doctrine like that. A person assuming all the authority that belongs to a supreme being, God Almighty Himself. *Jesus would not even do that.* He said, "I speak as the Father commands me to speak" (John 12:49).

I believe in the God of heaven that will forgive murderers, persecutors, idol worshippers, homosexuals, fornicators, sorcerers, those dead in sin, those without God, without Christ, without hope. But, I know that you and I had to meet His conditions to be forgiven. When I meet the fornicator, I am going to tell him, "Now, Mr. Fornicator, the first thing you need to do is get rid of that fornication. You are going to die with it unless God forgives it." "Well, how can I ever receive forgiveness." "I will tell you just what Peter did. 'Repent and be baptized in the name of Jesus Christ for the remission of sins.'" "You mean that is it? Why, that is *too easy."* That was the first argument I ever heard that favored brother Halbrook's position. "You make it *too easy* for the fornicator." Brethren, *I* did not. God said it to those fornicators over there; Paul preached to them in Acts 18. They heard, they believed, they were baptized. And everyone who was baptized left fornication behind. No fornicator is added to the church. God forgot all about it. But now this man comes along, he wants to avoid fornication. God says, "Have your own wife." Brother Halbrook steps up, "Now, Lord, you are making a mistake. I know this case. This man committed fornication back there ten years ago, and was divorced by his wife." God says, "I do not remember that." "What do you mean, Lord, you do not remember it?" "I forgave it." Brother Halbrook says, "I did not. I did not."

I will tell you that makes me want to weep — brethren who will set themselves up like that. God said, "I will remember their sins and iniquities no more." Brother Halbrook says, "Oh, he is forgiven, but I am going to see to it that he pays a penalty as long as he lives. He will live without a wife. And she will live without a husband." Oh, people who believe that and teach it ought to hang their head in shame. They are not as merciful as God is. You know when the prodigal son came home, his father went out to meet him with open arms. And we come. Our Father will step out and meet us with open arms if we meet his conditions.

Rebuttals:
Fourth Evening
Halbrook's Third Negative

Brother Freeman, gentlemen moderators, ladies and gentlemen, my opponent brings up the matter of brother Bassett and says that I lied about that, and he quoted Revelation 21:8 on it, about all liars. When I mentioned that problem when I was out at Las Vegas, I did not call Jerry's name because Jerry had not gone into print on it. Since then, *he has sent me a bulletin,* brother Freeman, in which he says when it comes to the matter of converting people who are in polygamy, that it ought to be *"handled in the same way the Apostles treated the unlawful practice of (per God's law) slavery" [Coberg Road Bulletin, Published by Church of Christ, Eugene, OR, Feb. 4, 1990].* You and I agreed in the debate that God did not demand people to get out of slavery in order to be Christians. Now, according to Jerry Bassett, then, *they do not have to get out of what?* Out of *what,* brother Freeman? *Polygamy!* I would look down, too. [The speaker referred to Freeman looking down at this point.] Now, you ought to get this and read it. He mailed them out. We have got copies out here. [Copies of several such statements were made available to the audience in Harry Osborne's "Polygamy & Repentance," *A Reason for Hope,* Bulletin of House St. Church of Christ, Alvin, TX, Feb. 25, 1990; revised and reprinted in *Gospel Truths,* Oct. 1990, pp. 232-234.] Yes sir, he committed himself on it. I do not know what he told you, but I know what he put *into public domain,* what he put *into print.*

Now, you talk about this matter of lying. Let's see my chart 15, please. It hurts me and gives me no pleasure at all to do this, but you and I are going to face each other in eternity and I will not leave this place without appealing to you as a

---

Not Authorized = Sinful

1. Things "not authorized within the doctrine of Christ are not only non-essential but sinful as well."

2. An author defended sponsoring church but had "no passage of Scripture to show that such a plan is authorized by the Lord" (Jack Freeman, <u>Gospel Guardian</u>, 28 April 1960, pp. 8-9).

3. No clear passage authorizes put-away fornicator or deserted believer to marry another.

4. Conclusion: such marriages are sinful!

Fourth Evening: Halbrook's Third Negative 301

brother and as a Christian to make this matter right. I want to give you one last chance, brother Freeman. I will give you part of my time to apologize if you will clear the record of this debate. You charged me with lying when I pointed out that you are the author of this. You said it had to be *somebody else,* and all of that stuff, and talked about how there could have been *two* Jack Freemans. And there *were* two Jack Freemans there at San Pablo, California — *both of them were you* [i.e., he lived there twice]. And the editor of the paper says this is *you.* Now, would you like to apologize and clear the record of this? Would you?

Freeman: I am not sure I can clear the record, but I really meant to deal with this and overlooked it. Brother Halbrook gave me the other evening some copies and other partial copies of articles that were written under the same name as *Jack Freeman,* not just one, but more than one from San Pablo, California. And I *cannot say* I did. I have read them. A part of it looks like my writing — I think we could recognize our own writing — and part of it does not. I called my own wife again. She does not remember it. No one else that I knew in that area at the time, preachers and others, remember it, that I wrote them. If I find out that I did, I will be happy to own these articles. *Brother Halbrook agrees, I believe, that they are good articles, and they teach the truth.* They have nothing to do, however, with divorce and remarriage. They have to do with another subject. *Institutionalism* was dividing the church then. They all have to do with that.

And, I am sorry, but that is the best I can do. I do not know if I wrote them or not. I have no memory. At that time I was editing my own paper. Now, if I believed I wrote them I would tell you — because, why not? I would be happy to take credit for them, but I do not want to take credit if they are not mine. If I learn they are mine, I will write to you, and you can pass it on if you like. That is all I can do about it.

Halbrook: And if you find that you did, *you are committed to apologize for what you said about me to the church in Las Vegas,* is that right?

Freeman: Yes, right, *publicly.*

Halbrook: You will do it?

Freeman: I will not travel down here; I will send writing and let you do it, or a tape. Is that okay?

Halbrook: I understand, alright.

Freeman: Okay, fine.

Halbrook: So, here is where we are leaving it folks. If I had written an article twenty years ago, and I could not remember for sure if I had done it, I would have to see the evidence. Here is evidence on chart 16-A. I see the articles with *my name* and *my address.* And, the people at the church where I lived, said, "Ron, remember you lived there *twice*, and you are the *only* Ron Halbrook that ever lived there." And, then the *editor* said, "Yes, it was you." And, the other Ron Halbrook was a schoolboy when this was written. Then, brother Freeman, I would quit making these *excuses*, and just say, "I wrote it, I am sorry that I called you a liar, and I ask forgiveness, and I want the record clear." But, he is going to let the debate end, and even after we gave him another opportunity, *without making that correction!* And so it will have to stand.

Gospel Guardian Articles by Jack Freeman
"WITHOUT FACILITIES, TRAINING, AND ADEQUATE FINANCIAL MEANS" Jack Freeman, San Pablo, California 25 July 1957 *Gospel Guardian*
"ARE YE NOW MADE PERFECT BY THE FLESH?" Jack Freeman, San Pablo, California 24 Oct. 1957 *Gospel Guardian*
"NOT CONFORMED – BUT TRANSFORMED" Jack Freeman, San Pablo, California 3 Mar. 1960 *Gospel Guardian*
"NECESSARY THINGS" Jack Freeman, San Pablo, California 28 Apr. 1960 *Gospel Guardian*

16 A

Now, he talks about his "mercy" argument again, and how that sin is forgiven. *Polygamy,* too, is polygamy forgiven, brother Freeman? Now, if we apply all your remarks about sin being forgiven, if polygamy is forgiven, they can *stay in* polygamy. Notice our chart 326, my friend. Here is his "mercy" argument: "Oh, God remits sin, but brother Halbrook remembers sin." Well, now, what about *polygamy?* Are *you* going to remember the poor old polygamist anymore, brother Freeman? *Remember your argument?* God adds him to the church and God does not add polygamists to the church. "Mercy" indeed — *you* answer it! You never did call for that chart, and I can see why.

Opponent Opposes Himself (2 Tim. 2:25)

What About These Cases?

1. "Doctrine of Devils" if forbid marriage.	Homosexual (1 Cor. 6:9-11)
2. "Mercy" remits sin, but "opponent remembers sin."	Polygamy (Gen. 2:24)
3. "Paul preached to aliens," "not say leave husband or wife to be saved."	Unscripturally divorced (Matt. 5:28; 19:9; 1 Cor. 7:10-11, 15)
4. "Demands impossible," "how do you know?"	Unscripturally remarried (Mk. 6:17-18; Mt. 5:28; 19:9)

326

He said, "Oh, we cannot be God," and would imply that Ron Halbrook is sitting in judgment on the word of God. Oh, my friend, *we cannot be God,* and that is why we cannot dismiss the requirement of *repentance*, and why we preach that people must *get out* of polygamy. *If we let them stay in it, we are pretending to be God. And, if we let people stay in unscriptural marriages, we are sitting in the seat of God.*

I want us to close by looking at the appeal we have made to Scripture. Notice our chart 60 [text, Matt. 5:32]. Our appeal has been that *Jesus said,* "Whosoever shall put away his wife, saving for the cause of fornication, causeth her to commit adultery: and whosoever shall marry her that is divorced committeth adultery." My friend, that means that if you put your wife away without cause, *you cause her to commit adultery when she marries again.* When I pointed that argument out, what did he say? *Not a thing* about it. Now, according to the way he interprets that, when you *put her away,* you *cause* her to *not* commit adultery. So, if you want your wife to not commit adultery, put her away and get her in another marriage! Now, my friend, he perverts that simple passage, the plain meaning, and even the young people tonight can see this.

Consider our chart 72 [text, Matt. 19:9]. *Jesus said,* "Whosoever shall put away his wife, except it be for fornication, and shall marry another, committeth adultery: and whoso marrieth her which is put away doth commit adultery." Now, my friend, I want you to notice that *if we put away our wife without cause, and marry another, we commit adultery.* And he says whoever marries the one put away commits adultery. Now, supposing I have been put away for fornication. What about that case? *Whoever marries that one put away for fornication commits adultery.*

Now, notice my chart 74. "Except" means *if and only if. I* did not put the *"only"* in it. When the Lord put "except" in there, the Lord put "only" in there. This is just like Matthew 18, *except* you become as a little child. What *force* does it have — that is what the equal sign means — what is the *force* of this expression? The force is that you *must* become as a little child. What is the *force* of this expression? The force is that you *must* become as a little child to enter the kingdom. You *must* be

---

Except = If & Only If!

* Matt. 18:3 Become as little child → Enter kingdom

* John 3:2 God with Him → Do miracles

* John 3:5 Born of water & Spirit → Enter kingdom

* Matt. 19:9 Put away wife for fornication & marry another → Not adultery

74

born of water and the Spirit to enter the kingdom. And, if you put away your wife for fornication and marry another, *you do not commit adultery*. That is the plain and simple meaning of it.

My young son suggested this parallel, our chart 74-A. "Except it be for fornication" is like "except it miss the hoop." Whoever shoots a basketball, *except it misses the hoop*, scores two points. The force is, *if and only if* your shot misses the hoop, you do *not* get two points. *If and only if* you put your wife away for fornication and marry another, you do *not* commit adultery.

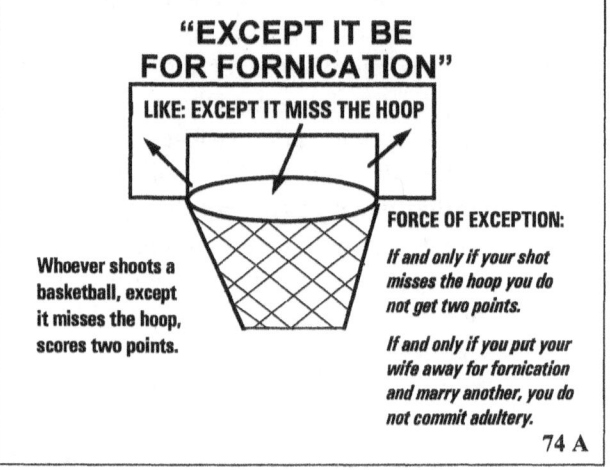

74 A

On our chart 122-A, we notice 1 Corinthians 7. I am trying to help you take *the text* home in your heart tonight. And the text said, *"Let every man have his own wife."* My opponent never ever did come back and deal with this because he knows this is what he is teaching [pointing to right side of chart] and this is what the text said [pointing to left side]. He has got this: "Every man who wrecks his marriage and throws away his wife by fornication can get another wife." And yes, *that will encourage the sin of fornication!*

It said in the text *"unmarried"* and *"widows,"* it did *not* say *"the put-away fornicator."* Then in verses 27 and 28, the man "loosed from a wife" and the "virgin" may marry, and it did *not* say the put-away fornicator may marry a put-away fornicator! Not at all.

Does 1 Cor. 7 Authorize
The Put-Away Fornicator To Marry Another?

Text Says This:	Not This:
Vs. 2 "Every man have his own wife"	Every man who wrecks his marriage & throws away his own wife by fornication or unscriptural divorce, gets another wife!
Vs. 9 "Unmarried...widows... better to marry than to burn"	Unscripturally divorced & put-away fornicator... better to commit adultery than fornication!
Vv. 27-28 A man "loosed from a wife" (free, never married) and "a virgin" (free, never married) may marry.	A man unscripturally divorced or a divorced fornicator may marry a woman in the same condition!

122 A

Then we have also talked about 1 Corinthians 7:10 and 11 on our chart 140-X [text, 1 Cor. 7:10-11]. They are not to depart, but if she departs "let her remain unmarried or be reconciled to her husband." My friend, if she *violates* this, the only way she can go to heaven is to *come back* to this. This idea that her husband can say, "Well, I do not want her anyway, and she can get in another marriage," which brother Freeman taught, *contradicts and violates the word of God*. We cannot play God and do that.

Next, on chart 150 notice that we are *slaves to Christ, not to men*. "If the unbelieving depart, let him depart. A brother or sister is not under bondage" — has not been enslaved — "in such cases." Now, my friend, this matter about the deserted believer does not involve *1/1,000th of one percent* of the cases with which we deal. And yet, he preaches and pounds on that, and you know the *reality* we are dealing with is this matter of *the put-away fornicator!*

Interpret Difficult Passage - Contradict Clear & Simple One

Matthew 5:32; 19:9 Clear and Simple	1 Corinthians 7:15 Interpretation of Difficult Text
"Whoso marrieth her which is put away doth commit adultery"	Whoso marrieth her which is put away doth NOT commit adultery

150

Now, then, I want us to notice our chart 190-X. Again, the text says, "concerning virgins," "good for a man so to be," "Art thou bound unto a wife? Seek not to be loosed" — if you are married stay — "Art thou loosed from a wife? Seek not a wife." Here is the man who never married. He is to stay in that condition, and then the same way for a virgin.

Read the text! The text is *plain* and the text is *simple. The text will stand when the world is on fire!*

We are facing the issue and the problem of *authority* again among the people of God. He said our chart 15 has nothing to do with the current controversy. Oh, my friend, yes, it does. Yes, it does. That which is *"not authorized"* is *"sinful,"* as shown on chart 15. Notice his expression, *his expression* showing that whatever is *"not authorized"* is *"sinful."* You have seen *there is no passage that will authorize the put-away fornicator or deserted believer to marry another.* Such marriages are *sinful!* Our chart 35 [page 307] shows the misuse of Romans 14 opening the door to digression, just as it happened in the last generation. And,

1 Corinthians 7:25-28

Now concerning virgins...	} Never Married
...for the present distress... good for a man so to be	} Never Married
Art thou bound unto a wife? Seek not to be loosed	} If Married, STAY
Art thou loosed from a wife? Seek not a wife. But and if thou marry, thou hast not sinned; and if a virgin marry, she hath not sinned [but best not to marry, vv. 28-38]	} If man never married, STAY } If woman never married, STAY

190 X

Not Authorized = Sinful

1. Things "not authorized within the doctrine of Christ are not only non-essential but sinful as well."

2. An author defended sponsoring church but had "no passage of Scripture to show that such a plan is authorized by the Lord" (Jack Freeman, <u>Gospel Guardian</u>, 28 April 1960, pp. 8-9).

3. No clear passage authorizes put-away fornicator or deserted believer to marry another.

4. Conclusion: such marriages are sinful!

15

Fourth Evening: Halbrook's Third Negative

Romans 14 - OR - 2 John 9-11	
Receive Him	**Receive Him Not**
Instrumental Music	Women Preachers
Church Supported Missionary & Benevolent Societies	Modernism
	Evolution
Church Suppers, Ball Teams, Gyms	Abortion On Demand
Premillennialism	Polygamy
Church Hospitals	Domestic Partners
A.D. 70 World Ended, Resurrection, Etc.	New Law On Marriage & Divorce: "Kingdom Law"
Choirs & Quartets	
Interdenominational Services	Baptism Removes Marriage Redefine "Adultery"
Boston Church Schemes	
Tongue Speaking	Fornicator Remarry
Open Membership	2nd Exception - Desertion
Fellowship With The Christian Church	Homosexual Marriage

35

we had better be crying out again. If we receive people that are teaching and practicing these things, the church will become like a veritable ark, full of every clean and unclean beast. Every doctrine true or false will be tolerated — it will not matter what it is.

Then, we notice our chart 333. Notice, my friend, this is *his* doctrine — *the remarriage of the guilty party* — but it *invites sin*. The *International Standard Bible Encyclopedia* did an article surveying the history of this problem. It warned that when courts allow remarriage to the "guilty and innocent alike," "we invite the very evils we seek to remedy. We make it the interest of a dissatisfied party to create" the grounds that "free" him to marry another. The law of Christ opens no such door to invite sin!

Remarriage Of Guilty Party Invites Sin!

I.S.B.E. article (II:865-866) warns that when courts allow remarriage to "guilty and innocent alike," "We invite the very evils we seek to remedy. We make it the interest of a dissatisfied party to create" the grounds that "free" him to marry another.

The Law of Christ opens no such door to invite sin!

333

Now, notice our chart 176, dealing with his idea that 1 Corinthians 7:15 gives another right to remarry. It opens the door according to the historians for the very mess we are in! "The floodgates are open." If your husband deserts you, marry another. If he is cruel, fails to support you, or is drunken, marry another. Now, that is where we are today. Isn't this where we are? This is where the rubber meets the road. These are the problems we are facing in trying to teach people. And how did it get like this, brother Freeman? *By the doctrine you are teaching*. That is how it got into this mess! Historically, that is the truth about the matter.

Now, notice our chart 108 again on *God versus Satan*. God versus Satan. If you eat, you shall die. If you eat, you shall *"NOT* surely die." God said, "Whoso marrieth her which is put away doth commit adultery." Satan says, *and my opponent joined hands with him to say,* "Whosoever marrieth her which is put away doth *NOT* commit adultery."

I am raising a ten year old, a thirteen year old and an eighteen year old. And I want them to know and do *what God said* and *not what Satan said.*

> **I.S.B.E. Article Warns**
> If use 1 Cor. 7:15 as right to remarry,
> "The flood gates are open" (II:865-866)
>
> **Steps of Progression:**
>
> "If your husband deserts you, you may have another. If he is cruel, you may have another. If he fails to support you, you may have another. If he is drunken, you may have another. If he is incompatible or makes you unhappy, you may have another" - and yet others beyond these.
>
> **Results: Careless Marriages, Divorce For Any Cause, Multiplied Miseries!**
>
> 176

You look at Adam and Eve and the sin they fell into, and then their children fell into, and we are not yet through reaping the horrible results. If we do not respect God's law of marriage, *we* will fall into these sins and *our children* will fall into these sins. There will not be an end to the horror, the sorrow, the error of it, yea, *even reaching into eternity.* These sins are already breaking up the foundations of justice and right and order and natural affection. And, my friend, it will mean we will spend eternity away from the living, loving God, away from the light of His presence and warmth of His presence!

> **God -vs- Satan**
>
> 1. If you eat, "surely die" (Gen. 2:17)
> 1. If you eat, "NOT surely die" (Gen. 3:4)
>
> 2. Believe & "Baptized shall be saved" (Mk. 16:16)
> 2. Believe and NOT baptized shall be saved
>
> 3. "Whoso marrieth her which is put away doth commit adultery" (Matt. 5:32; 19:9)
> 3. Whoso marrieth her which is put away doth NOT commit adultery
>
> 108

Don't you forget, even you little children, the difference presented in the debate you heard. *"Whoso marrieth her which is put away doth commit adultery."* But Satan said, "Whoso marrieth her which is put away doth *NOT* commit adultery." And, my friend, you do *what God said!* Live by the word of God. Thank you very much. Thank you, brother Freeman.

ADDENDUM No. 1:
Authorship Acknowledged by Freeman

Church of Christ
2424 McCarran
North Las Vegas, Nevada 89030
Phone: 642-3141
May 14, 1990

Dear Ron,

After searching through the files of the "Eye Opener" which I edited both in San Pablo and in Santa Ana, California, I have found all four articles to which you made reference during the debate.

These articles all appeared in the "Eye Opener" and also appeared in the Gospel Guardian. In going through the various issues of the "Eye Opener" there were several announcements in regard to gospel meeting in the San Pablo Area in which Yater Tant was to do the preaching. He was either given these articles while in that area, or they were mailed to him, or he copied them from the "Eye Opener".

I am happy to say that I did write the articles as they appeared in the "Eye Opener" with my name included as editor of each.

As I stated in the debate, there was no reference in any of the articles to marriage, divorce and remarriage. Copies of these articles will be supplied to any person who has an interest in them.

Jack Freeman

ADDENDUM No. 2:
Halbrook's Response to Freeman

Church of Christ
Jackson at 15th Street
West Columbia, Texas 77486
409-345-3818

28 August 1992nd Year of Our Lord

Mr. Jack Freeman
2424 McCarran
N. Las Vegas, NV 89030

Dear brother Freeman,

     As the book of our debate nears publication, I wanted to assure you that in all fairness to you the book will include an "Addendum: Authorship Acknowledged," publishing the full text of your 14 May 1990 letter. I am thankful that at long last your repeated denials that you authored the articles and your repeated charges that I lied by attributing them to you have finally been *withdrawn* by your acknowledging you are the author. I informed the church here of your letter, as I promised to do.

     You argued in the debate and implied in your letter that you had no direct contact with Yater Tant and the *Gospel Guardian*. It is interesting to note that he told me he remembers well knowing you. He published not only your articles but also news reports from you (see, for instance, *Gospel Guardian*, 13 June 1963, p. 107).

     On the last night of the debate here, you promised that if you decided you did write the articles, *you would apologize to the church at North Las Vegas for calling me a liar during the debate there* (15-19 Jan. 1990). Your letter says the articles appeared in a bulletin as well as in the *Gospel Guardian*, which was never disputed. You also say you are "happy" you wrote the articles, but argue they had no application to our debate, thus implying that I marred the debate by introducing them. *But your letter makes no apology for your harsh charges against me, and makes no mention of an apology before the church there.* North Las Vegas members who were present when you made your statement confirm that you briefly acknowledged your authorship of the articles on a Wednesday night, but you offered no apology and added that you "would make no further mention of these things again."

To acknowledge a deed is *not* to apologize for it. These are two distinct steps, as you well know. Cain finally acknowledged killing Abel after professing to know nothing about it, but there was no godly sorrow, repentance, or apology. Judas acknowledged that he was wrong to betray Jesus, but there was no godly sorrow, repentance, or apology. During the period of the 50th anniversary of Japan's bombing Pearl Harbor, the Japanese government acknowledged regret for the suffering experienced in Hawaii, but chose not to apologize and carefully framed their public statement without an apology. Although your letter is carefully framed in the same way, I harbor no bitterness or ill will toward you, but am willing to leave the matter as being between you and the Lord.

This failure to truly correct sin is the same basic error of your teaching on divorce and remarriage. Similarly, you angrily charged in our first debate that a "Judas" was in the audience, tried to cover it up by claiming you welcomed an honored guest by that name, and at other times have identified that "Judas" as several people who helped me in the debate. You see no more need to truly correct such matters than to truly correct *unscriptural, adulterous marriages*. Your concept of repentance is fatally flawed and false to the core.

With or without an apology, your acknowledgement of authorship at least clears away your aspersions against my character in the printed record of the debate. Such unfounded charges only served to cloud the issues between us. It was clear all along from abundant evidence that you did author the articles, and I was amazed that you denied them. I introduced them to show that *we share common ground in affirming the necessity of positive, divine authority in the Bible for what we preach and practice,* although you fail to properly apply that principle to divorce and remarriage. I never claimed the articles were written directly on the subject of divorce and remarriage.

I fervently pray and plead that you will accept the proper application of the principle stated so well in your articles, and make the needed corrections of your false teaching. Then, we could stand shoulder to shoulder, united upon the truth of the gospel of Christ, and proclaim it to a lost world (Phil. 1:27).

Yours for service to Christ,

Ron Halbrook

Freeman's Charts

Chart Number	Page Numbers
1	33, 79, 104, 138, 152, 159, 236
2	34, 105
3	34, 106
3A	106
4	35, 64, 107
5	65
6	65, 107
7	66, 129
8	133
9	67, 134
11	74, 126
12	75, 127
15	77, 136, 149, 220, 228, 273, 288
15/01	228, 289
16	78, 136, 150, 272, 287
17	134, 151, 198, 237, 254
18	135, 151, 198, 238
21	78, 137, 197, 273, 290
22	159, 184, 193, 213, 274
25	221, 240, 257
28	160, 185, 278, 297
30	156, 178, 238, 256
31	157, 179, 239, 256
32	164, 206, 244
33	164, 206
34	167, 195, 212, 245, 267, 286
35	195, 268, 284
35/01	213
36	196
37	196, 215, 269, 285
41	271
43	221, 240
44	222, 241
45	269
46	270, 286
47	162, 203, 243
48	162, 204, 243
48/01	204
49	32, 163, 205
56	158, 181
57	127, 165, 210
59	138, 219, 226, 242, 258
424	30

Chart Index

426	223
428	31, 51
430	32
451	165, 208
452	166, 211, 275
453	212, 276, 290
747	30, 49, 60
748	63, 277
749	63, 277
750	278
751	128
752	128
752/02	145

Halbrook's Charts

Chart Number	Page Numbers
Q3-1-90	170
Q3-2-90	249
1	1, 36, 80, 96, 109, 140
2	169, 200, 224, 246
3	37
4	169, 187, 214
6	2, 19, 39, 55
7	3, 19, 39, 55
8	3, 20, 40, 56
13	4, 20, 40, 56, 71, 76, 81, 99
15	6, 16, 22, 42, 62, 85, 175, 230, 300, 306
16	6, 16, 42, 62
16A	86, 302
23	5, 21, 41, 57
35	231, 307
37	4, 21, 41, 57, 176
41	7, 23, 43, 58
43	7, 23, 44
44	8, 24, 44
48	8, 24
51	177
51A	177
54	9, 17, 25, 46, 82, 95, 147, 175
59B	83
59X	70
60	9, 143
62	10, 26, 46
63	10, 27, 47
65	251, 282

67	11, 27, 47
67A	45, 58
67B	45
70	51
72	11, 28, 69
73	12, 28, 48
74	12, 29, 49, 59, 84, 99, 141, 148, 303
74A	84, 100, 141, 304
81	13
83	207, 259, 286
85	113, 174, 205
94	282
95	248
100	13, 61
100A	14, 61
101	14, 178, 185, 211, 247, 264, 281
108	52, 73, 229, 263, 295, 308
110	182
110A	183
113	50
114	182
121	89
122	87, 101
122A	88, 95, 102, 142, 171, 214, 260, 284, 304
125	90
126	90
129	91
130	91
133	225
135	92
136	92
138	93
139	93, 103
140	94, 104
140X	143
145	251
146	81, 94, 251
150	115, 131, 305
150X	68, 111, 114, 144
151	115
151A	116
152	116
154	117
154A	117
157	118, 133, 146
157A	171

Chart Index

162	119
165	120
165A	120
175	124, 231
176	124, 146, 231, 308
190	121
190X	121, 145, 306
191	257
191A	122, 180, 209
193	122
196	123, 180, 190, 209
197	123
198	181, 210
231	207, 258
234	203
235	227, 259
236	227
241	202
242	250, 280
243	253, 266, 283
250	216
252	216
254	217, 226
286	186, 194, 201, 252
301	287
314	183, 191
315	184, 192
316	72, 215, 254
317	291
318	292
321B	229
324	179
325	15
326	255, 288, 302
326A	255
330	292
330A	293
331	294
333	52, 232, 307
336	294
346	260, 279
346A	261
346B	261, 279
346C	262, 280
346D	263